MW00611201

Archaeology in the Land of 'Tells and Ruins'

Archaeology in the Land of 'Tells and Ruins'

A History of Excavations in the Holy Land Inspired
by the Photographs and Accounts of Leo Boer

Edited by
Bart Wagemakers

Oxbow Books
Oxford & Philadelphia

Published in the United Kingdom in 2014 by
OXBOW BOOKS
10 Hythe Bridge Street, Oxford OX1 2EW

and in the United States by
OXBOW BOOKS
908 Darby Road, Havertown, PA 19083

© Oxbow Books and the individual authors 2014

Hardcover Edition: ISBN 978-1-78297-245-7
Digital Edition: ISBN 978-1-78297-246-4

A CIP record for this book is available from the British Library

Library of Congress Cataloging-in-Publication Data

Archaeology in the land of "tells and ruins" : a history of excavations in the Holy Land inspired by the photographs and accounts of Leo Boer / edited by Bart Wagemakers.
     pages cm
  Summary: "Recently, a travel account and 700 photographs came to light by the hand of Leo Boer, a former student of the École Biblique et Archéologique Française in Jerusalem who, at the age of 26 in 1953-4 visited many archaeological sites in the area of present-day Israel and the Palestinian Territories. This unique collection of images and essays offers to scholars working in the region previously unpublished materials and interpretations as well as new photographs. For students of archaeology, ancient or Biblical history and theology it contains both a detailed archaeological historiography and explores some highly relevant, specific themes. Finally, the superb quality of Boer's photography provides an unprecedented insight into the archaeological landscape of post-war Palestine for anyone interested in Biblical history and archaeology"--Provided by publisher.
  Includes bibliographical references and index.
  ISBN 978-1-78297-245-7
  1. Israel--Antiquities. 2. Palestine--Antiquities. 3. Bible--Antiquities. 4. Excavations (Archaeology)--Israel. 5. Excavations (Archaeology)--Palestine. 6. Israel--Antiquities--Pictorial works. 7. Palestine--Antiquities--Pictorial works. 8. Boer, Leo, 1926-2009--Travel. 9. Israel--Description and travel. 10. Palestine--Description and travel. I. Boer, Leo, 1926-2009. II. Wagemakers, Bart.
  DS111.1.A74 2014
  933--dc 3
                    2013047767

All rights reserved. No part of this book may be reproduced or transmitted in any form or by any means, electronic or mechanical including photocopying, recording or by any information storage and retrieval system, without permission from the publisher in writing.

Printed in the United Kingdom by Berforts Information Press

For a complete list of Oxbow titles, please contact:

UNITED KINGDOM
Oxbow Books
Telephone (01865) 241249, Fax (01865) 794449
Email: oxbow@oxbowbooks.com
www.oxbowbooks.com

UNITED STATES OF AMERICA
Oxbow Books
Telephone (800) 791-9354, Fax (610) 853-9146
Email: queries@casemateacademic.com
www.casemateacademic.com/oxbow

Oxbow Books is part of the Casemate Group

Front cover: Photograph taken by Leo Boer at Khirbet Qumran on 21 March 1954
Back cover images, respectively: Jerusalem; Khirbet et-Tell; Samaria & Sebaste; Tell Balata (Shechem);
Tell es-Sultan (Ancient Jericho); Khirbet Qumran; Caesarea Maritima; Megiddo; Bet She'an
© Duby Tal (Albatross Aerial Photography Ltd.)

Contents

List of Contributors

BENJAMIN (BENNY) ARUBAS, M.A. is Chief Field Archaeologist, Surveyor, Researcher and Lecturer at the Institute of Archaeology of the Hebrew University, and Stratigrapher and Senior Member of the Expedition to Bet She'an-Scythopolis.

DR. WALID ATRASH acts as Academic Advisor to the Israel Antiquities Authority and was involved as Field Supervisor in the excavation of the Roman theatre in Bet She'an.

DR. FANNY BOCQUENTIN is a Bio-Archaeologist at the French National Centre for Scientific Research (CNRS) in Jerusalem. Since 2007 she has been Co-Director of the renewed excavation at Beisamoun (Upper Jordan Valley), a major Pre-Pottery Neolithic settlement of the eighth and seventh millennium.

PROF. EDWARD F. CAMPBELL, JR. is Emeritus Professor of Old Testament, McCormick Theological Seminary, Chicago. He joined the Drew-McCormick Expedition in Tell Balata (Shechem) as a graduate student in 1957. In 1964 he became Associate Director and served as Field Director in 1966–1968. After Ernest Wright's death in 1974, he took over the task of Publication Director and continues in that capacity to this day.

DR. NORMA FRANKLIN is currently Research Associate at the Zinman Institute of Archaeology, University of Haifa. She was a member of the Tel Aviv University's Megiddo Expedition for nineteen years, and her PhD dealt with state formation processes at Megiddo and Samaria in the Iron Age. In 2011 she resigned from the Megiddo Expedition in order to launch the Jezreel Expedition.

DR. SHIMON GIBSON has excavated in Jerusalem and at many sites in Israel. He is currently Head of the Archaeology Department at the University of the Holy Land and Senior Research Fellow at the Albright Institute of Archaeology in Jerusalem.

PROF. JAN GUNNEWEG is a retired Senior Staff Member of the Hebrew University of Jerusalem. As a representative of Israel in COST Action-G8 in 2001 he founded and still participates in the Qumran Project, which aims to apply science to the archaeology of the Qumran settlement and the Dead Sea Scrolls.

PROF. KENNETH G. HOLUM is Professor of History at the University of Maryland and has excavated at Caesarea since 1978. He organised the Combined Caesarea Expeditions with Avner Raban of Haifa University in 1989; the field work at this site continued up to 2003.

DR. GERRIT VAN DER KOOIJ is a retired Lecturer of Near Eastern Archaeology of the Faculty of Archaeology, Leiden University and Co-Director of the Tell Balata Archaeological Park Project.

DR. GABRIEL MAZOR works for the Israel Antiquities Authority and is Director of the Bet She'an Archaeological Project.

DR. NAVA PANITZ-COHEN is Researcher and Adjunct Instructor at the Institute of Archaeology of the Hebrew University of Jerusalem. She worked at the Tel Bet She'an excavations from 1989 to 1996 and as Supervisor of Area S from 1990–1996. She also co-edited the third volume of the final publication.

DR. LUCAS P. PETIT is Curator of the Near Eastern Department of the Dutch National Museum of Antiquities. Currently, he is studying the Iron Age settlement history of the Central Jordan Valley in Jordan.

DR. MAURA SALA is Research Assistant at Rome's "La Sapienza" University and Field Director of the University's Expeditions to Tell es-Sultan and to Khirbet al-Batrawy (Jordan). She is also Co-ordinator of the Project PADIS (Palestine Archaeological Databank Information system).

DR. MARGREET L. STEINER is an independent scholar living in Leiden, the Netherlands. Together with Henk Franken she has published a large part of the results of Kenyon's excavations in Jerusalem.

Dr. Hamdan Taha is Deputy Minister of Tourism and Antiquities of the Palestinian Authority and Co-Director of the Tell Balata Archaeological Park Project.

Prof. Ron E. Tappy is the G. Albert Shoemaker Professor of Bible and Archaeology at Pittsburgh Theological Seminary, Director of the James L. Kelso Museum, and Project Director of The Zeitah Excavations. He is a specialist in the archaeology of Israelite Samaria and has written two books and numerous articles on the subject.

Prof. Joan E. Taylor is Professor of Christian Origins and Second Temple Judaism at King's College London. She has published numerous articles on the archaeology and history of Khirbet Qumran and the Dead Sea environment.

Prof. Yoram Tsafrir is Emeritus Professor of Archaeology at the Hebrew University of Jerusalem and Co-Director of the Hebrew University Excavations at Bet She'an-Scythopolis.

Dr. Monique H. van den Dries is Assistant Professor of Archaeological Heritage Management at the Faculty of Archaeology, Leiden University. She joined the Tell Balata Archaeological Park Project in 2010, supervising the promotional aspects of the project and organising community involvement.

Bart Wagemakers, M.A. lectures on Ancient and Religious History at the Faculty of Education at the University of Applied Sciences Utrecht and is curator of the Leo Boer Archive.

Prof. Jürgen Zangenberg is Full Professor Interpretation of the New Testament at the Department of Religious Studies and researcher at the Faculty of Archaeology, Leiden University. Since 2007 he is the Director of the excavations at Horvat Kur, a sub-project of the Kinnret Regional Project.

Preface

Exactly 60 years before the publication of this volume Leo Boer, a young Dutch student, who was preparing for priesthood in Rome, was given the opportunity to stay in Jerusalem at the *École Biblique et Archéologique Française de Jérusalem*. They were turbulent times. The terror and devastation of the Second World War had ended less than ten years before and the British and French mandatory powers had already left the region. In 1948 the State of Israel had been founded alongside the young independent states of Transjordan, Syria, Lebanon and Iraq. Under the umbrella of the United Nations, itself a child of the post-Second World War era, the Near East was in a fundamental transitional period, and it was not yet certain how stable the new system would prove to be. Thousands of people were still in search of a new home, refugees fleeing from Europe as well as from area to area within the region itself due to a bitter war fought between nascent Israel and its Arab neighbours. As a result, new borders were set up and new conflict was looming on the horizon.

In the midst of all this, Leo Boer, eager to learn and travel, set off from Jerusalem to visit a region, which, to his knowledge, was saturated with biblical connotations and reminiscences. To me, his journeys with his fellow students resembled in many ways the adventures of the great nineteenth-century travellers, although motorcars and electricity alleviated the hardships considerably. And how 'empty' the landscape was even then!

In the 1950s Palestine as a region remained very much unvisited by Europeans. But being a student of the famous and renowned *École Biblique* and equipped with Vatican travel documents, Leo Boer was able to travel fairly freely in the Holy Land. Fortunately for us today, he carefully noted down everything he saw and – being an enthusiastic photographer with great camera skills – he shot many rolls of film covering sites and landscapes that form the inspiration for this book. Some of these sites were excavated before the Second World War. Others (Jericho and Qumran) were being excavated by two of the most famous archaeologists of the era, when Boer visited the sites: Dame Kathleen Kenyon and Roland de Vaux.

For several decades these film rolls lay unnoticed in Leo Boer's home waiting for their own re-excavation. It can therefore only be called a stroke of luck that Leo Boer met Bart Wagemakers on that day in 1999 at the National Museum of Antiquities in Leiden. For several years Bart worked to salvage this treasure and make it accessible to the public. The fruits of these efforts form the core of this book. In it Bart has not only documented various impressions from the 1950s, even though this in itself would have made an attractive publication. He has also invited renowned scholars from around the world – many of whom have themselves excavated at the sites which they describe – to report on what we know today about the sites that Leo Boer visited 60 years ago. It is precisely this contrast between the beginning of a new post-Second World War era and the huge progress that has been achieved since that I find particularly fascinating.

The many old and new photographs together with the skilled and careful hand of the editor and the expertise of many colleagues make this book a unique achievement, a pleasure to the eye and an inspiration for the mind. *Tolle lege!*

Leiden, November 2013

Jürgen K. Zangenberg
Professor for New Testament Exegesis and Early
Christian Literature
Professor of Archaeology
Leiden University

A Chance Meeting in a Museum

Bart Wagemakers

As an employee of the National Museum of Antiquities in Leiden, the Netherlands, I happened to meet the late Leo Boer at the museum on an ordinary weekday back in 1999. He approached me with some questions on the exhibition he was visiting. During our chat, the subject of our conversation gradually changed, and 30 minutes later we were discussing topics such as the history of the Levant, biblical archaeology and the Dead Sea Scrolls. It appeared that Boer had studied for the priesthood in Rome in the mid-1950s. In the course of his studies, he had the opportunity to stay in Jerusalem at the *École Biblique et Archéologique Française de Jérusalem* for one year (1953–1954), where he engaged in biblical studies, joined the third excavation led by Father Roland de Vaux at Khirbet Qumran, and participated in many archaeological excursions organised by the École Biblique.

Photographic films and a travel account

After our first meeting at the museum, he subsequently invited me to his home where I was able to ask him at length about his stay in Jerusalem and his studies at the École Biblique. During our conversation Boer suddenly produced two photo film canisters from his pocket and told me that these contained the photographs he had taken while excavating at Khirbet Qumran with de Vaux in March 1954. In his own words 'he never had the time to do anything with them' and that is why he had stored the film canisters in a small box in his garage for

decades! Some years later it occurred to me that these photographs could be of real significance for the archaeology of Qumran and some of them have now been published (Bart Wagemakers and Joan E. Taylor 2011, "New Photographs of the Qumran Excavations from 1954 and Interpretations of L.77 and L.86." *Palestine Exploration Quarterly* 143.2:134–56).

However, it was not until after his death in November 2009 that I realised that there might be more photo films stored in his garage. If he shot two films in just one week of excavation, how many photographs would he have taken during his stay in Jerusalem of a whole year? After contacting his wife Annemie and asking her to search for a box in the garage – she was not aware of its existence – another nineteen photo film canisters were found. In total we now have a collection of about 700 photographs taken of places in Lebanon, Syria, Jordan, Israel and Egypt in 1953 and 1954. Although Boer had not developed the photographs himself, he had carefully made a list of them during his stay in Jerusalem, including the numbers of the pictures, captions and the dates on which they were taken (see Appendix).

Boer also told me of the existence of a diary and travel account. After our first meeting in the museum and the subsequent conversation at his home, he became animated again about this phase of his life – which had drained away from his memory until that moment – and he decided to type up his handwritten diary and travel account. He and I then kept in touch over the years, and at one of our later encounters he showed me the result: an entire book work, consisting of about 140 pages, including a preface and index.

An archaeological historiography and themes

Boer's photographic collection and travel account are the sources of inspiration for this volume. The combination of his pictures and text provides us with an excellent spirit of the times, the years just after the Second World War and the foundation of the State of Israel. Moreover, it gives an account of the beginnings of a new phase in Palestinian archaeology, as will become clear in the chapters that follow. It raises interesting questions: what archaeological remains did Boer encounter on his visits to the sites; who were responsible for the actual archaeological results which he encountered, and what archaeological activities were undertaken subsequent to his visit?

Therefore, instead of focusing on the history of certain sites, the contributors to this volume – each of them an expert on the site they are writing about – focus on questions such as: who have excavated the site? What were the specific aims of these excavations? What kind of techniques and methods were used? What were the most noteworthy finds and interpretations of these archaeological campaigns? Did any major misconceptions occur in the past?

Since this volume concentrates on the history of archaeological campaigns from the beginning of the twentieth century up until today, it has become an 'archaeological historiography', which not only provides an overview of the most distinguished archaeologists and their work in this region, but also demonstrates the enormous development in archaeological methods and techniques as well as the change in archaeological approaches during the last 100 years.

This volume also discusses several themes which are typical for the archaeology and excavations of the selected sites, and which demonstrate the versatility of archaeology and its interdisciplinary character. In some chapters the theme is incorporated into the archaeological historiography, in others it appears as a separate section. The themes featured in this volume include: the identification of biblical sites; biblical interpretation of archaeological remains; regional surveys; underwater archaeology; archaeothanatology; excavation and restoration; archaeology and politics; archaeology and science; archaeology and heritage management.

The selection of archaeological sites

This volume follows in Leo Boer's footsteps. It describes the history of archaeological expeditions at nine selected sites, located in present-day Israel and the Palestinian Territories, which Boer visited in the mid-1950s. The arrangement of the chapters is based on the chronological order of Boer's visits of these locations. The following sites are discussed successively (see Fig. 1): Jerusalem; Khirbet et-Tell; Samaria & Sebaste; Tell Balata (Shechem); Tell es-Sultan (Jericho); Khirbet Qumran; Caesarea Maritima; Megiddo; Bet She'an.

Several criteria were used to determine the selection of these sites. First of all, the site is well documented by Boer with photographs and text. Second, the archaeological historiography of the site is noteworthy and, preferably, the location is of archaeological importance even today. Most of the selected sites are still being excavated (for instance, Caesarea, Tell es-Sultan, Megiddo, and Jerusalem) or their (biblical) identification or history is still being disputed (Khirbet et-Tell and Khirbet Qumran). Furthermore, by opting for this type of selection of the sites I tried to present the reader with a variety of archaeological teams and of some of the most well-known archaeologists working in this region during the last hundred years. This diversity of archaeologists is reflected in the wide range of different approaches, methods and techniques. Finally, the selected sites hopefully present a balanced collection of major archaeological campaigns (Bet She'an and Caesarea), of sites that attract many tourists (Jerusalem, Khirbet Qumran and Megiddo), and of more modest sites that are also well worth the attention (Khirbet et-Tell and Tell Balata).

Some challenges

Writing a history of archaeology in the Levant, an author inevitable encounters several 'challenges'. Even though the ancient sites have been situated at the same location for centuries, if not millennia, the territory in which the sites are located, changed hands numerous times in the past amongst different authorities. Consequently, most of the sites are known by several different names. They could be Arabic, Hebrew, Greek, Latin names or others, originating from the Bronze and Iron Ages, the Hellenistic,

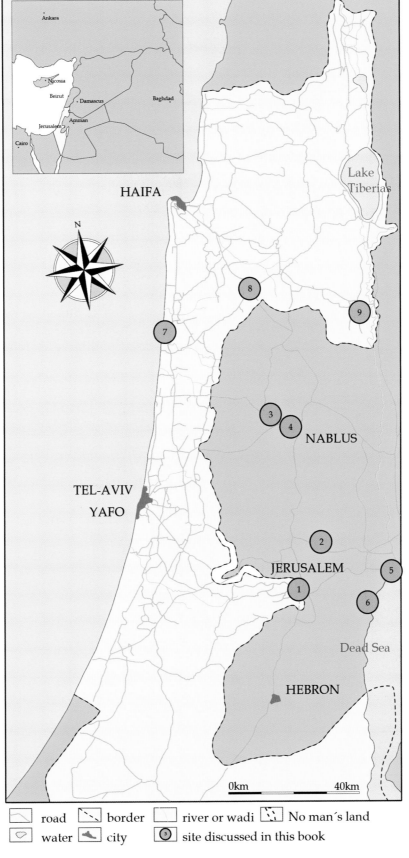

Figure 1: Overview of the sites discussed in this volume:
1. *Jerusalem*
2. *Khirbet et-Tell*
3. *Samaria & Sebaste*
4. *Tell Balata (Shechem)*
5. *Tell es-Sultan (Jericho)*
6. *Khirbet Qumran*
7. *Caesarea Maritima*
8. *Megiddo*
9. *Bet She'an*

Roman, Byzantine, Crusaders or Arabic periods. As this volume follows Leo Boer in his footsteps, I decided to adopt his use of place names when required, although in general the authors used their own preference.

The place names referred to on the maps in chapter 1, showing the routes of Boer's monthly excursions and his journeys through Israel and Jordan of that time, derive from topographical maps used by Boer himself which I came across in his study after his death in 2009.

The Leo Boer Archive

This volume contains a mere 70 of the almost 700 photographs that Boer took during his stay in the Levant. As the whole photographic collection may indeed have some significance for the study of the (archaeological) history of this region, it was decided to make all the photographs accessible to the public, not just the ones selected for this volume. Therefore the 'Leo Boer Archive' has now been founded (www.leoboerarchives.com) and it is most welcome that *The American Schools of Oriental Research* has been willing to locate the entire digital archive on their website. The photographs in the digital archive are all supplied with their negative numbers, captions, and dates on which the photographs were taken (see Appendix).

Acknowledgements

Finally, I would like to take this opportunity to show my gratitude to a number of people, without whom this project would never have been realised. First of all, I would like to thank Annemie Boer for her permission to publish Leo's photographs and accounts. I will remember Leo as a very cordial and kind man who had many interests and an excellent memory. Leo and Annemie always welcomed me with much hospitality to their home and I consider our friendship as very special.

Furthermore, this project received financial support from the University of Applied Sciences Utrecht, Stichting Jacques de Leeuw, Ms. T. Koning and Mrs. A. Boer. Their interest in this project and their confidence in a successful outcome are much appreciated. I would also like to show my gratitude to my employer, the University of Applied Sciences Utrecht. Especially to Huib de Jong and Dick de Wolff – former member of the Executive Board and director of the Faculty of Education respectively – who supported this project in every possible way, to Hans Werker, head of the History Department, who helped to create some space in my lecturing schedule and to my colleague Jaap Patist, with whom I was able to share my experiences of this project and who provided me with much useful feedback.

As I am fully aware of the extremely busy schedules the authors of this volume have, I am really grateful to them for participating in this project. They were willing to spend time going through Boer's account and photographic material and without their efforts this volume would not have come to fruition.

I would like also to express thanks to the following people for their help in this project: Laliv Happee-Doron, student at the ITV Hogeschool voor Tolken en Vertalen, who translated a large part of Boer's account into English. Vivien Hargreaves, another student at this institute, was responsible for editing the English texts and translated the lists of photographs into English (see Appendix). She did an excellent job. I want to thank Fieke Zijlstra, Fransien Kroon, and Alan Killip for their assistance of these students. Willem Beex used his expertise to generate accurate route maps of Boer's journeys in the Levant in the mid-1950s. I am grateful to Clare Litt, Val Lamb and Sam McLeod of Oxbow Books, for our pleasant and successful collaboration.

Special thanks I owe to Margreet Steiner for her help and advice during the entire project. Her enthusiasm was contagious and her critical comments were essential for the editing process. I really enjoyed our constructive teamwork.

Last, but certainly not least, I am very grateful to Hester and our daughters Nynke and Mirthe. During many years they coped with my fascination with the Leo Boer Archive and the excessive amount of time and energy I spent on researching it. Nevertheless, they showed understanding and compassion and they encouraged me in several ways to actually put the project in motion. Their support has been invaluable.

Utrecht, November 2013

Bart Wagemakers
University of Applied Sciences Utrecht

Chronological Table

Period	Approximate dates
Neolithicum	
Pre-Pottery Neolithic	10,000–6,500 BCE
Pottery Neolithic	6,500–4,300 BCE
Chalcolithic	4,300–3,300 BCE
Bronze Age	
Early Bronze Age	3,300–2,300 BCE
Intermediate Bronze Age	2,300–1,800 BCE
Middle Bronze Age	1,800–1,550 BCE
Late Bronze Age	1,550–1,200 BCE
Iron Age	
Iron Age I	1,200–1,000 BCE
Iron Age II	1,000–586 BCE
Babylonian Period	586–539 BCE
Persian Period	539–332 BCE
Hellenistic Period	332–64 BCE
Roman Period	64 BCE–313 CE
Byzantine Period	313–632 CE
Early Islamic Period	632–1099 CE
Crusader and Ayyubid Period	1099–1250 CE
Mamluk Period	1250–1516 CE
Ottoman Period	1516–1917 CE

Chapter 1

Leo Boer, a Dutch Student in the Near East (1953–1954)

Bart Wagemakers

Before focussing on several archaeological sites in Israel and the Palestinian territories dealt with in the succeeding chapters, it is worth taking a closer look at the background of Leo Boer himself and at the documentation of his activities in 1953–1954, which is the starting-point of this book. This chapter contains a biography on Boer, an account of his stay in Jerusalem in the mid-1950s, an overview of his photo collection and travel account, and ends by showing the significance of his documentation.

Leonardus Hermanus Cornelis (Leo) Boer (1926–2009)

Leo Boer was born in the city of Delft in the Netherlands on 23 July 1926. He grew up in a Catholic family and he had already decided, when he was quite young, to devote his life to religion. After having attended religious education colleges in Sint-Oedenrode (1938–1943) and Simpelveld (1943–1944), Boer started work as a novice, under the priest name of Barnabas, in Bavel on 31 August 1944. On 25 September 1945 he took his 'temporary vows' and became a member of the *Congregazione dei Sacri Cuori di Gesù e di Maria* (SS.CC. Picpus; Congregation of the Sacred Hearts of Jesus and Mary). From 1945 till 1947 he studied philosophy at the Major Seminary in Valkenburg (in the south of the Netherlands. After completing this study, he went to Rome to study Theology at the *Pontificia Università Gregoriana* (Pontifical Gregorian University). Having graduated in 1951, he then became a *Candidato al Dottorato* at the *Pontificio Instituto Biblico* (Pontifical Biblical Institute), which is located across the square from the Gregorian University. Four years later Boer completed his studies by writing his *exercitatio ad lauream*, about the 'The Sanctuary of Bethel in the Books of Judges and Samuel'.

It appears that Boer was a brilliant student. He graduated magna cum laude from the Gregorian University and his study results at the Biblical Institute were also on average above a 9 (on a scale to ten). For his *exercitatio* he even gained a 9.75. Hence, it is no wonder that the Biblical Institute awarded him his degree *maxima cum laude*.

In 1953, while he was working on his PhD at the Biblical Institute, the 26-year-old Boer was given the opportunity to study at the renowned *École Biblique et Archéologique Française de Jérusalem* for one year (Figs 1.1 and 1.2). There he chose to read 'Biblical study', instead of 'Archaeology', the other field of study available at this institute. This choice tended to determine the subjects which Boer studied, as the register of the École Biblique in 1953–1954 shows: 'Rev. Pat. Leonardus BOER, Congreg. Sacrorum Cordium (Picpus), Hollandus, S. Theol. Licens., S.S. Prolyta, Exeg. V.T.; Exeg. N.T.; Hist. Bibl.; Archaeologiae; linguarum agyptiacae et arabicae studens (cursus maior) nec non syriacae'.

Figure 1.1: *Leo Boer, aged 26, posing in the Jordan desert (19 October 1953).*

Figure 1.2: *Photograph of the École Biblique, taken from the Ben Shadad road (6 December 1953).*

Although Boer preferred biblical study to the field of archaeology, he was to encounter the archaeology of the Holy Land in several ways during his stay at the École Biblique.

After his year in Jerusalem Boer returned to Rome and wrote his *exercitatio ad lauream*. Shortly after that, in 1955, he moved back to the Netherlands where he held several offices in the church. Then on 28 July 1955 Boer was appointed professor in the Holy Scripture at the Major Seminary in Valkenburg, where he had been a philosophy student almost a decade earlier. His main teachings concerned the exegesis of the Bible and contained courses such as 'Luke 1 and 2', 'The travel accounts of John' and 'An introduction to the letters of Paul'.

Out of the blue, or so it seemed to people around him, his liturgical career came to an abrupt end in 1968. In November 1967 Boer applied for priestly dispensation, which was granted to him on 25 October 1968. His motives for applying become clear in a letter to his colleagues in June 1968:

'In November of last year, I applied for priestly dispensation. I have decided to do this, because for me the meaning of the priesthood has almost faded away in the way my life has changed. And I did not want to appear as someone who I am not anymore in my heart. Besides, I found my thoughts and myself to be no longer compatible with the existing notions and with the meaning of the office. I have no intention of leaving the church and I hope to give shape to the Gospel – which has been such an important part of my life because of my study – in a new way. Whether I will ever get married, I don't know. At the moment I have nobody in mind.'

After he was granted priestly dispensation, Boer's life changed completely, albeit gradually. He married Annemie Hakze in 1970 and they raised five boys (Fig. 1.3). He found work in the building trade, yet he never lost his interest in theology. Up until his death on 9 November 2009 he continued to give many lectures about topics relating to religion. Apart from giving lectures, he also worked as a volunteer for several charities.

Figure 1.3: Leo and Annemie Boer (August 2008).

Boer was an extremely kind person who was concerned about the needs of others. His social skills did not remain unnoticed while he was a lecturer at the Valkenburg seminary. Jan Wouters, one of Boer's former students, remembers Boer, besides lecturing on the Holy Scriptures, organising several film evenings for the students every year and arranging the annual carnival festivities at the seminary in the 1960s.

Not only former students remember Boer kindly. Also the people who got to know Boer in Jerusalem, were impressed by his cheerful character. One of those people was Th. C. Vriezen (1899–1981), Old Testament professor at Utrecht University, who travelled frequently to the Levant in the first half of the twentieth century. When Vriezen visited Jerusalem in the spring of 1954, he met with Boer several times; they had lunches and dinners together and they joined the same daytrip to the monastery of Latrun. In his letters to his family in the Netherlands, Vriezen mentions Boer several times as the 'cheerful Father Boer'. This jolly disposition of Boer was even the reason for Vriezen to place a bet. A letter he wrote to his wife on 29 June 1954 reads:

> '.... I must rectify my previous statements a bit; I have always been in the opinion that Father Boer, the cheerful Father, was a Jesuit; but now I have been told that he is not. He belongs to the Congregation of the Sacred Hearts of Jesus and Mary and somebody here (an Englishman who previously lived in a Catholic institute in Paris) said: "a Jesuit never smiles, and merely chuckles when he laughs, but this Father roars with laughter, so he could not be a Jesuit" (which was confirmed by two other Fathers here). Therefore, if you ever happen to meet the laughing Father, he is not a Jesuit as I wrongly assumed. It cost me two packets of cigarettes, because the Englishman wanted to bet...'[1]

Besides his cheery character, Boer was always meticulous and well-organised. An example: although he never developed the photographs he took during his stay in the Near East, he made a minutely detailed list of them including the numbers of the pictures, captions and the dates when they were taken. Moreover, in his travel account, Boer refers to the numbers of the corresponding photographs. Thanks to this list, it was possible to identify the names and locations of the places shown in the pictures.

Another example of his tremendous sense of organisation is the way in which he ordered his own office and study. Even after his death I was able to find all the documentation about his travels in the Near East without any difficulty: notebooks; maps; curriculum and code of conduct of the École Biblique; even a drawing of the routes of the four trips he made with his lecturers and fellow students at Petra.

One further aspect of his character I should like to mention here, namely his excellent memory. Every bit of information about his time in Jerusalem which he told me during the many conversations we had, and which I was able to check, appears to be correct. The following example is a perfect illustration of this. One day Boer mentioned to me that, on the last day of his stay during the third archaeological expedition of Father Roland de Vaux in Khirbet Qumran, on 27 March 1954, they found an artefact which was identified by someone as an inkwell. A few hours later Boer returned to the École Biblique and never heard of this 'inkwell' again. Oddly enough, the field notes of de Vaux do not mention any inkwell found *in situ* in 1954 (Humbert and Chambon 2003). Having searched in the field notes myself for a mention of an artefact that was found on 27 March and which could have been wrongly identified as an inkwell – possibly by one of the assistants or students present at the site – I came to the conclusion that there could only be one solution: on the day concerned the team excavated an *unguentarium* (archive number: 1500) at locus 96, a small flask used for preserving perfume, essential oils or other precious liquids.[2]

To try and find out whether what Boer had seen was indeed this same flask, I compared the available data in the archives of the École Biblique with the details Boer had given me of the object that was found in his presence 55 years ago. The resemblance of the data was astonishing! According to Boer, the 'earthenware artefact had the same colouring as the wall where it was found (a kind of yellow), had a length of approximately ten centimetres and the thickness of the rim was five millimetres'. The *unguentarium* that is stored at the École Biblique is also made of pottery, its length is 10.6 centimetres and the rim five millimetres in thickness. Even the colour mentioned on the data card of the flask corresponds with Boer's description: 'terre chamois' (Wagemakers 2009). These details of the flask have never been published before, and this story demonstrates how excellent Boer's memory was.

Following this brief biography on Leo Boer, it is important now to describe the new environment he entered into in October 1953, including the political situation of Jerusalem and daily life at the École Biblique in the 1950s, so as to have a proper understanding of his travel account and insight into the photographic material.

Israel, Jordan and Jerusalem in the 1950s

Boer visited the Near East in turbulent times: the Second World War ended nearly ten years earlier, yet the foundation of the State of Israel and the subsequent War of Independence took place only five years prior to Boer's arrival in East Jerusalem on 14 October 1953. During the years 1953–1954 this region was not at all peaceful and Boer's account gives several references to the tense political situation, including indications of anti-semitism during his journey from Rome to East Jerusalem. The first anti-semitic incident concerned a fellow passenger on the boat from Naples to Beirut – a Muslim from Cairo – who Boer visited because the man was ill. Boer writes that the man 'had been under the weather much in his lifetime, because his wife was a Jewess'. Further on, when Boer records his journey from Baalbek to Damascus, he writes: 'Useless formalities at the border. Everything went well. Hatred against Jews'.

The creation of new borders and the tense political situation since 1948 forced the Jordanians to move existing roads. For example, the road to Bethlehem and Hebron, which started at the Jaffa Gate in Jerusalem, ran through Israeli territory. For that reason the Jordanians decided to build a new road in 1952.[3]

On several occasions, the group from the École Biblique encountered a hostile, 'anti-Western' attitude from local residents. At times, this tension led to the cancellation of an intended visit to a site or village, such as the planned visit to Halhul (Alula), located in the neighbourhood of Hebron. At other times, the group did manage to visit a site as intended, but only in the company of armed policemen or soldiers, such as happened in Lachish. Another good example of this is their visit to the city of Hebron. Boer writes that, before entering the city, a policeman got onto the bus as a precaution. According to Boer, the inhabitants would sometimes be aggressive towards Westerners, and the group was strictly forbidden to take photographs of local residents. In addition, during an excursion in the Negev, the group was accompanied by an armed escort, although Boer does not mention whether this was for the same reason as the cases above refer to. During their visit to the caves of Marissa, near Beth Govrin in Israel, the same armed escort asked the party to leave the area immediately after shots were heard at close range.

This strained atmosphere was also present in Jerusalem. Between 1948 and 1967 the city was divided into an Israeli (West) and a Jordan section (East). The École Biblique was located in East Jerusalem and was separated from the Jewish section by a length of no man's land. The crossing-point was situated at the so-called Mandelbaum Gate (Fig. 1.4), about 150 metres to the north of the institute. Travelling from one section to the other required certain formalities, such as being in possession of two passports because it was not possible to have both an Israeli and a Jordan visa on one passport. On 26 April 1954 Boer crossed the gate, along with some of his lecturers and his fellow students, in order to make a trip through Israel. In his account he writes:

'After having divided some items of baggage among the various group members, we left the atrium at 8 a.m., all ready and raring to go. We walked towards the Mandelbaum Gate, approximately 150 metres north of the school. There was a great display of military presence on the Arab side of the border. The border checkpoint itself was no more than a small hut. The surrounding area, which looked as though it used to be a beautiful neighbourhood, offered a sad view: a square with roads leading onto it, and heavily damaged villa's with gardens that were beautiful once, now completely abandoned and neglected. Some 50 metres ahead we could see the Jewish checkpoint. We passed through quickly on the Arab side of the border; after our names were checked, we were allowed to move on. On the Jewish side, however, it took a lot longer. Our only comfort was that this was a decent, be it wooden, building where we could sit down at least. Everyone had to fill in a couple of forms, which were examined and stamped by some officials. Next, all cameras and other things had to be listed and our luggage was noted on our papers. Finally, just as we thought all the formalities were done, we had to be inoculated against smallpox. Then, at last, everything was ready and we were allowed to leave.'

All these examples indicate the tense environment which Boer encountered. It is clear that these incidents had an effect on him, as he wrote about them in his accounts. Initially, he made brief notes about events, encounters and experiences in two small notebooks. Then, a few times a week, he wrote out most of these notes into accurate accounts.

Figure 1.4: *The Mandelbaum Gate viewed from the Jordan sector. On the right is a sign which directs people to the right at the crossing (24 December 1953).*

Boer's intriguing accounts

As the accounts are quite substantial, about 145 pages long, Boer himself divided it into several sections. The following sections will feature respectively: the diary; historical and archaeological walks; monthly excursions; and journeys through Jordan and Israel.

The diary

The first section in his diary is concerned with daily occurrences, encounters, and ... the weather! Not every day is described in such an extensive way. Here follows a selection of some interesting descriptions and conclusions from his diary.

Travelling from Rome to East Jerusalem 60 years ago was not as easy as it is today. Boer left Rome on Sunday 4 October 1953 and arrived in Jerusalem ten days later. From Rome he travelled by train to

Naples, and from there he took a boat which was headed for Beirut. Three days after the boat had left Naples, it arrived at Alexandria, where some of the passengers disembarked. After a six-hour stop, the boat departed for Beirut, where it arrived on 8 October. Boer stayed in Beirut for three days at a monastery, run by Franciscan friars, and visited Baalbek, among other sites. Then, on 11 October, he was brought to Damascus by taxi, where he stayed with Franciscans for another two days. Finally, Boer took a taxi to East Jerusalem via Amman, where he arrived at the École Biblique on 14 October at 3 p.m.

In his account of his journey to East Jerusalem, he describes in detail the encounters he had on this journey, especially the ones on the ship, in which he emphasises the religious and cultural background of the people he met. It seems that there were a lot of clergy on board. The document also reveals a lot about the political circumstances in Egypt at the time. Boer writes that when the boat arrived in the harbour of Alexandria, the chief of the harbour police came on board to welcome the passengers to Egypt in a variety of languages, and to assure them that the current situation was under control thanks to Muhammad Naguib, the first president of Egypt (1953–1954). Boer noticed that the defeat of King Farouk was illustrated by the derelict royal palace which he could see from the boat.

From his diary it also becomes clear that Boer found the housing at the École Biblique pretty poor. He was staying with eleven other students in a separate building with one tap and a shower (a rope fastened to a bucket) which sometimes provided warm water. The door to Boer's room – which was also the front door – was too high at the bottom, too low at the top, and too narrow. There was no heating in the room. The cook at the institute used to be a veterinary surgeon. The story went that he often dished up meat from female camels, which had been cooked for hours in a pressure-cooker. Even so, the meat was foul, which made many of the residents go to the Dom Polsky hostel for dinner instead.

Another aspect evident from his diary, is that his stay at the institute offered Boer the opportunity to meet well-known and learned scholars as well as academics who were at the start of a promising career. At the École Biblique he was in touch with scholars such as Roland de Vaux (who, at the time, was also the director of the institute), Louis-Hughes Vincent and Józef Milik. The latter was back in Jerusalem in September 1953 to work on the fragments of the Dead Sea Scrolls that were found in Cave 4. One of Boer's student peers was Maurice Baillet – a student at the institute from 1952 to 1954 and from 1958 onwards the eighth member of the 'Cave 4 team' – and Boer was present at his farewell party at the École Biblique on 23 April 1954. Furthermore, Boer spent a great deal of time with Ernest-Marie Laperrousaz, the future director of the well-established École Pratique des Hautes Études in Paris, who participated in the excavations at Khirbet Qumran under the guidance of de Vaux during these years.

It seems that biblical and archaeological expertise came together in those days, not only in the École Biblique, but across the whole of Jerusalem. For example, Boer had several conversations with Frank Cross who had just been appointed as the 'annual professor' at the American School of Oriental Research – the present W. F. Albright Institute of Archaeological Research – for 1953–1954 and was also its acting director. Boer met Kathleen Mary Kenyon – then the Honorary Director of the British School of Archaeology in Jerusalem since 1951 – twice at Tell es Sultan nearby Jericho, where she was excavating at the time (see Sala in this volume). He was shown the *Homo Carmelitanus* at the Rockefeller Museum by Dorothy Garrod, who had directed the renowned campaign in 1929 at the foot of Mount Carmel, where several caves were explored and the remains of prehistoric humans were discovered (Garrod and Bate 1937).

Besides his encounters with these scholars, Boer also had the opportunity to acquire archaeological experience himself during his time at the institute. Despite the fact that he was a student of Biblical studies, he took part in numerous visits of archaeological sites that were organised by the École Biblique. The institute expected him to join the excavation at Khirbet Qumran for one week, where he participated in de Vaux's third expedition from 20 to 27 March 1954 (Fig. 1.5). It has become apparent only recently that his visit to Qumran was important in view of the present field research of Qumran archaeology. Boer took more than twenty photographs at the site during that week, and some of them appear to be of great significance: thanks to two of his photographs, existing theories concerning the 'dining room' and the 'pantry' as used by the Qumran community – L.77 and 86 – may need to be reconsidered (Wagemakers and Taylor 2011).

Historical and archaeological walks

The École Biblique used to organise walks to historical and archaeological locations in the Jordan sector of Jerusalem at an average rate of one every two weeks. Unfortunately, Boer does not give any detailed description of these walks in his diary, only their destinations and dates; from this we know that they visited (among other sites) the City of David, the Church of the Holy Sepulchre, Gethsemane, the Mount of Olives, the Garden Tomb, Cedron Valley, Hezekiah's Tunnel, Haceldama, Robinson's Arch and the 'former' Jewish Quarter (Fig. 1.6). Despite the fact that there is no comprehensive account available, we do at least have Boer's photographs of these locations at our disposal.

Figure 1.5: Tea break at Khirbet Qumran during de Vaux's third expedition from 20 to 27 March 1954. Boer is sitting on the far left, de Vaux (with beard) and Józef Milik on the right (25 March 1954).

Figure 1.6: The 'former' Jewish Quarter at the south-east sector of the Old City in Jerusalem. The Sidna Omar minaret is visible in the background. The domes of both the Tifaret Yisrael Synagogue and the Hurva Synagogue – which used to be part of the skyline of this quarter – are missing because they were demolished in the war of 1948 (1 June 1954).

Monthly excursions

At the institute Father Lemoine was responsible for conducting the excursions. Every month he used to organise an elective day trip. However, trips were frequently postponed in 1953-1954 because of poor weather conditions. All the excursions were to archaeological sites relating to biblical places and most of them had rather packed schedules: the participants left early in the morning, travelled long distances by a privately-hired bus, and did not return until the evening. Boer's accounts of the five excursions, which he joined (Fig. 1.7), are very detailed, but this is not the right place to explore their content in its entirety. Nevertheless, in order to give

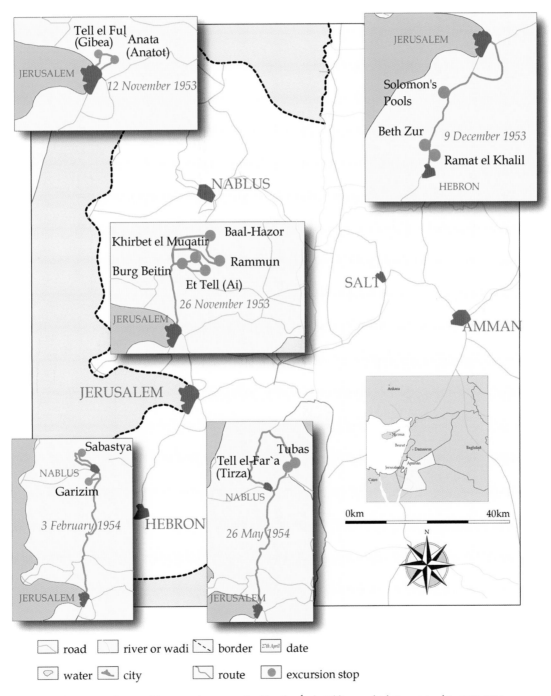

Figure 1.7: The monthly excursions organised by the École Biblique, which Boer joined in 1953-1954.

an impression of the type of these excursions, I will list some of the locations Boer visited and cite some remarks from his account. Please note that his remarks represent the (archaeological) views of the 1950s.

The first excursion that Boer joined was to Tell el-Ful (Gibeah). William Foxwell Albright excavated the site in 1922 and found (among other things) the foundations of a building which he attributed to King Saul. In 1927, parts of the walls collapsed as a result of an earthquake. According to Boer, the site was nothing more than 'a pile of stones' in 1953, yet he was able to photograph a corner of Saul's building (Fig. 1.8).

The first stop during the second excursion was at Khirbet et-Tell ('Ai), located 2.5 kilometres north-east of Bethel (Beitin). Judith Marquet-Krause excavated the site in 1933, 1934 and 1935 (see Petit in this volume). Boer describes the results of the campaign in fairly elaborate detail and mentions among other things three walls, a gate, an ancient sanctuary containing three constructions from different periods, a palace, and a few houses dating from the Iron Age. Later that day, the group travelled to Khirbet el-Maqatir – one kilometre due west of Khirbet et-Tell – where they explored the outlines and pieces of mosaic from a fourth century church and a monastery dating from the sixth century. Burğ Beitin was the next stop. There they saw a second-century *temenos* and a large part of a Crusader tower measuring 42 × 32.60 metres. Unfortunately, the 'modern' town of Beitin had been built exactly on top of the location of biblical Bethel, which meant that little could be seen of the campaign which Albright had directed in 1934. After their visit to Jebel el ʿAsūr (Baal-Hazor), they were caught in a heavy rain shower and decided to stop for a break at Et-Taiyibe. This village had not yet undergone any excavation, but they were able to visit the ruins of a Byzantine church and St. Elias, a Crusader castle, which was handed over by Baldwin IV to Boniface of Montferrat in 1185. Just outside the town stood

Figure 1.8: A corner of Saul's building in Tell el-Ful. About ten years after Boer took this photograph, King Hussein of Jordan decided to build a palace on top of this tell. This building project came to a standstill due to the Six-Day War in 1967 (12 November 1953).

the fifth-century church of St. George, which had been restored by the Crusaders (Fig. 1.9).

Another excursion was to Hebron and the sites on the road leading to the city. The group stopped at Solomon's pools after visiting the cistern of 'Ein 'Arrub. In Hebron, they were able to enter the mosque despite being non-Muslims thanks to the permission of the Jordan Ministry of Awqaf. After they visited the pool of Hebron (2 Samuel 4:12), the bus then took them to Jebel Rumeide where they saw the city walls of ancient Hebron, with the Deir Arbain monastery at the top. In the afternoon, they arrived at Ramet el Khalil, which is ancient Mambre. Boer makes a reference to the excavations of Evaristus Mader some 25 years earlier, summarising them as follows:[4] '(1) the hedge, which measured 65 × 49 metres, dated from the time of Herod; (2) at the time of Emperor Hadrian (117–136), a temple was built which was dedicated to Hermes; (3) the 'altar of Abraham' was found; (4) a church was built on the orders of Constantine I (324–337); (5) the ancient

floor found beneath the first construction dates from the period of the Kings.'

Jordan and Israel

During Boer's stay at the École Biblique, he went on two extended trips, organised by the institute: one through Jordan (18–29 October 1953) and one through Israel (26 April–13 May 1954). Figures 1.10 and 1.11 show the itineraries of these excursions. The group traversed the greater part of the accessible areas of the two countries. In his accounts Boer noted carefully the exact number of kilometres they covered each day. He also gives a detailed description of the routes they followed; he even mentions the smallest and insignificant sand tracks in the Jordan desert. As he also listed the names of all the participants on the excursions and the religious order to which they were affiliated, we now know who joined Boer on these journeys and, indeed, who was studying at the École Biblique during 1953–1954.

Figure 1.9: Et-Taiyibe, with the ruins of the church of St. George in the background (26 November 1953).

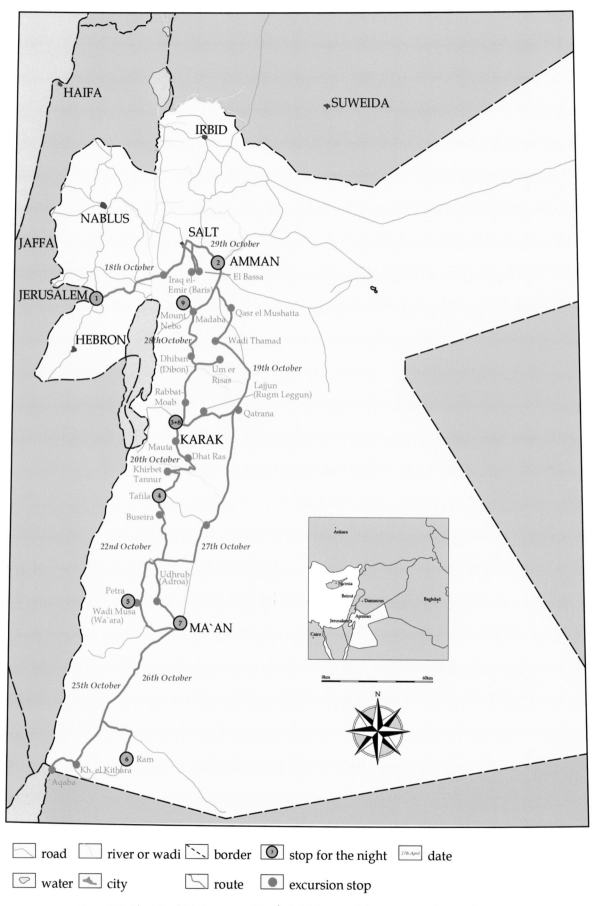

HAIFA

SUWEIDA

IRBID

NABLUS

JAFFA

SALT
29th October

18th October

AMMAN
El Bassa

JERUSALEM ①
Iraq el-
Emir (Baris)

⑨
Qasr el Mushatta

HEBRON
Mount
Nebo
Madaba

28thOctober
Wadi Thamad

Dhiban
(Dibon)
Um er
Risas
19th October

Rabbat-
Moab
Lajjun
(Rugm Leggun)

3+8
Qatrana

KARAK

Mauta
Dhat Ras

20th October
Khirbet
Tannur

Tafila ④

Buseira

22nd October
27th October

Udhrub
(Adroa)

Petra
⑤
Wadi Musa
(Wa`ara)
⑦ MA`AN

25th October
26th October

⑥ Ram
Kh. el Kithara
Aqaba

Ankara
Nicosia
Beirut
Damascus
Baghdad
Jerusalem
Amman
Cairo

0km   60km

N

road   river or wadi   border   ③ stop for the night   27th April date

water   city   route   ● excursion stop

Figure 1.10: The trip which the group of the École Biblique made between 18 and 29 October 1953.

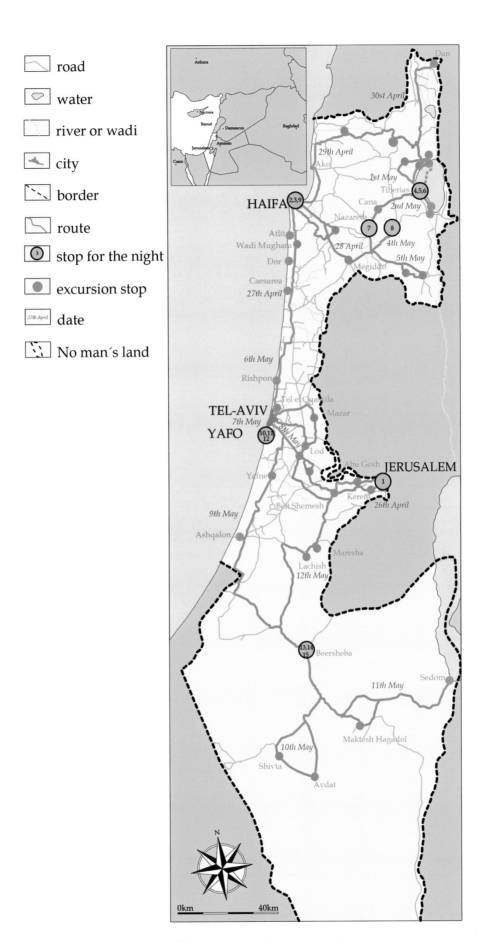

Figure 1.11: The route of the Israel journey between 26 April and 13 May 1954.

Despite the difference in destination, there are many similarities to the journeys. In both cases, the group was led by Father Louis Lemoine, and visited numerous archaeological and religious sites, came into contact with many local people, travelled long distances every day, and – despite the full programme – reserved a relatively large amount of time for lunch (Fig. 1.12). Furthermore, one can deduce some general points from reading the extensive account of the two journeys:

1) There were a number of particular requirements for travelling through Jordan and visiting its archaeological sites. For instance, the group had to be in possession of recommendations from the local police or preferably from the Arab Legion (the Jordan army). In addition, the group leader was supposed to reserve time for drinking coffee with the local official before visiting the site;

2) When the group arrived at the sites in Jordan, they were frequently welcomed by members of the Antiquities Guard who acted on instructions from Gerald Lancaster Harding, the Director-General of the Department of Antiquities. As a result of his recommendations, the group was not only granted access to every part of various sites, they were also given free entry: 'Do not forget', Boer writes, 'that the admission fee for Petra is one whole Dinar!'. Unfortunately, Lancaster Harding was not there when they visited the recently-built Museum of Antiquities in Amman, to thank him for his help;

3) The group had good contact with the police posts in Jordan: on several occasions, they ate and slept at the posts;

4) Some of the Israeli sites were closed for visitors in the 1950s, because of the army presence. The ruins of Crusader castle Migdal Aphek in Antipatris, for example, were not accessible because soldiers had taken up post there. The famous Byzantine Monastery of the Cross, on the outskirts of Jerusalem, had become a military station too. The group was also prohibited from visiting 'Atlit, which housed 'one of the best preserved Crusader castles in the region' according to Boer, because the army had a camp there which served as a depot.

Figure 1.12: Lunch at Shobak (21 October 1953).

5) Boer was absolutely not familiar with the way of life in Israeli kibbutzim. In his account he notices the 'strange' customs he encountered at these places. Especially the position of women in the kibbutzim caught his attention. After visiting kibbutz Ayelet Hasharar, for instance, Boer remarked that the kibbutz itself looked like a small paradise (neat, well-maintained houses, small gardens and trees everywhere, and the sound of birds filling the air), and that 'women and young girls were walking around in shorts or trousers, showing with their behaviour and attitude that they were extremely emancipated'. He gives a similar remark after his visit of the kibbutz Beth Yerah: 'A young lady showed us around, typical for Israel where women are extremely emancipated. This is particularly striking in the eyes of those who have lived in the Arab district for some time, where women do not count for much'.

6) On another level and just a hilarious note: the bus they hired for their trips through Israel was of a poor quality. It gave them some serious problems when driving over Mount Carmel and Mount Tabor. At the latter site the group had to get out off the bus and walk the rest of the way to the top of the hill. During this particular journey the bus also had to be repaired several times. This was the reason that the visit of Megiddo was shortened. The same happened when the group tried to reach the monastery of the Carmelites on top of Mount Carmel, where they were supposed to stay overnight: the bus was unable to take them up due to some repairs and a taxi was ordered so as to take the cook and his cooking utensils up to the monastery, the rest of the party, however, had to walk up.

The photo collection

Remarkably, Boer never again thought about his travel account nor his photographic material after he returned to Rome and, later, to the Netherlands. He stored the film negatives in a box in his garage where they lay for almost 55 years before being picked up!

Thanks to the accurate photo lists, including all the captions, which Boer had made and the references in his account to the photographs, we know exactly what they show to us and when they were taken.

The collection of about 700 photographs – of a stupendously good quality – can be divided into several categories. In contrast with his account, this division into categories has been made by the author and not by Boer himself. A brief summary of the categories follows below in order to give an impression of the photo collection.

First of all, Boer photographed various landscapes in the Levant. These photographs perpetuate views of hills, rivers, deserts, plains, etc. Besides landscapes, he also took panned out pictures of cities and villages giving an impression of the skylines in those days. Some of the locations have not changed much since then, while others have grown and developed into a complex infrastructure and show higher buildings (Fig. 1.13). The third category is that of rural life, showing us beautiful pictures of ploughing, fishermen, and shepherds with their sheep. On the other hand, Boer also photographed the daily life of residents and streets in villages and cities. These photos vary: from a shot of the Christian quarter in Damascus to craftsmen in Jerusalem; from an almost desolate street in Lydda (Fig. 1.14) to the old harbour in Jaffa; from people cycling in Bethlehem to people standing in front of the Damascus gate in Jerusalem. It is not a surprise that Boer, as a student for the priesthood at the Pontifical Biblical Institute at Rome and of the École Biblique in Jerusalem, took many photographs of locations with a religious function or context (fifth category), such as the synagogue at Capernaum, the mosque in Hebron, the graves in the Kidron Valley, the Church of Saint Anna and Bethesda pool, the Dome of the Rock, a Palm Sunday procession on the Mount of Olives, the tomb of Lazarus in Bethany (Fig. 1.15) and the Western wall (which was located in the Jordan section in those days).

Finally, he took photos of archaeological sites that he visited on the historical and archaeological walks, the monthly day excursions and the longer journeys through Israel and Jordan. For instance, Boer visited Herodion before the start of the excavations by Victor Corbo (1962–1967) and later by Ehud Netzer (1972–1987; 1997–2000; 2005–2010). In his travel account we read that the group were guided around by a Bedouin and, as a matter of fact, the photo shows a Bedouin tent on the lower part of the hill pitched between the stones of the site. It looks like the photo was taken from the west side of the hill, later excavated by Netzer (Fig. 1.16). In Megiddo

Figure 1.13: The boulevard of Tiberias. The present upper city had not yet been built (1 May 1954).

Figure 1.14: Street in Lydda (8 May 1954).

Figure 1.15: Tomb of Lazarus in Bethany (30 May 1954).

Figure 1.16: A Bedouin tent in front of Herodion (23 May 1954).

Boer and his companions saw the results of the campaigns of Gottlieb Schumacher (on behalf of the German Society for Oriental Research, 1903–1905) and the Oriental Institute of the University of Chicago between 1925 and 1939 when four of the uppermost strata of the tell were excavated. Despite their being in a hurry – as their bus had to be repaired that evening, as mentioned before – Boer took photos of the Northern gate, the 'stables', an altar, and some cross-cuts. In his diary he noted that it was hard to distinguish the constructions on the tell because of the intensive vegetation which is clearly visible in these pictures (see Franklin in this volume). According to Boer, the site in Caesarea was hardly excavated when they visited the location on 27 April 1954 (see Holum in this volume) and when the group of the École Biblique was guided around by Kathleen Kenyon at Tell es-Sultan (ancient Jericho) during her third campaign, Boer concludes that 'the situation in Jericho is very complicated and requires much study, and I must admit that I do not understand much of it'. Fortunately, during their visit to Tell es-Sultan he took an important picture of skeleton remains that were still *in situ* (see Bocquentin and Wagemakers in this volume). Lastly, as I mentioned before, Boer was expected to join the excavation at Khirbet Qumran for one week, where he participated in de Vaux's third expedition from 20 to 27 March 1954. He took several pictures that week and they demonstrate clearly how the site has changed in the last 55 years.[5]

The significance of the account and the photographs

There are several ways in which the travel account and photographic material of Leo Boer offer scholars – in particular historians, archaeologists, and theologians – notable sources for their fields of interest. First of all, the combination of the account and pictures provides an excellent spirit of the times for historians. As has already been demonstrated, Boer describes the daily life in an area of the world that has a strained atmosphere. His work gives a good impression of what life was like in a divided city characterised by political tension, and what travelling was like through a state that had just been founded and whose right to exist was not undisputed. He also brings into the picture the archaeological and religious academic world in

Jerusalem of the 1950s. Boer does not only describe the activities and circumstances at the École Biblique, he also gives insight into the social networks that the scholars and students had, and the ongoing scholarly discussions that took place. Finally, the account also shows how a Dutch 26-years old Theology student experienced life in the Middle East 60 years ago. From his work we learn about what he was used to and what norms and values he had.

Archaeologists in particular benefit from Boer's writings and photographs. As Boer stayed at the École Biblique he was able to visit many archaeological sites accompanied by members of this institute, at a time when Palestinian archaeology was at the beginning of a new phase. After the Second World War and the foundation of the State of Israel in 1948, a new generation of archaeologists, approaches and methods came into being in Palestinian archaeology. Also, several new developments – such as the so-called 'Wheeler-Kenyon' method – marked a new phase in archaeology as will be demonstrated in the following chapters. By visiting numerous archaeological sites Leo Boer witnessed the results of these new approaches. In that sense his account and photographs give an interesting overview of the state-of-the-art archaeological techniques of that time. For example, the photograph of the skeleton remains *in situ* in Tell es-Sultan gives us an interesting insight into a new way of studying human remains as demonstrated by I. W. Cornwall, and provides a strong testimony of advanced field methodology as employed by him. In the 1950s Cornwall's field work was not only modern in his day but his general approach to human remains was definitively well-suited to the interpretation of complex burials. Therefore, it marks the beginning of a real interest in funerary archaeology (see Bocquentin and Wagemakers in this volume).

Another reason why Boer's work is valuable for archaeologists, is that it gives a detailed report of the views uttered by his lecturers during excursions and visits of sites and which did not always get published. It appears that they often did not mince their words about things and told the students exactly why they felt other scholars were wrong. In the account of his visit to Khirbet et-Tell, for instance, Boer mentions a difference of opinion between Judith Marquet-Krause and Roland de Vaux. Marquet-Krause, who led the excavations from 1933 until 1935, found a double wall behind which the inhabitants could entrench themselves (see Fig. 3.1 in Petit's contribution in this volume). In her opinion, the space between the walls had been used as a corridor. Boer writes that de Vaux fully disagreed with her and postulated that this construction was similar to the defence system at Tell Fara, and that the space used to be filled with sand in order to prevent the walls from collapsing.

Boer also mentions archaeological discoveries that were made during or just prior to his stay in the Middle East. This is illustrated by the following two examples: on 9 December 1953, during one of the monthly excursions, the group encountered a burial chamber in the stony bottom of the road from 'Ein ed Dirwe to Beth Zur. This chamber had been discovered only a few months earlier. The entrance, a set of steps, was blocked, and the ceiling had collapsed. Boer counted twelve tombs, and noted that some of the bones were exposed. The wall of this cavern was decorated with a symbol of the Christian cross. This was all he said at the time.

When, on 2 May 1954, during the trip through Israel, the participants were in the vicinity of Tiberias, they passed an excavation which was raising a lot of questions in the archaeological world at the time. In his account, Boer calls it the 'Place of the Bath', as it seems that the location did not yet have an official name. Some Arabic layers had already been excavated at the site, but the place also included Byzantine elements. According to Boer, the location contained a hall of which the floor was paved with mosaics of flowers, birds and other animals, including two donkey heads and an elephant. Other mosaics featured birds and fish. The images were placed in a kind of framework, which was more compacted than the ones in Tabgha, which were older, according to Boer. In addition, the site had a complicated system of waterworks and several *hypocausts*. A system of pipes was used to heat the second floor. There was a water reservoir with two canals, in which archaeologists found fifteen jars, the openings of which all pointed in the same direction. Finally, 24 columns were found that had been re-used in other buildings.

It is now certain that the site which the group was visiting are the ruins of the bathhouse of ancient Tiberias, excavated by Bezalel Rabani in the early 1950s, because many similarities are found between the details in Boer's account and the archaeological reports. At the time of Boer's visit, several Islamic

layers, a Byzantine layer and a layer from the late Roman period had already been revealed. Both halls that had been discovered in the bathhouse were decorated with mosaic floors dating from the sixth century CE, i.e. the second building phase of this complex (Hirschfeld and Galor 2007, 217, 220). The list of representations that Rabani provided includes animals (namely elephants, leopards, griffins, donkeys, birds and fish) and flowers. In addition, he exposed a brick oven that was connected to a *hypocaust* cellar with vaults through which pipes ran (Rabani 1953, 265). The water reservoir containing the fifteen jars has now been identified as a fish pond which might have been used to breed fish and has been dated to the third century CE (Hirschfeld and Galor 2007, 215).[6]

Aside from these matters of archaeological debate and discoveries, the photo collection also provides a valuable historic record of buildings and locations. A considerable number of photographs were taken from unusual angles, such as the picture of the assumed Roman aqueduct between Nablus and Samaria-Sebaste. This building has only been sporadically photographed from that side. This picture gives rise to the hypothesis that it does not show an aqueduct, but a water mill (see Gibson in this volume).

Moreover, most of the locations photographed by Boer have since changed irreversibly, which makes the material even more valuable. An example of this is the photograph of the Church of St. Anne and the Bethesda Pool in Jerusalem (Fig. 1.17): numerous excavations were conducted in the area of the Crusader-period Church of St. Anne, following the acquisition of property next to the church by the Catholic White Father's community in 1863 and onwards (Gibson 2011). The photograph shows a view of the Bethesda Pool excavation area towards the south-east and the well-preserved Church of St. Anne in the background; the ruins of the Crusader-period Chapel of the Sheep Pool are visible in the foreground. The open area seen on the left, showing some walls and a palm tree, which is to the east of the apse of the ruined church, was substantially excavated in the 1960s – only a few years after Boer's visit – and revealed remains of a large Byzantine church with Early Roman houses beneath. Additional excavations visible in the foreground of this picture brought to light remains of the northern basin of the Bethesda Pool. The structure on the right of the photograph (labelled 'Akourah' by the excavators) was dismantled

Figure 1.17: The Church of St. Anne and the Bethesda Pool (3 June 1954).

to make way for excavations which subsequently brought to light a corner of the deep southern basin of the Bethesda Pool.[7]

Boer even took a photograph of an artefact that disappeared shortly after. When Boer and his companions from the École Biblique were travelling through Jordan, during their visit to Aqaba on 26 October 1953, they were shown by an English Major a stone with a Greek inscription, which had been found by soldiers just a few days earlier. The inscription on the stone was difficult to read, and after trying very hard for an hour to decipher it, they gave up. As it turns out, the students of the École Biblique were not the first ones to study this inscription. Archaeologist Nelson Glueck had encountered the block of stone on his journey through the Aqaba area in late 1936. Based on his account, it seems that this re-used building block was found within the ruins of Khirbet el-Khâldeh (Khirbet el-Khalidi), approximately 40 kilometres north-east of the military base where Boer and his companions subsequently came across

it![8] A photograph of the block was published in the third volume of *Explorations in Eastern Palestine* (Glueck 1939, 18). Unfortunately, due to the poor quality of the picture, the inscription is difficult to read. And this was the only published photo of the inscription until now. At some point in time after 1953, the block disappeared from the artifactual record and has since not been found. This meant that all subsequent scholars have had to depend on Glueck's photograph. Although the quality of Boer's picture might be better than Glueck's original photograph, it is obvious that the inscription has weathered much more extensively in the seventeen years between Glueck's initial documentation and the later, fortuitous photograph taken by Boer in 1953 (see Wagemakers and Ameling 2012, for a revised reading of the text).

Leo Boer's documentation offers valuable access to the archaeological past of the Holy Land. The combination of the account and the photographic material gives an impression of the state of affairs in the Middle East of almost 60 years ago and may provide the field of archaeology of the Holy Land with new data. Unfortunately, Boer died in November 2009, and so is unable to witness the scholarly benefits that have resulted from his documentation which he stored in his garage all those years ago.

Notes

1 I would like to thank Dr. Karel Vriezen, son of Prof. Th. C. Vriezen, for providing this letter and relating information about his father in personal communication. The author is responsible for the English translation.

2 I am grateful to Prof. Mladen Popović, director of the Qumran Institute at the University of Groningen, for pointing out this possibility.

3 Thanks to these building activities, a part of a water pipe that ran from 'Ein 'Arrub to Jerusalem and dates from the time of Pontius Pilate, the fifth Roman prefect of Judaea (26–36 CE), was uncovered one kilometre from Sur Baher. Boer and his lecturers and fellow students visited this location on 9 December 1953.

4 These observations by Boer correspond fully with the conclusions in Mader's final report, published three years later (Mader 1957, 48, 77–78, 81, 99–115).

5 In 2011 all of Boer's pictures of Qumran were published on the website of the Palestine Exploration Fund (http://www.pef.org.uk/qumran). Some of them – where possible – are accompanied by recent photos (taken by the author in June 2009). In this way you are able to see what has happened to the site in half a century.

6 Hirschfeld and Galor mention two fish ponds in this area of ancient Tiberias: one is located in Area C, and the other underneath the bathhouse in Area A (see Fig. 2 in Hirschfeld 2007, 213). When reading Boer's description, it is clear that he saw the pool beneath the bathhouse.

7 The author would like to thank Dr. Shimon Gibson for pointing out these details in personal communication.

8 It is unclear as to how the stone was relocated in the period between 1936 and 1953; a reasonable assumption would be that British soldiers found the block at Khirbet el-Khâldeh during patrols prior to Boer's visit and brought it back to their base at nearby Aqaba.

Bibliography

Garrod, D. A. E. and Bate, D. M. A. 1937. *The Stone Age of Mount Carmel, Vol. I: Excavatations at the Wady el-Mughara.* Oxford: Clarendon Press.

Gibson, S. 2011. "The Excavations at the Bethesda Pool in Jerusalem. Preliminary Report on a Project of Stratigraphic and Structural Analysis (1999–2009)." *Proche-Orient Chrétien* 61:17–44.

Glueck, N. 1939. *Explorations in Eastern Palestine, III.* The Annual of the American Schools of Oriental Research 18/19. New Haven: American Schools of Oriental Research.

Hirschfeld, Y. and Galor, K. 2007. "New Excavations in Roman, Byzantine, and Early Islamic Tiberias." In *Religion, Ethnicity, and Identity in Ancient Galilee: a Region in Transition*, edited by J. Zangenberg, H. W. Attridge and D. B. Martin, 207–30. Tübingen: Mohr Siebeck.

Humbert OP, J.-B. and Chambon, A. 2003. *The Excavations of Khirbet Qumran and Ain Feshka. Synthesis of Roland de Vaux's Field Notes.* English Edition Translated and Revised by Stephen J. Pfann. Fribourg: University Press Fribourg & Göttingen: Vandenhoeck & Ruprecht.

Mader, E. 1957. *Mambre: die Ergebnisse der Ausgrabungen im Heiligen Bezirk Râmet el-Halîl in Südpalästina, 1926-1928.* Freiburg im Breisgau: Wewel.

Rabani, B. 1953. "Notes and News." *Israel Exploration Journal* 3:265.

Wagemakers, B. 2009. "Zoektocht Naar een Mysterieuze Inktpot. Verhaal van een 'Verdwenen' Bijzondere Vondst bij een Opgraving." *Archeologie Magazine* 6.5:54–58.

Wagemakers, B. and Taylor, J. E. 2011. "New Photographs of the Qumran Excavations from 1954 and Interpretations of L.77 and L.86." *Palestine Exploration Quarterly* 143.2:134–56.

Wagemakers, B. and Ameling, W. 2012. "A New Photograph and Reconsidered Reading of the Lost Inscription from Khirbet el-Khalidi (IGLSyr 21, 4 137)." *Zeitschrift für Papyrologie und Epigraphik* 183:176–78.

CHAPTER 2

Jerusalem

The history of the city is a long and complicated one. The name Jerusalem may already be mentioned in Egyptian sources dating back to the nineteenth century BCE, and in the Bible its name appears more than a thousand times. The biblical narrative reads that king David conquered the Jebusites' fortress on Mount Zion and named his new residence the 'City of David'. Under king Solomon's rule a new acropolis was erected, with a magnificent temple crowning the top of the Temple Mount. However, not much remained of these supposedly grandiose buildings. Later in the Iron Age the town expanded to the west and north. It was eventually destroyed by the Babylonians in 587 BCE, rebuilt in Persian times, enlarged and embellished by King Herod the Great, and again destroyed by the Romans in 70 CE. After the Roman Emperor Hadrian ordered the rebuilding of the town in 135, Aelia Capitolina was erected, the plan of which is still visible in the Old City today.

A grandiose city in Byzantine times, Jerusalem was taken over by Muslim forces under Caliph Umar in 638, after which the Dome of the Rock and Al-Aqsa mosque were built on the former temple platform, now called the Haram al-Sharif. The town saw many invaders since then: Mongols, Crusaders, Ayyubids, Mamluks, Ottomans, British, Jordanians and Israeli. In the twentieth century the city greatly expanded, was divided by a wall, and then re-united again.

Tens of thousands of books have been written on the history of Jerusalem, and hundreds of archaeological reports highlight the finds of the many archaeological excavations conducted during the last 150 years. Today Jerusalem is one of the most densely excavated and most hotly disputed areas in the Levant. And nowhere else is archaeology interlaced with politics so intimately.

This chapter focuses on the history of the archaeological excavations in the city and discusses the increasingly difficult relationship between archaeology and politics in Jerusalem.

One Hundred and Fifty Years of Excavating Jerusalem

Margreet L. Steiner

When Leo Boer travelled to Jerusalem in 1953, he arrived in a divided city. Boer stayed at the École Biblique in East Jerusalem, from where it was easy to visit most ancient and Christian sites, including the Old City and the Haram al-Sharif, the City of David (which he called Ophel) and the Mount of Olives. Most of the photographs of Jerusalem were taken at these locations.

No other site in the Middle East has been researched more intensively during the last two centuries and by more nationalities than ancient Jerusalem.[1] Nevertheless, when Leo Boer came to Jerusalem in 1953, all was quiet on the archaeological front.

Large excavations were out of the question in those troubled days. The last major excavation had taken place in 1934–1940 in the Citadel of David near Jaffa gate (see below). In 1953 and 1954 only the Franciscan Father Bellarmino Bagatti was excavating, because some workers, while laying the foundations for the Dominus Flevit Church on the western slope of the Mount of Olives, had stumbled upon several tombs (Bagatti and Milik 1958). Leo Boer visited the excavations on 23 February 1954 and took a photograph of one of the caves (Fig. 2.1).

These rock-cut tombs date from the second century BCE to the first century CE, while some tombs had been re-used in the Byzantine period. Numerous ossuaries (small stone chests, meant for human bones) were found in the tombs, among which 43 with inscriptions in Hebrew, Greek and Aramaic. Some claim that Saint Peter was buried here, as the name inscribed on one ossuary read: 'Shimon Bar Yonah' – Simon, the Son of

Figure 2.1: An excavated tomb at the Dominus Flevit Church excavations.

John – which is the name of the disciple Peter in the gospel of John (John 1:42; 21:15,17). If the ossuary is indeed that of Peter, that would be quite sensational, as traditionally the tomb of Saint Peter is located in Rome.[2] Other names on the ossuaries at Dominus Flevit include Jesus, Joseph, Judas, Mathew, Martha, Mary and Mariamne. Some consider this site to be the cemetery of the earliest Christians, others argue that these were common names in the first century CE and have not necessarily anything to do with the Christians. The same controversies concerning the identification of the names on other ossuaries have plagued Jerusalem ever since – compare, for example, the Talpiot tomb, of which some argue that this is the tomb of Jesus' family,[3] and the ossuary that bears the name of 'James, son of Joseph, brother of Jesus'.[4]

Hardly any excavations, thus, were carried out at Jerusalem in 1953. However, as a biblical scholar, Boer must have been well acquainted with the archaeology of ancient Jerusalem, if only because during the previous year, in 1952, the Dutch scholar Father Simons had published a book titled *Jerusalem in the Old Testament, Researches and Theories,* which contained a compilation of all the biblical and archaeological studies concerning ancient Jerusalem up to the Second World War. After its publication, the book became the 'Jerusalem Bible' for historians, biblical scholars and archaeologists alike. Despite its title, the book also discussed 'New Testament' questions, such as the location of Josephus' Second and Third Walls and the 'problem of the Holy Sepulchre'.[5]

The history of the archaeological excavations of Jerusalem is a fascinating story, not only because of the flamboyant men and women who worked in the city and the exciting discoveries they made, but also because this history is closely related to and entangled with the contemporary political situation.

The nineteenth century

Maybe we should salute empress Helena as being the first 'archaeologist' working in Jerusalem. When she came to live in the city in the beginning of the fourth century CE, she identified the holy places of the gospels under divine inspiration and built several memorial churches, such as the Rotunda over the Holy Sepulchre. It was only at the beginning of the nineteenth century that scholars started to doubt the authenticity of these and other holy places. Much of the early research in Jerusalem, such as the identifications established by E. Robinson (1838) and the survey of Ch. Wilson (1867–1868), was meant to prove or disprove theories about the location of the temple of Solomon or the tombs of the kings of Judah, the identification of Golgotha, and the course of the ancient city walls. In 1863 L.-F. C. de Saulcy conducted the first 'scientific' excavation in Jerusalem. On behalf of the Louvre museum he cleared the so-called Tomb of the Kings, a monumental tomb thought to contain the graves of the kings of Judah with all their riches. Now the tomb is thought to belong to Queen Helena of Adiabene, who converted to Judaism and settled in Jerusalem in the first half of the first century CE.

Excavating in Jerusalem in those days meant digging underground, using tunnels and shafts, a method developed to overcome two difficulties: working in a densely-populated city and coping with the prohibitions of the Ottoman authorities against westerners approaching Muslim sanctuaries. That is why in 1867 the British engineer Charles Warren dug vertical shafts at some distance from the walls of the Temple Mount, and from there tunnelled his way towards the ancient walls. He then went on to dig horizontal galleries along the walls. He also explored the underground water system of the south-eastern hill or City of David, which includes the shaft leading to the Gihon Spring (now aptly called Warren's Shaft; see Fig. 2.2) and the tunnel carrying the Gihon water to the Siloam Pool at the south end of the hill. His book *Underground Jerusalem* (1876) makes fascinating reading. Warren's Shaft was more fully explored during the 1909–1911 expedition conducted by the unfortunate M. Parker, who was accused of trying to steal, among other things, nothing less than the Holy Ark. Parker fled Jerusalem, and the results of his explorations were published by Pere L.-H. Vincent (Vincent 1911; Reich 2004).

This method of working underground was practised little elsewhere in the country, a Jerusalemite speciality, used, even when there was no specific need for it. Thus in 1894–1897 the archaeologist Frederick Jones Bliss and architect Archibald Campbell Dickie still worked completely underground, while excavating the relatively empty hill south of the Old City on behalf of the Palestine Exploration Fund (Bliss and Dickie 1898). Their work gave the first indications that the town of early biblical times had not been

Figure 2.2: Location of the main archaeological excavations mentioned in the text (Courtesy of Margreet Steiner): 1. Dominus Flevit; 2. Warren's Shaft / Spring House excavations; 3. Bliss and Dickie; 4. Weill; 5. Macalister / Kenyon / Shiloh / Eilat Mazar; 6. Crowfoot; 7. Benjamin Mazar / Temple Mount excavations; 8. Avigad; 9. Eilat Mazar: Ophel; 10. Givat Parking Lot.

located within the present city walls, but on the south-eastern hill, now called the City of David. They were able to follow a complicated system of fortifications that surrounded this hill and which they dated to the time of Solomon. Although later research showed that these walls probably belonged to the Byzantine period, the idea of the extramural location of the ancient town (i.e. outside the city walls surrounding the Old City) had by then been firmly established.

First half of the twentieth century

This assumption led to the next phase of archaeological research, which consisted of exposing large areas to fill in the ground plan of ancient Jerusalem. The excavations of Raymond Weill (1913–1914 and 1923–1925), sponsored by Baron Edmond de Rothschild, uncovered a large area in the south part of the City of David, yielding many interesting discoveries, including fortifications and a mass grave, all of an unknown date (Weill 1920; idem 1947; Reich 2004). However, this part of the hill had been used intensively as a quarry over the ages, and, to his frustration, Weill excavated large stretches of worked bedrock without exposing any architecture. One of his intriguing finds, however, consisted of a series of long narrow tunnels that penetrated the rock at the south side of the hill. The tunnels were empty: no objects or inscriptions were discovered there. However, Weill interpreted the tunnels as the tombs of the kings of Judah, who, according to several biblical texts, were buried in the City of David.[6] Boer visited the tunnels on 1 December

Figure 2.3: Tunnels excavated by Weill in the City of David (1953).

Figure 2.4: Photograph taken at the same location in 2013 (Photograph by Bart Wagemakers).

1953 (Fig. 2.3). The tunnels were cleared again and made accessible in 1995, on the occasion of the celebration of 'Jerusalem 3000' (Fig. 2.4).[7]

One of Weill's most famous discoveries was the Theodotus inscription, a stone slab with an inscription commemorating the dedication of a new synagogue in Jerusalem. The inscription is in Greek and dates to the first half of the first century CE, before the destruction of Jerusalem by the Romans.

During 1923–1925 the British archaeologist R. A. S. Macalister exposed a large area on top of the City of David, north of Weill's area. This excavation revealed many buildings and fortifications, the dating of which remained problematic as it was based more on information from the Bible than on an analysis of the excavated pottery (Macalister and Duncan 1926). Although Macalister was familiar with the method of establishing pottery sequences, he considered the stratigraphy of Jerusalem's soil to be too muddled to yield any results. Thus Macalister dated the large tower he excavated to the time of King David (conventionally considered to be the beginning of the tenth century BCE), and the stone ramp running up to

the tower to the Jebusites who lived in the city before the occupation of the ancient Israelites, according to several biblical texts.

Leo Boer visited the site on 1 December 1953 and climbed the ramp with his fellow students (Fig. 2.5). Boer wrote a very short report on this visit to what he called Ophel, now the City of David: 'There is not much to see as the Romans used this site as a quarry. At the east site some remains of a wall are visible, which is partly Jebusite, partly Solomonic and partly from the time of Nehemiah. The tower may also be from Nehemiah's time.'[8]

Although Figure 2.5 betrays Boer's disinterest in the archaeology of Jerusalem, as it highlights the gymnastics of the visitors rather than the architectural remains, it is an interesting picture nonetheless, because it shows the southern edge of the so-called Jebusite ramp. Most of the photographs, whether they were taken by Macalister, Kenyon, Shiloh or more recently, are taken from north to south, showing the relationship of the ramp with the tower. This one, however, is taken from south to north, and suggests that the ramp is filled with stones. Later excavations,

Figure 2.5: Boer and companions at the City of David, climbing the 'stepped stone structure' (1953).

however, have established that the ramp (or 'stepped stone structure' as it is now called), is just a mantle of stones laid over earlier fill, at least in that spot. Kenyon reported that the Jordanian Department of Antiquities had at a certain point restored the ramp to prevent it from further erosion, and this may account for the fill of stones, so eagerly climbed by the École Biblique students. I only found one photograph taken from almost the same position; it is from Macalister's campaign, and shows the tower and the ramp during excavation (Fig. 2.6).

The photograph shows Macalister's rather untidy way of digging, not giving much attention to the clearing up of excavation trenches or the straightening of sections. It also shows Macalister's grave sin of trenching along the foot of the walls (notice the cuts in the foreground of the photograph), thereby destroying the connection of a wall and the surfaces running up against it, which makes it impossible to date the wall.

In 1927 J. W. Crowfoot, the newly-appointed director of the British School of Archaeology in Jerusalem, was invited by the Palestine Exploration Fund to continue Macalister's work in the City of David. Crowfoot chose a revolutionary new approach. In contrast to the tunnelling or the clearing of large areas carried out by his predecessors, he cut deep trenches in the western slope of the hill, where he uncovered a line of fortification walls with a large gateway. He dated the gate to the Late Bronze Age on account of the building technique of roughly hewn blocks of stones, notwithstanding the discovery of a cache of Maccabaean coins from the reign of Jannaeus (103–76 BCE), which he considered to be intrusive (Crowfoot and Fitzgerald, 1929).

After that time, no large-scale excavations were carried out. The period of the grand excavations was over, at least for the time being, and research concentrated on specific sites within the city, using modern methods like deep-trenching and careful

Figure 2.6: The same structure during the 1923–1925 excavations carried out by Macalister (Courtesy of the Palestine Exploration Fund, London).

small-scale excavation. R. W. Hamilton excavated north of the Damascus Gate (1937–1938) and C. N. Johns started digging in the Citadel near Jaffa Gate (1934–1940), while from 1925 until 1927 E. L. Sukenik from the Hebrew University of Jerusalem uncovered stretches of wall and towers along the line of the Josephus' Third Wall (Hamilton 1944; Johns 1950; Sukenik 1927). Most of the problems concerning the city of biblical times remained unsolved, however, and the debate continued in the form of an ingenious re-analysis of existing evidence combined with new research into Bible texts, culminating in Father Simons' book.

Second half of the twentieth century

It was only in 1961, when the British archaeologist Kathleen Kenyon together with A. D. Tushingham and Père de Vaux started to excavate in Jerusalem, that new information came to light on the ancient city. Kenyon described her reason for focusing on Jerusalem as follows (1962):

> 'When the British School of Archaeology in Jerusalem completed in 1958 its excavations at Jericho, it had the not very easy task of deciding what should be the next site it would tackle. Jericho had been such a success that there was a risk that work at any other place would be bathos. Jerusalem seemed to be the only other site that in importance could compete with Jericho.'

Kenyon's idea was to apply the Wheeler-Kenyon method of careful stratigraphical research, which had been so successful at Jericho, to Jerusalem's complex situation. She was confident that it would be possible in this way to solve every unsolved riddle once and for all. Therefore she dug small squares all over the city, as these riddles concerned many unrelated problems. For instance, Kenyon wanted to know why the entrance to Jerusalem's ancient water shaft was located outside the contemporary city walls, she aimed to establish the correct chronology of the fortifications on the City of David and wanted to establish a date for the extension of the ancient town over the western hill. But she was also interested in the exact course of the Second and Third city walls, as mentioned by Josephus, as well as the location of King Herod's palace and the size of the city in Roman times. Thus her excavation squares were located in several places in the City of David (Fig. 2.7), in the

Old City, north of Damascus gate and just south of the Haram al-Sharif (Kenyon 1967; idem 1974).

Unlike archaeologists before her, Kenyon was not a 'biblical archaeologist', someone who conducts archaeological research as part of Bible studies. To her the archaeology of Palestine was a branch of general world archaeology, and its task was to expand our knowledge of the ancient world by systematic research and strict application of scientific methods. In other words, Kenyon's objectives were not specifically biblical, but rather historical in its broadest sense.

Unfortunately, these excavations, which continued until 1967, did not manage to end the controversies. Although some problems were solved satisfactorily, many were not, and the debate carried on as before. The reason for this was Kenyon's way of digging; she excavated small squares of five by five meters, with little attention to architectural units; not one house, not even one room within a house, was completely cleared. And she constantly used the *pars-pro-toto* principle: 'If I don't find it in this small area, it doesn't exist at all'. These weaknesses were fully revealed in Jerusalem's churned-up soils. The important question of when the city started to expand over the western hill therefore remained unsettled.

Shortly after the Six-Day War of 1967, Israeli archaeologists conducted several large-scale excavations in Jerusalem. From 1968 till 1978, Benjamin Mazar excavated large areas near the Temple Mount, uncovering remains from the first century CE as well as buildings from the Byzantine and later periods. This area had never before been excavated because of its location at the foot of the Haram al-Sharif. In 1969, Nahum Avigad started his explorations of the Jewish Quarter in the Old City, where he unearthed remains of fortifications, public buildings and domestic dwellings from the end of the Iron Age until the Ottoman period. From 1978 until 1985 Yigal Shiloh tackled the City of David again, picking up where Kenyon and Macalister had left off.

These excavations were characterised by excellent organisation, an intensive use of technical appliances, a preference for the exposure of large areas with much attention to architecture and little to stratigraphy, and the composition of a corpus of complete pots from floors instead of the detailed analysis of sherd material. Their foremost aim was the reconstruction of both a visible and a visitable national history, mainly

Figure 2.7: This photograph of Kenyon's excavation in the City of David shows the difficulty of digging stony layers on the slope of the hill. The stones visible in this photograph range in date from the twelfth till the second centuries BCE (Courtesy Council for British Research in the Levant CBRL).

from the so-called First and Second Temple periods, encompassing the Iron Age and the Herodian/Roman period. Although these excavations proved to be an enormous success, the hastened method of digging with the help of inexperienced volunteers as well as the often hurried and controversial interpretations have been criticised repeatedly.

In the 1980s and 1990s the large-scale Israeli excavations came to an end, and only smaller-sized rescue excavations took place. These were the years of consolidation, of study and analysis. Several series with final publications came out in this period: Kenyon's excavations were presented in the series *Excavations by K. M. Kenyon in Jerusalem 1961-1967*, the first one of which was published in 1985 (Tushingham 1985; further Franken and Steiner 1990, Eshel and Prag 1995; Steiner 2001; Franken 2005; Prag 2008). From 1984 onwards Shiloh's dig was published in *Excavations at the City of David 1978-1985* (Shiloh 1984, Ariel 1990; idem 1996; idem 2000a; idem 2000b; De Groot and Ariel 1992), while the series *Jewish Quarter Excavations in the Old City of Jerusalem*, on Avigad's excavations, saw the light in the year 2000 (Geva 2000–2010). Benjamin Mazar's extensive work around the Haram al-Sharif was published from 1989 onwards: *The Temple Mount Excavations in Jerusalem 1968-1978: Final Reports* (Mazar and Mazar 1989; Mazar 2003–2011).

Twenty-first century

The political controversies concerning excavations in Jerusalem have deepened recently. Many large and small excavations are under way which lay bare the deep rift between Israeli and Palestinian claims to the land and to their respective heritage. From the point of view of the Israel Antiquities Authority, the excavation of 'Jewish' remains from the Iron Age and the Herodian/Roman periods highlights the Jewish history of the city. From the point of view of the Palestinian inhabitants of the areas that are being excavated, these excavations not only ignore théir history and ties to the past, but also threaten their very existence in Jerusalem as land is appropriated not only for excavations but also for tourist centres, carparks and footpaths.[9] Several examples (see Fig. 2.2):

Excavations in the City of David

In what is now consistently called the City of David, several large-scale excavations are being conducted in areas which were tackled previously by Weill, Macalister, Kenyon and Shiloh. Weill conducted his excavations without any fuss on a parcel of land that was bought by Baron de Rothschild. Macalister, being a Briton and a gentleman, had no trouble digging in an area that was relatively empty, with the permission and goodwill of the powers that be, the British Mandate rulers. The local Silwanis had no say in the matter. Kenyon dug in the final years prior to the Six-Day War, when the Hashemite Kingdom of Jordan controlled the area. As the local population had expanded, there was less open space available and she had to drive a hard bargain to hire the land from a reluctant and at times hostile population. After the war she conducted one more season of excavations under Israelite occupation, with permission given by the Jordanian Department of Antiquities.

The Israeli excavations in the City of David under the direction of Shiloh had a relatively easy task. The Palestinian population had not yet found their voice of protest, and the area was considered to belong to Israel proper, with Israeli and foreign volunteers flocking to the excavations. I was one of them, in 1982, and (very naively or stupidly) it did not occur to me that there were rules of international law in force that prohibited such an excavation.

Not so in the twenty-first century. Following two intifada's, Israeli ànd foreign archaeologists have become acutely aware of the legal controversies surrounding digging in occupied areas and against the will of the local population.

The recent excavations in the City of David are sponsored by the City of David Foundation or 'Elad', an organisation 'devoted to Judaizing East Jerusalem', according to the Israeli newspaper *Haaretz* of June 1, 2008. On its website Elad describes itself as 'committed to continuing King David's legacy'.[10]

On top of the hill, near the *City of David's Visitor's Center*, Eilat Mazar has been directing excavations, searching for the 'palace of David', which, in her opinion and based on biblical texts, should be located there. In 2005 she announced that she was excavating a monumental building on top of the hill. Based on the size of the building and the associated finds, she interpreted it as the palace of king David (Mazar 2009). This interpretation evoked many a passionate comment, if only because digging 'with a trowel in one hand and the Bible in the other' may have been fashionable in the nineteenth century, but is now considered to be completely unscientific.[11] In 2009 Mazar started excavations at the Ophel, just south of the Haram al-Sharif, where she claimed to have uncovered, amongst other things, the 'Solomonic' city wall of Jerusalem.

Just outside of Dung gate is the *Givati Parking Lot excavation*. This is the largest archaeological project ever carried out in Jerusalem. Since 2007, Doron Ben-Ami of Hebrew University and Yana Tchekhanovets of the Israel Antiquities Authority have been conducting excavations there, sponsored by Elad. Large buildings (palaces?) from the first and the second/third centuries CE have been uncovered, as well as a Byzantine residential quarter (fifth–sixth centuries) (Ben-Ami 2011). Later periods are not deemed of much interest. The Elad website just notes that 'above these layers, a number of layers of settlement from the Muslim period were found'.

Further to the south *the Spring House excavation* are being conducted from 1995 onwards. Ronny Reich from Haifa University and Eli Shukron from the Israel Antiquities Authority have been working near the Gihon Spring where they found large fortifications surrounding the spring, dating to the Middle Bronze Age, and connected to Warren's Shaft (Reich 2010). The excavators have also been conducting a systematic excavation of the main water drainage tunnel of the city of Jerusalem from the Second Temple period: the *Siloam Pool excavations* (Reich 2011b). This channel gathered and drained water from the city of Jerusalem southwards, passing the Siloam Pool and out of the city.

Excavations in the Old City

South of the Haram al-Sharif the extensive *Ophel excavations* are currently being conducted, continuing where Kenyon and Benjamin Mazar left off. The excavation team unearthed, among other things, some graves from the Abbasid period (eighth–ninth centuries CE), large structures (palaces or administrative buildings) from the Umayyad period (seventh–eighth centuries CE), a residential quarter from the Byzantine period (fourth–seventh centuries CE) and finds from the Roman period (first–fourth

centuries CE), as well as the street that ran along the ancient temple complex in the Herodian period (first century BCE). A new archaeological park and museum, the Jerusalem Archaeological Park and Davidson Center, has been opened here. Digging so close to the Haram has, expectedly, created tension between the authorities and the local Palestinian population.

Even more controversial to both sides is the work on the Haram al-Sharif. In 1996 the Waqf, the Muslim trust that takes care of the Haram al-Sharif, started work on the area below the al-Aksa mosque, in the so-called Solomon's stables, which are in fact part of the foundations of the large podium on which the temple built by king Herod stood. A new prayer hall was created there, and truck loads full of soil were removed from that area and dumped in the Kedron Valley. According to some archaeologists (Palestinian and Israeli), the soil consisted of ancient fill, once brought to the site from elsewhere, and it contained no important archaeological artefacts. Others, most prominently the archaeologist Gabriel Barkay, considered the soil to originate from the Temple Mount. Since 2004 he has been sieving the hundreds of tons of dumped soil, together with volunteers. They retrieved several interesting objects.[12]

Some conclusions

The esteemed Jerusalem art of digging underground has made its come-back. Not so much in the form of digging new tunnels under densely-occupied areas to prevent clashes with the authorities, but of cleaning and emptying old tunnels dating from antiquity that transverse the city, and now it is done with the official approval of the authorities. Clashes, however, still occur: this time with the local Palestinian population. In 1996 the clearance of a passage-way running along the Haram al-Sharif and appearing above ground in the Via Dolorosa, led to an uproar of the Palestinian inhabitants, ending in the deaths of several people.

Digging with 'Bible and spade' seems to be fashionable once more, such as it was in the nineteenth century. Starting an excavation in search of King David's palace, or interpreting finds in Jerusalem in the framework of biblical stories, is deemed proper archaeological practice again.

There also seems to be a return to nineteenth-century colonialist perspectives. In Jerusalem excavations and heritage management seems to concern itself foremost with the ancient remains of a (supposedly grandiose) Israelite and Jewish past. The Palestinian population of East Jerusalem and Silwan are not considered to have any connection with ancient Jerusalem, and Palestinian land is appropriated for excavation work and the building of tourist centres and carparks.

Not just later (post-Jewish) remains are being neglected, however; earlier remains face the self-same fate. At the foot of the hill of the City of David, below the entrance to the spring Gihon, one of the oldest remains of Jerusalem is to be found: a stretch of the Middle Bronze Age town wall, dating around 1800 BCE and excavated by Kenyon. Although the area around the spring has been transformed into an archaeological park by Elad, the oldest town wall of Jerusalem was not included in the park and has been sadly neglected. The excavation trench, in which the wall was discovered, has been used as a rubbish dump over many years; the wall is covered by debris and trees are growing between the stones and dislodging them. Leo Boer never saw this wall, as it had not yet been excavated at the time, but very soon no one will be able to see this important part of Jerusalem's rich archaeological heritage (Fig. 2.8).

Notes

1 See also Avigad 1983; Auld and Steiner 1996; Ben-Dov 1985; Bieberstein and Bloedhorn 1994; Galow and Avi 2011; Geva 1994; Reich 2011a; Yadin 1975.

2 Both pope Pius XII (in 1950) and pope Paul VI (in 1968) officially announced that the bones found in the tomb in Rome belong to Saint Peter.

3 In this tomb ten ossuaries were found, six of which bore epigraphs, including the name 'Jesus, son of Joseph', although this has since been contested. These ossuaries were published in the 'Catalogue of Jewish Ossuaries in the Collections of the State of Israel' (numbers 701–709) in 1994 and they have attracted much attention from 1996 onwards. In 1996 the BBC produced a documentary on the subject and in 2007 the Discovery Channel issued a documentary titled, 'The Lost Tomb of Jesus'.

Figure 2.8: The Middle Bronze Age city wall in recent times (Photograph by Margreet Steiner).

4 On the controversies surrounding this ossuary, see (among many others) http://www.biblicalarchaeology. org/daily/biblical-artifacts/artifacts-and-the-bible/ why-did-the-james-ossuary-forgery-trial-verdict-find-oded-golan-and-robert-deutsch-not-guilty and http:// www.bibleinterp.com/articles/James_Ossuary_essays. shtml.

5 The location of Calvary and the tomb of Jesus are uncertain. The Holy Sepulchre is one of several possible locations.

6 The interpretation of the shafts as the tombs of the kings of Judah has re-surfaced from time to time. The most recent publication is Zorn 2012.

7 This refers to the celebration in 1995 of 'David's capture of the city'.

8 Kathleen Kenyon's excavation showed that the tower is Hellenistic in date, while Yigal Shiloh was able to prove that the ramp is Iron II in date.

9 More information on these matters is to be found on the website of Emeq Shaveh: www.alt-arch.org and in the booklets they have produced.

10 http://www.cityofdavid.org.il

11 For an overview of Mazar's finds and some of the comments see my article on the website 'Bible and Interpretation': http://www.bibleinterp.com/articles/ palace_2468.shtml.

12 Read more: http://www.smithsonianmag.com/history-archaeology/What-is-Beneath-the-Temple-Mount. html#ixzz1yiY8ytMs; and: http://templemount. wordpress.com; and: http://www.robat.scl.net/ content/NAD/press/jerusalem/adnan_husseini.php.

Bibliography of Jerusalem

Ariel, D. T. 1990. _Excavations at the City of David 1978–1985 Directed by Yigal Shiloh, Vol. II: Imported Stamped Amphora Handles, Coins, Worked Bone and Ivory, and Glass._ Qedem 30. Jerusalem: Israel Exploration Society.

Ariel, D. T. (ed.). 1996. _Excavations at the City of David 1978–1985 Directed by Yigal Shiloh, Vol. IV: Various Reports._ Qedem 35. Jerusalem: Israel Exploration Society.

Ariel, D. T. (ed.). 2000a. _Excavations in the City of David 1978–1985 Directed by Yigal Shiloh, Vol. V: Extramural Areas._ Qedem 40. Jerusalem: Israel Exploration Society.

Ariel, D. T. (ed.). 2000b. _Excavations in the City of David 1978–1985 Directed by Yigal Shiloh, Vol. VI: Inscriptions._ Qedem 41. Jerusalem: Israel Exploration Society.

Avigad, N. 1983. _Discovering Jerusalem._ Nashville, Camden, New York: Thomas Nelson Publishers.

Auld, A. G. and Steiner, M. L. 1996. _Jerusalem I, from the Bronze Age to the Maccabees._ Cities of the Biblical World. Cambridge: The Lutterworth Press.

Bagatti, B. and Milik, J. T. 1958. _Gli scavi del "Dominus Flevit" - Parte I - La Necropoli del Periodo Romano._ Gerusalemme: Tipografia dei PP. Francescani.

Ben-Ami, Doron. 2011. "Has the Abiabene Royal Family "Palace" Been Found in the City of David?" In _Unearthing Jerusalem: 150 Years of Archaeological Research in the Holy City_, edited by K. Galor and G. Avni, 231–39. Winona Lake, Ind.: Eisenbrauns.

Ben-Dov, M. 1985. _In the Shadow of the Temple; the Discovery of Ancient Jerusalem._ Jerusalem: Keter Publishing House.

Bieberstein, K. and Bloedhorn, H. 1994. _Jerusalem: Gründzüge der Baugeschichte vom Chalkolithikum bis zur Frühzeit der osmanischen Herrschaft._ Beihefte zum Tübinger Atlas des vorderen Orients, Reihe B, Geisteswissenschaften, 100, 3 Vols Wiesbaden: Ludwig Reichert Verlag.

Bliss, Frederick J. and Dickie, A. C. 1898. _Excavations at Jerusalem, 1894–1897._ London: Palestine Exploration Fund.

Crowfoot, J. W. and Fitzgerald, G. M. 1929. _Excavations in the Tyropoeon Valley 1927._ London: Palestine Exploration Fund.

De Groot, A. and Ariel, D. T. (eds). 1992. _Excavations at the City of David 1978-1985 Directed by Yigal Shiloh, Vol. III: Stratigraphical, Environmental, and Other Reports._ Qedem 33. Jerusalem: Israel Exploration Society.

Eshel, I. and Prag, K. (eds). 1995. _Excavations by K. M. Kenyon in Jerusalem 1961-1967, Vol. IV: The Iron Age Cave Deposits on the South-East Hill and Isolated Burials and Cemeteries Elsewhere._ British Academy Monographs in Archaeology No. 6. Oxford: Oxford University Press.

Franken, H. J. 2005. _A History of Pottery and Potters in Ancient Jerusalem._ London: Equinox.

Franken, H. J. and Steiner, M. L. 1990. _Excavations in Jerusalem 1961-1967, Vol. II: The Iron Age Extramural Quarter on the South-East Hill._ British Academy Monographs in Archaeology No. 2. Oxford: Oxford University Press.

Galor, K. and Avi, G. (eds). 2011. _Unearthing Jerusalem, 150 Years of Archaeological Research in the Holy City._ Winona Lake, Ind.: Eisenbrauns.

Geva, H. 1994. _Ancient Jerusalem Revealed._ Jerusalem: Israel Exploration Society.

Geva, H. (ed.). 2000–2010. _Jewish Quarter Excavations in the Old City of Jerusalem Conducted by Nahman Avigad, 1969-1982_, 4 Vols Jerusalem: Israel Exploration Society.

Hamilton, R. W. 1944. "Excavations Against the North Wall of Jerusalem, 1937–8." _Quarterly of the Department of Antiquities of Palestine_ 10.

Johns, C. N. 1950. "The Citadel, Jerusalem. A Summary of Work Since 1934." _Quarterly of the Department of Antiquities of Palestine_ 14:121–88.

Kenyon, K. M. 1962. "Biblical Jerusalem." _Expedition: the Bulletin of the University Museum of the University of Pennsylvania_ 5 (fall):32–35.

Kenyon, K. M. 1967. _Jerusalem. Excavating 3000 Years of History._ London: Thames and Hudson.

Kenyon, K. M. 1974. _Digging Up Jerusalem._ London: Benn

Macalister, R. A. S. and Duncan, J. G. 1926. _Excavations on the Hill of Ophel, Jerusalem, 1923-1925: Being the Joint Expedition_ of the Palestine Exploration Fund and the "Daily Telegraph". London: Palestine Exploration Fund.

Mazar, E. (ed.). 2003–2011. *The Temple Mount Excavations in Jerusalem 1968-1978: final reports*, 4 Vols Jerusalem: Institute of Archaeology, The Hebrew University of Jerusalem.

Mazar, E. 2009. *The Palace of King David: Excavations at the Summit of the City of David: Preliminary Report of Seasons 2005-2007.* Jerusalem: Shoham Academic Research and Publication.

Mazar, E. and Mazar, B. (eds). 1989. *Excavations in the South of the Temple Mount: The Ophel of Biblical Jerusalem.* Qedem 29. Jerusalem: Israel Exploration Society.

Prag, K. (ed.). 2008. *Excavations by K. M. Kenyon in Jerusalem 1961-1967, Vol. V: Discoveries in Hellenistic to Ottoman Jerusalem. Centenary volume: Kathleen M. Kenyon 1906-1978.* Levant Supplementary Series 7. London/Oxford: Council for British Research in the Levant and Oxbow Books.

Reich, R. 2004. *The City of David: Revisiting Early Excavations/ English Translations of Reports by: Raymond Weill and L.-H. Vincent (notes and comments by Ronny Reich; edited by Hershel Shanks).* Washington: Biblical Archaeology Society.

Reich, R. 2010. "A New Segment of the Middle Bronze Fortification in the City of David." *Tel Aviv* 37.2:141–53.

Reich, R. 2011a. *Excavating the City of David Where Jerusalem's History Began.* Jerusalem: Israel Exploration Society.

Reich, R. 2011b. "The Pool of Siloam in Jerusalem of the Late Second Temple Period and its Surroundings." In *Unearthing Jerusalem: 150 Years of Archaeological Research in the Holy City*, edited by K. Galor and G. Avni, 241–55. Winona Lake, Ind.: Eisenbrauns.

Shiloh, Y. 1984. *Excavations at The City Of David I, 1978-1982: Interim Report Of The First Five Seasons.* Qedem 19. Jerusalem: Israel Exploration Society.

Simons, J. J. 1952. *Jerusalem in the Old Testament, Researches and Theories.* Leiden: Brill.

Steiner, M. L. 2001. *Excavations by Kathleen M. Kenyon in Jerusalem 1961-1967, Vol. III: The Settlement in the Bronze and Iron Ages.* Sheffield: Sheffield Academic Press/Continuum Press.

Sukenik, E. L. 1927. "Note on the North Wall of Jerusalem." *Bulletin of the American Schools of Oriental Research* 26:8–9.

Tushingham, A. D. (ed.). 1985. *Excavations in Jerusalem 1961-1967, Vol. I.* Toronto: Royal Ontario Museum and Leiden: Brill.

Vincent, L.-H. 1911. *Jerusalem sous Terre – Les recentes fouilles d'Ophel.* London: Horace Cox.

Warren, Ch. 1876. *Underground Jerusalem; an Account of Some of the Principal Difficulties Encountered in its Exploration and the Results Obtained. With a Narrative of an Expedition through the Jordan Valley and a Visit to the Samaritans.* London: Richard Bentley and Son.

Weill, R. 1920. *La Cité de David: Compte-Rendu des Fouilles Exécutées à Jérusalem sur le Site de la Ville Primitive: Campagne de 1913-1914*, 2 Vols Paris: Geuthner.

Weill, R. 1947. *La Cité de David: Compte-Rendu des Fouilles Exécutées à Jérusalem sur le Site de la Ville Primitive: Campagne de 1923-1924*, 2 Vols Paris: Geuthner.

Yadin, Y. (ed.). 1975. *Jerusalem Revealed: Archaeology in the Holy City 1968-1974.* Jerusalem: Israel Exploration Society.

Zorn, J. 2012. "Is T1 David's Tomb?" *Biblical Archaeology Review* 38.6:45–52, 78.

CHAPTER 3

Khirbet et-Tell ('Ai?)

The ruins of Khirbet et-Tell (Arabic for 'heap of ruins') are situated about three kilometres east of the modern city of Beitin and about six kilometres north-east of Jerusalem. In the beginning of the Early Bronze Age, around 3100 BCE, an unfortified village of about 2.4 hectares was established. Later in the Early Bronze Age the settlement grew to urban proportions and its approximately eleven hectares were surrounded by a defence wall. This flourishing regional centre was destroyed, probably by an earthquake, around 2700 BCE. After a short period the settlement was rebuilt and strengthened by a second wall. In 2400 BCE the city was completely destroyed by fire. Twelve hundred years later, in about 1200 BCE, an unwalled village of not more than one hectare was built in the acropolis area. This village was occupied until 1050 BCE after which it was abandoned for good.

Although the site has been identified with the biblical city of 'Ai since 1838, when Edward Robinson first proposed this suggestion, it was not until W. F. Albright's endorsement of this identification that it has been accepted by most scholars. The city of 'Ai (in Hebrew 'the ruin') is mentioned several times in the Bible. According to the biblical narrative the Israelites attacked and conquered the city under the leadership of Joshua, killed its inhabitants and finally destroyed the city (Joshua 8:28). However, the results of the archaeological campaigns at Khirbet et-Tell do not confirm this narrative, as will be demonstrated in this chapter.

An Archaeological Historiography of Khirbet et-Tell and the Ongoing Search for the Biblical City of ʹAi

Lucas P. Petit

The following commentary, triggered by the wonderful pictures of Leo Boer (Figs 3.1–3.6), deals with Khirbet et-Tell and the search for the biblical city of ʹAi. Not a biblical scholar, I found myself, during the writing process, blindfolded in a huge basin filled with biblical citations, each of them apparently equally important in the identification of the biblical city. It was difficult studying the different opinions and suggestions when not acquainted with hardly any of the purely biblical arguments. It seems to me to be appropriate at this stage to apologize for my interfering in an almost completely biblical dispute and for the somewhat coarse use of the data. Additionally, I may have to disappoint some readers. This synthesis will not provide a solution for the still-pending identification of ancient ʹAi, but aims to provide a view from the 'outside', from an archaeologist who admires the archaeological value of an ancient residential house with broken pottery more than the fact that it may have been inhabited by Israelites. Hopefully, it will provoke the reader to reconsider whether or not a correct identification is essential for the understanding of the intriguing occupation history of the Southern Levant.

Environmental setting

Khirbet et-Tell is situated in the highlands of the Palestinian Territories north of Jerusalem and west of Deir Dibwan. Boer's personal notes in 1953 give us an excellent description of the site's location:

'We take the main road to Ramallah and pass Tell el-Ful on our left and Tell en-Nasbeh on our right. Before passing Beitin and reaching et-Tell, we drive over the runway of the airport of Qalandiya and turn right just before reaching Ramallah. It is 7.45 pm. We are halfway between Beitin and Deir Diwan and 22 kilometres away from Jerusalem. The ruins that we are planning to visit are located to the left. To get there, we need to climb the mound, which lies 850 metres above sea level. It is chilly and windy there. Et-tell means 'ruins', and is similar to the Hebrew word Ha ʹAi mentioned in the Old Testament. The ruins are located East-South-East of Bethel (2.5 kilometres) and are described as being located north of Michmas close to Bethhaven (possibly Deir Diwan) (Gen. 12:8; Josh. 8:9; 12:9; 7:2; Isa. 10:28). In the book of Joshua the place is described as a very old ruined town (8:28) and according to Nehemiah (11:31) the region itself was inhabited after the Babylonian Exile.'[1]

Leo Boer's visit in November 1953

Boer's visit in November 1953 occurred in a period in which Khirbet et-Tell was slowly retracting itself from the centre of a heavy dispute between biblical and non-biblical scholars about the possible identification of the site with the biblical ʹAi. Many had tried to solve the puzzle, but failed due to too many uncertainties and knowledge gaps. But still, you can almost hear the excitement of Leo Boer in his description of climbing up the steep hill and looking over the excavated wall stumps. It was this site that was 'causing trouble for the exegetes'.

In Boer's notes, it seems clear that he intermixed the things he saw with the things he knew. Those who have visited a previously excavated site know the inherent difficulties in identifying the buildings described in their original publication. Erosion, dense vegetation and deliberate filling can change the outlook considerably. This problem was also noticed by Leo Boer. He mentioned that the excavation units were filled. However, it is not likely that all the trenches of Marquet-Krause (see below) were purposely filled, since she had wanted to return to the site in 1936. Also, the excavator Callaway, who worked on the site after her, mentioned that she 'left it excavated to bedrock and open' (Callaway 1980, 12). However, some units may have been refilled. Callaway

Figure 3.1: Two parallel walls at Khirbet et-Tell. According to Boer's notes, the walls are part of the Early Bronze Age defensive system.

Figure 3.2: The gate or postern of the Early Bronze Age wall at Khirbet et-Tell (cf. Marquet-Krause 1949, pl. XXX, 2).

mentioned that 'most of the area had been excavated in 1934 and filled in again' (1980, 63). In his personal notes, Boer writes:

'In 1933, '34 and '35 six months of excavations in total were conducted under the direction of the Jewish archaeologist Judith Marquet-Krause. She found out that in around 3000 BCE the place was inhabited by Semites who were protected by a double city wall: the first was five or six metres thick and stood two and a half metres away from a second wall with a thickness of one to two metres [Fig. 3.1]. She assumed that there were passages between those walls, but, as was pointed out by de Vaux, it was more likely to be similar to that found at Tell Far'a. The space between the two walls was filled with debris to prevent the walls from collapsing.

In front of those two walls, a third wall had been constructed of about one metre thick. But this one seems to have been much later in time. Some dwellings were built on top of the other two walls. This third wall contained a rampart. The south-east corner of the older two walls was destroyed deliberately. On the inside of those walls some sort of temple or palace was found, seemingly older. During the construction of the wall this building had been spared. In the same corner one can see the remains of a gate [Fig. 3.2].

More to the west, we come to the remains of a very old sanctuary of which the oldest phase (there are three) is even older than the largest city wall. In this sanctuary, which consisted of a portal and one room, several incense jars were discovered. Those are now exhibited in the Rockefeller Museum [in Jerusalem]. A few Egyptian vases made of alabaster were also found. In the north we reach a palace that was constructed on the bedrock. The palace building itself is surrounded by a hallway and a courtyard. The size of the palace and hallway is 25 by 15 meters. The palace consisted of a large hall, of which the floor is still visible, and more than likely had a second storey, as four pillar bases would suggest. Those pillar bases stand parallel to the longest side of the palace. One can assume that the large hall was used for the public, which is common in the Near East, whereas the upper storey was for private use. One difficulty of this interpretation is that no two-storey buildings have as yet been found. In the south-western corner of the hall a niche was found with two jars from the Early Bronze Age. This feature might have been used for honouring the house god. In

Figure 3.3: A fragment of the palace or temple wall at Khirbet et-Tell.

Figure 3.4: The Iron Age village of Khirbet et-Tell.

Figure 3.5: The Early Bronze Age defensive system at Khirbet et-Tell (cf. Marquet-Krause 1949, pl. XXXII).

Figure 3.6: Parallel walls at Khirbet et-Tell.

the wall of the hallway we can still see the pillar bases that had borne the roof or a second storey.

Intriguing is the beautiful construction method of the palace walls built with flat white stones [Fig. 3.3]. East of the palace an open courtyard was located, of which some remains are still visible. A few hundred metres away from the north-east corner of the palace, the remains of Iron Age houses were discovered. Many of those dwellings have a hole in the ground that led to a cistern for water storage. It is a pity that most of the excavation units have been refilled. But what we see is enough to get a good picture of this ancient and powerful city, which, however, causes problems for the exegetes.'

The photographs of Leo Boer

The photographs of Leo Boer show the excellent condition of the excavated structures at that time (Figs 3.1–3.6). Comparing his photographs with the official excavation pictures of Marquet-Krause a few points are worth mentioning. According to Boer's notes, Figure 3.1 displays the parallel wall system that protected the Early Bronze Age city around 3000 BCE. Since it was the first photograph taken that day in 1953, it seems likely that it was indeed made near the gate and tower (seen on Fig. 3.2). However, the exact location remains uncertain. Also the position of the last photograph, Figure 3.6, could not be identified.

Figures 3.2 and 3.5 show the small gate or postern through the Early Bronze Age defensive system (cf. Marquet-Krause 1949, pls XXX–XXXII). Hardly any damage or changes can be identified. A similar good condition is visible on the photograph of the Iron Age village (Fig. 3.4). Marquet-Krause's rooms 150, 183, 184, 186 and 208 (cf. Fig. 3.7) can be identified. The third picture taken by Leo Boer (Fig. 3.3) is most likely of the palace or the temple wall.[2] The worked limestone blocks contrast clearly with, for example, the Iron Age village or the Early Bronze Age city wall. Far from certain though it is, I propose that the photograph shows the southern face of Callaway's Wall A (Callaway 1965).

Archaeological research at Khirbet et-Tell prior to 1953

Although Boer refers frequently to the excavations of Marquet-Krause, she was not the first excavator at Khirbet et-Tell. The first archaeological explorations at the site were conducted by the British archaeologist John Garstang in the autumn of 1928. He was a leading archaeologist with work experience in many areas, from Turkey in the north to the Sudan in the south. Among his most notable accomplishments were the excavations at Tell es-Sultan – ancient Jericho (see Sala in this volume) – and the discovery of Hazor. The excavation campaign at Khirbet et-Tell was funded by Sir Charles Marston. Eight trenches were opened; five on the outer face of the southern city wall and three within the city itself (cf. Fig. 3.8). It was a short and hastily executed excavation with only limited supervision. Garstang left us with a five-page, unpublished summary (1928; see Callaway 1980). According to Garstang, his expedition showed convincingly that Khirbet et-Tell was an important city during the Early Bronze Age and continued to flourish until its destruction in the Late Bronze Age. In his opinion this proved that Khirbet et-Tell was ancient 'Ai.

A few years later, Garstang mentioned the discovery of 'Late Bronze Age fragments upon the surface' (Anonymous 1936b, 129) and of a fragment of a Cypriot bowl in the excavation (Garstang 1931, 356). However, none of these finds were mentioned in his report of 1928. Of the five boxes packed by Garstang, only one was found back in the Rockefeller Museum in Jerusalem and a few selected pieces ended up in the Albright Institute in Jerusalem. Neither assemblage contained any Late Bronze Age specimens (Winter 1970; Callaway 1980, 3; idem 1992). The presence or absence of Late Bronze Age pottery at Khirbet et-Tell played and would continue to play an important role in the identification of the site (see below). Garstang received support from Albright who combined his own study of surface pottery from the site with Garstang's excavation results: 'There can be no doubt

Figure 3.7: Loci 190, 189, 188, 181, 184 of the Iron Age village of Khirbet et-Tell, published by Judith Marquet-Krause (Courtesy of Librairie Orientaliste Paul Geuthner).

that the site was occupied before 2000 BC, in the Early Bronze Age proper, and that it was occupied more or less continuously through the Middle into the Late' (Albright 1929, 11).

Only a few years later, the conclusions of these two famous archaeologists were seriously challenged by an Israeli orientalist named Judith Marquet-Krause. After her education in France she joined the Jericho excavations directed by John Garstang in 1932 and 1933. This was the start of her, sadly short, archaeological career. Baron de Rothschild appointed her in 1933 as the director of the renewed excavations at Khirbet et-Tell. Marquet-Krause's aim was to confirm Joshua's conquest of Canaan.

Marquet-Krause worked with an enormous team of about 80 to 100 workmen in the first two seasons and almost 160 workers during 1935. She focused mainly on the upper areas of the site, i.e. the acropolis (cf. Fig. 3.9). It was covered by an almost six-meter high heap of stones which had to be removed laboriously. Underneath it lay a sanctuary containing some Egyptian alabaster vessels. Khirbet et-Tell revealed itself as having been a large fortified Early Bronze Age city that ended abruptly as a result of some severe destruction around 2400 BCE. On top of the ruins, Marquet-Krause discovered the remnants of an unfortified village. But it did not date from the Middle or Late Bronze Age. The village was founded around 1220 BCE and lasted no more than two centuries (Marquet-Krause 1934; idem 1935; idem 1949). At the time of Joshua's campaign, dated in the 1930s by most scholars to the Late Bronze Age, Khirbet et-Tell

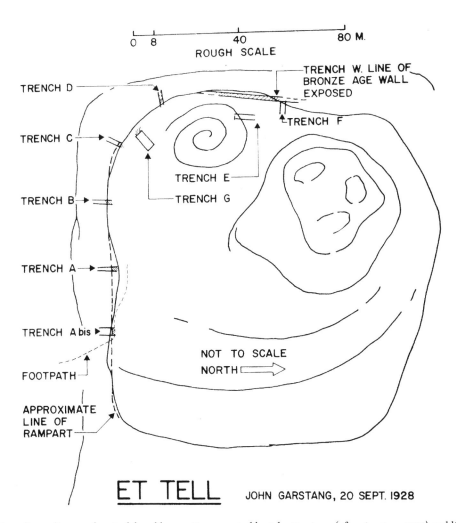

Figure 3.8: Sketch plan of soundings at the citadel and lower city excavated by John Garstang (after Garstang 1928), published by Callaway (© 1980 American Schools of Oriental Research. All rights reserved. Published here by permission of the American Schools of Oriental Research).

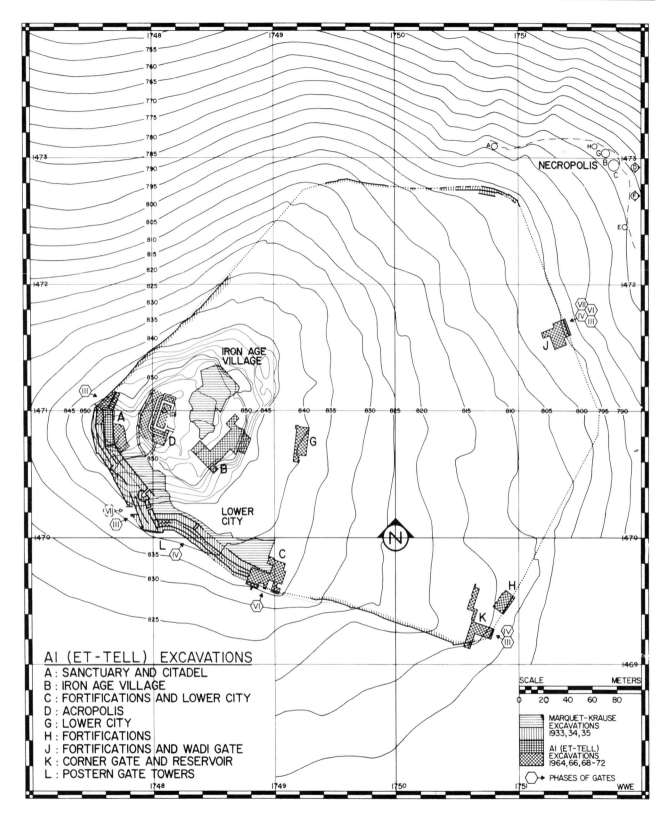

Figure 3.9: Site plan of the early Bronze Age citadel and lower city at et-Tell published by Callaway (© 1980 American Schools of Oriental Research. All rights reserved. Published here by permission of the American Schools of Oriental Research).

was a heap of stones. Her results were immediately questioned by the ruling class of archaeologists, among them Albright and her teacher Garstang. They announced on several occasions that they *had* found Late Bronze Age pottery, questioning the reliability of Marquet-Krause's excavation.[3]

Her unexpected death in July 1936 meant the end of the excavations at Khirbet et-Tell. A catalogue of the objects and three preliminary excavation reports were published by Marquet-Krause's husband in 1949, making the discoveries available to the scientific world.

Even though the excavations at Khirbet et-Tell questioned the foundations of the biblical narratives (see below), most scholars have acknowledged the excellent work of Marquet-Krause. The Palestine Exploration Fund Quarterly Statement of 1936 pointed out that 'these excavations have, in the opinion of competent judges, been carried out perfectly', but also 'the results of the recent excavations at ʿAi will cause some perplexity for those who pin their faith too simply to the spade' (Anonymous 1936a, 54). All the hope of identifying biblical places had been pinned by biblical scholars on archaeologists. Suddenly, archaeology was causing a threat.

Martin Noth (1935) was one of the first who agreed with Marquet-Krause's interpretation, later supported by others (e.g. Vincent 1937). He questioned the historicity of the biblical account and pointed out that these stories were aetiological legends rather than historical events. At the end of the 1930s there were three separate groups: 1) scholars who acknowledged the excavation results and searched for explanation without touching on the biblical narratives, 2) those, like Noth, who rejected the historicity of the Old Testament and placed the archaeological data above the biblical narratives, and 3) a group questioning the results of the excavations. This dispute went on for many years, until most came to the agreement that 'since the case of Ai is an equal embarrassment to every view on the Exodus, and cannot be integrated at present into any synthesis of biblical and non-biblical material, it must be left out of the account' (Rowley 1950, 20).

This was the archaeological state of affairs when Boer visited Khirbet et-Tell in November 1953, wrote his personal notes and took his photographs. But what happened here after he had left the site and gone back to Jerusalem, Rome, and later, back to the Netherlands?

Archaeological research at Khirbet et-Tell after 1953

It was of course only a question of time before someone would return to Khirbet et-Tell. Eleven years after Boer's visit and 29 years after Marque-Krause's last campaign, the American biblical scholar Joseph Callaway started new research at Khirbet et-Tell. In 1960 Callaway worked for several weeks on the excavation at Beitan – probably Bethel – and on the Drew-McCormick excavations at Tell Balata – Shechem (see Campbell in this volume). He became more and more intrigued by Kathleen Kenyon's stratigraphic analysis. Callaway had taken some courses in stratigraphic excavation at the University of London Institute of Archaeology, and it was here that he had first-hand contact with Early Bronze Age material from Khirbet et-Tell (Callaway 1964). After his return to the Middle East and some more excavation seasons in Jerusalem and Tell Balata, he initiated a pilot season at Khirbet et-Tell in 1964. This was very promising, and excavations continued during the following years. It was a joint project, financed by the American School of Oriental Research in co-operation with other research institutes. Callaway conducted five major expeditions until 1970, followed by two that he called, 'closing-down operations' in 1971 and 1972 (Callaway 1992; idem 1993).

Besides his familiarity with the site and the material, the divergence between the archaeological record and the biblical narratives intrigued him. He was convinced that with his training and new stratigraphic techniques he could solve some of the stratigraphic problems that Marquet-Krause and Vincent had encountered in the 1930s (Vincent 1937; Callaway 1980, 10). Callaway opened eight excavation areas, most of which were adjacent to the trenches of Marquet-Krause. A few new areas were chosen along the eastern fortifications (Fig. 3.9). During all the years of excavations (1964–1972), he worked in small squares with very neatly trimmed baulks. His stratigraphic control over the excavation supported by a very experienced supervisory staff are also clearly evident in his excellent final reports (1972; 1980). But he, too, died before he could publish all the results.

Early Bronze Age

The earliest remains of occupation date to the Early Bronze Age IB. Buildings were set on bedrock forming an unfortified village of about 200 metres in diameter. Most of the pottery is indigenous, having antecedents in Chalcolithic forms. But the foreign elements in the ceramics increased over time, pointing to immigrants settling there at the end of this phase. The inhabitants were buried in tombs on the north-eastern slope of the site.

During the Early Bronze Age IC, the settlement of Khirbet et-Tell grew to urban proportions and the approximately eleven settled hectares were surrounded by a wall. The layout indicates a degree of planning which is different from the pre-urban phase (Callaway 1976, 20). Excavations exposed a walled citadel, a sanctuary on the highest point and a residential quarter on the east side. The pottery traditions gradually show more and more northern influences. The next phase, which dates to the Early Bronze Age II, is a continuation of the same culture, but with apparent Egyptian influence. It was probably an earthquake which ended this flourishing regional centre in around 2720 BCE.

After a short period of desolation, the city was rebuilt at the beginning of the Early Bronze Age III. The large city wall of the previous phase was strengthened with a second wall. Houses were constructed directly on top of the ruins, and the acropolis together with the sanctuary was repaired. The city wall had at least two gates. A massive water reservoir inside the walls provided rainwater to the inhabitants. Material culture and building techniques again show affinities with Egypt. Around 2550 BCE, the city experienced a short disruption and some damage. But the fortification and sanctuary seem to have been repaired almost immediately. The inhabitants of Khirbet et-Tell were not very fortunate: the city was destroyed completely by a fire in 2400 BCE.

Iron Age

After this violent destruction, Khirbet et-Tell lay in ruins for more than 1000 years. Callaway did not discover any Middle or Late Bronze Age pottery, nor found evidence of any temporary occupation during this period.[4] In accordance with the findings of Marquet-Krause, he encountered the remnants of a small and unfortified village of not more than one hectare. It was founded in 1250 BCE at the earliest. The communal way of life in the Early Bronze Age was exchanged for a more individual or family-based living strategy. The village suffered some damage and

was abandoned for a short period around 1125 BCE (Callaway 1976, 30). The next settlement, still within Iron Age I, was smaller and only visible in several flimsy walls. At the end of the eleventh century BCE, Khirbet et-Tell was abandoned for good (Callaway 1993, 44–45).[5]

Identifying Biblical places: the case of 'Ai

The persistent fascination scholars have with Khirbet et-Tell is certainly traceable to its early identification with the biblical city of 'Ai. Had the ruins been situated on the eastern side of the Jordan River or elsewhere in the Middle East, I would not be surprised if they would still have been hidden under a thick layer of debris today. The site's appearance is far from impressive and the archaeological findings are relatively limited when compared to many other sites in the Southern Levant.

The city of 'Ai in the Bible

The fact that ancient 'Ai plays a prominent role in the biblical narratives about the Israelite conquest certainly motivated nineteenth-century travellers in their quest for identification of the site. From the total of 42 citations this place name in the Bible, 36 references can be found in the book of Joshua 7–12 describing the Israelite conquest.[6] But there are several other references too. In Genesis the city is mentioned twice as a place next to which Abraham had set up a camp (Genesis 12:8; 13:3) and in Isaiah 'Ai was attacked by the Assyrian army at the end of the eighth century BCE (Isaiah 10:28). The latest references, chronologically speaking, can be found in Ezra and Nehemiah. Deportees from the area returned from Babylonia in the second half of the sixth century BCE, among them were inhabitants from 'Ai (Ezra 2:28; Nehemia 7:32).

The biblical references contain a wealth of information about the location, that is to say, *if*, of course, you consider the information to be historically correct. 'Ai must be situated to the east of and not too far from Bethel; the towns are even considered twin-cities (Joshua 12:9). 'Ai is located beside Beth-Aven, which is east of Bethel (Joshua 7:2) and west of Michmash (1 Samuel 13:5). There was a hill between Bethel and 'Ai (Genesis 12:8), a valley north of 'Ai

(Joshua 8:11) and a plain in the vicinity. From the city of ʿAi, one could descend to Jericho (Joshua 7:5). At first glance, it would seem obvious where the city of ʿAi should be found, but the geographical information fits more than one location.

According to the description of Joshua's attempts, the city of ʿAi was small, since only two or three thousand Israelites were able to conquer this sparsely populated city (Joshua 7:3). However, the next passage mentions that the soldiers killed 12,000 inhabitants, which indicates a pretty large town (Joshua 8:25). Another intriguing piece of information is that Joshua destroyed the city, making it a heap of rubble (Joshua 8:28). This means that at the time of writing the biblical text, the site must have been abandoned and left in ruins.[7]

Identifying ʿAi as Khirbet et-Tell

The first person to associate ancient ʿAi with Khirbet et-Tell was the American adventurer, topographer and theologian, Edward Robinson. He visited large parts of the Southern Levant in 1837 and 1838, primarily in search of biblical cities. Khirbet et-Tell was an obvious choice, but certainly not Robinson's favourite candidate for ancient ʿAi. That was Khirbet Ḥaiyan (Robinson and Smith 1841, 312–13). Carel van de Velde visited Khirbet et-Tell in 1852 and declared that it had to be ancient ʿAi (1854, 278–79); Charles Wilson (1869–1870, 123) and Samuel Anderson (1871, 469–70), too, were convinced of this identification (see also Wood 2008, 209). Those identifications were based on biblical narratives, as well as the geographical situation and etymological evidence. Scholars easily favoured Khirbet et-Tell as the Arabic name 'et-Tell' equates with the Hebrew word 'ha-ʿAi', both referring to 'the ruin' (e.g. Albright 1934, 11).[8]

This dispute was more or less settled by the American archaeologist William F. Albright. After studying the geographical situation and surface pottery from the site, he strongly endorsed the site as being ancient ʿAi (Albright 1924, 141–49; idem 1929). From the moment the famous scholar Albright had expressed his verdict, the rest of the world accepted this identification. In the 1920s and early 1930s this proposition was never seriously challenged. Only a few scholars, such as the German archaeologist Ernst Sellin, pointed out that only

excavation work could prove the identification as being correct (Sellin 1900).

The sole reason for John Garstang's fascination with Khirbet et-Tell was this identification. His short and hastily executed excavation convinced him that Albright was right. He discovered a large Early Bronze Age town which had continued to be inhabited at least until Joshua's time (Garstang 1928). Around 1400 BCE, a fire destroyed the city after which it was abandoned. He was convinced that this destruction was caused by the Israelites.

Cracks in the identification

Until 1933, the equation of Khirbet et-Tell with ʿAi was hardly disputed. This changed immediately after the excavation results of Marquet-Krause became known (1934; 1935; 1949). Khirbet et-Tell had *not* been continuously occupied until the end of the Late Bronze Age, as had previously been suggested by Albright and Garstang. The site saw a long occupational gap between the destruction of the Early Bronze Age III town and the Iron Age I. The conquest of the Israelites, traditionally dated to the Late Bronze Age, could therefore not be the reason of the destruction of ʿAi. Not only was Khirbet et-Tell uninhabited during the Late Bronze Age, Marquet-Krause also failed to discover Late Iron Age remnants, a time during which, according to the biblical narratives, ʿAi was a thriving city, besieged both by the Assyrians and Babylonians.

Leo Boer, too, was aware of these discrepancies: 'Because, as the excavations have revealed, the town became derelict around 2000 BCE and was not resettled prior to the Iron Age. And how can it be explained that Joshua had so much trouble capturing this city after leaving Jericho? In his time et-Tell was a ruin, not a thriving city (Joshua 7:1–8).'

The results of Marquet-Krause's excavations shocked the biblical world. 'Archaeology has raised more problems than it has solved' (McKenzie 1966, 56). You would expect that scholars would have responded immediately by criticising the identification of Khirbet et-Tell as the biblical city of ʿAi. Strangely enough, however, most people were convinced that the identification was justified and were looking for other reasons why the archaeological evidence did not match the biblical narratives.

Searching for explanations

One of the most radical hypotheses proposed to solve the difficulties so far was that Joshua's campaign was not meant to be historical but aetiological. Noth suggested that the writers of the Bible noted the presence of the local ruin and sought to explain this destruction in terms of a legendary ancestor (Noth 1935). The excavator of the site, Marquet-Krause, had a similar explanation. She believed that Khirbet et-Tell was 'Ai, but concluded that the conquest was more a legend than history (Marquet-Krause 1934, 341).

The period after Marquet-Krause's excavations saw scholars trying to protect the historicity of biblical narratives, some agreed on the identification of 'Ai with Khirbet et-Tell others wanted to save both. Albright, Wright and Filson were among the last group, suggesting that the later writers of the biblical narratives had confused the conquest of 'Ai with that of Bethel (Albright 1939; Wright and Filson 1956). Also the suggestion by Vincent, that a military outpost of Bethel was hastily constructed on the ruins of Khirbet et-Tell – and that the conquest of 'Ai was actually the overrunning of the outpost – kept both the identification and the historicity of the Bible intact (Vincent 1937, 262–66; Owen 1961). It was, however, not only difficult to explain the absence of Late Bronze Age material, but also the gap during the Late Iron Age. Albright proposed that the name 'Ai may have been transferred from Khirbet et-Tell to Khirbet Ḥaiyan after the Iron Age I city had come to an end (Albright 1939).[9]

Besides the idea that remains of the Late Bronze Age city had simply not withstood the long period of erosion, another solution was brought in to keep both the historicity of the biblical narratives and the identification of 'Ai in place: re-dating the time of the Israelite arrival. Khirbet et-Tell was settled in the Early Iron Age. If the conquest was dated to this period, for example the twelfth or eleventh century BCE, the story would fit the archaeological record (Zeyit 1983, 28; Negev and Gibson 2003). The suggestion that the Iron Age I village of Khirbet et-Tell was biblical 'Ai was also concluded by Callaway in 1969. He pointed out that the site must have been occupied prior to the conquest by Joshua's group, in other words, that the conquest should be dated to the Iron Age I. In the short gap between the two Iron Age phases (see above) the Israelite conquest took place (Callaway 1969b, 60–61; idem 1992, 130).[10] Others have

pushed back the period of the conquest even to the Early Bronze Age (Aardsma 1993).

Searching for alternatives

It therefore proved hard to solve the puzzle without destroying one of its pillars: either the identification was incorrect, or the biblical narratives should be re-interpreted. The easiest strategy, supported by most scholars, was to search for another candidate site that did match the biblical stories (Fig. 3.10). Although the identification of Khirbet et-Tell as 'Ai had been taken for granted for more than a century, it now appeared that not all biblical data backed this identification. Khirbet et-Tell was located too far from Bethel, it was too large, and it did not have a valley to the north and was not situated to the west of the biblical town of Michmash (e.g. Simons 1959, 270; Livingston 1994). Biblical scholars now started to search for 'gaps' in the traditional identification and to look for alternatives.

Khirbet Ḥaiyan

The earliest alternative was proposed by Edward Robinson. Instead of Khirbet et-Tell, he chose Khirbet Ḥaiyan for the identification, at the southern edge of Deir Dibwan (Robinson and Smith 1841, 312–13). Others, too, were convinced that Khirbet Ḥaiyan was ancient 'Ai (Conder and Conder 1882; Saunders 1881, 95–97). Even though Callaway was sure Khirbet et-Tell was biblical 'Ai, he surveyed and trenched Khirbet Ḥaiyan in 1964 and 1969. The soundings revealed evidence of habitation from the Roman through to the Omayyad Periods with only a few Early Bronze Age sherds (Callaway and Nicol 1966; Kallai 1972, 178–79; Finkelstein and Magen 1993, 183). The site was most intensively used during the fifth century BCE and could therefore hardly be the city that Joshua had destroyed (Callaway and Nicol 1966).

Khirbet el-Khudriya

A different suggestion was made by Victor Guérin (1869, 59; see also Grintz 1961, 203). He proposed Khirbet el-Khudriya as being ancient 'Ai, a site situated east of Khirbet et-Tell.[11] Callaway made some soundings in 1966 and 1968, revealing only Byzantine ruins, including a church, an industrial complex and

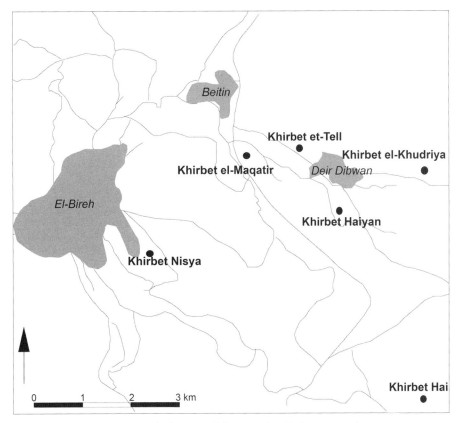

Figure 3.10: The location of the sites identified as ancient 'Ai.

numerous Herodian and Roman tombs (Callaway 1968, 315; idem 1969a, 4–5; Bagatti 2002, 35–38). Only one Middle Bronze Age IIB-tomb was discovered far down in the valley, to the east of the site. Some of the cisterns contained Early Iron Age pottery (Callaway 1970; idem 1969a, 4).

Khirbet Ḥai

A third proposition was Khirbet Ḥai, located to the south-east of Michmash (Kitchener 1878, 94–96). A later survey showed that all of the surface pottery and architecture belong to the Mamluk Period, while only a few sherds were dated Byzantine (Callaway 1968, 315; Kallai 1972, 182; Finkelstein and Magan 1993, 38). Even if earlier material had been discovered at Khirbet Ḥai, its identification with 'Ai would be questionable because of geographical reasons.

Khirbet el-Maqatir

A much more probable candidate for 'Ai is the site of Khirbet el-Maqatir. The site was already mentioned

by Edward Robinson, who explained that the local inhabitants believed it to be biblical 'Ai (1841, 126). Ernst Sellin had also heard those rumours when he visited the site in 1899 (1900, 1). Khirbet el-Maqatir is located one kilometre west of Khirbet et-Tell and approximately fifteen kilometres north of Jerusalem. Bryant Wood, research director of the Associates for Biblical Research, started archaeological excavations at the site in 1995 (Wood 1999a; idem 1999b; idem 2000; idem 2008). The site reveals five periods of occupation, ranging from the Middle Bronze Age to the Byzantine Period. Wood discovered a ruin border fortress dating to the fifteenth century BCE. The settlement was surrounded by a wall with a gate complex. Sling stones found in the excavation trenches suggest that a battle had been fought there. After a gap of two centuries, the town was rebuilt by, according to Wood, Israelites. They cleared some of the structures for re-use. The settlement was poorly constructed and never reached the same level of wealth as in the Late Bronze Age. Remains of later occupation include buildings from the Hasmonean Period, a Byzantine monastery and a storage pit from the sixth century BCE. Wood is convinced that Khirbet el-Maqatir meets all the requirements 'to be Joshua's 'Ai' (Wood 2008, 231).

Khirbet Nisya

After excavating Khirbet Nisya between 1979 and 2002, a site situated two kilometres south-east of the modern village of El-Bireh, David Livingston became convinced that it must be ancient 'Ai. Not only the settlement history, but also the topography of this site corresponds closely to the narratives of Joshua (Bimson and Livingston 1987, 48–51; Livingston 1994, 159; idem 1999; idem 2003, 203–22). The excavation results produced remains of occupation with varying intensities from the Middle Bronze Age right through to the Islamic Period, including some Late Bronze Age and Late Iron Age material (Livingston 2003, 36–43).

Conclusions

From the nineteenth century right through to the first part of the twentieth century scholars equated Khirbet et-Tell with the city that was the focus of Joshua's men during the Israelite conquest. This identification was based on the geographical and topographical position of the site. Even surface explorations by Albright and a sounding by Garstang in the beginning of the twentieth century did not alter this identification. For almost 100 years, biblical scholars were convinced that the heaps of stones at Khirbet et-Tell were the outcome of Joshua's attack. This changed in the year 1933, when Marquet-Krause announced that Khirbet et-Tell did not reveal any evidence of Late Bronze Age occupation, nor any material from the Late Iron Age. One can imagine the impact these results had on the biblical as well as the non-biblical world.

The divergence between the archaeological record and the textual evidence was resolved in different ways. Only a few scholars criticized the result of the archaeological research itself. The most radical solution was to challenge the historical credibility of the biblical narratives: the stories must have been legends. Others tried to explain the texts in such a way that they fitted the archaeological record, or started to look for other candidate-sites, such as

Khirbet el-Maqatir or Khirbet Nisya. But these new identifications are not universally nor unambiguously accepted.

Has the search for biblical 'Ai brought us closer to a better understanding of the Bronze and Iron Age society of the Southern Levant? Perhaps. But we have to read between the lines of the publications and consider that they were written to convince the reader of a certain interpretation. A biblical scholar searching for the city of 'Ai, logically, looks differently at the archaeological record than, for example, a prehistorian does (cf. Finkelstein 2007, 110). This makes it extremely difficult to judge the scientific value of the various reports. Which interpretations are solely based on the archaeological record and which ones are constructed upon religious motives or preconceived ideas? It is often hard to tell.

In the 'Ai discussion, there is one question that has never been asked: why should we *want* to know where the city of 'Ai was located? In every research project, archaeologists have to explain why certain research activities are undertaken, why one concentrates on certain things and not on other things, why money is spent on investigating a heap of rubble, and what information one expects to find. The identification of biblical cities with modern sites remains speculative and notoriously uncertain. Then, why should it be put at the centre of a scientific programme? One may question whether a purely biblical project aim can justify the irreversible damage caused by archaeological excavations. Similar objections may be raised to the search for a synagogue or Iron Age layers with Black Burnished Ware. If the focus of an archaeological excavation is too narrow, the whole project may be criticised.

But I am aware of one important aspect. If you excavate a site mentioned in the Bible, it will increase the chances of receiving funding and other kinds of support. Hundreds of professional archaeologists and interested volunteers are willing to search for remains from biblical periods in Israel, but are not so eager to walk through the eastern Jordanian deserts in search of ancient nomadic campsites.

It seems time for biblical and non-biblical scholars to start working together. This will help to avoid preconceived ideas and to stimulate different views on each archaeological record. Scholars are then able to study the biblical relevance of the site *and* the occupation levels that have no relation to the

Bible. We need to be aware that each archaeological record is unique in every aspect and that it is the honourable task of the excavator to unravel as many aspects as possible.

Acknowledgements

I wish to thank Bart Wagemakers for providing me with the opportunity to participate in this publication. Without the excellent descriptions and photographs of Leo Boer, this paper would never have been written. Furthermore, I am indebted to Laura Crowley for editing this paper. I remain responsible for any failures and discrepancies in the text.

Notes

1　Leo Boer, 26 November 1953. Boer's notes have been translated into English by the author of this paper.

2　Wright argued that it was not a palace as Marquet-Krause suggested, but a temple (Callaway 1965, 31; idem 1980, 41).

3　Discussions concerning the presence or absence of Middle and Late Bronze Age pottery at Khirbet et-Tell are ongoing, due to ambiguous descriptions in publications and difficulties the excavators had with sequence dating (Kennedy 2011, 149–50; cf. Marquet-Krause 1949, 11; Yeivin 1971, 51; Callaway 1968, 316). Albright would later admit that the Late Bronze Age cooking pot sherds he had discovered could also belong to the Early Iron Age (1934, 11).

4　Remember the comments of Albright and Garstang in which they described finding Late Bronze Age pottery at Khirbet et-Tell (Albright 1929, 11; Garstang 1931, 129). See also note 3.

5　Not all scholars agree with the dating of the Iron Age phases (Finkelstein 1988, 72; idem 2007). The most problematic element is that the Iron Age pottery of Callaway's excavation has not yet been published and that so far only sherd material from Marquet-Krause's excavations is known (Marquet-Krause 1934; idem 1935; idem 1949). Finkelstein mentioned a few complete vessels, 'hidden in the plates among the hundreds of Early Bronze Age vessels and sherds' (Finkelstein 2007, 107). There is hardly any evidence for human presence in the very Early Iron Age I, and the latest item found at Khirbet et-Tell should be dated to the second half of the tenth century BCE. The Iron Age occupation should, according to Finkelstein, be placed between the eleventh century BCE and the late tenth century BCE.

6　One reference in the Bible mentions the fall of 'Ai years later (Jeremiah 49:3).

7　The date and authorship of the book of Joshua are still disputed. The more liberal scholars assume that the stories were written almost 1000 years after the Israelite conquest, whereas others have suggested that the text was written close to the time of the events, around 1400 BCE (e.g. Davis 2007, 181).

8　Not all scholars agree on this theory. (e.g. Grintz 1961, 211). According to Zevit there is no relationship at all between 'ha-'Ai' and the Hebrew word for 'ruin'. Support for this thesis is found in the Septuagint, which uses the spelling of 'Ai as Aggai (Zevit 1983, 25–26; idem 1985, 62).

9　Khirbet Ḥaiyan is not a very likely suggestion, since no Late Iron Age occupation has been revealed (Callaway and Nicol 1966).

10　However, note that Finkelstein challenged the absolute chronology of those two phases. Parallels of well-dated assemblages place the phases almost a century later, from the eleventh century till the late tenth century BCE. According to him, the archaeology was dictated by the Book of Joshua, fixed 'according to the excavators' view on the early Israelite conquest' (Finkelstein 2007, 110).

11　Albright (1924, 141) and Wood (2008, 209) have suggested that Guérin had confused Khirbet el-Khudriya with Khirbet Ḥaiyan.

Bibliography of Khirbet et-Tell

Aardsma, G. 1993. *A New Approach to the Chronology of Biblical History from Abraham to Samuel.* El Cajon: Institute for Creation Research.

Albright, W. F. 1924. "Excavations and Results at Tell el-Ful (Gibeah of Saul)." *Annual of the American Schools of Oriental Research* 4:iii–160.

Albright, W. F. 1929. "The American Excavations at Tell-Beit Mirsim." *Zeitschrift für die Alttestamentliche Wissenschaft* 47:1–17.

Albright, W. F. 1934. "The Kyle Memorial Excavation at Bethel." *Bulletin of the American Schools of Oriental Research* 56:1–15.

Albright, W. F. 1939. "The Israelite Conquest of Canaan in the Light of Archaeology." *Bulletin of the American Schools of Oriental Research* 74:11–23.

Anderson, S. 1871. "The Survey of Palestine." In *The Recovery of Jerusalem. A Narrative of Exploration and Discovery in the City and the Holy Land*, written by Ch. W. Wilson, Ch. Warren, and others, 438–71. London: Palestine Exploration Fund.

Anonymous. 1936a. "Notes and News." *Palestine Exploration Fund Quarterly* 68 (April):51–58.

Anonymous. 1936b. "Seventy First Annual General Meeting." *Palestine Exploration Fund Quarterly* 68 (July):121–40.

Bagatti, B. 2002. *Ancient Christian Villages of Judaea and the Negev.* Studium Biblicum Franciscanum Collectio Minor 39. Jerusalem: Franciscan Printing Press.

Bimson, J. J. and Livingston, D. 1987. "Redating the Exodus." *Biblical Archaeology Review* 13.5:40–53, 66–68.

Callaway, J. A. 1964. *Pottery from the Tombs at 'Ai (Et-Tell).* Monograph Series (Colt Archaeological Institute), Vol. 2. London: Bernard Quaritch.

Callaway, J. A. 1965. "The 1964 'Ai (Et-Tell) Excavations." *Bulletin of the American Schools of Oriental Research* 178:13–40.

Callaway, J. A. 1968. "New Evidence on the Conquest of 'Ai." *Journal of Biblical Literature* 87.3:312–20.

Callaway, J. A. 1969a. "The 1966 'Ai (et-Tell) Excavations." *Bulletin of the American Schools of Oriental Research* 196:2–16.

Callaway, J. A. 1969b. "The Significance of the Iron Age Village at 'Ai (et-Tell)." In *Proceedings of the Fifth World Congress of Jewish Studies*, Vol. 1, 56–61. Jerusalem: World Union of Jewish Studies.

Callaway, J. A. 1970. "The 1968–1969 'Ai (et-Tell) Excavations." *Bulletin of the American Schools of Oriental Research* 198:7–31.

Callaway, J. A. 1972. *The Early Bronze Age Sanctuary at 'Ai (et-Tell).* London: Bernard Quaritch.

Callaway, J. A. 1976. "Excavating at Ai (Et-Tell): 1964–1972." *The Biblical Archaeologist* 39:18–30.

Callaway, J. A. 1980. *The Early Bronze Age Citadel and Lower City at 'Ai (et-Tell). Report of the Joint Archaeological Expedition to 'Ai*, Vol. 2. Cambridge, MA: American Schools of Oriental Research.

Callaway, J. A. 1992. "'Ai." In *The Anchor Bible Dictionary*, Vol. 1, edited by David Noel Freedman, 125–30. New York: Doubleday.

Callaway, J. A. 1993. "'Ai." In *The New Encyclopedia of Archaeological Excavations in the Holy Land*, edited by Ephraim Stern, 39–45. New York, NY: Simon and Schuster.

Callaway, J. A. and Nicol, M. B. 1966. "A Sounding at Khirbet Haiyan." *Bulletin of the American Schools of Oriental Research* 183:12–19.

Conder, Francis R. and Conder, C. R. 1882. *A Handbook to the Bible.* London: Longmans and Green.

Davis, C. 2007. *Dating the Old Testament.* New York, NY: RJ Communications.

Finkelstein, I. 1988. *The Archaeology of the Israelite Settlement.* Jerusalem: Israel Exploration Society.

Finkelstein, I. 2007. "Iron Age I Khirbet et-Tell and Khirbet Raddana: Methodological Lessons." In *"Up to the Gates of Ekron": Essays on the Archaeology and History of the Eastern Mediterranean in Honor of Seymour Gitin*, edited by Sidnie White Crawford, Amnon Ben-Tor, J.P. Dessel, William G. Dever, Amihai Mazar, and Joseph Aviram, 107–13. Jerusalem: W.F. Albright Institute of Archaeological Research and Israel Exploration Society.

Finkelstein, I. and Magen, Y. 1993. *Archaeological Survey of the Hill Country of Benjamin.* Jerusalem: Israel Antiquities Authority.

Garstang, J. 1928. "Et-Tell: Ai. Report on the 1928 Soundings at Ai Submitted to the Department of Antiquities, Jerusalem, September 21, 1928." 5 pages. Unpublished report.

Garstang, J. 1931. *Joshua-Judges.* London: Constable.

Grintz, J. M. 1961. "Ai Which is Beside Beth-Aven: A Reexamination of the Identity of 'Ai." *Biblica* 42:201–16.

Guérin, V. 1869. *Description Géographique, Historique et Archéologique de la Palestine.* Paris: L'Imprimerie nationale.

Kallai, Z. 1972. "The Land of Benjamin and Mt. Ephraim." In *Judaea, Samaria, and the Golan: Archaeological Survey 1967-68*, edited by Moshe Kochavi, 153–93. Jerusalem: Carta [Hebrew].

Kennedy, T. M. 2011. *The Israelite Conquest: History or Myth? An Archaeological Evaluation of the Israelite Conquest during the Periods of Joshua and the Judges.* Unpublished MA Thesis, University of South Africa.

Kitchener, H. H. 1878. "The Site of Ai." *Palestine Exploration Fund Quarterly Statement* 10.2:74–75.

Livingston, D. P. 1994. "Further Considerations on the Location of Bethel at el-Bireh." *Palestine Exploration Quarterly* 126:154–59.

Livingston, D. P. 1999. "Excavation Report for Khirbet Nisya." *Bible and Spade* 12:3.

Livingston, D. P. 2003. *Khirbet Nisya: The Search for Biblical Ai 1979-2002.* Manheim, PA: Associates for Biblical Research.

Marquet-Krause, J. 1934. "The Ai Excavations." *News of the Hebrew Society for Research of Eretz Israel and its Ancient Artifacts* 1.4:28–30.

Marquet-Krause, J. 1935. "La Deuxieme Champagne de Fouilles a Ay (1934). Rapport Sommaire." *Syria* 16.4:325–45.

Marquet-Krause, J. 1949. *Les Fouilles de 'Ay (et-Tell), 1933-1935: Le Resurrection d'une Grande Cité Biblique.* Bibliotheque

Archéologique et Historique, Vol. 45. Paris: Librairie Orientaliste Paul Geuthner.

McKenzie, J. L. 1966. *The World of the Judges*. Englewood Cliffs, NJ: Prentice-Hall.

Negev, A. and Gibson, S. 2003. *Archaeological Encyclopedia of the Holy Land*. New York, NY: The Continuum International Publishing Group.

Noth, M. 1935. "Bethel und Ai." *Palästina-Jahrbuch* 31: 7–29.

Owen, G. F. 1961. *Archaeology of the Bible*. Westwood, NJ: Fleming H. Revell Company.

Robinson, E. and Smith, E. 1841. *Biblical Researches in Palestine, Mount Sinai, and Arabia Petraea. A Journal of Travels in the Year 1838*. Boston: Crocker and Brewster.

Rowley, H. H. 1950. *From Joseph to Joshua: Biblical Traditions in the Light of Archaeology*. The Schweich Lectures. London: Oxford University Press.

Saunders, T. 1881. *An Introduction to the Survey of Western Palestine: Its Waterways, Plains and Highlands*. London: Richard Bentley and Son.

Sellin, E. 1900. "Mitteilungen von Meiner Palästinareise 1899." *Mitteilungen und Nachrichten des Deutschen Palästina-Vereins* 6:1–15.

Simons, J. J. 1959. *The Geographical and Topographical Texts of the Old Testament*. Leiden: E.J. Brill.

Van de Velde, C. W. M. 1854. *Narrative of a Journey through Syria and Palestine in 1851 and 1852*. Utrecht: Kemink.

Vincent, L.-H. 1937. "Les fouilles d'et-Tell='Ai." *Revue Biblique* 46:231–66.

Wilson, Ch. W. 1869–1870. "On the Site of 'Ai and the Position of the Altar Which Abram Built Between Bethel and Ai." *Palestine Exploration Fund Quarterly Statement* 1:123–26.

Winter, W. W. 1970. "Biblical and Archaeological Data on Ai Reappraised." *The Seminary Review* 16.4:73–83.

Wood, B. G. 1999a. "Kh. El-Maqatir 1999 Dig Report." *Bible and Spade* 12:109–14.

Wood, B. G. 1999b. "The Search for Joshua's Ai: Excavations at Kh. El-Maqatir." *Bible and Spade* 12:21–30.

Wood, B. G. 2000. "Kh. El-Maqatir 2000 Dig Report." *Bible and Spade* 13:67–72.

Wood, B. G. 2008. "The Search for Joshua's Ai." In *Critical Issues in Early Israelite History*, edited by Richard S. Hess, Gerald A. Klingbeil and Paul J. Ray Jr., 205–40. Winona Lake, IN: Eisenbrauns.

Wright, G. E. and Filson, F. V. 1956. *Westminster Historical Atlas*. Philadelphia: Westminster Press.

Yeivin, S. 1971. *The Israelite Conquest of Canaan*. Leiden: Nederlands Historisch-Archeologisch Instituut te Istanbul.

Zevit, Z. 1983. "Archaeological and Literary Stratigraphy in Joshua 7–8." *Bulletin of the American Schools of Oriental Research* 251:23–35.

Zevit, Z. 1985. "The Problem of Ai". *Biblical Archaeology Review* 11.2:58–69.

CHAPTER 4

SAMARIA AND SEBASTE

Samaria was the capital of the Northern Kingdom of Israel. According to the biblical record the city was founded by Omri, King of Israel, who bought the hill from a man named Shemer (1 Kings 16:24). This is traditionally dated to 876 BCE. A shrine and altar to Baal were erected at Samaria by Omri's son Ahab (1 Kings 16:32), who also built a palace at the site, that was referred to as an 'ivory house' (1 Kings 22:39). It was during this period that the city was attacked on a number of occasions by Arameans from Damascus, but without success (1 Kings 20; 2 Kings 6:24–7:20). Omri's dynasty ended at the time of the revolution of Jehu in 842 BCE.

Following a sustained Assyrian attack on the Israelite city, it was captured in 721 BCE and its inhabitants deported (2 Kings 17:6). The city was subsequently repopulated with people from different origins. Samaria remained an important settlement throughout the Persian period (539–332 BCE) when it served as a provincial capital for much of central Palestine.

In 332 BCE the city was eventually taken by force following Alexander the Great's invasion of the Near East, and from that time onwards the city came to acquire a fairly cosmopolitan flavour, with Hellenism at the forefront of cultural endeavour and enterprise. It was a target for the Hasmonean rulers and was destroyed by them in 109 or 108 BCE. When Pompey arrived in the region (63 BCE) the city became part of the Roman province of Syria; restoration of its buildings began between the years 57–54 BCE under Gabinius, the Roman proconsul of Syria.

Yet another drastic change occurred: when Samaria was granted to Herod the Great by Augustus in 27 BCE, Herod poured funds into the embellishment of the city, with the construction of many beautiful buildings, including a temple and a palace. He renamed the city 'Sebaste', in honour of his benefactor (*sebastos* is Greek for 'Augustus'). The Arab name for the present-day village, Sabastiyeh, preserves the ancient name of the site. Two of Herod's sons were executed in this city. Following the death of Herod the Great, Sebaste came under the brief rule of his son Archelaus and then under a Roman procurator (from 6 CE). During the First Jewish War (66–73 CE) the city was destroyed, but it was rebuilt and gained the status of a Roman colony from the hands of Septimus Severus in 200 CE.

By the time that Christianity became the dominant religion, Sebaste was already deteriorating and after the Arab conquest in the first half of the seventh century CE it was left in ruins.

The history of the archaeological campaigns in Samaria and Sebaste, which is discussed in this chapter, shows that archaeologists in this region frequently tended to focus on the biblical traditions when interpreting archaeological finds.

A Visitor at Samaria and Sebaste

Shimon Gibson

All visitors, pilgrims and explorers travelling in the Holy Land, eventually turn up at the hill of Samaria, next to the Arab village of Sabastiyeh, to have a look at its impressive Iron Age and Classical ruins, and, not surprisingly, so did Leo Boer and his fellow travellers from the École Biblique in February 1954 (Fig. 4.1).[1] They arrived at the site having first been to Nablus, which seemed to Boer to be 'fairly modern' and 'a city of no biblical connotations'. In fact, there is a mound on the outskirts of the city, Tell Balata, which is identified as biblical Shechem (see Campbell in this volume).[2] From Nablus, the travellers drove on towards Samaria, arriving there mid-morning.

The archaeological campaigns at Samaria and Sebaste

When Leo Boer travelled to the biblical city of Samaria, he was only one on a long list of travellers who had gone there before him to have a look at its impressive antiquities. Substantial archaeological excavations had been conducted at the site by the time of Boer's arrival. One of the earliest scholars to visit Samaria was Edward Robinson, who explored the site in 1838. Explorers working for the Palestine Exploration Fund mapped the site, in July 1872 and again in June 1875, as part of the Survey of Western Palestine (Robinson 1860; Guérin 1874, 189–209;

Figure 4.1: Members of the group resting in the basilica situated at the west end of the forum.

Conder and Kitchener 1882, 212–13). Some visitors were not as impressed by the site as the explorers. Mark Twain, for example, described the place as 'hot and dusty' when reaching the village in 1867: 'There was nothing for us to do in Samaria but buy handfuls of old Roman coins at a franc a dozen, and look at a dilapidated church of the Crusaders and a vault in it which once contained the body of John the Baptist. This relic was long ago carried away to Genoa.' (Twain 1869, 397).

Substantial archaeological digging operations were undertaken at Samaria between 1908 and 1910 by a Harvard University expedition led by G. A. Reisner and C. S. Fisher (Reisner, Fisher and Lyon 1924). This was followed by a joint expedition from 1931 to 1935 under the general directorship of John Winter Crowfoot, representing the British School of Archaeology, the Hebrew University, and Harvard University (Crowfoot, Kenyon, and Sukenik 1942). These expeditions brought to light substantial remains of the city dating from the Iron Age through to the Byzantine period. The original Iron Age acropolis was on the summit of the hill; further parts of the city and its fortifications were uncovered on the east slope (just south of the later basilica). The acropolis was expanded and re-fortified during the Hellenistic period, and an extremely prominent tower was uncovered on the north-east side. The Roman city was impressive and had massive fortifications, with two or perhaps three gates. This city and its defences continued to exist until the Byzantine period. Among the important monuments identified by the expeditions, one must include the foundations of the Temple of Augustus, the theatre, the basilica and the stadium.

Additional excavations, albeit on a much smaller scale, were subsequently conducted at the site in the 1960s by F. Zayadine on behalf of the Jordanian Department of Antiquities, and by an Australian team headed by J. B. Hennessy in 1968, who excavated a number of areas on the western side of the hill (Fig. 4.2).

Crowfoot (1873–1959), the director of the second major expedition to Samaria, was originally a graduate of Brasenose College in Oxford, where he trained in the fields of Classical Archaeology and Early Christianity. He then shifted direction to successful postings in education in Cairo and Sudan, before ending up as Principal of Gordon College at Khartoum. This experience in administration eventually served

Figure 4.2: Photograph taken during the excavation of J. B. Hennessy in 1968 (Courtesy of Daniel Gibson).

him well when he was appointed Director of the British School of Archaeology in Jerusalem in 1927. Strange as it may seem, Crowfoot, who excavated so many important sites, such as Jerash, Bosra and at the Ophel in Jerusalem (see Steiner in this volume), seems to have disliked dirt archaeology. Kathleen Kenyon, the famous British archaeologist and future director of the British School in Jerusalem, diplomatically described him in 1960 as follows: 'his firm hand, unlimited tact and equable temperament provided ideal leadership...', but she was not being completely honest about Crowfoot. At Samaria Crowfoot was constantly at odds with his archaeological staff, including Kenyon, about what needed to be done on the dig. On one occasion Crowfoot turned up just as a staff member, Betty Murray, was trying to uncover two mixed levels. She wrote: 'He proceeded to change all the plans about what was to be photographed the next day, to mess up what had been prepared before by pulling down a lot more and further irritating me by proclaiming as discoveries things that I had pointed out to him two days ago. By which time, as you may gather, I was in a thoroughly bad temper.'[3] On another occasion, Murray reports:

'However during breakfast Mr Crowfoot began to fuss and soon after breakfast down he came criticizing everything and objecting to everything. I don't think he really knows much about it himself, but he is governed by two principals: a) He is terrified of destroying anything. This is the natural position of anyone looking on and not doing the thing himself. The worst of excavation is that only the actual workmen really sees and knows what is happening and as the responsibility rests on someone else, that someone else always feels uneasy and wonders if things are really as they look. But one has to take the plunge somehow and destroy if one is ever to know; b) He has learnt a lot from Kathleen [Kenyon]'s good slow methods, and wants to apply them on every occasion. Today he suddenly got cold feet and thought I was mismanaging things and wanted the dig done by trenching and not by layers. It isn't a suitable dig for that method as it really isn't much more than a trial trench itself, a very small area in which there isn't room for trial trenches. Anyway having upset everything – complained of every bit of work and that there were too many workmen and the place wasn't clean – he went off after leaving instructions with me, with the Raise [foreman], and with the workmen.'

The buildings at the site visited by Boer

Arriving mid-morning at Samaria, Leo Boer and his companions made a tour around the ruins at the site (see Fig. 4.15 in the contribution of Tappy in this chapter), and Boer mentions in his diary seeing the results of both Reisner's and Crowfoot's excavations on the acropolis: 'vast ruins echo the different eras of Samaria. Parts of it have disappeared underground again, but some of Omri's castle walls are still standing.' (Fig. 4.3). Reisner and Crowfoot had distinguished six Israelite layers with architectural remains in the area of the acropolis, dated to between the foundation of the city by Omri in 876 BCE and the destruction of the city by the Assyrians in 721 BCE (see Tappy in this chapter). Discussion about the nuances of the dating of these layers continues among scholars (Stager 1990; Finkelstein 1990; Tappy 1992; idem 2001; Franklin 2004). Within this complex of walls are a number of subterranean caves which Norma Franklin has recently suggested may be the Omride royal tombs (Franklin 2003). According to the biblical account six kings of Israel were buried at Samaria: Omri, Ahab,[4] Jehu, Jehoahaz, Joash and Jeroboam II[5] (1 Kings 16:28, 22:37; 2 Kings 10:35, 13:9, 14:16, 29). To the east of the acropolis, close to the basilica (see below), are the remains of a defence wall or fortified building, built with well-dressed stones (ashlars), which is attributed to the Israelite city (Fig. 4.4; Finkelstein 2011).

Figure 4.3: Walls of Omri's castle.

Figure 4.4: The remains of a defence wall or fortified building.

Boer and his companions also examined a round Hellenistic tower excavated by Crowfoot on one side of the summit of the hill (see Fig. 4.22 in the contribution of Tappy), and walked along the impressive colonnaded street from the Roman period (Fig. 4.5) which extends from a gate in the fortification wall on the west side of the city all the way towards a gate in the east fortification wall of the city (now beneath the Sabastiyeh village, see Fig. 4.15, number 5).[6] Some of the other prominent classical buildings at the site were also examined, notably a theatre, a stadium, a Temple of Augustus (Fig. 4.6), and a very well-preserved basilica situated at the west end of the forum (Fig. 4.7). The basilica is dated primarily to the Roman period (circa second century CE), but the building has discernible earlier phases to it, and it deserves a renewed investigation. At the northern end of the nave is a platform with a semi-circular niche and benches; it was here that Boer and his companions gathered to talk about the site (Fig. 4.8).

Samaria and John the Baptist

Having spent about an hour wandering around the ruins at Samaria, Boer and his friends reached the Chapel of the Invention of the Head of John, which is situated on the southern brow of the acropolis and on a terrace just above the main colonnaded street of the ancient town (Fig. 4.15, number 15). Boer wrote about it in his diary:

'Around the year 350, the story passed into legend among Christians that the body of John the Baptist, who had been murdered in Macheronte, in Transjordan, was buried here; so a church in his honour was built over a crypt with murals depicting the decapitation of John the Baptist. A bit further on, there was a monastery connected to another church where, according to a later legend, the missing head was found. This church, a former basilica now serving as a mosque, contained, again according to several legends, the graves of the prophets Zacharias, Abdias and Eliseus.'[7]

Figure 4.5: The colonnaded street.

Figure 4.6: Stairs leading to the Temple of Augustus.

Figure 4.7: Basilica situated at the west end of the forum.

Figure 4.8: The group of the École Biblique resting in the basilica.

There are two sites at Sebaste connected with the death and burial of John the Baptist.[8] The first is the small chapel of the Invention of the Head of John marking the supposed spot of the palace where John was imprisoned and later beheaded. This site was found and excavated by Crowfoot (1937, 24 ff.). The second site, located some 600 metres further to the east (Fig. 4.15, number 23), is the very large cathedral of St John located in the midst of the present-day village of Sabastiyeh, marking the alleged spot of the tomb of John (Fig. 4.9).[9] While Boer definitely visited the Chapel of the Invention of the Head of John, taking a photograph there (Fig. 4.10), he probably did not go into the large cathedral of St John in the village, though he would have passed it when leaving the village with his companions.

The ruined Chapel of the Invention of the Head of John the Baptist was first seen by officers of the British Royal Engineers, C. R. Conder and H. H. Kitchener, during their survey of the site in the 1870s, who marked it on the topographical map that they prepared of the site and its antiquities.[10] I am

Figure 4.9: The large cathedral of St John marking the spot of the tomb of John.

Figure 4.10: The Chapel of the Invention of the Head of John in 1954.

not sure that Crowfoot, who excavated the building, realised that it had already been visible to explorers in the nineteenth century, otherwise he would not have written that he had 'stumbled more or less by chance in 1931' on an 'undiscovered' church' (Crowfoot 1937, 26). Explorers in the nineteenth century, Edward Robinson among them, had tried to identify signs of a Christian edifice among the ruins outside the village because of the references given in the writings by Phocas and Burchard, but without visiting it.

Crowfoot originally tackled the excavation of this area of fields – known to the locals as 'Aqtan el Deir' (Lands of the Monastery) – because he wanted to find a continuation of a much earlier Israelite wall that he was tracing. Almost immediately, he came down upon a jumble of walls, patches of decorated mosaic floors and water cisterns, which he identified as the remains of a Greek monastery of the sixth or seventh centuries CE, though medieval pottery and a coin of King Amaury (1162–1173) were also found in one of the cisterns. Further traces of monastic buildings could be identified (but were not excavated) to the north and west, and

the working theory that Crowfoot developed was that the lands of this Byzantine monastery stretched for a distance of some 220 metres along the terrace. The church was apparently located at the heart of this monastic complex.

Access to the church was from the west, via a paved *narthex*-like porch and an entrance that could be barricaded from the inside with a slot-bar (Fig. 4.11). The interior of the church is almost square (14.6 by 13 metres) and a single apse, square on the outside, protruded towards the east. The ceiling of the building was originally domed and was supported on four columns, which were later encased in masonry in the form of piers. In appearance this church largely dates from the final stage of its construction in the twelfth century. Nothing much has survived of the first Byzantine basilical-church except for the foundation slabs (*stylobates*), which supported the colonnades and patches of decorative floor mosaics, one of which has a fragmentary Greek dedicatory inscription (Fig. 4.12).[11]

What happened to this early church, whether it was eventually destroyed in an earthquake or

Figure 4.11: A recent picture of the Chapel of the Invention of the Head of John the Baptist. On the left the entrance to the subterranean crypt is visible.

Figure 4.12: A drawing of the Greek dedicatory inscription found in the Byzantine basilical church.

dismantled by human hands, is not known. However, it did have quite a long history, surviving into Abbasid times, even after the main Byzantine church (in the area of the village) had become a heap of ruins. The *Commemoratorium de Casis Dei* (circa 808) mentions the church 'where the prison was and [where] he

[John] was beheaded' and that ceremonies were still conducted there by Bishop Basil and 25 presbyters, monks and clergy. Its destruction may have been the work of Caliph Hakim (1009–1114) (Pringle 1998, 297–301: Site No. 226). The church was substantially rebuilt sometime at the end of the eleventh century with *spolia* from ancient buildings at the site. The four columns that support the domed ceiling of the church date from this time, as well as the oldest visible portions of the walls, and column shafts with red-painted graffiti and crosses. A badly-weathered wall painting of a row of saints (?), dated on stylistic grounds to circa 1080, was visible in the north-west corner of the church. The church was restored and rebuilt probably during the Crusader period (twelfth century) and it was during this stage that the Chapel of the Invention of the Head was constructed in the north-east corner of the church with the restoration of an underground crypt below it.

A flight of eight steps led from the north aisle of the church down to the crypt (only 2.3 metres high from floor to ceiling) and there were crosses cut by pilgrims in the walls. A hole was visible in the ceiling of the crypt, which must have extended down from the floor of the chapel above it; perhaps holy effluences ascended through this hole to the worshippers above. Crowfoot, the excavator, described the moment when he first entered the crypt in a very dry and matter-of-fact fashion, which is quite disappointing: 'The crypt was quite empty when we entered it except for insignificant accumulations of dust below the hole in the roof and at the foot of the steps; the painting on the east wall was all that had survived of its former decoration, and this had been mutilated.' (Crowfoot 1937, 36).

The paintings were in a very bad state of preservation when Crowfoot first entered the crypt, and, subsequently, after the discovery, some unknown person broke the lock on the door and slashed the faces of the two monks. The paintings can hardly be made out in the photographs from the 1930s and so we are lucky that a crayon rendering was made by Muriel Bentwich at the time of the excavation (Fig. 4.13), otherwise it would be almost impossible to discuss this unique painting. New photographs taken in the 1980s and published by Kühnel in a book on Crusader-period paintings are also useful in

the reconstruction of the original appearance of the painting. The niche in the east wall was subdivided by a stone shelf into two areas, with representations of kneeling angels on either side. The painting in the top register shows the first martyrdom of John the Baptist that is the scene of his decapitation. On the left is the figure of a soldier, wearing a red tunic and a blue cloak billowing down from his shoulders, with his right arm stretched out above the bent figure of John. The painting in the lower register of the niche represents the second martyrdom of John the Baptist, which is the scene of the desecration of his tomb. The paintings have been attributed by Kühnel to a local school of Byzantine artists, because of their typical Middle Byzantine style, and dated them to the third quarter of the twelfth century at the latest. However, not all scholars agree: Folda believes that they are the work of western artists instead, suggesting that they predate 1160 (Kühnel 1988, 195–204, plates LXXII–LXXV; Folda 1995, 313–15, plates 8B.16 b–e).

The buildings of the Greek church and monastery continued to survive following the capture of Sebaste by Saladin in 1187. In the church various changes were made to the altar and to the various structural parts of the building, including the walling up of the *narthex*. Crowfoot also uncovered evidence of cooking. Based on Crowfoot's findings this phase must be Mamluke in date (i.e. thirteenth to fifteenth centuries).

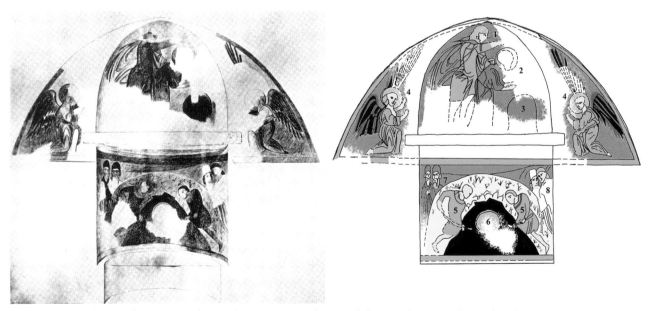

Figure 4.13: Muriel Bentwich's crayon rendering of the paintings in the crypt (after Crowfoot 1937, plate 16c); and a new reconstruction of the painting by Shimon Gibson (drawing: Fadi Amirah).

Figure 4.14: The remains of a watermill between Samaria and Nablus. These remains had frequently been misidentified in nineteenth-century travel accounts as a Roman aqueduct.

Watermills

Before leaving the area of Samaria, Boer took pictures of two medieval or Ottoman watermills in the valley south of Samaria. The better preserved of these two mills (Fig. 4.14) had frequently been misidentified in nineteenth-century travel accounts as a Roman aqueduct. The Reverend C. T. Wilson described this kind of mill in 1906:

> 'In valleys where there are powerful perennial springs or permanent streams there will usually be found several watermills for grinding corn. A winding channel, carried along the side of the valley, conducts a stream of water to a point at which it is high enough above the floor to give the needful pressure. Here the mill is built. It consists of a single room, in the floor of which the lower millstone is firmly embedded. Under the room is a vaulted space in which works the wheel or turbine which drives the mill.' (Wilson 1906, 249–51).[12]

Having completed their one and a half hour excursion of Samaria, Boer and his companions eventually 'drove north where we had a meal along the road,

near the village of Burqa'. Thus ended Boer's first trip to Samaria.

Notes

1 Boer made two visits to Samaria: on 3 February 1954 and 1 April 1954. My thanks to Bart Wagemakers for inviting me to write about Boer's visit to Samaria.

2 Impressive archaeological remains have been uncovered at Tell Balata particularly from the Middle Bronze Age. Recent excavations at the site have been undertaken by Leiden University in conjunction with the Palestine Department of Antiquities and Cultural Heritage (see Van der Kooij and Taha in this volume). I am grateful to Dr. Gerrit van der Kooij for showing me around these new excavations.

3 Letters written in 1933 by Betty Murray to her mother: PEF Archives, London.

4 Ahab built a palace at the site that was referred to as an 'ivory house' (1 Kings 22:39). The reference to 'ivory' may be an indication that there were substantial

furnishings in Ahab's palace decorated with bone and ivory plaques.

5 During the reign of Jeroboam II (783–742 BCE) we hear of 'houses of ivory' and 'beds of ivory' (Amos 3:15; 5–6); not surprisingly, in the excavations of Samaria large numbers of carved inlay ivories were uncovered, with various decorative themes, including floral motifs, animals, a winged sphinx, and one with a depiction of a 'woman at the window' (Crowfoot and Crowfoot 1938, 29–30, pl. XIII: 2). The woman at the window is usually thought to represent Ashtart or Asherah.

6 For a summary of the Classical and Late Antiquity remains at Sebaste, see Avigad 1993.

7 Boer seems to have mixed up the information he received regarding the John the Baptist traditions for the two church sites at Sebaste.

8 At the time of Jesus, Sebaste was mainly a pagan city, though this did not exclude the presence there of Samaritans and Jews. Jesus visited the Samaria region himself, according to Luke (9:52; 17:11) and John (4:4–5), but according to Matthew (10:5) he did not allow his disciples to go there. The appearance of Jews in the Samaria region was exceptional at that time and probably also dangerous for them. At one of the watering-holes (Jacob's Well), Jesus encountered a woman who had come to draw water and he asks for water which amazed her since Jews were not supposed to interact with Samaritans (John 4:9). Much later, we hear that Philip the apostle goes to Samaria (circa 33 CE) and finally manages to baptise some of the inhabitants (Acts 8:5). Also Peter and John visit the city when they hear 'that Samaria had received the word of God' (Acts

8:14). While there was some Christian presence in the Samaria region during the following centuries, it would not appear to have been very substantial until the early Byzantine period (about mid-fourth century CE).

9 New excavations are being conducted in the area of the Church of St John and in the village of Sabastiyeh by Hani Nur el-Din, and restoration and conservation work is being undertaken by architect Osama Hamdan and Carla Benelli. I am grateful to them for showing me the new finds. See: Benelli, Hamdan and Piccirillo 2007.

10 The survey took place in July 1872 and June 1875: Conder and Kitchener 1882, 211.

11 Crowfoot dated the inscription to the sixth century, but wrote that it 'is too fragmentary to give an intelligible meaning'. Dr Leah Di Segni, in a letter to me, wrote: 'I believe something can be made of the text: on the first line you can see very clearly the word *euch]aristo[n*, "giving thanks" (or perhaps *eucharistontes* in the plural, if the participle is continued in line 2). It is a common term in dedicatory inscriptions: somebody built this or that in thanksgiving. The letters in line 2 suggest very strongly then *st[oan*, which goes quite well with the fact, that you mention, that the inscription was found in the southern aisle of the church. *Stoa* is one of the terms for aisle in late antiquity. The last N may be the ending of the word "Amen"'. The inscription probably dates to the fifth century or to the beginning of the sixth at the latest. My thanks to Dr Di Segni for her help.

12 See also Dalman 1902, 13–14. For modern literature on watermills: Avitsur 1960; Hill 1984, 155–62; Cresswell 1993; Ayalon 1998.

Israelite Samaria: Head of Ephraim and Jerusalem's Elder Sister

Ron E. Tappy

A site of natural and artificial formations

The earliest remains discovered on the summit of Samaria (Fig 4.15) consist of numerous rock cuttings (cups, pits, etc., hollowed out of the bedrock), which the first excavators dated to the Early Bronze Age. The fragmentary base of one large vessel included a spout and may have functioned as a separator vat. These features seem to indicate the systematic production of olive oil at pre-Omride Samaria. In fact, the city may represent one of the earliest (already by the late fourth millennium BCE) places in Canaan where this industry occurred.

The next significant period of occupation occurred during the Iron Age I. Archaeologists have identified many more rock cuttings from this era as press platforms, vats, collecting basins, connecting bowls, and mortars that reflect the household economy of a family-owned estate belonging to the lineage of Shemer (or Shomron), from the tribe of Issachar (see the discussion in Tappy 2001, 4). The storage capacity of the bell-shaped cisterns alone argues in favour of this new understanding. Many more such features undoubtedly exist in the unexcavated portions of the site. Analysts estimate that these facilities would have accommodated the yield from 3,200–4,800 olive trees covering an area of 32–48 hectares on the slopes and in the valleys around the summit. The annual production rate would have supported an overall population of at least 150–200 individuals.[1] Re-evaluations of the pottery from Samaria have confirmed this Iron Age I occupation of the hill and have corrected the excavators' view that an occupational gap existed from the Early Bronze Age to the time of King Omri in the early ninth century BCE (see below). In fact, the earliest Iron Age pottery at Samaria dates to the late twelfth and eleventh centuries BCE.

During the Iron Age II period the site became the capital of the northern kingdom of Israel. The topography of the excavated portion of the summit reveals that ancient workers significantly reshaped the rock summit of the site (Fig. 4.16). Lateral and longitudinal rock scarps ran along the northern, the western, and probably also the southern perimeters of the royal compound. Although portions of these ledges – which often drop as much as 3.5 metres in elevation – represent natural formations, workers expanded and connected them through extensive quarrying activities. The resultant split-level summit provided a rectilinear dais of solid rock measuring roughly 72 metres by 93.5 metres (circa 0.67 hectares; the entire area inside the grand Casemate Wall system covered circa 19,600 m², or 1.96 hectares; see Tappy 2001, 170–71, n. 633). The vertical face of these scarps provided backing for the foundation courses of the city's earliest walls (e.g., the so-called Enclosure Wall 161, north of the courtyard area). This elevated, central platform distinguished the central summit from peripheral areas that encircled the royal quarter at least on the northern and western sides. The raised area accommodated only the principal housing (main palace; Fig. 4.17) and activity areas (northern official buildings and main courtyard) of the royal family and attendants (see Tappy 2001, 2: fig. 1). It did not incorporate domestic housing in the royal compound proper.

The palace itself sat near the south-western corner of the summit plateau, and a series of official buildings lined the northern edge of the area. Two large rock-cut chambers immediately beneath the northern portion of the palace may represent the burial tombs for at least some of the Israelite kings who ruled from Samaria, although this proposal remains uncertain (cf. Franklin 2003; idem 2007; Ussishkin 2007). According to biblical traditions, at least Omri, Ahab, Jehu, Jehoahaz, Joash, and perhaps Jeroboam II were interred in the royal centre at Samaria (see 1 Kings 16:28; 22:37; 2 Kings 10:35; 13:9; 14:16, 29). A series of interconnecting cave-tombs, situated both

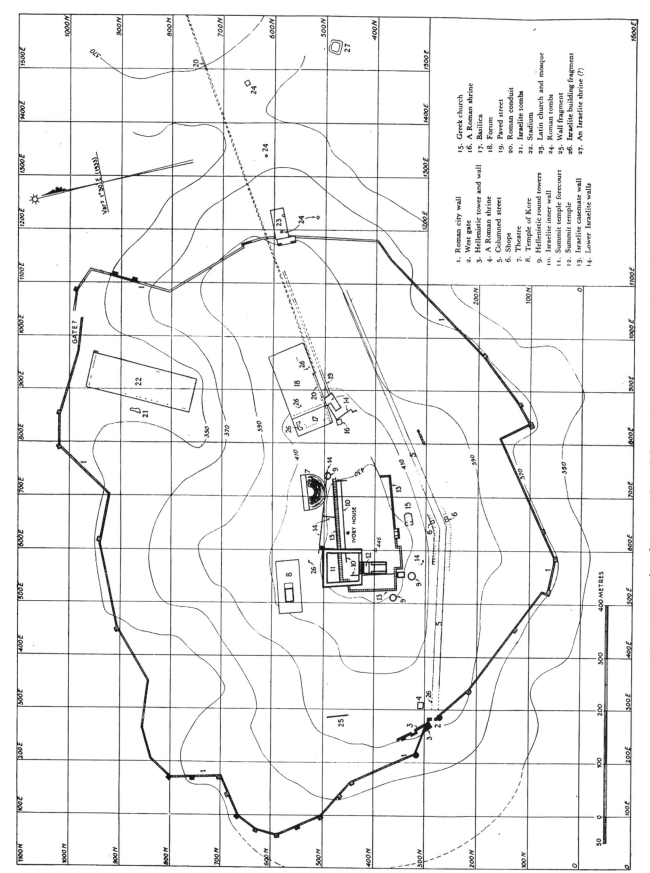

1. Roman city wall
2. West gate
3. Hellenistic tower and wall
4. A Roman shrine
5. Columned street
6. Shops
7. Theatre
8. Temple of Kore
9. Hellenistic round towers
10. Israelite inner wall
11. Summit temple forecourt
12. Summit temple
13. Israelite casemate wall
14. Lower Israelite walls
15. Greek church
16. A Roman shrine
17. Basilica
18. Forum
19. Paved street
20. Roman conduit
21. Israelite tombs
22. Stadium
23. Latin church and mosque
24. Roman tombs
25. Wall fragment
26. Israelite building fragment
27. An Israelite shrine (?)

Figure 4.15: Site plan of Samaria-Sebaste (after Crowfoot, Kenyon and Sukenik 1942, plate 1).

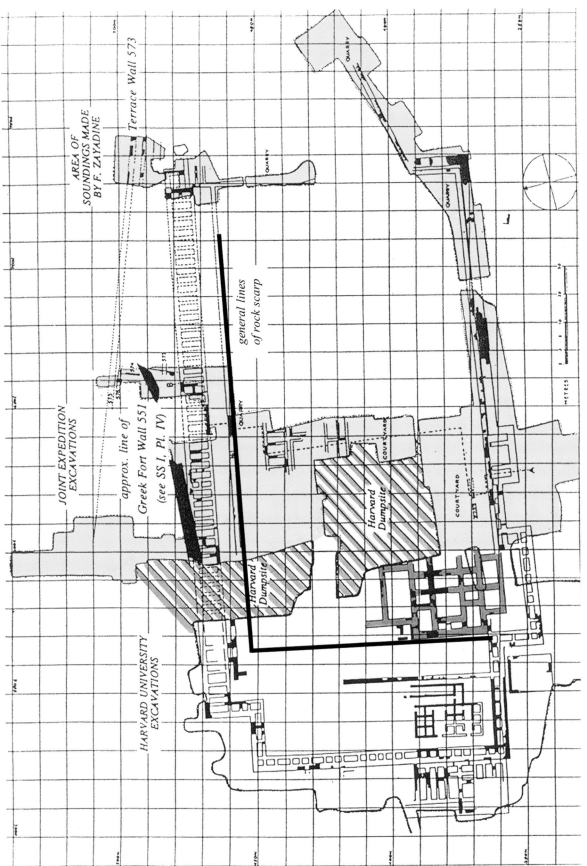

Figure 4.16: Summit plan of Samaria (after Crowfoot, Kenyon and Sukenik 1942, plate II).

Figure 4.17: Partial view of Israelite palace remains looking south-west on 2 November 1910. Strip 2 IV – 10, 11, 13, 14 (after Reisner, Fisher and Lyon, Vol. 2, plate 8.4).

on the north-western slopes of the mound nearly 100 metres below the royal acropolis and on the nearby hill of Munshara, may have served as burial places for the wealthier occupants of Samaria. A large courtyard extended eastward from the palace and southward from the public buildings. The main city gate lay still farther to the east in a part of the summit that has so far received less archaeological attention than the palace area. A threshing floor likely existed somewhere just outside the city gate (cf. the Micaiah ben Imlah narrative in 1 Kings 22; in ancient cities, the threshing floor and the city gate sometimes shared a judicial function and, consequently, constituted a word pair in some ancient poetry). Located over 650 metres east of the gate area, a trapezoidal-shaped, rock-cut trench (labelled E207) apparently represents an Israelite shrine (Steiner 1997). It remains unknown, however, whether this facility relates in any way to the *asherah*

or to the temple and altar reportedly built by Ahab and dedicated to Baal as mentioned in 1 Kings 16:25–33.

The core of this royal city remained considerably smaller than commentators have usually recognised. The compound itself probably could not have accommodated more than 200 individuals. The king and his court, the royal attendants, and the 'young men of the governors of the districts' (1 Kings 20:15) who resided within the city walls would themselves have taxed the city's available space. The 7,000 others alluded to in that verse – and certainly the 27,290 'Samarians' who Sargon ultimately claims to have deported from the city – undoubtedly lived in outlying areas around the royal compound. One former excavator's suggestion that the city itself could have accommodated 30,000 to 40,000 citizens remains quite untenable (Crowfoot, Kenyon, and Sukenik 1942, 1–2).

A site of archaeological exploration and interpretative debates

Representing Harvard University, Gottlieb Schumacher directed the first official archaeological exploration of Samaria in 1908. George Andrew Reisner, along with architect Clarence Fisher, succeeded Schumacher in 1909 and 1910. The Harvard excavations, which focused on the western half of the summit, revealed much of the Israelite royal palace and, immediately to its west, the so-called 'Ostraca House' (see below; Reisner, Fisher, and Lyon 1924).

A consortium of institutions, mostly from England and Israel, renewed excavations at Samaria from 1932 to 1935 (Crowfoot and Crowfoot 1938; Crowfoot, Kenyon, and Sukenik 1942; Crowfoot, Crowfoot, and Kenyon 1957). John Winter Crowfoot directed this 'Joint Expedition', while Kathleen M. Kenyon supervised all the work in the royal quarter and introduced new techniques of debris-layer analysis to the project's field methodology. Kenyon cut a large north-south section across the entire summit east of the earlier excavations by Schumacher and Reisner. Based on the pottery removed from this area, Kenyon attempted to lower the chronology of the stratigraphic history and ceramic traditions at other major Iron Age II sites in Palestine, such as Megiddo and Hazor (Kenyon 1964). Her official report, which did not appear until 1957, offered a new chronological framework against which to understand this period, not only at Samaria and in Palestine generally, but at sites in the Aegean world as well (Crowfoot, Crowfoot, and Kenyon 1957).

Although, as noted above, the rock surface yielded clear signs of Early Bronze Age I occupation, most of the material remains pointed to Iron Age cultures (the period of the Old Testament or Hebrew Bible). The date of the earliest Iron Age settlement, however, became the subject of considerable controversy. Appealing to 1 Kings 16:24, Kenyon concluded that no occupation had occurred at the site prior to the time when Omri purchased the hill from Shemer in the early ninth century BCE. From there to the sixth and fifth centuries BCE, she outlined eight major building phases (labelled Periods I–VIII) and assigned Periods I–VI to the time from Omri to the Assyrian capture of Samaria in 722/721 BCE. Furthermore, she believed that new ceramic traditions accompanied each new building phase, which, in turn, arose as each new king ascended to power. In other words, Kenyon

tied her archaeological phasing and, by extension, her historical reconstruction to her understanding of Samaria's list of kings as presented in the Hebrew Bible. The notice in 1 Kings 16:24 of Omri's purchase of the site undergirded and served as the starting point for her archaeological interpretations; based primarily on this single verse, she argued decidedly against any Iron Age occupation of the site before the early ninth-century BCE reign of King Omri.

Even prior to Kenyon's official publication in 1957 of the Samaria pottery and objects, however, Roland de Vaux compared the Samaria repertoire with that of Tirzah, where he was excavating, and concluded that the two earliest ceramic phases at Samaria actually predated all Omride building activities and indicated an Iron Age I presence at the site (de Vaux 1955). Though de Vaux's comparisons merely questioned the direct correlation of architectural and ceramic periods, they sparked a longstanding debate regarding both the field methods and historical conclusions espoused by Kenyon at Samaria. Within the next two years, George Ernest Wright and others, such as W. F. Albright, Yohanan Aharoni, and Ruth Amiran, expanded de Vaux's recommendations by drawing an official distinction between the ceramic and architectural developments at Samaria and dating the earliest Iron Age pottery to a modest, pre-Omride occupation (Aharoni and Amiran 1958; Albright 1958; Wright 1959a; idem 1959b; idem 1962). By the 1990s, Lawrence Stager showed that this pre-royal occupation actually reflects the remains of a private, family estate belonging to the clan of Shemer, from whom Omri purchased the property (Stager 1990).

The debate that swirled around the fieldwork at Samaria resulted mainly from differences in archaeological method and interpretation. Kenyon's assertion that 1 Kings 16:24 precluded any occupation on the hill of Shomron prior to King Omri compelled her to correlate the earliest Iron Age ceramic remains with the earliest royal architecture and to assign both to Omri. Although the earliest Omride courtyard lay several depositional layers above bedrock, Kenyon's system demanded that she would associate all the Iron Age pottery lying directly on bedrock (and often mixed with scrappy, Early Bronze Age remains) with that higher floor level. Having begun her method of dating this way, she continued to assess the chronology of all discernible floor levels based on the material trapped beneath them (sometimes by as much as several depositional layers). Since her method of dating worked in the opposite direction (i.e. from bottom upwards) from the actual process of excavation (which naturally progressed top down by first exposing the floors and then the make-up beneath them), it seems clear that Kenyon established her interpretative method only after the close of the fieldwork, during the process of analysis and publication.

Meanwhile, Wright and others continued to date floors and surfaces according to the material found lying directly on top of them. In reality, each method addresses different aspects of chronology. While Kenyon's system offers the *terminus post quem* (or earliest possible date) of a surface's existence, Wright's approach helps ascertain a *terminus ante quem* (or latest possible date) for the functional life of the floor, i.e., the span of time during which it was actually in use. In chronological terms, Kenyon's approach focused on the *construction* date of a given floor, while the approach of Wright and others related to the *occupational* dates of that floor.

Recent re-evaluations of the Samaria evidence, from both ceramic and stratigraphic perspectives, have confirmed an Iron Age I occupation of the site, but have also shown (with Kenyon) that this phase lacked any monumental architectural features (Tappy 1992; idem 2001). Instead, installations either resting on or cut into the rock surface confirm Stager's suggestion that here the Shemer clan maintained a modest family estate that already produced oil and wine during the late pre-monarchic era. Contrary to Kenyon's uncritical reading of the Hebrew Bible (Tappy 1992, 68–69 n. 185, 214–15 n. 1), then, the text of 1 Kings 16:24 does not preclude this conclusion.

The early studies that challenged Kenyon's principles of dating were only able to use her *published* pottery for evaluation. More recent studies, such as those dealing with the natural and artificial formation of the rock surface and others offering a full-bodied ceramic and stratigraphic investigation, have augmented earlier approaches by adding *unpublished* material to their study sample (Stager 1990; Tappy 1992; idem 2001; Franklin 2004). By allowing a clearer picture of the original find spots of the pottery, these studies have settled lingering questions concerning the site's depositional history. The results have confirmed a pre-Omride occupation of Samaria and

have associated the Iron Age I pottery there with various non-monumental architectural features resting immediately on or, more often, set into the rock surface (remains of a possible beam press, numerous rock cuttings, storage pits, separator vats, cisterns, etc. – i.e. all features one would normally expect at a locally-owned estate that produced wine and oil for surrounding areas).

A narrow reading of 1 Kings 16:24, then, can no longer support, on several different levels, Kenyon's proposed chronological framework for Israelite Samaria. First, her narrow dating of floors merely on the basis of the material trapped beneath them resulted in a skewed chronological picture.

Second, the collective attributes of vessels such as bar-handle bowls, cup-and-saucer forms, lentoid flasks, collar-rim storage jars, early Iron Age krater and chalice forms, and a significant series of cooking pot rims point to a noteworthy Iron Age I occupation for many of the levels, that Kenyon lumped into her 'Periods I–II'. So while she correctly linked the first *monumental* building activities to the early ninth-century Omride dynasty, she misread the earliest deposits and pottery, which date as early as the eleventh (possibly even the late twelfth) century BCE. It does not follow, however, that we should automatically shift the ceramics from Pottery Period 3 to fill the resultant gap created in the Omride era. In fact, only some of the Pottery Period 3 wares relate to the Omrides. Other vessels from that assemblage must remain in the latter half of the ninth century, in the time of King Jehu. And some of these vessel forms, in fact, extend into the early eighth century BCE.

Third, recent studies have shown that much of the published pottery derived from secondary or disturbed contexts (Tappy 1992; idem 2001). Moreover, fragments recovered from primary contexts often came from deposits situated several layers above or below the floors and the architecture to which they purportedly relate. Still, when analysed typologically against ceramic groups from traditional and more recently excavated sites, the pottery found in these deposits supports the new stratigraphic analysis.

Besides these significant adjustments to our understanding of the earliest Iron Age levels at Samaria, a recent re-evaluation of the later depositional history of the site has called for a new understanding of the final phases of Israelite control over the city (Tappy 2001). In her popular account of the royal cities in ancient Israel, Kenyon once again appealed to a single biblical text (2 Kings 17:23–24) in support of the 'wholesale transference of populations [that] was basic to Assyrian policy' during the late eighth century BCE (Kenyon 1971). She went on to say that, based on her excavation data from Samaria, 'the archaeological record is equally eloquent of the complete destruction of the capital city'. According to Kenyon's final report, the buildings assigned to Period V represent the latest Israelite structures on the north side of the summit. Among others, these structures (labelled Rooms hk, hq, j, and n) should bear the traces of this pervasive Assyrian assault.

Yet close examination of the local stratigraphy and published finds associated with these chambers raises important new questions regarding the nature of the transfer of civil authority from Israelite to Assyrian leadership. In fact, the diverse layers from which excavators removed the purportedly latest Israelite materials can hardly represent a homogeneous matrix or a depositional history centred on a single episode, whether a devastating destruction by military force or a subsequent, wholesale levelling for purposes of new construction. Rather, the stratigraphic record reveals a wide array of accumulation types: clean levelling fills; the tumble of rubble-filled matrix; pockets of possible occupational debris; hard-packed floor levels from disparate periods; at least two post-Israelite pit fills; a late foundation trench backfill; other very late (Hellenistic and Roman) disturbances of earlier surfaces; and so on. Many of these deposits represent secondary contexts, a fact that urges discretion when attempting to draw firm historical conclusions based on the pottery assemblages published by the Joint Expedition.

In sum, the archaeology of Samaria and, by extension, the political history it reflects, have emerged as vexing topics for those interested in both the opening and closing decades of Israelite use of and sovereignty over this once grand capital city. Today, we must make important adjustments in our new understanding of each of these periods. Clearly, we have many archaeological data that are less stratigraphically secure pertaining to the ninth century BCE than the excavation reports imply. We must, therefore, exercise caution when relying on the published materials from Samaria to establish or adjust chronologies at sites elsewhere in the Levantine and Aegean worlds. Also, it now appears that both the Syro-Ephraimite conflict around 732 BCE[2] and the events attending the final collapse of Israelite authority between 722–720 BCE (when Sargon II established full Assyrian control over the capital city) caused minimal physical destruction to Samaria. In fact, neither the Assyrian texts nor the archaeology of Samaria points to a physical destruction of the city near the close of the third quarter of the eighth century BCE (Tappy 2007).

During these years, the neo-Assyrian leaders commonly blockaded the capital city of a region while ravaging the countryside, with no further intention of capturing or destroying the political centre itself. Moreover, a consistent pattern of activity emerges from the archaeology of various northern sites around Samaria. Following their first substantial wave of military engagements throughout the northern valley areas during the decade of the 730s BCE, the Assyrians appear to have delayed regional administrative and building programmes until after the final, political collapse of Israelite control over the capital in the late 720s.[3] Following Stratum V at Hazor (destroyed by Tiglath-pileser III in 732 BCE), even that site did not return to a substantial citadel under the Assyrians until the time of Stratum III, with the intervening Stratum IV showing merely a small, unfortified settlement. Yet once the Assyrians had firmly established control over a particular region and had selected (probably on the basis of economic considerations) the most strategic sites they wished to rebuild and expand, a much smoother transition between successive strata appears.[4] While a programme to resettle foreign populations in Samaria and elsewhere began during the rule of Sargon II (from 716 BCE onwards; Na'aman 1990), then, the physical refurbishment of selected provincial centres emerges from the archaeological record only during the late eighth and seventh centuries BCE. Few traces of such a rebuilding effort have appeared in the archaeology of Samaria, apparently because of very minimal destruction of the site by the Assyrians when they first 'conquered' (*kašādu*) the city.

A site of biblical history and historiography

Just as one recognises both natural and artificial processes behind the physical formation of Samaria, one must also acknowledge various forces (historical and theological) at work in the creation of a literary Samaria. Israelite culture began and flourished in the hill country of Ephraim. Following the collapse of the monarchy ruled over by David and Solomon, northern leaders declared their independence from the authority of Jerusalem. But their own emergent kingdom experienced a precarious beginning. The new capital city shifted between the sites of Shechem and Tirzah (Fig. 4.18) and the crown of kingship passed to three claimants within the monarchy's first couple of decades. Then, in the early ninth century BCE, Zimri's failed coup (1 Kings 16:8–20) against King Elah, who was drinking himself drunk in Tirzah, beset the kingdom with political turbulence that threatened the stability of the entire realm. The claim on royal power had proven short-lived in both Shechem and Tirzah. But Omri, the commander of the army who enjoyed popular acclaim among his troops, responded decisively. Leading his forces from their camp in Gibbethon, he besieged and controlled strife-ridden Tirzah, overcame threats from another contender for the throne (Tibni), and became King of Israel around 884 BCE (1 Kings 16:21–24).

Omri quickly purchased a modestly-sized, family-owned estate that lay on the seaward slopes of the Ephraimite hills, opposite the eastern-oriented Shechem/Tirzah, transferred his political capital there, and called the new city Samaria. To the end of the Israelite kingdom, no other city usurped Samaria's place as political hub. Even the surrounding region took on its name (1 Kings 21:1; 2 Kings 1:3), and over 160 years later leading nations continued to refer to the city as the 'House of Omri'. The symbolism and status of Samaria became so impressive that later biblical writers spoke of the city as the undisputed 'head of Ephraim' (Isaiah 7:9), or as Jerusalem's 'elder sister' who ruled and influenced numerous 'daughters', outlying villages, of her own (Ezekiel 16:46, 53, 55, 61; 23:4–5). The choice of Samaria both freed Omri from the baggage of earlier political turbulence and reoriented his kingdom's economic outlook westward toward the lucrative trade moving along coastal routes and throughout the Mediterranean world. Under the watchful eye of Omri, the family-villa-turned-royal-centre succeeded in assuming its place as the undisputed seat of northern power.

Following Omri's transformation of Samaria into a political capital, his son and successor, Ahab, ruled as one of Israel's most powerful kings (circa 873–851 BCE). He expanded the summit of Samaria and constructed a massive casemate fortification (Fig. 4.19) enclosing lavishly appointed royal buildings, including the 'ivory house' (1 Kings 22:39; Amos 3:15). But following Ahab's marriage to the Sidonian princess Jezebel (1 Kings 16:31), the religious and political culture of Samaria grew more diverse. While Ahab's Samaria may have included a temple to Yahweh (Hosea 8:5; Kuntillet ʿAjrud inscriptions), it also appears to have contained a temple or shrines to Canaanite Baal and Asherah (1 Kings 16:32–33; 2 Kings 13:6). Thus the cult of Yahweh at Samaria was, at best, monolatrous; from its inception, and especially from the reign of Ahab, the city appears to have had a syncretistic approach to local religions. The fact that the biblical writers mention only shrines to Baal and Asherah, and not the temple to Yahweh, underscores the historiography behind their theological critique of the king, queen, and capital.

The opulent lifestyles of the royals further evoked the ire of Israel's prophets. Hundreds of ivory fragments from wall panels and furniture inlays recovered from Samaria depict Israelite, Phoenician, and Egyptian motifs (Fig. 4.20). The city might even have housed a production centre for these carvings, which date from the time of Ahab and reflect two distinct styles – one in low relief with simple borders and backgrounds, the other in deeper relief with fewer traces of coloured insets. The former group sometimes appeared so lavishly decorated with gold foil and inlays of lapis lazuli that precious little of the gleaming-white ivory actually remained visible. Such conspicuous opulence undoubtedly inflamed orthodox Yahwists such as Elijah and other early writing prophets (e.g., Amos) who focused on social justice and the poor.

So while Ahab brought Israel to the fore of international politics by fighting protracted wars against the Aramaeans of Damascus (1 Kings 20), struggling for hegemony over Transjordan (1 Kings 22; Meshaʿ Stele), and participating in an anti-Assyrian league at Qarqar in the Orontes Valley (Assyrian records), he and the rulers after him all received criticism in the Bible. Direct references to Samaria

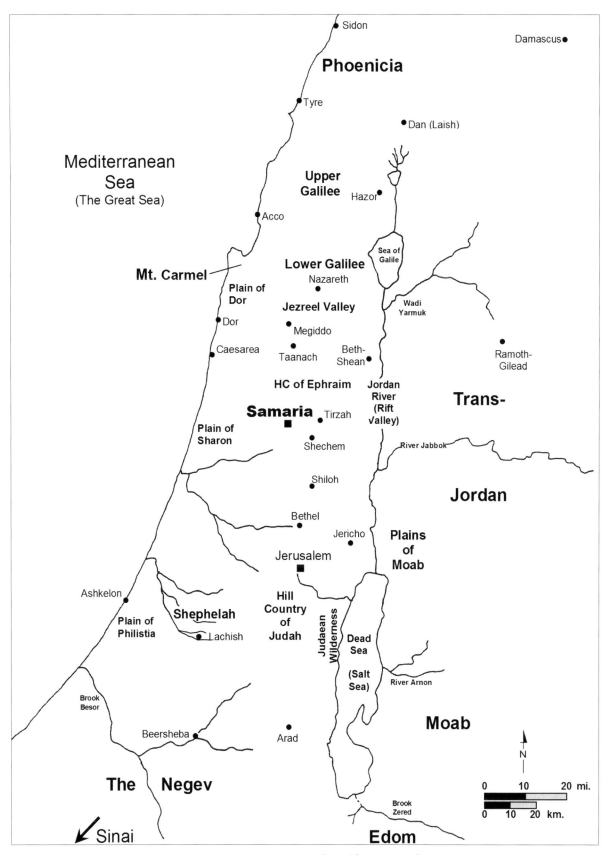

Figure 4.18: Map of Israel (Ron E. Tappy).

Figure 4.19: Aerial view of the Israelite casemate wall on the north side of the summit, at excavation grid 658 E. (after Crowfoot, Kenyon and Sukenik 1942, plate XXII: 1–2).

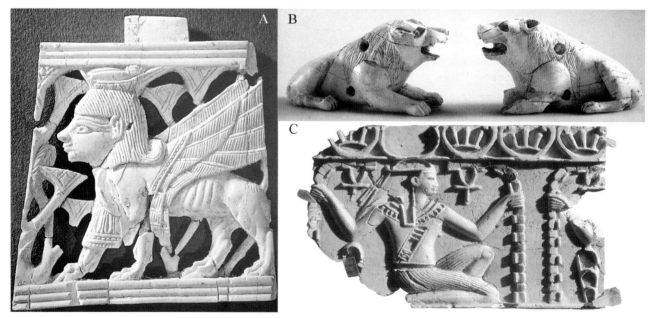

Figure 4.20: Ivory fragments from the 'Ivory house': A) Sphinx standing in a lotus thicket; B) lions carved in the round; C) plaque showing the Egyptian god Hah (after Crowfoot and Crowfoot 1938, plate V:1; IX:1, 1a, 1b; plate II:2, respectively).

first occur in the Historical Books, and the books of 1–2 Kings alone account for 62% of all such notices in the Old Testament (72% including the Chronicler's history). An ominous chord sounds with the very first mention of Samaria (1 Kings 13:32) in a context that anticipates the ultimate downfall of the city and its outlying kingdom. Following this dire pronouncement, the biblical writers focus nearly two-thirds of their references to Samaria on periods of external and internal political turbulence (1 Kings 16, 20, 22; 2 Kings 6, 10, 13, 15, 17). A significant percentage of the remaining narratives highlights the perceived social and religious atrocities perpetrated by the city's rulers (1 Kings 21; 2 Kings 1) or brought on by periods of economic hardship (1 Kings 18; 2 Kings 6). In general, this history draws much more heavily on harshly critical prophetic and popular traditions (Micaiah ben Imlah; Elijah; Elisha) than on available annalistic records. Four of the six chapters devoted to Ahab's reign (1 Kings 16:29–22:40) rely primarily on narratives that highlighted the prophets Elijah (1 Kings 17–19, 21) or Micaiah ben Imlah (1 Kings 22). Ahab's fleeting moment of popular acclaim and competent leadership appears only in 1 Kings 20:1–34. But even this snatch of text receives a sudden, severe critique in a vignette drawn from prophetic traditions (1 Kings 20:35–43). So while archaeology and extra-biblical sources (the Mesha' Stele; Assyrian annals) point to the capital's grandeur and its political, military, and economic successes, most people's perception of Samaria derives from the biblical censure of this famous royal couple, Ahab and Jezebel.

Becoming increasingly syncretistic under their influence, the political leadership incurred the greatest scorn from the prophet Elijah (1 Kings 17–19). Ultra-conservative factions with both religious and political aspirations arose. The populist Jehu seized the throne of Samaria in 842 BCE (2 Kings 9–10) – with backing from the prophetic leadership and, undoubtedly, conservative social groups and zealous segments of the military (Albertz 1994, 150–56) – but he quickly committed his new government to a pro-Assyrian posture by paying tribute to Shalmaneser III (an act recorded in relief and writing on the Black Obelisk).

Commentators have generally assumed that this revolt and the resultant death of the queen and former Sidonian princess (1 Kings 16:31), Jezebel, jeopardised Samaria's political and commercial ties with Phoenicia. The material remains and depositional history of Samaria, however, do not permit definitive conclusions on this matter. The phasing of levels from the time of Jehu and the following periods received only sparse documentation in the final excavation report and therefore remains somewhat cloudy (Crowfoot and Crowfoot 1938; Crowfoot, Kenyon, and Sukenik 1942; Crowfoot, Crowfoot, and Kenyon 1957). In any event, it is clear that the capital's wealth and influence continued to flourish throughout most of the eighth century BCE. Omri's design distinguished Samaria as a seat of royal administration and power focused exclusively on the king and his family. Excavators have not identified any clearly-defined residential and domestic quarters on the summit area. As noted above, throughout its life as capital of Israel, Samaria remained a small, royal compound. While its palace and other official buildings occupied the rock crest, storage and food-processing facilities, workshops, and other service-related areas existed on the lower ground around the perimeter of the summit.

One auxiliary structure, the 'Ostraca House', lay west of and below the palace level. Rooms connected to this building yielded 63 legible administrative ostraca (Fig. 4.21), which were shipping dockets and date to the early eighth-century reign of Jeroboam II. They record small shipments of wine and oil to the capital from clan-based communities in the surrounding countryside (including Shechem but not rebuilt Tirzah). Personal names attested on these dockets belonged either to absentee landlords temporarily residing in the royal compound of Samaria and receiving the shipments from their own local estates, or to clan heads sending tax payments to the king. Either way, these records corroborate Samaria's continuing wealth and centripetal force during the peaceful and prosperous reign of Jeroboam II. As the number of villages increased on the seaward slopes of the Ephraimite hill country, sparsely-populated Samaria was preserved for the elite. It remained a 'forbidden city' to local Hebrew prophets (Elijah; Amos), except for those imprisoned there (Micaiah ben Imlah) (e.g. 1 Kings 22).

Ultimately, however, this seat of power became increasingly unstable as it suffered during a period of virtual anarchy under competing leaders such as Shallum, Menahem, his son Pekahiah, and finally Pekah (from roughly 750 to 733 or 731 BCE; 2 Kings 15:8–31). All but one man, Pekahiah, seized the throne through regicide, as they contended for the right to

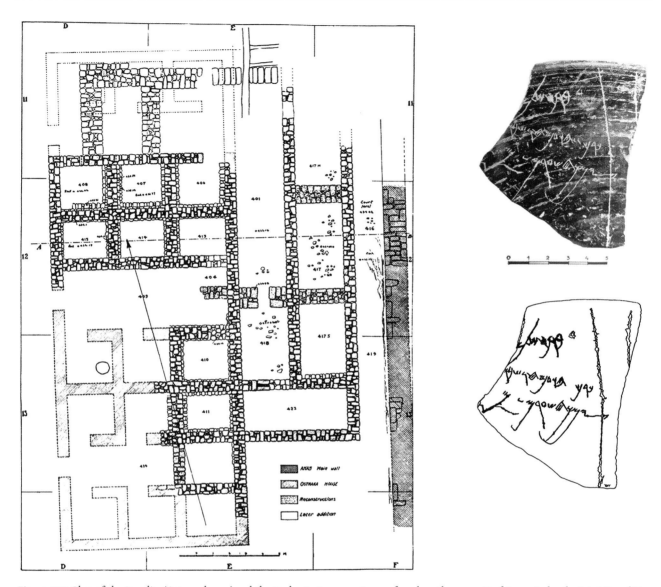

Figure 4.21: Plan of the Israelite 'Ostraca house' and the Barley Letter, an ostracon found on the summit of Samaria by the Joint Expedition (after Reisner, Fisher and Lyon, Vol. 1, 64, figs 15 and 114, fig. 42 (plan) and Crowfoot, Crowfoot and Kenyon 1957, plate I:1 (ostracon); drawing by Ron E. Tappy).

rule from Samaria in the face of an emergent empire in Assyria. Local events during the Syro-Ephraimite War (734–732 BCE; see Isaiah 7) helped place the ultimate fate of Israelite Samaria in Assyrian hands. So while Samaria exemplified the northern kingdom's cultural and political prowess, it ultimately fell to the Assyrians, who continued to refer to the capital city as the 'House of Omri'.

When the Assyrians finally conquered Samaria in the late eighth century BCE, they reorganised the city as the capital of Province Samerina rather than destroying it. Those who were not deported during

the Assyrian and Babylonian exiles came to be known as Samaritans. According to the Hebrew Bible, the Assyrians eventually sent a priest whom they had deported from Samaria back to Bethel to teach 'the fear of Yahweh' (2 Kings 17:24–28). Following the decline of Assyria in 612 BCE, Josiah annexed to Judah the southern extent of Samerina as far as Bethel (2 Kings 23:4) and perhaps also the entire province (2 Kings 23:29–30; 2 Chronicles 35:20–24).

While few architectural remains have survived from the Babylonian period, Jeremiah 41 alludes to the continued occupation of the city by people who worshipped Yahweh. The fact that, after the fall of Jerusalem to Nebuchadnezzar in 587/586 BCE, the Babylonian-appointed governor of Judah established his administrative centre at Mizpah rather than Jerusalem (Jeremiah 41:1) may belie the orientation of the south as much toward Samaria as toward Jerusalem, since those who survived the scourge of Judah needed the stores of grain, honey, and oil that apparently remained available in the north (Jeremiah 41:4–8). The city of Samaria continued to exist as an administrative centre under Persian occupation in the late sixth and fifth centuries BCE.

The discovery of Greek red- and black-figured ware, Hellenistic red- and black-glazed pottery and terracotta figurines, Rhodian amphorae, and abundant coinage from Samaria suggests that local and international economies continued to flourish there throughout the turbulent Hellenistic era.

Large-scale, defensive architecture, constructed over the course of this period, bears witness to political vicissitudes as the Ptolemies and Seleucids competed for control over the region. A series of beautifully-built round towers (8.5 metres in height; 13 to 14.7 metres in diameter; see Fig. 4.22), originally misdated to the Israelite period, belongs to the late-fourth century BCE. Eventually, the second-century BCE Greek Fort Wall, a massive defensive element (four metres thick) with square towers, replaced the old Israelite casemate wall system that had remained in use (with extensive repairs) throughout the early Hellenistic period. Notwithstanding these strategies, around 111–108/107 BCE, the Hasmonean priest John Hyrcanus mounted a destructive, year-long siege against the city and brought the entire region temporarily under Judean control (Josephus, *Antiquities* 13.275–281; *Wars* 1.64–65).

Figure 4.22: The round Hellenistic tower excavated by Crowfoot (photograph by Leo Boer, 1 April 1954).

Notes

1   For these calculations, see Stager 1990, 97–98.
2   Circa 732 BCE, Tiglath-Pileser III deposed Pekah as Israelite king and installed Hoshea as puppet king; Tadmor 1994, 140–41: Summary Inscription 4, ll 17'–18'.
3   Compare the transitions from Megiddo IVA to III, Ta'anach IV to V, Yoqne'am 10 to 9, Tell Abu Hawām III to II, the occupation gap at Keisan to level 5, etc.
4   Compare Megiddo III–II, Tell Keisan 5–4a, 4b, etc.

Bibliography of Samaria and Sebaste

Aharoni, Y. and Amiran, R. 1958. "A New Scheme for the Sub-Division of the Iron Age in Palestine." *Israel Exploration Journal* 8:171–84.

Albertz, R. 1994. *A History of Israelite Religion in the Old Testament Period, Vol. I: From the Beginnings to the End of the Monarchy.* Old Testament Library Series. Louisville, KY: Westminster/John Knox.

Albright, W. F. 1958. "Recent Progress in Palestinian Archaeology: Samaria-Sebaste III and Hazor I." *Bulletin of the American Schools of Oriental Research* 150:21–25.

Avigad, N. 1993. "Samaria (City)." In *The New Encyclopedia of Archaeological Excavations in the Holy Land*, Vol. 4, edited by Ephraim Stern, Ayelet Lewinson-Gilboa, and Joseph Aviram, 1300–1310. Jerusalem: The Israel Exploration Society & Carta.

Avitsur, S. 1960. "On the History of the Exploitation of Water Power in Eretz-Israel." *Israel Exploration Journal* 10.1:37–45.

Ayalon, E. 1998. "Water-Driven Flour Mills." In *Water Installations in Antiquity*, edited by S. Gibson and D. Amit, 58–60. Jerusalem: IAA Conference Proceedings (Hebrew).

Benelli, C., Hamdan, O. and Piccirillo, M. (eds). 2007. *Sabastiya: History, Conservation and Local Community.* Jerusalem: Edkadek.

Conder, C. R. and Kitchener, H. H. 1882. *The Survey of Western Palestine. Vol. II. Sheets VII–XVI. Samaria.* London: Palestine Exploration Fund.

Cresswell, R. 1993. "Of Mills and Waterwheels: The Hidden Parameters of Technological Choice." In *Technological Choices: Transformation in Material Cultures Since the Neolithic*, edited by P. Lemonnier, 181–213. London: Routledge.

Crowfoot, J. W. 1937. *Churches at Bosra and Samaria-Sebaste.* British School of Archaeology in Jerusalem. Supplementary Paper 4. London.

Crowfoot, J. W. and Crowfoot, G. M. 1938. *Samaria-Sebaste II: Early Ivories from Samaria.* London: Palestine Exploration Fund.

Crowfoot, J. W., Kenyon, K. M. and Sukenik, E. L. 1942. *Samaria-Sebaste I: The Buildings at Samaria.* London: Palestine Exploration Fund.

Crowfoot, J. W., Crowfoot, G. M. and Kenyon, K. M. 1957. *Samaria-Sebaste III: The Objects.* London: Palestine Exploration Fund.

Dalman, G. 1902. "Grinding in Ancient and Modern Palestine." *The Biblical World* 19.1:9–18.

Finkelstein, I. 1990. "On Archaeological Methods and Historical Considerations: Iron Age II Gezer and Samaria." *Bulletin of the American School of Oriental Research* 277/278:109–19.

Finkelstein, I. 2011. "Observations on the Layout of Iron Age Samaria." *Tel Aviv* 38:194–207.

Folda, J. 1995. *The Art of the Crusaders in the Holy Land, 1098–1187.* Cambridge: Cambridge University Press.

Franklin, N. 2003. "The Tombs of the Kings of Israel. Two Recently Identified 9th-century Tombs from Omride Samaria." *Zeitschrift des Deutschen Palästina-Vereins* 119:1–11.

Franklin, N. 2004. "Samaria: from the Bedrock to the Omride Palace." *Levant* 36:189–202.

Franklin, N. 2007. "Response to David Ussishkin." *Bulletin of the American Schools of Oriental Research* 348:71–73.

Guérin, V. 1874. *Description Géographique, Historique et Archéologique de la Palestine, Vol. II: (part 2) Samarie.* Paris: Impr. Impériale.

Hill, D. 1984. *A History of Engineering in Classical and Medieval Times.* London and New York: Routledge.

Kenyon, K. M. 1964. "Megiddo, Hazor, Samaria and Chronology." *Bulletin of the Institute of Archaeology (University of London)* 4:143–56.

Kenyon, K. M. 1971. *Royal Cities of the Old Testament.* New York: Schocken.

Kühnel, G. 1988. *Wall Painting in the Latin Kingdom of Jerusalem.* Berlin: Mann.

Na'aman, N. 1990. "The Historical Background to the Conquest of Samaria (720 BC)." *Biblica* 71:206–25.

Pringle, R. D. 1998. *The Churches of the Kingdom of Jerusalem: A Corpus, Vol. II: L–Z (excluding Tyre).* Cambridge: Cambridge University Press.

Reisner, G. A., Fisher, C. S. and Lyon, D. G. 1924. *Harvard Excavations in Samaria 1908–1910.* Vols I–II. Cambridge: Harvard University Press.

Robinson, E. 1860. *Biblical Researches in Palestine and in the Adjacent Regions. A Journal of Travels in the Year 1838.* Boston: Crocker and Brewster.

Stager, L. 1990. "Shemer's Estate." *Bulletin of the American School of Oriental Research* 277/278:93–107.

Steiner, M. 1997. "Two Popular Cult Sites of Ancient Palestine." *Scandinavian Journal of the Old Testament* 11:16–28.

Tadmor, H. 1994. *The Inscriptions of Tiglath-pileser III King of Assyria. Critical Editions, with Introductions, Translations and Commentary.* Jeruslaem: The Israel Academy of Sciences and Humanities.

Tappy, R. E. 1992. *The Archaeology of Israelite Samaria. Early Iron Age through the Ninth Century B.C.E.* Vol. I, Harvard Semitic Studies 44. Atlanta: Scholars Press.

Tappy, R. E. 2001. *The Archaeology of Israelite Samaria, Vol. II: The Eighth Century B.C.E.* Harvard Semitic Studies 50. Winona Lake, Indiana: Eisenbrauns.

Tappy, R. E. 2007. "The Final Years of Israelite Samaria: Toward a Dialogue between Texts and Archaeology." In *Up to the Gates of Ekron: Essays on the Archaeology and History of the Eastern Mediterranean in Honor of Seymour Gitin*, edited by S. White Crawford, A. Ben-Tor, J. P. Dessel, W. G. Dever,

A. Mazar, and J. Aviram, 258–79. Jerusalem: The W. F. Albright Institute of Archaeological Research and the Israel Exploration Society.

Twain, M. 1869. *The Innocents Abroad or the New Pilgrims Progress.* New edition 1966. New York: New American Library.

Ussishkin, D. 2007. "Megiddo and Samaria: A Rejoinder to Norma Franklin." *Bulletin of the American Schools of Oriental Research* 348:49–70.

de Vaux, R. 1955. "Les Fouilles de Tell el-Far'ah, Près Naplouse, Cinquième Campagne." *Revue Biblique* 62:541–89.

Wilson, C. T. 1906. *Peasant Life in the Holy Land.* London: Murray.

Wright, G. E. 1959a. "Israelite Samaria and Iron Age Chronology." *Bulletin of the American Schools of Oriental Research* 155:13–29.

Wright, G. E. 1959b. "Samaria." *Biblical Archaeologist* XXII:67–78.

Wright, G. E. 1962. "Archaeological Fills and Strata." *Biblical Archaeologist* XXV:34–40

CHAPTER 5

TELL BALATA (SHECHEM)

Tell Balata (Shechem) dominates the pass between Mount Gerizim and Ebal in the central hill country of Palestine, but is curiously elusive in ancient literary records. Shechem is mentioned only in the list of pharaoh Sesostris III's raids of the mid-nineteenth century, as king Lab'ayu's city-state centre in the fourteenth-century Amarna archive, and in the Bible. In the stories of the biblical patriarchs, it appears regularly in connection with famous old shrines: Abraham (Genesis 12:6–8); Jacob (Genesis 33:18–20 and the conflict story in Genesis 34); Joseph (Genesis 37:14, buried there according to Joshua 24:32). It is listed as a Levitical city and a City of Refuge in Joshua 20 and 21. In Joshua 8 and 24, and Judges 9, the city and its region are central to vital religious-political remembrances; Rehoboam goes to Shechem to woo the north as the kingdom splits in two after Solomon's reign. Shechem, fortified by Jeroboam, became for a while the capital of the new kingdom (1 Kings 12:1; 14:17; 2 Chronicles 10:1). Jeremiah 41:5 and Hosea 6:9 hint that Shechem was an old pilgrimage site.

In the classical period Shechem was the main settlement of the Samaritans, whose religious centre stood on Mount Gerizim, just above the town. The city was destroyed during the First Jewish-Roman War and a new city (or Neapolis) was built nearby by the Roman emperor Vespasian in the year 72 CE. Eventually, this name turned into the Arabic Nablus.

Elusive but crucial indeed, it begs to be better-known – to historians, theologians and its modern inhabitants.

Apart from the history of archaeological campaigns at Tell Balata, this chapter will also discuss the aspect of heritage management at archaeological sites, illustrated very well by the current Balata Archaeological Park Project.

Archaeological Campaigns at Shechem (1913–1973)

Edward F. Campbell, Jr.

In 1954 Leo Boer together with the École Biblique field trip travelled to Nablus, where they met the Samaritan priest and visited the Samaritan Synagogue. Then, travelling on from Nablus, they came to the east end of the pass between Mount Ebal and Mount Gerizim. They then took a narrow road leading up to Askar village, which lies on the slopes of Mount Ebal. There they looked down on the ancient site of Shechem from the north-west, from where Boer took his first photograph.

Opposite Mount Gerizim is visible and the watch tower memorial of Sheikh Ghanim on its summit. On the slope of Gerizim, speckled with trees, lies Tell er-

Râs, site of the temple of Hadrian, which was later brought to light by the excavation campaigns led by the American Joint Expedition. On the other side of the brow lie the Hellenistic site of Luza and the Samaritan High Place. The road from Nablus turning south round Mt. Gerizim towards Jerusalem runs close beneath the Middle Bronze II site of Tananir, below the modern house. This site was partially uncovered by Gabriel Welter of the German expedition in 1932 and re-excavated in 1968 and published by Robert G. Boling (1975). Shechem's tell can be seen in the foreground, the southern half of which is covered by the village of Balata. The northern portion of the

Figure 5.1: Leo Boer's photograph taken from the flanks of Mt. Ebal looking south across the site of Shechem (compare this with Fig. 5.9 in the contribution by van den Dries).

ruins clearly shows the large-scale German excavation effort of the acropolis.

The huge piles of dumped soil mask the western face of Shechem's fortification which is why the Cyclopean Wall, stretching to 15.20 metres, is not visible in Boer's photograph. This wall was first noted in 1903 by Hermann Thiersch and named as the western defence wall of the ten-acre near-circular site. Boer took his photograph in 1954, nineteen years after the Germans had ended their work and three years before the American Joint Expedition began theirs.

Leo Boer at Tell Balata (Shechem)

Boer's Figure 5.2 was taken near the Cyclopean 'Wall A' (Fig. 5.4, number 1) looking south through the structure which the German team had called a palace, neatly positioned between the top of Wall A on the right and Wall E, the last Middle Bronze Age attempt at fortification, on the left. If Boer had expanded his exposure two metres to the right, he would have

shown the face of the sloping Wall A, rising nearly ten metres above the plain of the city. Boer is standing on the south wall of the Northwest Gate (Fig. 5.4, number 3), and his colleagues are in a colonnaded hall further south. The modern factory building behind the young man who is looking down at Boer's colleagues can be seen in Figure 5.1 on the right hand side.

The oblong rock in the centre of the 'Palace' is noteworthy. An identically shaped rock was found in Wall E; W. G. Dever carried out a new investigation of the place in 1972 and rejected the palace interpretation and found instead a small sanctuary complex. The floor in Boer's photograph pertains to a drawback in German record-keeping: on top-plans they failed to portray floors and surfaces and did not indicate their elevations above the site's horizontal datum.

In Figure 5.1 the north-eastern wing or side of the fortifications is difficult to discern. There the fortification system, defined by Wall B (Fig. 5.4, number 6), reaches the Middle Bronze IIC East Gate of the city (Fig. 5.4, number 8), pictured in Boer's Figure 5.3 with its remarkable orthostats that once anchored the wooden gates. The end of the rented

Figure 5.2: Boer's photograph taken from the south wall of the North-West Gate at Shechem, looking south through Sellin's 'Palace', with the field trip members standing in the colonnaded hall.

Figure 5.3: Boer's photograph of the East Gate at Shechem looking east onto the plain of Askar (compare this with Fig. 5.12 in the contribution by van den Dries).

plot, marked out by E. Sellin, can be found on the right (south) side of the cleared area of the gate, and once again the marcation of any road or path through the gates has been poorly defined. The drop to the plain of Askar which forms Shechem's bread-basket hints at approach systems providing access to town.

The tell plan in Figure 5.4 and the 1966 photo (Fig. 5.5) help to visualize what Boer saw. Note the three different places that are indicated, on the slope of Mt. Ebal, near the thick wall of the North-West Gate and near the north-west corner of the East Gate.

The Sellin/Welter Expedition (1913–1934)

Hermann Thiersch, a classical archaeologist later to become famous for his work on the lighthouse of Pharos, was serving a brief term as director of the German Archaeological Institute in Jerusalem. On an exploratory trip somewhat like the one Leo Boer took part in, he noticed the top of the Cyclopean Wall in 1903 and correctly assigned it to ancient Shechem.

This knowledge then circulated among a few scholars in Germany. Ernst Sellin of the University of Rostock who was soon to be appointed as Professor of Old Testament at Kiel University, and who had fieldwork experience from Taanach and Jericho, visited Tell Balata in 1911 and took up the challenge of mounting an expedition to the site with his architect colleague Camillo Praschniker in 1913. Having hired around 100 workers, he embarked on a two-fold approach to the excavation work: first clearing along the Cyclopean Wall, northwards from Thiersch's sighting which led him to locate the North-West Gate, and, second, opening trial trenches into the heart of the tell, in order to probe the stratigraphy. He continued this method through a second campaign in 1914, by which time the work crew, now consisting of nearly 150 workers, had found the North-West Gate. They had also widened Trench H (Fig. 5.4, number 2) at the north end and along its 50-metre length had identified at least four layers of stratigraphy, and they had cut an east-west trench from the North-West Gate into an area which would ultimately be regarded as the acropolis. Guided by a report of a site of a hoard of weapons in 1908, they also opened a sounding in the south-east of the site, which later became known as Trench K. The German work, supervised by two scholars and six experienced foremen who had previously worked with Sellin at Taanach and Jericho, had succeeded in bringing the site of Shechem to the world's attention.

Since it is not the purpose of this volume to report on the finds as much as it is to assess the development of archaeological techniques used at Shechem spanning almost a century, it is important to note the inadequacies of the work carried out during the first two seasons. The trenches themselves, as deep as they are wide, showed a lattice-work of superimposed short segments of walls which were

part of at least four stages of stratigraphy. On the rare occasion that a whole dwelling was found, no full documentation was carried out. Any connection between surfacing or floors of the mound and the walls of the structures was lost by cutting trenches along the walls. Rich artefacts were unearthed without careful assignment to the floors of the chambers. Poorly supervised, men, women and children from Balata unwittingly destroyed the contexts of their archaeological finds. Sellin and Praschniker had, however, succeeded in establishing the validity of Thiersch's identification of Shechem, and had probed the layers of the Middle Bronze ('Canaanite') Age.

Excavation was interrupted by the First World War and due to the Mandate the responsibility of the site and excavation of the land came under British

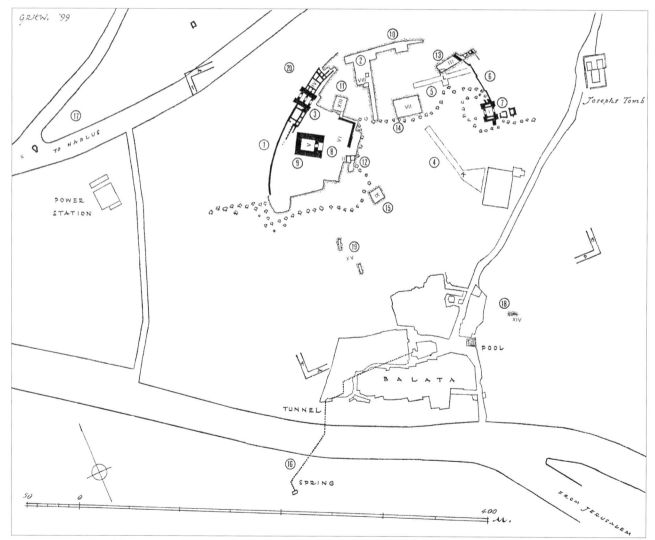

Figure 5.4: Key plan of the progress of excavation at Tell Balata from 1913 to 1968, prepared in 1999 by G. R. H. Wright. Note the locations mentioned throughout the text (Courtesy of the Joint Expedition to Tell Balâṭah/Shechem Archive, Semitic Museum, Harvard University).

control. Economic recovery for Germany took at least a decade. By 1925, Dutch biblical scholar Franz M. Th. Böhl of Groningen University had become part of the team, and it was he who first managed to combine the 1913–1914 archaeological information with literary evidence, using prevalent literary analysis of the Bible, the Amarna letters, and the nineteenth-century BCE (Sesostris III) mention of *škmm* also noted in Boer's diary on 3 February 1954 (Böhl 1926). This method introduced a trait inherent in all 'biblical archaeology' and soon became controversial: can a biblical scholar like Sellin, later pejoratively called 'the Theological Director', be trusted to bracket issues of biblical apologetic from the practice of rigorous archaeological method?

In 1926 Böhl brought Dutch resources to two more fruitful campaigns and joined Sellin in his return to the field. After his full-scale participation in both 1926 campaigns, Böhl wrote a 40-page illustrated monograph (1927) about the site which both described and prescribed important changes in archaeological method. He spent the interval between the two 1926 campaigns at Tell Beit Mirsim, where W. F. Albright and James Kelso had begun their excavation work, and there he encountered the emerging American emphasis on pottery typology which heightened his appreciation of the broken potsherd.

Böhl influenced Sellin's approach on another point as well. He urged him to turn from using trial trenches, to open up wider excavation plots,

Figure 5.5: Aerial view from above Mt. Gerizim showing Balata village and the tell from the south in 1966. Note the locations from which Boer took his photos, marked as B-1, B-2, and B-3 (Figs 5.1, 5.2 and 5.3 respectively; photograph by Lee C. Ellenberger, courtesy of the Joint Expedition to Tell Balâṭah/Shechem Archive, Semitic Museum, Harvard University).

in order to seek out more coherent architectural units and – in Böhl's own words – to see how people lived in these buildings. These are the first hints of engagement with anthropological disciplines, of attention to *la longue durée* – matters too long neglected in Palestinian archaeology.

Böhl advocated what he called the *Afschilferingsmethode*, which means peeling back the layers by strata to open up a wider spread of coherent architecture. After the spring 1926 campaign had revealed huge blocks of a temple structure inside and to the south of the gate, later to be called the 'Fortress Temple', this peeling method was applied to the acropolis and the North-West Gate region in five subsequent campaigns in the spring and summer of 1926 and 1927, and the spring of 1928. Attention now turned to understanding the Temple, its forecourt and the precinct or '*temenos*' in front of it, and bringing all of it in relation to the fortifications. Work was started at the North-West Gate and continued with as many as 200 workers removing huge amounts of soil (Fig. 5.4, numbers 7, 8 and 9). This region reportedly contained Hellenistic, Late 'Israelite' (Iron II), and Early 'Israelite' housing, but virtually no records of these layers were kept, and any plans made by the young draughtsman Heinz Johannes have been lost or were never completed. Johannes did produce plans of the Middle Bronze IIC and B layers once they had been laid bare. The question arises: how were the various peelings of the *Afschilferingsmethode* defined? Were floors and surfaces noted down and separated? How thoroughly could that be carried out, given the pace at which work proceeded?

Thus, Sellin found the temple, traced the fortifications along the northern perimeter of the site, followed the walls around leading to the East Gate, revealed the eastern wing of the 'Palace', opened Trench K (with rich content) in the south-east and cut another trench (L) into the heart of the tell from east to west (Fig. 5.4). Method here reverted to the use of the trial trench and to tracing walls; only rarely did large segments of entire houses come to light and were then cleared; work proceeded in much the same fashion as of the work in 1913–1914, with the focus on interesting, small finds, including pottery vessels and decorated pottery fragments. Many of these objects were granted to the Dutch in return for their financial support, and were brought to Leiden by Böhl. Vera Kerkhof (1969) set up a catalogue of the collection at

the request of the American Joint Expedition, using the 'Finds Registries' that survived, and did her best to place finds in their contexts.

In the summer of 1926, an architect with classical archaeological experience in the Aegean, Gabriel Welter, joined the staff. While busy on several fronts in the classical world, Welter excavated the East Gate to the outer limits of the land, rented for the expedition, and worked on the interpretation of the acropolis. It is hard to establish what the co-operation was like between Welter and Sellin, but by the end of the 1927 seasons Sellin was removed from his leadership by the *Notgemeinshaft der Deutschen Wissenschaft*, the 'emergency' organisation for German scientific endeavors since 1920 and Welter was put in charge instead. In 1928 Sellin was only a visitor, yet he and Welter disagreed vehemently about whether the Fortress Temple was indeed a temple or not. Sellin observed that a large fragment of a standing stone (*maṣṣebah*) fitted appropriately into what had previously been deemed a watering trough, and had it erected in place, relating it to the stones in Joshua 24 and Judges 9. Sellin put it up; Welter pushed it over. Later excavation work seems to support Sellin's idea, as can be seen in Figure 5.6.

Welter's work in the years 1928 to 1931 included an important study of the temple/fortress and its foundations, where he identified two earlier phases of fortification from Middle Bronze IIB. He also expanded his work to the flank of Mt. Gerizim where he discovered the structure at Tananir and suggested that it was the Shechem temple of the Abimelek story in Judges 9. Welter then proposed placing the location of ancient Shechem back beneath the modern city of Nablus to the west. His plans and section drawings of the Fortress (Temple) are invaluable. But Welter's work has also been severely criticized, as has Sellin's, notably in three separate evaluations, by Johannes Hempel (1933), Hermann Thiersch as reported by Hempel, of having said that he 'almost wished' he had not spotted the Cyclopean Wall, and by G. Ernest Wright (1965, 23–34). Wright ends his evaluation of the entire German work by mentioning two crucial faults: that the staff was woefully inadequately equipped to supervise the huge undertaking, and that the record-keeping of the stratigraphy and of the finds was virtually counter-productive in its effectiveness.

Sellin returned to the site in 1934, supported by Hans Steckeweh who had also worked with

Figure 5.6: Fields V and VI, the Fortress Temple and the Courtyard Complex, as they looked in 1968. The wall retaining the fill on which the temple stands was constructed by the Joint Expedition to hold things in place. Note the standing stone/maṣṣebah in front of the temple, as placed by Sellin and remounted by the Joint Expedition (Photograph by Lee C. Ellenberger, courtesy of the Joint Expedition to Tell Balâṭah/ Shechem Archive, Semitic Museum, Harvard University).

Albright at Bethel where G. E. Wright himself was a colleague, and peeled the stratigraphy just north of the acropolis (Fig. 5.4, number 11), but then the German work came to an end. As one of the great ironies of the whole story, an American bombing attack on Berlin in 1943 completely destroyed Sellin's home, and all his records, including his reportedly finished final report. Sellin, always the gentleman and since then somewhat vindicated for his efforts, died on New Year's Eve 1945.

The Drew-McCormick/Joint Expedition (1956–1973)

In the autumn of 1954, G. Ernest Wright of McCormick Theological Seminary of Chicago began planning a new endeavour together with Dean Bernhard W. Anderson and Professor William Farmer of Drew University, in what was by now Jordanian-controlled central Palestine, based out of the American School of Oriental Research in Jerusalem (later called the W.F. Albright Institute, the AIAR). Shechem was nominated. They envisioned a 'learn-as-you-go'-field school which would take on and train a new generation of scholars, thus encouraging an American surge in archaeology. In July 1956, Wright and Anderson enlisted Robert J. Bull of Drew and Douglas Trout of McCormick Seminary, and the four of them met with Hasan ʿAwad of Jordan's Department of Antiquities to prepare Shechem for a new excavation project (Trout became afflicted with polio at the dig, but remained a financial benefactor of future seasons). They excavated parts of the East Gate and took stock of the logistical needs for a lengthy expedition. They found the East Gate exactly as shown in Boer's photograph (Fig. 5.3). Bull, a multi-talented Early Church Historian, assumed the role of draughtsman and architect. Wright and Anderson were both already heavily engaged in biblical theological interpretation.

Between 4 July and 16 August 1957, a huge staff gathered at Shechem, most of them American graduate students or young professors with no digging experience, along with Balata residents who remembered Sellin. More seven-week sessions took place in the summers of 1960, 1962, 1964, 1966 and 1968. Between autumn 1968 and that of 1973, targeted projects were conducted on Tell er-Râs (Bull), at Tananir (Boling), and again on Tell Balata (Seger in 1969, and Dever in 1972–1973), all technically salvage operations. An unpublished salvage probe under Israeli auspices in the late 1980s may have touched the fortifications and even a possible gate on the south side along the eastern swing, but any records are lost.

Campbell and Wright 2002, 6–7 lists the 115 participants of the now-expanded Joint Expedition, which later included Harvard Semitic Museum, Southern Baptist, Austin, and Garrett Theological Seminaries, and other institutions participating on a smaller scale. Most staff came from seminaries, or were preparing for seminary and college or university teaching and not just representing biblical studies. More than 30 came only for one or two seasons, by then having been exposed to rigorous field experience. Others became key staff at Tel Gezer under William G. Dever, at Tell Ta`annek under Paul Lapp, at ʿAi under Joseph A. Callaway (see Petit in this volume) and at Tell Ḥisbân under Siegfried H. Horn. Twenty Jordanians and Palestinians served as representatives and trainees of the Antiquities Department, including the famous 'Jericho Men' about whom I will mention more below.

Twenty-five of the staff became the backbone of the Shechem project, providing continuity to field supervision and registry of finds, contributing to published reports, and developing field technique. In addition to Anderson and Ernest Wright the following should be especially named: George R. H. Wright ('Mick' – chief architect and draughtsman); Lawrence E. Toombs (stratigraphic expert and associate director); Lee C. Ellenberger (photographer); Vivian Bull (manager); Ovid R. Sellers (object registrar); Nancy Lapp (pottery registrar); Robert G. Boling, Roger Boraas, Robert J. Bull, Edward F. Campbell, Jr., Dan P. Cole, John S. Holladay, Jr., Siegfried H. Horn, H. Neil Richardson, James F. Ross, Henry O. Thompson and Prescott H. Williams (field supervisors, all of whom published on the Expedition).

By fulfilling the aim of training future American field archaeological leadership, Wright and Anderson had exposed crucial shortcomings in the German work. They supplied adequate staff to supervise every aspect of the excavation. Another major improvement was the application of the 'Wheeler-Kenyon' method of soil deposition analysis, an approach that would go far in answering the questions left open in the German work.

Toombs (1965) trained the team in the new field methods. The emphasis lay on the layering of the soil and the connection of horizontal layering to vertical features, inside, outside, over and under any feature. It comprised a package of techniques. Primary focus was upon the nature of each soil accumulation: texture, colour, natural ingredients, and artefacts. This required close attention to any changes and to any intrusions visible in the layers. Supervisors of any undisturbed bank of earth learned in practice how to separate soil layers from one another and how to isolate the soil character and artefact content of each deposit for separate recording. Sifting of the soil was carried out whenever necessary.

One contribution to this detailed analysis came from the 'Jericho Men' who had been trained by Kenyon, augmented by several Balata residents, notably among them the incomparable Nasr Dhiab Mansoor ('Abu `Issa'). Often a probe trench was cut through a portion of each layer to see what lay underneath, and peeling to the next layer followed. The edge of any such cut was trimmed back to reveal layers already encountered, producing a vertical section which could then be drawn to scale. Whenever a wall or feature was encountered, care was taken to leave a control bank of earth against it.

This description applies not only to the three sites where the Expedition broke new ground, but also to the vastly complicated task of finding undisturbed earth where German digging had preserved banks of it among the public buildings and along the fortifications. Such banks were first trimmed to expose a fresh face, thereby guiding careful separation of phases.

Supervisors kept notebook sketches of section drawings of such faces. These were connected, wherever possible, with the section on the major control earth bank, which is called a 'baulk', in order to form a virtual vertical road map of each project. A baulk was not to be removed until the section drawing of it was completed, drawn by those who had actually dug it, and then included in a final presentation by architect Mick Wright. Drawings of 60 sections of various locations are included in his volume II of Campbell and Wright 2002, and another 24 are in the Text volume.

Tracing soil layers and recording vertical sections were combined with separating sherds, other artefacts and puzzling objects found within each locus – a Latin term used to designate any distinctive feature, be it a wall, an installation, a layer of destruction debris, or a floor. After cleaning, these were 'read' by Ernest Wright and staff members who were developing expertise in pottery form identification, where 'indicators' – rims, handles, bases, decorated pieces and some 'body sherds' – were set aside for drawing. Staff members spent a lot of time each day in the local school house drawing profiles of sherds at a scale of 2:5.

At the Fortress Temple site (Field V), the German work had left in place the walls of an Iron Age building (now posited as a 'granary') on top of the massive foundations. Removal of these walls meant that undisturbed banks of earth were left behind. Study of these banks and renewed study of the walls brought to light an intermediate phase of the structure, pottery-dated to the Late Bronze Age, as well as two phases of the Temple itself. In front of the Temple (Field VI), where the German team had removed masses of stratified materials down to MB IIB strata, phases of structures representing Strata XXII to XV were disentangled. Just on the edge of the German clearance at the west of the tell, a fine Hellenistic House was brought to light (Field II), which, when combined with evidence from Fields VII and IX, brought the Hellenistic strata IV-I into focus. The soil deposits in Field III, located so as to check German Trench L, confirmed the four phases of Middle Bronze A fortifications, as did the work at the East Gate – Welter's four phases were confirmed as surrounding the tell, with Wall D built in the mid-eighteenth century, the C Rampart in use from 1725 till 1650 BCE, Wall A in use in the second half of the seventeenth century and Wall B in use during 1600–1550/1530 before being destroyed definitively. Three rectangular fields (VII, IX and XIII) were dug from the modern surface, refining the inner-city stratigraphy which the Germans had probed in Trenches H, L and K, and yielding domestic housing complexes. Especially noteworthy are the LB complexes in Field XIII, the fine 1727 Iron IIB house in Field VII, buried under the Assyrian destruction of the eighth century BCE, and the complete run of the stratigraphy to bedrock through 24 strata in Field IX.

This account of methods employed at Tell Balata has so far focussed on the work in the valley at the foot of Mt. Gerizim. Another major aspect of the work carried out by the Joint Expedition took place on Tell er-Râs on a spur of Mt. Gerizim. There the same excavation strategies were employed to deal with the ruins and foundations of the Zeus Temple built under Hadrian, meticulously excavated by Robert J. Bull, who began with soundings in 1964 and carried out full-scale work here in 1966–1971. Since Leo Boer could not have seen it, its story is reserved for another occasion. The same is true with the other endeavour started in 1964, a regional typographical survey by myself and Shechem staff members of the environs of the Shechem Plain. The two projects were first described in Bull and Campbell (1968). The survey was published by Campbell (1991) and the full report on Tell er-Râs is now in its final stages of publication.

The Joint Expedition left the field in 1973 and Ernest Wright died in 1974. Soon developments in field method and interpretive approach started off a series of reconceptualizations, in the literature often referred to as 'paradigm shifts'. We should recall Böhl's hope cited earlier in this chapter and expressed in 1926, that archaeology would come to focus on the everyday life of local inhabitants. Influence from 'Processual Archaeology' dominated during the following decades, and the lack of sophisticated equipment – the Shechem field expedition had neither computer facilities nor a university base with laboratory equipment – has meant that all the records retrieved at Shechem have now become part of a vast pool of data available to reconstruct its 'social history' and daily life. The Joint Expedition, for example, had failed to adequately record human bones *in situ* (in contrast with the campaigns of Kenyon at Tell es-Sultan; see Bocquentin and Wagemakers in this volume), although its staff recognized their pertinence to diet and health considerations in other expeditions which they later joined. The Expedition saved most of the indicator sherds, too many for developing period typologies, but not enough for satisfactory frequency analyses – how many cooking pots were found in a given dwelling, for example. More data are still being culled from ongoing ceramic studies and fabric analysis which will permit conclusions about native and non-native clay sources.

Early stages of the paradigm shifts were accompanied by a deepened mistrust of written sources, especially of the biblical historical narrative, and this attitude has continued to dominate in some of the current debates, notably those about the Davidic and Solomonic period. Ernest Wright's pursuit at Shechem of the relation of the courtyard complex in front of the Fortress Temple with the biblical Patriarchs remains severely questioned. A new and more sophisticated effort at linking philological study with archaeological data has emerged (cf. Stager 1999) and the availability of the entire Shechem archive at Harvard Semitic Museum and of the artefacts in Leiden (Kerkhof 1969), promise continued participation in the interpretation of the archaeological record. New light from an old dig will undoubtedly be shed. And with the new Dutch-Palestinian preparations for greater and more informed access to the site, the facts on the ground are ready for all to see (see Van der Kooij and Taha in this chapter).

Tell Balata Archaeological Park Project: Fieldwork in 2010 and 2011

Gerrit van der Kooij and Hamdan Taha

The American Joint Expedition left the site of Tell Balata in 1973 after a period of intensive fieldwork. Hardly any archaeological excavations were carried out at the site since then, yet many publications appeared, dealing with the excavated remains of the past, and in particular discussing their interpretations. A purely archaeological interpretation was not always sufficient, since several 'archaeological periods' could be related to written data, including biblical ones.

There were many factors leading to the start of a 'heritage management' project at Tell Balata: scholarly and public discussions were held about the historical 'value' of the site; the archaeological remains had been suffering from physical neglect and damage was done to them in the last decades, including a wide road-cut through its south-western part. In fact, Tell Balata is one of the first sites the Palestinian Authority focussed on since its establishment in 1994.

The 'Tell Balata Archaeological Park' project (2010–2012) is funded by the Dutch government and is being implemented jointly by the Department of Antiquities and Cultural Heritage (of the Palestinian Ministry of Tourism and Antiquities), the Faculty of Archaeology of Leiden University, and the UNESCO-Ramallah office, and directed by the co-authors of this chapter.

Heritage management of a site generally concerns aspects such as clearance, consolidation, restoration, and public facilities. The criteria used for deciding on how these aspects should be managed are partly based on the archaeological and historical significance of the site; this is the reason why the various interpretations of the remains must be looked at. This meant, in the case of Tell Balata, that previous archaeological work had to be assessed, for which not only surface clearance was necessary (done in 2010), but also some further excavations (in 2011). The archaeological aspects of the project will be discussed in this contribution, the management and public aspects in the next one by Monique van den Dries.

The archaeological aspects of the project

After clearance of the site's surface, the archaeological remains became visible again. The remains were compared with the circumstances in which they were left by previous excavations: they were assessed as far as any damage was concerned (for example see Fig. 5.7), as well as their archaeological and historical interpretations. Subsequently, the joint Palestinian-Dutch team excavated four of the chosen spots for the purpose of assessment, checking and exploration (see the orange indications in Fig. 5.8). Squares of five by five metres were used as basic units and each had test trenches for the purpose of predictive stratigraphy.

1) Area 2 (partly supervised by Mohammad Ghayada): west of the North-West Gate, a long interrupted trench, perpendicular to the Cyclopean Wall, was excavated two meters wide in order to check two issues. Firstly, the results indicated, that the north-west end of the site was suitable for building the visitor's centre, with no archaeological remains expected to be found underneath. Secondly, the stratigraphy of the layers of lime-debris showed that the original lime-earthen works were located on the slope just beneath the Cyclopean Wall and were made before fifth-fourth century BC late Iron Age and Hellenistic times, when a building was constructed on top of the foot of the slope.

2) Area 23 (supervised by Wael Hamamreh): recently an east-west road had been paved through the western end of the site, towards its centre, cutting through dump layers left by the German expedition and through the original town accumulations beneath them. The northern side of the cut had clear stratigraphic information, and a trench was excavated a few metres further north parallel to the cut. The sections of the cut, together with the landscape context and data from previous excavations, indicate an oval, rather than the often quoted circular, shape of the ancient town

Figure 5.7: Comparison of the 1954 (see Fig. 5.2 in contribution Campbell) with the 2010 photographs of Area 4, taken from the North-West Gate towards south-west, shows a great difference in the damage caused, after the German expedition had exposed the stone bases of the walls. For example, the upper half of the left-hand wall (which is an Iron Age construction on top of the Middle Bronze Age wall foundation) has fallen down to either side. The stone in the middle of the room (a column base of the Middle Bronze Age room) was turned in its position and recently used as a picnic table (Courtesy of the Tell Balata Archaeological Park Project).

with a longer east-west axis (see Campbell and Wright 2002, Vol. 2, ill. 2 and 6). This area also revealed deposits with Late Chalcolithic and/or Early Bronze I remains (ca. 4000–3000 BCE). In combination with similar remains found earlier, we may conclude that a village covering an area of at least one hectare existed alongside the bottom of the valley and near a water source.

3) Area 14 (supervised by Mohammad Ghayada): at the German west to east trench following the northern part of the city wall contour. This trench had been cut through a two metres thick layer of burnt mudbrick debris, which needed dating. Two squares were excavated and the result is that the burnt debris had to be connected with the final stages of the Late Bronze Age (early twelfth century BCE), rather than with earlier destructions. Some artificial levelling indicated

a new inhabitation phase during the Iron Age I period.

4) In Area 11 – west of American Field XIII – (supervised by Laurens Jansen): a stratigraphic sequence between the Middle Bronze Age '*temenos*' wall and the wall remains on the surface, as left by the German excavations, between the North-West Gate and Field XIII, was to be recorded, including the wall remains.

This was partially successful. It provided some clarity about the complex stratigraphy of the Late Bronze Age phases at this spot, but the extension of the *temenos* wall was not found.

Some of the goals were not achieved: the need for finding botanical remains, to serve as Carbon-14 samples for dating, was not satisfied; hardly any such remains were found in unmixed deposits.

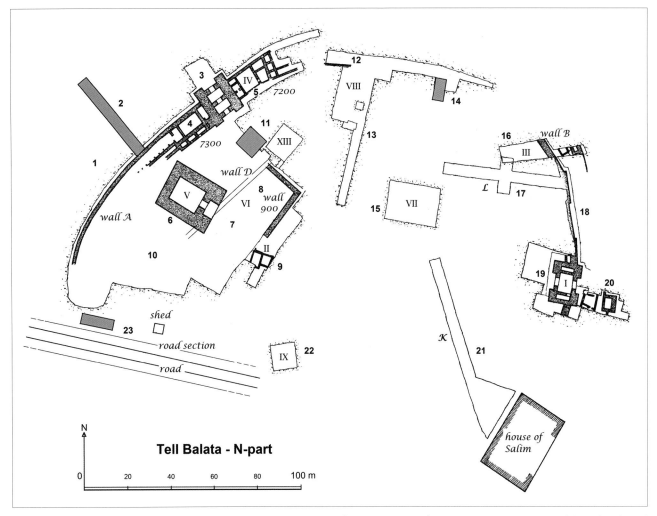

Figure 5.8: Key plan of the progress of excavation at Tell Balata in 2010-2011 (orange indications); based on the composite plan of the archaeological campaigns from 1913 to 1968, published by Campbell and Wright 2002, Ill. 2 (Courtesy of the Joint Expedition to Tell Balâṭah/Shechem Archive, Semitic Museum, Harvard University and the Tell Balata Archaeological Park Project).

Analysis of the remains

Interpretations of the archaeological remains (contexts, buildings, objects, etc.) at Tell Balata (Shechem) have changed during the past century of research. A major issue are the identifications of the site with biblical descriptions and events. Discussions occurred during the German and American expeditions (see Campbell in the previous contribution) and are still taking place up to this day. It is interesting to see what view Leo Boer and his group from the École Biblique had on this.

Two remarks in his notes are relevant in this respect. Firstly, he made an easy connection of the archaeological remains from the Middle Bronze Age with historical population groups, namely the

Hyksos for the early stage, and the Amorites for the later stage of the fortified town. Especially since the 1970s archaeologists have been more reluctant to accept these connections, because they suggest a population migration and through this a diffusion of cultures. Moreover, it has become known from the discipline of anthropology that innovations in a culture generally tend to be the product of a local development in combination with an external stimulation. Furthermore, the identity of both the Hyksos and Amorites became less well described and more diffuse, which made them less applicable in these cases.

Boer's second remark concerns the direct connection, between on the one hand the story of

Abimelech at Shechem in the biblical book of Judges, Chapter 9, its Beth-Millo (taken as the Migdol-Shechem) and its temple of Baal-Berith, and on the other the archaeological remains at Tell Balata, conveniently called the *Fortress Temple* inside the city's *acropolis*. We are currently more hesitant to accept such identifications, especially since it is difficult to assess the biblical narrative as a historical source, and, when dated traditionally, it is difficult to bridge the time gap created by the Middle Bronze date of the structures referred to.

At the present time, the Tell Balata Archaeological Park project focusses, for the public, on the archaeological remains, not only including the still visible, magnificent Middle Bronze Age architecture, with a partially extended use during the Late Bronze Age, but also the Late Chalcolithic-Early Bronze I culture. The Iron Age and Hellenistic remains left on the site are barely visible, since much, dating from these periods, was excavated and removed, by the German team in particular. Objects dating from these periods are stored e.g. in the Rijksmuseum van Oudheden (National Museum of Antiquities) in Leiden, The Netherlands. Nowadays, they are important not just because of their supposed biblical connections, but mostly because of their intrinsic value. The Tell Balata Archaeological Park project aims to put all periods present at the site in their wider Near-Eastern context, rather than focussing on its value for biblical studies.

Heritage Management at Tell Balata

Monique H. van den Dries

When Leo Boer visited Tell Balata in the 1950s, the site looked quite different from how it looks today. As his photographs (Figs 5.1–5.3 in the contribution of Campbell) show us, the area around the site was at that time open and green, and a large part of the site was still underground, much more than it is today (compare Figs 5.9 and 5.1). After the excavations in the 1970s (as described by Campbell in this chapter) no further excavation work was done and over the years the exposed ancient structures were neglected and became covered by vegetation and waste. In addition, the site has since been encroached on by modern buildings and is now completely encapsulated by them (Fig. 5.9).

However, Tell Balata has not been forgotten. On the contrary, it is still considered one of the most important heritage locations on the West Bank. In an attempt to stop any further decay and to preserve the site for the future, a joint project was started in 2010 by the Palestinian Department for Antiquities and Cultural Heritage, the Faculty of Archaeology of Leiden University and UNESCO, aiming to turn the site into a visitor-friendly archaeological park. At the time of writing, work is still in progress, and final results are yet to be published. However, some light can be shed on the work that has been done recently to prepare the site for the future.

Archaeological heritage management

As this book clearly illustrates, archaeology as a science has gone through a tremendous development. In contrast to the old days, archaeology is no longer focused only on collecting finds or reconstructing habitation histories and cultural development. Over the last three to four decades, the management of archaeological sites has become a major point of attention. It deals with the way we handle and preserve in the present the (visible and invisible) remains from the past. This started roughly in the United States in the 1960s, when people became aware that archaeological sites have a unicity and are non-renewable, and yet were being destroyed rapidly and on a large scale, due to extensive building and development activities. It was then called 'archaeological resource management' or 'public archaeology', the latter referring to the need for public support to safeguard archaeological remains.

In Europe, an important step was taken towards the development of archaeological heritage management when the Council of Europe signed the *European Convention on the Protection of the Archaeological Heritage* in 1992 in Valletta (Malta). Its aim is to render the preservation of the archaeological remains by a statutory law, preferably within its original context (*in situ*). Another important aspect of the Convention is that anyone who disturbs a site will be urged to take responsibility and to finance the archaeological research, prior to the destruction of the site. Additional aims are to give more public exposure of the sites and to raise public awareness of the vulnerability of the remains of the past.

Today, in Europe, almost all member states of the Council of Europe have signed the Convention. For most European countries this implies that archaeological research is focused mostly, and sometimes exclusively, on sites that are endangered by development or building activities. Increasingly, this means that the management of sites must also involve the interests of the general public and other stakeholders. Consequently, aspects of heritage management are integrated in most academic archaeological training.

This practice is not yet as extensively implemented in the Near East as it is in Europe, nor is it rendered by law. It is, however, standing policy of the Palestinian Department of Antiquities and Cultural Heritage (MOTA-DACH) to preserve archaeological sites as effectively as possible *in situ* and to apply a participatory approach in safeguarding cultural heritage, in other words, fostering the roles of official bodies, academics, non-governmental organizations as well as the local community (Taha 2010). Examples of this are: implementing facilities for the public,

Figure 5.9: Tell Balata in 2011, seen from Mount Ebal (as Leo Boer did in the 1950s, see Fig. 5.1 in the contribution by Campbell). The tell is now located in the middle of a lively community and is slowly encroached on by housing (Photograph: G. van der Kooij, archive Tell Balata Archaeological Park Project).

such as providing information panels, on-site maps, leaflets, etc. This policy has not only been applied at Tell Balata but also, for instance, at Tell es-Sultan (see Sala in this volume) and Hisham's Palace in Jericho, Sebaste, Bethlehem (listed as World Heritage in 2012), and in several other important archaeological places on the West Bank.

Working towards sustainable management at Tell Balata

One of the most important aims of the Balata Archaeological Park Project, funded by the Dutch Ministry of Foreign Affairs, is to set up a long-term management strategy for the site. Together with the historic town of Nablus and several other ancient locations in the surrounding area, Tell Balata is part of a heritage group which is on the tentative list for World Heritage (Taha 2009). The management plan entails

the preservation and conservation of the site itself, construction of a visitor centre and promotion and publicity of the site. Promotion of the archaeological park meant raising awareness in the local community of its invaluable archaeological heritage and developing a strategy to encourage tourism so as to render the park economically self-reliant and thus create a sustainable community development.

Why community involvement is a main aim of the project, is illustrated by Figure 5.9. It shows the location of the tell in the middle of Balata village, surrounded by houses, roads and small garages. Its many neighbours have a direct view onto the site and feel connected with it. Many local people also use the site as a short cut from one part of the village to the other; olive and fig groves provide subsistence to some farmers. The slopes of the site were also used as a dumping-ground for car tires and wrecks (Fig. 5.10). But most importantly of all, the tell serves as an oasis in the middle of the town:

Figure 5.10: Notice the car wreck at the front of the picture. Also the white standing stone/maṣṣebah is clearly visible at the centre of the picture, next to the people. When comparing this photograph with Campbell's Figure 5.6, it is clear that the Courtyard Complex, located in front of the people, has been filled up after 1968 (Photograph: M. van den Dries, archive Tell Balata Archaeological Park Project).

children play and fly their kites there, students use the serenity of the place to study, and adults enjoy picnics in the shade.[1]

These are important factors to keep in mind when developing the site into an archaeological park. The tell has a particular meaning to each of its local users, and it is considered to be paramount to involve them in the care and management of the site. They are interested in helping with the management, guarding the site and providing visitor facilities. It is therefore very important to discuss with the local inhabitants the ideas and plans for the site, any consequences and benefits they may have and to involve them in the whole process and management of the site. As a result, there is now close co-operation between the project team and the local community, represented by the Multipurpose Community Resource Centre at Nablus.

Community work

The first contacts with the community and its representatives were made in 2010. Then, during the summer campaign of 2011, priority was given to the involvement of the community in the project. One of the first activities during that time was to interview local inhabitants and record their oral history (Van den Dries and Van der Linde 2012). In this way the project team intends to document and preserve valuable information about the recent history of the site and its archaeological past (see Campbell in this chapter). Additionally, due to the fact that the people who had been involved in the German and American excavation campaigns, are now quite old, it has become paramount to record their memories as soon as possible and collect as much information as possible. Secondly, we used the interviews as a way to provide local inhabitants with on-going information on the project and in turn to acknowledge their opinions and wishes concerning the park and its future management. Thirdly, we collected material to be exhibited in the visitor centre, such as photographs of the former and current workers, film footage of children playing on the site, and some old documents.

Our team carried out 25 interviews in total. We talked to all kinds of people who had a direct link with the tell, such as those who live next to the site, workmen who took part in former excavations, land owners, children, people from the Balata refugee camp, and representatives of the local authorities (Rhebergen and Nogarede 2012, 17). Many interesting and wonderful stories have been collected, giving valuable information about how the archaeologists had carried out their work at the site – specifically, how they had found workers and divided the labour between them, what their dump policy had been and how they had focussed on finding ancient artefacts[2] – and information about the various views about the support for the park. One of these views concerned the ways in which pollution can be prevented by the owners of the garages located around the site. It is clear that the local community is well-informed about the site, enjoys using it, and appreciates its value. People are happy that the site is being preserved. The plans for a visitor centre are also well-received and community members are interested in providing some tourist facilities. At the end of the campaign a booklet, entitled 'Stories about Tell Balata', bilingual in Arabic and English, was produced, including photographs of the participants who were interviewed and quotes from their testimonies. A copy of the booklet was then presented to each participant.

Another way of involving the community was achieved by means of a logo competition. Just as local architects had been invited to design the visitor centre, so local students, from Najah University in Nablus, were asked to design an appealing logo for the park. Several promising designs were selected for further development.

We also tried to involve a larger part of the community by organising a family day on the site. With the help of the Community Centre of Nablus all sorts of people were invited from various parts of the community. As excavation work was still going on, families were able to explore the excavation pits, admire the finds and talk to the archaeologists. There

were children activities such as a drawing competition and fixing potsherds. Also, the plans for the visitor centre and the results of the logo competition were on show, and a leaflet and the oral history booklet were handed out to all the families.

Another way of engaging the community was to set up education programmes for schools. It was evident that the community was keen to learn more about the site, yet hardly any information was available in Arabic. In particular, the children of Nablus knew very little about the history of the site and its cultural value to their region. As 44 percent of the population is aged younger than fifteen, the education of schoolchildren will allow the information to reach a large part of the community.[3]

It is not just our intention to run the education programme while the project work is still going on, because this implies that as soon as the project ends, the education will stop too. Instead, the project team wants to ensure that the attention for heritage in education becomes consolidated. We are currently developing a teacher's handbook intended to inspire elementary school teachers to use the available information as teaching material in their lessons. The book will offer an introduction to archaeology and the value of heritage as well as ready-made lessons (including teaching and learning objectives, ideas for educational materials, field trips and testing methods) which can be integrated in the school curriculum. The success of such a book is entirely dependent on the commitment of the local teachers and whether or not it fits in with their curriculum and training methods. For that reason it is being developed in co-operation with local teachers and the Palestinian Ministry of Education.

In 2010 and 2011 a pilot was run in a summer school on the site. Hanneke van der Kooij, a Dutch school teacher, developed some pilot lessons and – in co-operation with a Palestinian archaeologist and an interpreter – she taught several groups of children in the summer school at the site (Fig. 5.11). Together with one of the students from Leiden University she tested and further developed different lessons for children aged nine–twelve and thirteen–fifteen. One of the things she discovered was that the children knew very little about the animals on the site and were mostly afraid of them. Information about the flora and fauna has now also been included in the handbook.

Figure 5.11: Children from summer school enjoying the heritage and history lessons given at the site. The experiences of such pilots are being used to develop a teacher's handbook which aims to give structural attention to heritage education (Photograph: G. van der Kooij, archive Tell Balata Archaeological Park Project).

Preservation work

In 1996 the Department of Antiquities and Cultural Heritage placed a fence around the northern part of the site, a first step towards protecting the site and preventing it from being used as a dumping ground. Visitors were still able to enter the site at two different places on the old popular route across the site. On the site itself dangerous or vulnerable parts were fenced off by means of an 'open' fence. Additionally, signs and garbage bins were placed to encourage people not to use it as a dumping ground. Gradually over time, the fence collapsed in certain places but has recently been repaired.

Next, the Tell Balata Archaeological Park project placed information panels on the site to show that the site is being rehabilitated. Also, guards have been appointed to look after the site and to receive visitors.

Thirdly, the summer campaign of 2010 focussed on clearing and cleaning the site from vegetation and rubbish, which consequently led to getting a clear picture of the current state of the site and establishing exactly what type of consolidation and restoration work was required. The clearing of the site from vegetation has also improved the visibility of the archaeological remains and its accessibility to visitors (for example, compare Campbell's Fig. 5.3 with Fig. 5.12 here). Keeping the site free from vegetation is also important for its preservation. The roots of trees have a strong disruptive power when growing between the stones of the walls and in old excavation areas.

The clearing showed that the dry stone wall, supporting the superficial terrace in front of the temple, was in urgent need of repair, in order to prevent soil erosion and ensure safety for visitors. This repair therefore became a priority in the 2010 campaign.

Local architects worked out a design for the visitor centre and during the summer of 2011 a test pit was dug just outside the rampart wall and the North-West Gate, in order to verify that no archaeological remains would be threatened or damaged by the building plan (see Van der Kooij and Taha in this volume).

Figure 5.12: The East Gate in 2010, when almost all the vegetation had been cleared. It is clear that even more structures are at present uncovered and exposed to decay and that modern buildings are encroaching on the site (Photograph: G. van der Kooij, archive Tell Balata Archaeological Park Project).

Promotion

The aim of the project is that the park will eventually generate its own income and become self-reliant as much as possible. Visitors, especially tourists, could contribute to this by paying an entrance fee and buying souvenirs in the visitor centre. In fact, tourism is now considered to be one of the main pillars of the Palestinian economy. In 2011 alone, the site already received 150 visitors every month, yet an even higher number is now feasible. In 2010 1.8 million tourists visited the Palestinian territories, but only a tiny percentage comes to visit Tell Balata, as it is still not that well-known. Moreover, the number of tourists who visit the Palestinian Territories was only half of that of Israel's and roughly a third of that of Jordan's, which means that a larger number of tourists could also visit the West Bank if more resources were utilized for tourism (World Bank 2008).

One of the major challenges for tourism in the Palestinian Territories and Israel however is caused by the political situation. The West Bank does not have a very positive image internationally and travel to the area can be difficult at times. Unfortunately, we are unable to influence these matters but we *are* able to improve the information about the site: we are currently working on a tourism development plan as part of the management plan. The main objective is to develop a promotion strategy in order to attract more visitors, both from the Palestinian Territories and abroad, and to provide the best tourist facilities possible. An inventory has been made on the one hand of the sources that already provide information, which may need to be updated (such as guide books, websites of tour operators etc.), and on the other, of potential new sources and places to distribute information to, like hotels, museums and other places that tourists already visit on the West Bank.

We have conducted interviews with visitors and tour guides, in order to establish exactly what they expect from a visit to the site. We asked them about their reason for their visit – often the reason being that the site is included in tours with a biblical topic

Figure 5.13: The site map at Tell Balata (Photograph: G. van der Kooij, archive Tell Balata Archaeological Park Project).

– and about what kind of information and type of facilities they would like to see. The tour guides appeared to know little about the site and were keen to receive training (Szalanska 2012, 21).

As part of the promotion of the site, various types of publicity have been set up, including a (bilingual) leaflet, a site map (Fig. 5.13) and a website (www. tellbalata.com). The website hosts a site description, visitor information and a news section with progress updates of the project. Road signs on the two major routes leading to Nablus clearly indicate the direction to the site and publicity material for the visitor centre has been organised, including blue prints for posters and entrance tickets.

Back to the future

A lot of progress has been made, but there is still quite a lot of work left before the project ends in 2013. In fact, the main task for people involved in the site will only begin *after* the project is finished. The Palestinian local community will face the challenge of running their Balata park successfully. This will not be easy, but the prospects are now enhanced by the fact that the Palestinian Territories have at last been acknowledged as a member state of UNESCO.[4] This has finally given the Palestinian people the chance to proudly present their astonishing heritage and to encourage tourists to follow Leo Boer's example by visiting the site. He probably could not have imagined what Tell Balata would have looked like, 60 years after his visit, but if he had been able to visit it today, he would have had many reasons for not returning hastily to Jerusalem but rather for staying to enjoy the city oasis of Tell Balata, the bustling town of Nablus, and the overwhelming warm hospitality of the Palestinian people for as long as possible.

Notes

1   With a surface of only 6.020 km² and a population of four million, the West Bank is one of the most densely populated countries of the world, with 625 habitants per km² (source:http://www.pcbs.gov.ps/Portals/_PCBS/Downloads/book1432.pdf).

2   One of the interviewees mentioned that during the American excavation a competition was held between the workmen to find the most valuable antiquities and that there was a prize for the winner.

3   http://www.pcbs.gov.ps/Portals/_PCBS/Downloads/book1432.pdf

4   http://www.unesco.org/new/en/media-services/single-view/news/general_conference_admits_palestine_as_unesco_member_state/

Bibliography of Tell Balata (Shechem)

Böhl, F. M. Th. 1926. *De geschiedenis der Stad Sichem en de Opgravingen Aldaar*. Mededeelingen der Koninklijke Akadamie van Wetenschappen, Amsterdam, Afd. Letterkunde. Deel 62, Serie B:1–24.

Böhl, F. M. Th. 1927. *De Opgraving van Sichem: Bericht over de Voorjaarscampagne en de Zomercampagne in 1926*. Zeist: G. J. A. Ruys Uitgevers-Mij.

Boling, R. G. 1975. "Excavations at Tananir, 1968." In *Report on Archaeological Work at Suwannet eth-Thaniya, Tananir, and Khirbet Minha (Munhata)*, edited by G. M. Landes. Bulletin of the American Schools of Oriental Research Supplemental Studies 21, 25–85. Missoula, Montana: Scholars Press.

Bull, R. J. and Campbell, E. F. Jr. 1968. "The Sixth Campaign at Balâṭah (Shechem)." *Bulletin of the American Schools of Oriental Research* 190:2–41.

Campbell, E. F. Jr. 1991. *Shechem II: Portrait of a Hill Country Vale: The Shechem Regional Survey*. American Schools of Oriental Research Archaeological Reports Number 2. Atlanta: Scholars Press.

Campbell, E. F. Jr. and Wright, G. R. H. 2002. *Shechem III: The Stratigraphy and Architecture of Shechem/Tell Balâṭah* 2 Vols American Schools of Oriental Research Archaeological Reports Number 6. Boston: ASOR.

Dever, W. G. 1974. "Stratification in the Northwest Gate Area at Shechem." *Bulletin of the American Schools of Oriental Research* 216:31–52.

Hempel, J. 1933. "Balâṭa." *Festschrift für die alttestamentliche Wissenschaft* 51:156–69.

Kerkhof, V. I. 1969. "Catalogue of the Shechem Collection in the Rijksmuseum van Oudheden in Leiden." In *Oudheidkundige Mededelingen* L:28–109.

Rhebergen, A. and Nogarede, S.-J. 2012. "Stories about Tell Balata: Community Involvement Through an Oral History Project." In *Out in the field, Internships Master Students Archaeological Heritage Management 2011-2012*, edited by J. van Donkersgoed, L. Elemans, and A. Rhebergen, 16–19. Leiden: Side Stone Press (Graduate School of Archaeology Occasional Papers 10).

Stager, L. E. 1999. "The Fortress-Temple at Shechem and the 'House of El, Lord of the Covenant'." In *Realia Dei: Essays in Archaeology and Biblical Interpretation in Honor of Edward F. Campbell, Jr., at His Retirement*, edited by P. H. Williams, Jr. and T. Hiebert, 228–49. Atlanta: Scholars Press.

Szalanska, M. 2012. "Tell Balata Archaeological Park Project: Perspectives and Challenges of Tourism on the West Bank, Palestine." In *Out in the field, Internships Master Students Archaeological Heritage Management 2011-2012*, edited by J. van Donkersgoed, L. Elemans, and A. Rhebergen, 20–22. Leiden: Side Stone Press (Graduate School of Archaeology Occasional Papers 10).

Taha, H. (ed.). 2009 (2nd edition). *Inventory of Cultural and Natural Heritage Sites of Potential Outstanding Universal Value in Palestine*. Ramallah: Ministry of Tourism and Antiquities.

Taha, H. 2010. "The Current State of Archaeology in Palestine." *Present Pasts*, vol. 2 (http://www.presentpasts.info/article/view/pp.17/34).

Taha, H. and Van der Kooij, G. et al. Forthcoming. *Tell Balata Archaeological Park project 2010-2012*. Ramallah: Department of Antiquities and Cultural Heritage, Ramallah.

Toombs, L. E. 1965. "Appendix 1: Principles of Field Technique." In *Shechem: The Biography of a Biblical City*, by G. E. Wright, 185–90. New York and Toronto: McGraw-Hill.

Van den Dries, M. and Van der Linde, S. 2012. "Collecting Oral Histories for the Purpose of Stimulating Community Involvement at Tell Balata, Palestine." In *Integrating Archaeology, Science – Wish – Reality. Social Role, Possibilities and Perspectives of Classical Studies*, edited by N. Schücker, 49–56. Frankfurt: Römisch-Germanische Kommission.

World Bank. 2008. The Economic Effects of Restricted Access to Land in the West Bank. Accessed June 2012.http://siteresources.worldbank.org/INTWESTBANKGAZA/Resources/EconomicEffectsofRestrictedAccesstoLandintheWestBankOct.21.08.pdf

Wright, G. E. 1965. *Shechem: The Biography of a Biblical City*. New York and Toronto: McGraw-Hill.

CHAPTER 6

TELL ES-SULTAN (JERICHO)

Tell es-Sultan is the site of ancient Jericho. The tell lies 250 metres below sea level in the Jordan Valley, near the northern end of the Dead Sea. Here, a flourishing spring ('Ain es-Sultan, also known as Prophet Elisha's Spring) gave life to a large oasis, inhabited since the Natufian Period (10,500 BCE), and provided one of the oldest settlements in the world the conditions for life.

The Jerichoan community was one of the first to become sedentary and rely on agriculture for subsistence and it offers very early evidence of ancestors worship. At the beginning of the third millennium BCE, the town was defended by mighty fortifications. The monumental ruins of these Bronze Age fortifications, still visible after their final destruction around 1550 BCE, may have inspired the biblical author of the Joshua account to name Jericho as one of the main towns conquered by the Israelites (Joshua 6). The identification of Tell es-Sultan with biblical Jericho has been controversial, as the site was hardly inhabited at the end of the Late Bronze Age, when 'the walls came tumbling down'.

This chapter sketches the fascinating archaeological history of Tell es-Sultan and describes I. W. Cornwall's research of the numerous human remains that were found *in situ* at Tell es-Sultan and his role as pioneer of archaeothanatology.

The Archaeological Expeditions to Tell es-Sultan (1868–2012)

Maura Sala

Leo Boer visited Tell es-Sultan in 1954, during the second British Expedition directed by Kathleen M. Kenyon (1952–1958). He met Kenyon (1906–1978) twice at the tell: the first time when he was travelling around with two friends; the second time when he visited the site in the company of his lecturers and fellow students of the *École Biblique et Archéologique Française de Jérusalem*. At that time, Kenyon had just started her large-scale excavations at the tell and the nearby necropolis. On his visits to these excavations Boer witnessed the use of innovative methods and techniques applied at a site with a rich archaeological history which will be discussed in this contribution.

Leo Boer at Tell es-Sultan during the second British Expedition (1952–1958)

Kenyon carried out her excavations at Tell es-Sultan – ancient Jericho – between 1952 and 1958 under the Jordanian administration (1948–1967), on behalf of the *University College of London*, the *British School of Archaeology in Jerusalem* and the *Palestine Exploration Fund* (PEF) (Kenyon 1957; idem 1981; Kenyon and Holland 1982; idem 1983; King 1983, 125–28; Drinkard, Mattingly and Maxwell Miller 1988, 48–52; Moorey 1991, 94–99). After the division of the region between Israel and Jordan at the end of the British Mandate in 1948, the West Bank fell, in fact, within the Jordanian borders.

Kenyon organized a large-scale expedition with an international team and set a new standard in archaeology by introducing the stratigraphic digging method of Sir Mortimer Wheeler[1] to the Near East. This method included the digging of deep squares and trenches, reading their vertical sections, so that the chronological history of the site could be reconstructed; as well as systematically collecting and studying the materials (in particular, pottery) according to their stratigraphic context.

Kenyon's expedition was the second British Expedition working at Tell es-Sultan (following the one directed by J. Garstang in the 1930s; see below), and it investigated all the occupational phases of the settlement, from the Natufian to the Byzantine Period, establishing the chronological sequence of the site, and producing a full re-evaluation of the archaeology of Tell es-Sultan.

Kenyon's excavations were launched with three main aims in mind: firstly, to obtain additional evidence on the date of the fall of the Bronze Age city and its related fortifications, traditionally associated with the Israelite invasion under Joshua according to the biblical account (just as Garstang had confirmed at the end of his campaigns at Tell es-Sultan); secondly, to expose more of the very important Neolithic occupation levels that were first revealed by Garstang; and finally, to investigate more tombs in the nearby necropolis, that was also first discovered by Garstang in the 1930s.

Kenyon excavated three main trenches, expanding the cuts made by previous expeditions on the western (Trench I), northern (Trench II) and southern (Trench III) flanks of the tell, and a series of squares five by five metres and ten by ten metres on the mound itself (Fig. 6.1).

Among the main results of her expedition is the discovery of the Pre-Pottery Neolithic circular Tower in Trench I (Fig. 6.2) and the extensive exposure of the prominent Neolithic phases at the site (Kenyon 1957, 51–76); furthermore, the systematic exploration of the huge cemetery located to the north and west of the site, where they uncovered more than 600 tombs, ranging in date from the Early Bronze Age I to the Roman Period, and often containing rich funerary equipment (Kenyon 1960a; idem 1965); and, eventually, the investigation of the Bronze Age fortifications, defining the morphology and, above all, the chronology of the city walls which had been placed at the heart of the biblical account of Joshua (Kenyon 1957, 169–82, 214–21, 256–65). The examination of the

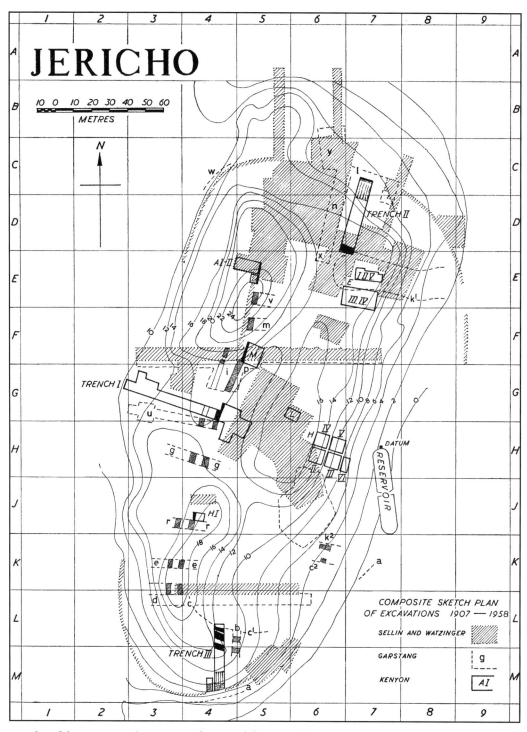

Figure 6.1: Plan of the excavations by K. Kenyon (1952-1958) (Courtesy of the Council for British Research in the Levant, CBRL).

Bronze Age defences started in 1952 from Trench I, which was opened at the middle of the western side of the mound, as well as in Site A, near its north-western corner. In Trench I, the whole sequence of Early and Middle Bronze Age fortifications could be unearthed, investigated and dated, based on an accurate analysis of associated pottery materials (Kenyon 1981, text, 97–103, 108–11).

The photograph taken by Boer from the Mount of Temptation (Fig. 6.3) offers an overview of the tell

Figure 6.2: Work at Kenyon's Trench I and PPNA (8500-7500 BCE) Tower at the time of Kenyon's excavations in 1952-1958 (Courtesy of the Council for British Research in the Levant, CBRL).

during Kenyon's excavations in 1954, showing the cut of Trench I open since 1952. When Boer visited Tell es-Sultan, Kenyon's excavations in Trench I had already exposed the whole sequence of Bronze Age fortifications (Kenyon 1953, 8–10; idem 1954a, 47, 58–

60). In the adjacent Squares DI and FI they had brought to light the Pre-Pottery Neolithic B layers,[2] exposing a settlement characterized by houses of a considerable size with both walls and floors covered with a smooth lime surface, by burials beneath the floors (as the

Figure 6.3: General view of the site of Tell es-Sultan from the Mount of Temptation (Jebel Quruntul) in 1954. Note the deep cut of Kenyon's Trench I across the western side of the mound (white arrow), and the refugee camp located next to the northern side.

ones portrayed in the photograph taken by Boer; see Figure 6.13 in the contribution of Bocquentin and Wagemakers in this chapter), and by plastered skulls associated with funerary rituals (Kenyon 1957, 60–64; idem 1981, plates 50b–59c). These houses had a multi-room rectangular plan, showing a main room with inner partitions constructed with cross-walls (opened both along the central axis and against the side-walls), and adjoining storage bins, as well as floors laid upon a bed of reeds, and inner walls and floors refined by burnished coloured plaster (Kenyon 1957, 52–56). Characteristic sun-dried, handmade, cigar-shaped mudbricks were used, showing a herringbone pattern of thumb-impressions on the surface, laid as stretchers and set in thick layers of clay (Kenyon 1981, plates 115–116a, 138b–c, 170a).

When Boer visited the site in March 1954, many other areas were under investigation apart from Trench I and Squares DI and FI (Kenyon 1954a):

namely Squares EI–EII, opened inside the huge North-Eastern Trench excavated by Garstang, where they continued the examination of the earliest Pre-Pottery Neolithic layers;[3] Square EIII, south of Garstang's Trench, where they examined the lay-out of the Early Bronze Age city; Squares HII–HIII, located on the eastern slope of the Spring Hill (which had already been extensively excavated by Sellin and Watzinger's and Garstang's expeditions), where a few Middle Bronze Age houses, positioned along a street, were excavated, as well as a flimsy, superimposed Late Bronze Age floor with an oven (which was the first identification of Late Bronze Age layers during Kenyon's excavations); Square MI, opened at about 30 metres north of Trench I, enlarging a pre-existing trench where the Germans and Garstang had worked previously, in which they investigated both Early Bronze Age and Pottery Neolithic layers; and, finally, Trench II and Trench

Figure 6.4: The refugee camp north of Tell es-Sultan during Boer's visit at the site in 1954; in the foreground, the northern slope of the tell.

III, opened across the northern and the southern sides of the tell respectively, in which the northern and southern boundaries of the ancient settlement could be established (Fig. 6.4).

Pilgrims and travellers from the Late Roman period to the Renaissance

Because of its religious role and significance, the site of Tell es-Sultan, and, more extensively, the Jericho Oasis, attracted pilgrims and travellers well before the twentieth century, in fact since late antiquity. Travellers started visiting Jericho during the Late Roman and Byzantine Periods as one of the major holy places in Palestine (Hunt 1982). It was mentioned by the Pilgrim of Bordeaux in 333 CE, as well as pilgrims Egeria (381–384 CE), Paula (404 CE), the archdeacon Theodosius (530 CE), and the Anonymous Pilgrim from Piacenza (570 CE). Each of them has left a written account of the places and the numerous churches and monasteries they visited in the Oasis, among which was the church 'Ain es-Sultan, built near the Elisha's Spring, east of the ancient site of Tell es-Sultan.

After the transit of the Persian army in 614 and the arrival of the Arabs in 638, Jericho fell into decline, which meant that in 670 the French pilgrim Arculf saw nothing but ruins there. When the Crusaders occupied Palestine in 1099, Jericho was nothing more than a 'Saracen Village', as defined by the Russian abbot Daniel in 1106–1107. After the Crusaders had gone, Jericho once again fell into decline and was reduced to a small hamlet, due to the perilous nature of its surroundings: travellers, who visited the Oasis during the Late Medieval and Renaissance Period, recorded a few houses, probably belonging to the village of 'Ain Hajla, or the remains of the Byzantine centre of Tell el-Hassan, a small cluster of houses grouped around a tower. Since the Middle and Late Islamic Periods the site of Tell es-Sultan itself was abandoned definitively and was reduced to a heap of ruins. Nonetheless, memory of it was preserved.

Travellers and pioneer archaeologists of the eighteenth and nineteenth centuries

European travellers began to visit Jericho from the seventeenth century onwards. It was Napoleon's campaign to Egypt and the Southern Levant (1798–1799) that launched journeys throughout the Near East for the sake of exploration. The nineteenth century thus saw a growing number of European and also American voyagers visiting the Near East, they would often be artists, painters and photographers, who would leave precious descriptions and information about ancient sites and monuments.[4] The American biblical scholar E. Robinson (1794–1863) opened the way for a modern approach to biblical topography. He made his first trip to Palestine in 1838, and a second trip in 1852, together with his pupil E. Smith: they identified more than 100 sites, and they also visited Tell es-Sultan, identifying it with biblical Jericho (Robinson and Smith 1856).

The foundation in 1865 of the *Palestine Exploration Fund* (PEF), and its aim of 'promoting research into the archaeology and history, manners and customs and culture, topography, geology and natural sciences of biblical Palestine and the Levant' (Bliss 1906, viii), launched a new phase of exploration in Palestine, involving not only individual researchers, but teams of specialists supported by the Royal Engineers of the British War Office (King 1983, 7; Moorey 1991, 19).[5]

C. Warren's (1868–1869) and J. F. Bliss' (1894) soundings

The first preliminary excavations at Tell es-Sultan were undertaken in 1868, within the framework of activities carried out in the Southern Levant by the newly born PEF, by Captain C. Warren (1840–1927), an officer of the Corps of Royal Engineers.[6] He cut the site with east-west trenches of 2.4 metres wide and six metres deep, destroying the double mudbrick city wall on the southern edge of the tell, and missing the Pre-Pottery Neolithic Tower in Kenyon's Trench I by less than one metre. Warren's excavations at Tell es-Sultan did not produce any archaeological results, which led him to conclude that the site lacked any proper historical interest (Warren 1869a; idem 1869b, 14–16).

Investigations at Tell es-Sultan were subsequently renewed in 1894, again on behalf of the PEF, by F. J.

Bliss (1857–1939), who made soundings at the bottom of the tell and – according to the biblical perspective current at that time – believed to have found the remains of the mudbrick walls which 'tumbled down at the sound of Joshua's trumpets' (Bliss 1894, 175–77; King 1983, 20–23).

The first systematic excavation carried out by the Austro-German Expedition directed by E. Sellin and C. Watzinger (1907–1909)

Renewed archaeological activities at Tell es-Sultan were supported at the beginning of the twentieth century by the *Deutsche Palästina Verein* (DPV), a German cultural institution founded in 1877. Two of its members, the biblical scholar E. Sellin (1867–1946) and the classic archaeologist C. Watzinger (1877–1948), focused their interest on the Jericho Oasis, and resumed investigations at Tell es-Sultan with the support of *Deutsche Orient-Gesellschaft* (King 1983, 14–15, 46–47).

During the years 1907–1909 they undertook at Tell es-Sultan the first scientific and systematic archaeological excavation, which resulted in a detailed report within just a few years, complete with photographs and accurate architectural sections and plans (Fig. 6.5), whereby, for the first time, finds were arranged by periods and classes of evidence (Sellin, Watzinger and Langenegger 1908; Sellin, Watzinger and Nöldecke 1909; Sellin and Watzinger 1913).

The Austro-German Expedition excavated the tell extensively (Fig. 6.6). The main results of these excavations were: the discovery of the EB II–III city walls made of sun-dried mudbricks along the summit of the mound; the excavation of the MB III rampart at the bottom,[7] consisting of a monumental structure made out of big limestone blocks (the so-called 'Cyclopean Wall'); the exploration of the EB III residential quarter on the northern plateau; the excavation of superimposed buildings (from the Iron Age down to Early Bronze Age) on the top and western side of the *Quellhügel* (the Spring Hill). Furthermore, two east-west trenches were cut across the site north and south of the Spring Hill, reaching, in some spots, the deepest Early Bronze Age layers. Another achievement of the Austro-German excavations was the establishment of an Iron Age sequence on

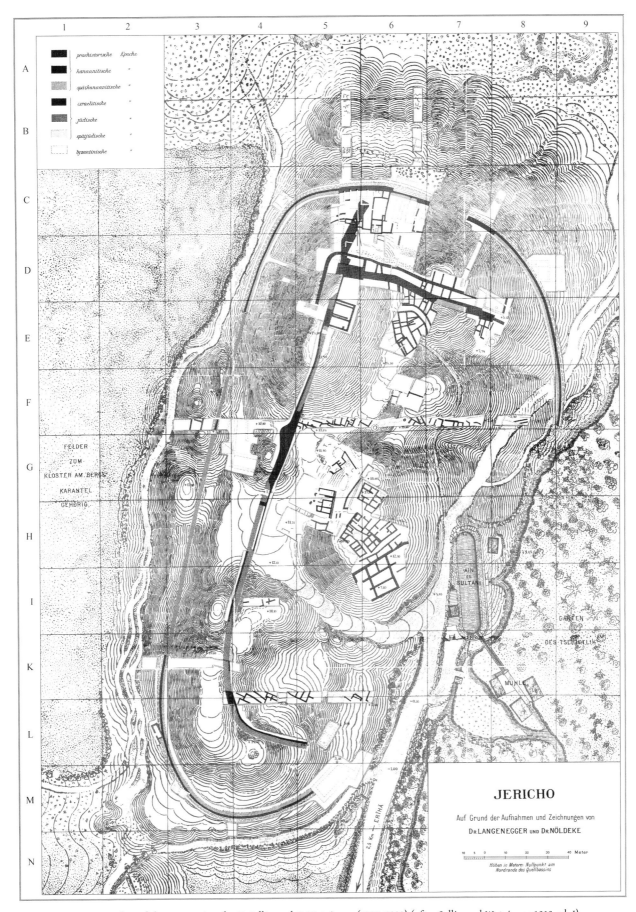

Figure 6.5: *Plan of the excavations by E. Sellin and C. Watzinger (1907-1909) (after Sellin and Watzinger 1913, pl. I).*

Figure 6.6: General view from the west of Tell es-Sultan during the Austro-German excavations in 1908 (after Sellin and Watzinger 1913, pl. 1a).

the eastern slope of the Spring Hill, which was later reassessed by M. and H. Weippert (1976), suggesting that Jericho was occupied continuously from the tenth to the sixth century BCE.

A periodisation of the site was also developed, which comprehended the *prähistorische, kanaanitische, israelitische* and *jüdische* periods. The methodology employed in constructing the chronological grid was very advanced for that time, but the historical reading of it was affected in some instances by the biblical narratives, which led them to adopt an incorrect chronological sequence: they attributed the Cyclopean Wall to the Israelites and the double mudbrick city wall to the Canaanite city conquered by Joshua, according to the biblical account (Nigro 2004, 224–25). Nonetheless, in the light of W. F. Albright's results at Tell Beit Mirsim, C. Watzinger later rectified his original chronological setting (with remarkable, intellectual honesty), suggesting an almost exact attribution of the Cyclopean Wall to Middle Bronze III, and of the double mudbrick city wall to the Early Bronze III (Watzinger 1926).

The first British Expedition carried out by J. Garstang (1930–1936)

Archaeological excavations at Tell es-Sultan were resumed between the years of 1930 and 1936 by J. Garstang (1876–1956), on behalf of Liverpool University and under Sir Charles Marston's patronage,[8] its major aim being to verify Watzinger's claims concerning the chronology of the mudbrick fortifications encompassing the summit of the tell, and demonstrating

the reliability of the biblical account in the Book of Joshua (Garstang 1927; idem 1930). At that time Palestine was under the British Mandatory Government and a Department of Antiquities had been set up in 1920.[9]

The British Expedition led by Garstang began a systematic exploration of the tell, cutting a series of trenches across the line of the double mudbrick city wall to check the chronology of the Jericho fortifications (Fig. 6.7; Garstang 1930; idem 1931; idem 1932, 6–15). Garstang also cut a big trench on the north-eastern plateau of the mound (Garstang, Droop and Crowfoot 1935; Garstang, Ben-Dor and Fitzgerald 1936), achieving two major results: for the first time an archaeologist exposed and identified the Neolithic layers at the site, the period in which Jericho was one of the most significant sites of the whole Levant (Mesolithic layers were also reached in small sounding); secondly, he investigated the Early Bronze Age layers covering a large area, offering a clear and coherent picture of the Early Bronze Age I village (Fig. 6.8), and of the Early Bronze Age II–III fortified town. Part of the earliest Middle Bronze Age I fortifications, together with a huge mudbrick tower (the so-called 'Eastern Tower') facing the spring of 'Ain es-Sultan, and the Middle and Late Bronze Age buildings on the eastern side of Spring Hill, were also brought to light by Garstang's expedition (Garstang 1932, 15–17; idem 1933, 41–42; idem 1934, 99–130). Finally, he discovered the large necropolis west and north of the site, excavating a series of family tombs from the Early, Middle and Late Bronze Ages, among which is the renowned EB I–III Tomb A (Fig. 6.9; Garstang 1932, 18–21, 41–54; idem 1933, 4–40).

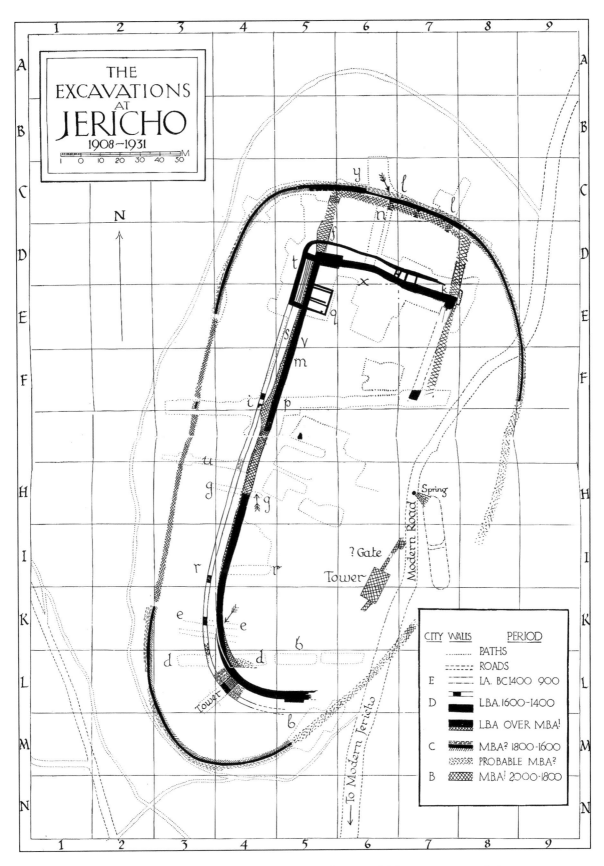

Figure 6.7: Plan of the excavations by J. Garstang (1930–1936) (after Garstang 1931, pl. I).

Figure 6.8: Tell es-Sultan: work at the EB I (3300–3000 BCE) village in Garstang's North-Eastern Trench at the time of Garstang's excavations in 1936 (Courtesy of the Palestine Exploration Fund, London).

Figure 6.9: General view from the west of Tell es-Sultan during Garstang's excavations in 1931; in the foreground, the necropolis with the cut of the Early Bronze Age Tomb A excavated by J. Garstang (Courtesy of the Palestine Exploration Fund, London).

Garstang's expedition thus revealed very important aspects of the multi-stratified history of the site. Nonetheless, in light of the biblical controversy, Garstang eventually attributed the double mudbrick city wall to the Late Bronze Age, thus relating this city wall to the one destroyed by Joshua according to the biblical narrative (Garstang 1935), and he never changed his mind on this subject. The results of Kenyon's excavations would later demonstrate that this interpretation was mistaken (see above).

Archaeological activities during the Israeli administration (1967–1993)

After the Six Days War (1967), the West Bank fell under Israeli control and the administration of the archaeological activities was taken over by Israeli institutions (Greenberg and Keinan 2009, 3–10). During the 25 years of Israeli control (1967–1993), the Jericho Oasis was surveyed intensively. Tell es-Sultan became one of Israel's National Parks, and was opened to the public in 1984 and exploited as a tourist site (although this caused some severe damage to the monuments on the site itself): a fence was put around the site; a tourist path was laid down; a shade shelter for tourists was built at the highest spot of the site; and some facilities (such as toilets and a parking area) were also set up.

A sounding directed by S. Riklin was conducted at Tell es-Sultan in 1992, on behalf of the Staff Officer for Judea and Samaria, on the west side of the mound south of Kenyon's Trench I (Riklin 1996): it brought to light a stretch of the double mudbrick city wall, which had already been traced along the summit of the mound in 1907–1909 by Sellin and Watzinger.

The Italian-Palestinian Expedition (1997–2012), and the archaeological park of the Jericho Oasis

After the Oslo (1993) and Madrid (1994) Peace Agreements, the district of Ariha was handed back to the Palestinian National Authority. Monuments, antiquities and other items of cultural heritage in the Jericho area thus fell under the administration of the Department of Antiquities and Cultural Heritage (MOTA-DACH) of the PNA.[10]

In 1997 this Department and 'La Sapienza' University in Rome started a new project of excavation, restoration and rehabilitation at the site of Tell es-Sultan (Fig. 6.10). A preliminary survey was carried out in the oasis in the area east of Tell es-Sultan by the joint Italian-Palestinian Expedition. Since then excavation and restoration works were carried out jointly at Tell es-Sultan during eight seasons (1997–2000, 2009–2012), with an interruption between 2000 and 2009, during which, however, research and work on the publication continued steadily. In 2005 and 2008 two international workshops on site management, conservation and sustainable development of Tell es-Sultan were organized in Ariha.

Excavations were resumed in fourteen areas of the site, mainly focusing on the Bronze Age city fortifications and residential quarters. The basic contribution of the Italian-Palestinian Expedition has been to present an overall periodisation of the site, re-examining and matching data produced by all the previous expeditions. In addition, some important monuments of the Early and Middle Bronze Age city were uncovered, both on the summit and along the southern and eastern edge of the tell (Marchetti and Nigro 1998; idem 2000; Nigro and Taha 2009; Nigro *et al.* 2011). The Italian-Palestinian Expedition continued the excavation of the Early Bronze Age quarter on the northern plateau, and the exploration of the Early Bronze Age III double fortification wall – the double mudbrick city wall – at the south-western corner of the site; it unearthed the Early Bronze Age III Royal Palace on the Spring Hill (Fig. 6.11), and excavated a Middle Bronze Age I built up tomb underneath it, which yielded a scarab inscribed with the ancient Canaanite name of the city (*Ruha*) in hieroglyphs characters (Nigro 2009). It also brought to light the Middle Bronze Age I–II defence tower A1 and a stretch of the Middle Bronze Age III Cyclopean Wall at the southern foot of the tell, as well as uncovered the imposing Middle Bronze Age II Curvilinear Stone Structure (Fig. 6.12). Finally, it identified the Bronze Age Lower City south and east of the mound (including the spring).

In the meantime, a new Pilot Project was announced by Rome 'La Sapienza' Expedition during the 2005 Workshop, called PADIS (The Palestine Archaeological Databank and Information System), which aims to create a reliable and accurate catalogue of archaeological sites in the West Bank. The project

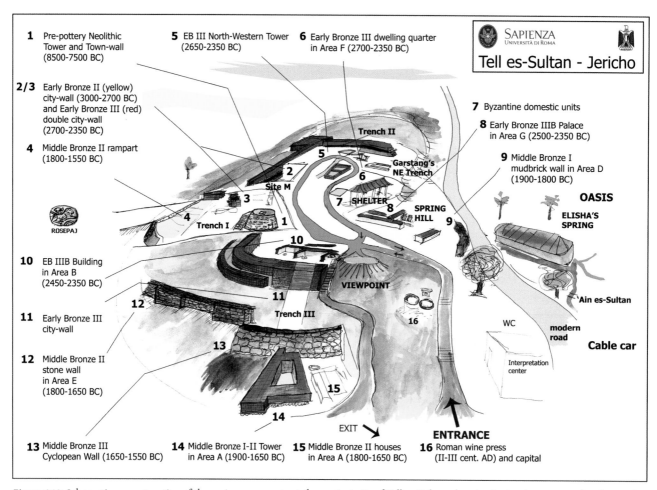

Tell es-Sultan - Jericho
SAPIENZA — Università di Roma

1 Pre-pottery Neolithic Tower and Town-wall (8500-7500 BC)

2/3 Early Bronze II (yellow) city-wall (3000-2700 BC) and Early Bronze III (red) double city-wall (2700-2350 BC)

4 Middle Bronze II rampart (1800-1550 BC)

5 EB III North-Western Tower (2650-2350 BC)

6 Early Bronze III dwelling quarter in Area F (2700-2350 BC)

7 Byzantine domestic units

8 Early Bronze IIIB Palace in Area G (2500-2350 BC)

9 Middle Bronze I mudbrick wall in Area D (1900-1800 BC)

10 EB IIIB Building in Area B (2450-2350 BC)

11 Early Bronze III city-wall

12 Middle Bronze II stone wall in Area E (1800-1650 BC)

13 Middle Bronze III Cyclopean Wall (1650-1550 BC)

14 Middle Bronze I-II Tower in Area A (1900-1650 BC)

15 Middle Bronze II houses in Area A (1800-1650 BC)

16 Roman wine press (II-III cent. AD) and capital

ROSEPAJ

Trench II · Trench I · Site M · Garstang's NE Trench · SHELTER · SPRING HILL · VIEWPOINT · Trench III · OASIS · ELISHA'S SPRING · Ain es-Sultan · WC · modern road · Cable car · Interpretation center · EXIT · ENTRANCE

Figure 6.10: Schematic reconstruction of the main monuments at the ancient site of Tell es-Sultan; drawing by L. Nigro; copyright of Rome "La Sapienza" Expedition to Palestine and Jordan (www.lasapienzatojericho.it).

Figure 6.11: Tell es-Sultan: work in EB IIIB (2500–2350 BCE) Palace G, on the eastern flank of the Spring Hill, during the Italian-Palestinian excavations in 2010; in the background, the Mount of Temptation (Jebel Quruntul) (copyright of Rome "La Sapienza" Expedition to Palestine and Jordan).

Figure 6.12: General view of the site of Tell es-Sultan from south, with the Middle Bronze Age (1900–1550 BCE) fortifications excavated by the Italian-Palestinian Expedition at the southern side of the tell in years 2009–2011 (copyright of Rome "La Sapienza" Expedition to Palestine and Jordan).

is now in its first stage consisting of the publication of the volume *Archaeological Heritage in the Jericho Oasis. A systematic catalogue of archaeological sites for the sake of their protection and cultural valorization* (Nigro, Sala and Taha 2011), which is a comprehensive listing of the archaeological and historic-cultural sites in the Jericho Oasis from pre-historic to modern times, thus establishing their protection and conservation.

A constant endeavour is being carried out by the MOTA-DACH to protect all of the archaeological and historical monuments in the Jericho Oasis from any modern agricultural and building activities, while excavations are currently carried out by the Italian-Palestinian Expedition at Tell es-Sultan, which now forms the core of one of the two archaeological parks of the Jericho Oasis. Each year around 250,000 tourists continue to visit the ancient mound of Tell es-Sultan. Many more than in 1954, when Boer and his fellow students of the École Biblique visited Kenyon's excavations at the site.

Acknowledgements

I wish to address a special thanks to both Prof. Lorenzo Nigro and Dr. Hamdan Taha, directors of the Italian-Palestinian Expedition to Tell es-Sultan/ancient Jericho, and to all the staff of the Palestinian MOTA-DACH for their support and hospitality during the joint work carried out at Tell es-Sultan by the Italian-Palestinian Expedition, in which the present author has participated since 2005.

Notes

1   Wheeler's excavation method was based upon square probes of five by five metres with preserved baulks of one metre, which ensured safe, readable vertical sections. Sections were then carefully drawn in order to reconstruct the exact stratigraphic chronological sequence of each spot of the site.

2   During this campaign, Pre-Pottery Neolithic A layers were also reached (Kenyon 1954a, 47–53).

3   Here Garstang had extensively exposed the uppermost
    PPNB layers and also reached the underlying PPNA
    layers until the Mesolithic in a small sounding (Garstang,
    Droop and Crowfoot 1935, 166–67; Garstang, Ben-Dor
    and Fitzgerald 1936, 67–70).

4   Among the best-renowned contributions are the
    descriptions by Charles Wilson (1836–1905) and
    photographic collections by James Robertson (1813–
    1888) in the second half of the nineteenth century.

5   Among the major enterprises of the newly born PEF was
    The Survey of Western Palestine, set up under the direction
    of Marquess F. W. R. Stewart (1805–1872), followed by
    Lieutenant C. R. Conder (1848–1910) and Lieutenant
    H. H. Kitchener (1850–1916), lasting from 1871 to 1878
    (King 1983, 7–8), and ending up in the publication of
    a map of the Southern Levant in 1880, and of the nine
    volumes of *Memoirs* edited in 1881–1886. During the
    survey about 9,000 Arab toponyms were registered,
    many of them for the first time, providing the basis for
    future work on topography and historical geography of
    ancient Palestine. Many sites in the Jericho Oasis were
    recorded in the *Survey*, including Tell es-Sultan itself,
    identified with biblical Jericho.

6   He carried out his probes with the same techniques used
    for digging tunnels employed in military operations,
    as he had done in Jerusalem during the previous year.

7   This massive wall was thought to be a freestanding
    structure by Sellin and Watzinger and its function
    as the inner retaining wall of the Middle Bronze Age
    III (1650–1550 BCE) rampart has subsequently been
    clarified by the Italian-Palestinian Expedition in the
    years 1997–2000 (Marchetti and Nigro 1998, 135–54;
    2000, 217–18; Nigro and Taha 2009, 734).

8   For a general presentation of the excavation results
    see Garstang and Garstang 1948.

9   The British Mandatory Department of Antiquities
    was established in 1920, and the law of antiquities
    was sanctioned in 1929. Afterwards, the Palestine
    Archaeological Museum (nowadays called the
    Rockefeller Archaeological Museum) was built in East
    Jerusalem and opened in 1938, to house the collection
    of artefacts discovered in the excavations carried out
    in Palestine during the British Mandate (1920–1948).

10 A dramatic moment coincided with the political hiatus
    in 1993–1994, when Israeli authorities abandoned
    territorial control, and the absence of any law caused
    some tragic damages to the archaeological sites: for
    instance, a large part of the Middle Bronze II Lower
    Town of the ancient Canaanite city of Tell es-Sultan
    was cleared off south of the tell by bulldozing activities
    for the realization of a parking area. Especially the
    necropolis of Tell es-Sultan suffered severe looting.

I. W. Cornwall at Tell es-Sultan: Pioneer in Archaeothanatology

Fanny Bocquentin and Bart Wagemakers

In the latest annual report of her archaeological campaign at Tell es-Sultan, Kathleen M. Kenyon notes explicitly the interest in her excavations shown by the members of the École Biblique de St Étienne in Jerusalem. During the campaign directed by Kenyon from 1952 until 1958, the fathers (including Roland de Vaux) and students from the institute, also known as the *École Biblique et Archéologique Française de Jérusalem*, used to visit the site each year (Kenyon 1960b, 88). Leo Boer was amongst those students, joining the group on their annual visit of de Vaux on 10 March 1954. During his visit of Tell es-Sultan, Boer was an unintentional witness to the beginning of a new approach to studying human remains at an archaeological site. In this chapter we will examine a photograph taken by Boer that illustrates the significant contribution Dr. I. W. Cornwall has made to the development of funerary archaeology.

Leo Boer at Tell es-Sultan

At Tell es-Sultan, Kenyon welcomed the group and showed them around the site. Boer writes in his diary that 'the whole situation at Jericho is so complicated and requires so much study that I have to confess that I do not understand it quite well enough. The excavation is immense. They have already reached a depth of 15 metres. They have found a Neolithic layer. A skeleton was exposed *in situ*. It is certain that Jericho will be the touchstone for the chronology of the whole of Palestinian archaeology, especially concerning the early periods. Final results have not yet been published and therefore it is better not to speculate at this moment. Anyway, the excavations have not cleared up the conquest by Joshua.'

Despite it not being a lengthy account and the fact that Boer admits that the story was too complicated for him, it contains some useful details that will be discussed later on. However, the content of the account seems to be consistent with Kenyon's reports which were published after Boer's visit to the site. Kenyon writes that the excavating team of 1954 found a wall of which the foundations were laid at a depth of 14.5 metres from the surface (Kenyon 1954a, 51; idem 1957, 67). The digging activities during that year concerned mainly the Neolithic period (Kenyon 1954a, 47–58) and did not supply any relevant information about the conquest of Jericho by Joshua (Kenyon 1954a, 61; idem 1954b, 82). Besides, Kenyon maintained that Jericho could be considered the oldest town in the world (Kenyon 1954b, 76). In that way the chronology of this city was imminent for Palestinian archaeology at that time.

Beside his short note on the excavation at Tell es-Sultan, Boer also took a photograph during his visit of the site (Fig. 6.13). Although Kenyon did not appreciate hasty, amateur photography of excavations at all – in her opinion 'views are taken of inadequately prepared subjects, the view does not cover the subject properly, the scale is not correctly aligned, and many similar faults creep in' (Kenyon 1956b, 135) – Boer's picture gives us an interesting insight into the way human remains were being studied at Tell es-Sultan in 1954.

The photograph: skeleton remains and stone artefacts

The picture was taken from a high position, the top of which shows two low wall structures. In the middle of the photograph a young local labourer is posing for Boer's photograph. On the boy's right-hand side, adjacent to one of the walls, skeleton remains are lying *in situ*. On his left-hand side, beneath the floor level on which the boy is standing, three stone artefacts can be seen lying next to each other.

There are several reasons for presuming that we are looking at a stratum that belongs to the Neolithic period. First of all, Boer's account of what he saw implies a connection between the Neolithic layer that was found and the skeleton that was still exposed *in situ*. Furthermore, the annual report states that the archaeological activities during the 1954 campaign were mainly related to the Pre-Pottery Neolithic period (PPN). It is therefore most probable that the bones and artefacts also belong to that period. In that case they must be linked to the PPN B period, because the PPN A phase in Tell es-Sultan was not revealed until 1956 (Kenyon 1956a, 72; idem 1956c, 188–89; idem 1957, 70). This dating seems to be supported by the identification of two of the artefacts as trough querns (Fig. 6.13). In total, 36 querns or fragments of this type were found at PPN B levels; only one item was excavated in a PPN A layer (Dorrell 1983, 534).[1] Since trough querns are typically PPN B, the presence of two specimens near the skeleton remains strengthens the supposition of a PPN B dating for these bones in the first instance.

Dating and locating the skeleton remains

We are able to determine the exact location of the spot where Boer saw these bones and artefacts. Comparing Boer's photograph (Fig. 6.14B) with one taken by Cornwall, that was published in 1956 (Fig. 6.14A, Cornwall 1956a, plate XX, 4B; Kenyon 1981, plate 61A), it becomes clear that they both show the same skeleton remains. The remains in both photos clearly show similarities as well as differences. There are two main explanations for the differences. First of all, the pictures were taken from a different angle, which causes a distortion of the position of the bones. Secondly, each photo shows a different phase of the removal of the bones, as will be explained below. On the other hand, the contours of the debris in both pictures are very similar and some of the bones are visible in both of them, as the added numbers in Figures 6.14A and 6.14B show.

Figure 6.13: The photograph Leo Boer took while sightseeing at Tell es-Sultan on 10 March 1954. The two white-coloured stone artefacts on the left-hand side of the boy are typical PPN B trough querns. The third artefact might be a grinding stone.

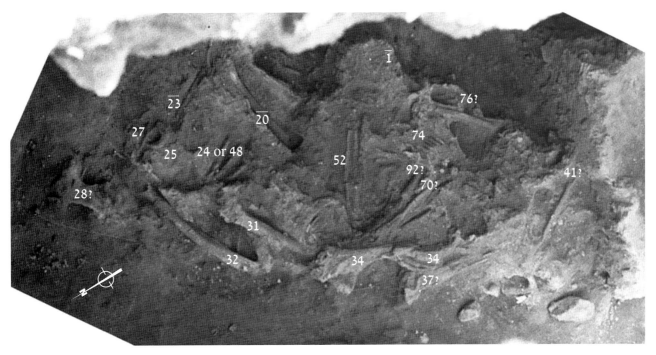

Figures 6.14A and B: Top (6.14A): photograph of Grave FI 3-4 in F I XVII.xxxi (Courtesy of the Council for British Research in the Levant, CBRL). Below (6.14B): photograph of the same skeleton remains taken by Boer. The numbers in both photographs are added by the authors of this article (according to Figure 6.17). Over lined numbers show imprints left on the ground after removal of bones.

According to the caption of Cornwall's published photograph, the remains were found at Square FI and relate to stage XVII A.xxxi (Cornwall 1956a, plate XX, 4B; Kenyon 1981, plate 61A). A plan of Square FI in Kenyon's field notes – nowadays held in the archives of the Museum of Archaeology and Anthropology (MAA) at the University of Cambridge – reveals the exact location where the burials concerned were found (Fig. 6.15). The wall, west of which the bones were found, has been numbered as wall 18 in the final publication (Fig. 6.16). The level of F 4.22b, in which these skeleton remains are located, as mentioned in the field notes, correspond to stage XVII.xxxi in the final publication.

Taking into account the position of the bones drawn by Cornwall (Fig. 6.17), we can conclude that

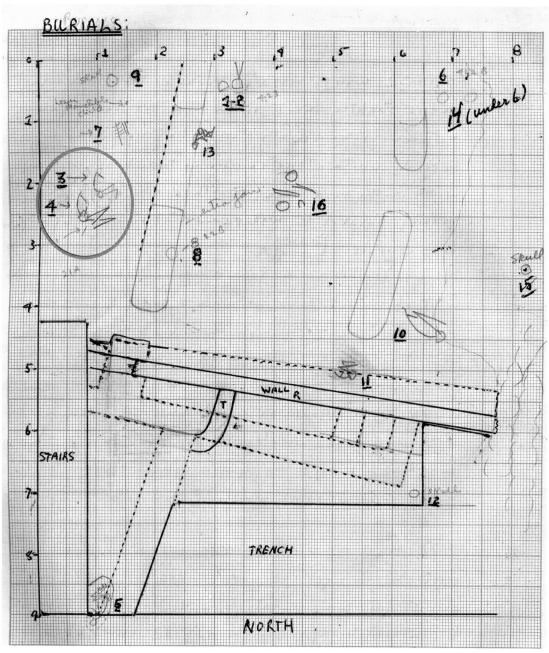

Figure 6.15: Plan of square FI in the Kenyon field notes (book F, page 50). The concerning skeleton remains are labelled as number three and four at top left (Courtesy of the Museum of Archaeology & Anthropology, Cambridge, archive number BR6/3/1).

Boer was standing on the east baulk, mentioned in another plan of FI in the field notes (BR6/3/1, book F, 46), and which runs parallel in an easterly direction along wall 18. In the first instance, it is hard to believe that Boer took his photograph from this point, because the wall structures visible in his picture do not match the walls drawn in Figure 6.16. When reading the description of Kenyon, it becomes clear that in stage XVII this specific part of the square was a bricky fill (Kenyon 1981, Text, 79–80).[2] The drawings of the east-west cross sections (Kenyon 1981, plates, 236, 240c, and 240d) confirm that the bones were discovered on the east side of wall 18. It can probably be ascertained that the stone artefacts lie on the floor of stage XVI.

Having located the human remains and stone artefacts, we will now focus on the way these remains were studied and excavated in March 1954.

Excavating human remains at locus FI at Tell es-Sultan in the early 1950s

During the 1954 campaign a large number of skeleton remains were found beneath the floors of Neolithic houses in Squares DI, FI and EI. As the remains were tremendously fragile, it was almost impossible to excavate them without causing damage. For that reason, arrangements were made for Ian Cornwall of the Institute of Archaeology in London to fly to

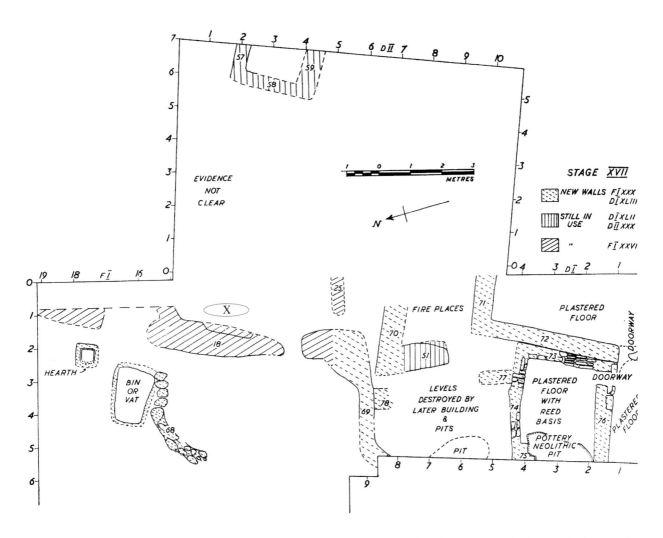

Figure 6.16: Plan of loci FI, DI, DII in stage XVII (Courtesy of the Council for British Research in the Levant, CBRL). The X marks the spot where the authors think that the skeleton remains were found.

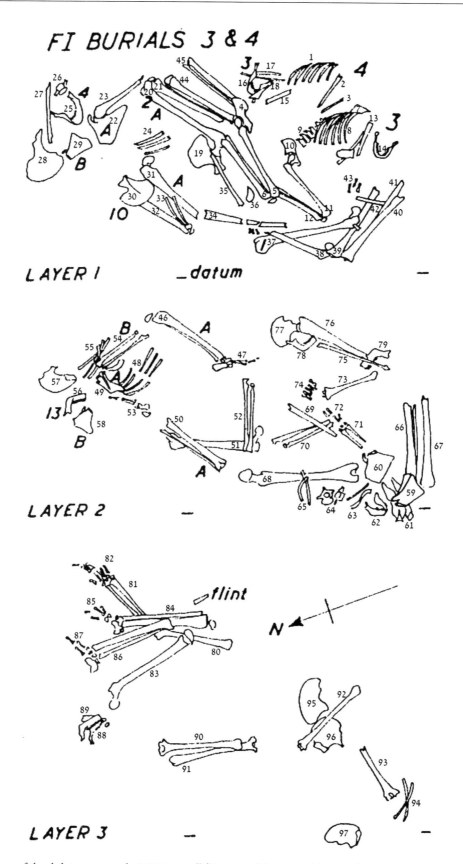

Figure 6.17: Drawings of the skeleton remains by I. W. Cornwall (Courtesy of the Council for British Research in the Levant, CBRL). The small numbers are added by the authors, the other ones are originals.

Transjordan immediately. He spent a fortnight at Tell es-Sultan studying and measuring the remains *in situ* (Kenyon 1954a, 48–49; Cornwall 1956a, 111). Before the bones were studied and – if possible – measured, they were left undisturbed. When Cornwall first visited the site, he noticed that 'several areas in which burials occurred had been painstakingly cleared already and the bones exposed and cleaned for photography' (Cornwall 1956a, 112).

The study of the remains caused some serious delay to the campaign, because of the large quantity of them and because of the intensive procedure required for studying them. Before measurements could be taken, it was necessary to let the bones dry to improve their hardness so they could be cleared from the surrounding earth without incurring further damage. After that the bones were impregnated with an aqueous emulsion before the excavators were able to lift them out (Cornwall 1956a, 111–12; idem 1956b, 207–17).[3]

It should be emphasized that identification of bones *in situ* was complicated, especially concerning a complex burial like this one: 'Bones found under the floors and between the debris of houses at Tell es-Sultan were surrounded with extremely compacted earth, and even sticky when moist, while the bones were weak and crumbly, the shafts reasonably firm, though soft, but the articular ends extremely delicate' (Cornwall 1956a, 112). Grave FI 3-4, as photographed both by Cornwall and Boer, clearly demonstrates the poor state of preservation of the remains. The articular extremities as well as the shafts of the long bones are all mostly crushed; in some other areas smashed quantities of bones are perceptible but unidentifiable.

Ongoing work on grave FI 3-4 on 10 March 1954

While Boer visited the tell, grave FI 3-4 was being excavated. The picture taken by Boer is a unique document which shows the work in process. This burial, located in a pit cut into earlier levels and extending over an area of two by one metres, seemed to contain a tangled mass of human remains dispersed over several layers. From the many disarticulated leg- and pelvis bones, only two bodies stood out reasonably clearly from the rest. Those were labelled by Cornwall as 'Square F. I, Nos. 3 and 4' (Cornwall 1956a, 117;

idem 1981, 396). While excavating this group of bones, Cornwall distinguished three successive layers: a, b and c (renamed I, II, III in the final publication: Cornwall 1981, 405). Layer by layer the bones were cleaned, drawn and removed from its location. Boer's photograph demonstrates this procedure very well. At the moment of him taking the picture, the uppermost layer (a) was partly removed and the second layer (b) was in the course of being exposed. The published picture of grave FI 3-4 (Fig. 6.14A) shows layer a, but not fully exposed: the north-east part of the grave was excavated later and is still *in situ* in Boer's picture (Fig. 6.14B) where n° 25 (mandible), 27 (long bone) and probably 28 (coxae) can be recognised. N° 23 (humerus), by contrast, was already removed and we can still see in Boer's picture its imprints left on the ground as well as the negative of n° 20 (femur) and n°1 (thoracic cage).

The best-represented skeletons (named n° 3 and 4: cf. Figures 6.14A and 6.18) lying on their left side, were already lifted, just as the majority of the bones found at the southern part of the grave. Others are visible in both pictures: either exposed (n° 31: femur, 32: tibia?, 34: femur, 41: fibula) in Boer's picture or already partly removed (n° 37 femur). Finally, a few bones from layer b are partially discernible such as n° 52 (articulated forearm) and n° 74 (ribs?) and possibly others (cf. Fig. 6.14B).

The picture of Boer provides a strong testimony of advanced field methodology as employed by Cornwall. At that time, few digs, if any, benefited from such delicate handling of the graves. Moreover, Cornwall's field work was not only modern at that time but his general approach to studying human remains was definitively well suited to the interpretation of complex burials. It marks the beginning of a real interest in funerary archaeology.

Excavation and recording methods: the efficient 'serial section' technique

Considering the very bad state of preservation of the bones at Tell es-Sultan, Cornwall was therefore very much concerned about getting the maximum information *in situ*, including anthropological measurements. The bones were carefully exposed, documented, restored and finally lifted out one by one. He greatly benefited from a special team, dedicated to the examination of graves (diggers, a drawer, a photographer, and a person in charge of strengthening the bones *in situ* and removals), which demonstrates that Kenyon herself attached great significance to the burial issue.

Grave FI 3-4 caused specific difficulties, because of the commingling of the bones lying on each other to a certain depth, which led Cornwall to apply what he called the 'histological technique of serial sections' (Cornwall had a background in biology). Therefore, each layer of bones they exposed was drawn to scale on tracing paper and the drawings were superimposed (Cornwall 1956a, 118; idem 1981, 396). He hoped that by using this technique 'the exact relations of the remains found in each layer to those underneath would be shown and this would perhaps make it possible to assign bones to their proper owners' (Cornwall 1956a, 118). These words reveal Cornwall's main goal which was to understand the organisation of the pile of bones at the time of discovery: namely, to what degree the skeletons were disturbed, how and why. The drawings were not his sole source for answering those questions. As an excellent osteologist, Cornwall identified *in situ* a majority of the bones and noted down details of their anatomical relation.

Finally, despite the mass of commingled bones, Cornwall's articles reveal that he recognised an important number of anatomical segments. Fourteen clusters of bones are described by him (Fig. 6.18). The first four (n° 3, n° 4, A and B) were labelled by Cornwall while the other ten were labelled (from C to L) for the purpose of this article, as well as each set of bones was re-numbered (from 1 to 97) to gain clarity in the current description.

Individuals 3 and 4 were recognized by Cornwall as soon as the first layer started being exposed. They were labelled following on from the previous grave, which was discovered in sector FI with burials of individuals 1 and 2. Skeletons 3 and 4 are described as a pair of burials flexed on the left side and considerably disturbed. The detailed position of each of them is given, together with a list of bones that were likely to belong to them, along with some remarks on articular preservation or dislocation. One of these remarks is particular interesting as it gives the relative chronology of the two burials: 'the right leg [of n° 4] was almost complete, the knee over the ankle of n° 3, patella in position' (Cornwall 1956a, 118).

The right lower limb of skeleton A was exposed in layer a and thanks to the technique of 'serial sections' digging and drawing, its lower left limb was found lying exactly under the right one, in layer b. Assuming the body was buried on its left side, other bones, partially connected, were attributed to the same individual. Finally, dislocated bones 'quite out of position but, from their large size' were also 'attributable' to skeleton A (Cornwall 1956a, 118).

A pair of small scapula was considered being in primary position, and consequently testified of a body, skeleton B, lying on his back. Other small bones, found in the surrounding area, may also have belonged to this individual.

Two more individuals were buried there, according to Cornwall. Although no indication of their initial position is available, he provides very interesting descriptions. He identified a pair of femur, mutually reversed in position, together with a pair of tibia possibly belonging to the same individual (cluster C) but isolated from the rest of the skeleton. Beneath it, in layer b, another cluster of bones was found (cluster D) which included a pair of scapulae, loose ribs, vertebrae, clavicle, two disjointed tibia, one together with its fibula.

A seventh individual (cluster E) was recognized by Cornwall at the north-east corner of the grave, there were two lower legs, undisturbed and overlapping a complete right upper leg. According to him the remains belonged to a burial contracted to the right, with the head pointing to the south.

Finally, seven more isolated bone clusters are described lying in the middle of the grave in layers b and c: a possible pair of tibiae lying parallel to each other (cluster F), three cases of ulnae and radii still in correct articulation (clusters G, H, I), a pair of humeri side by side (cluster J), another pair of humeri (cluster K) possibly belonging to cluster I, and a disjointed pair of innominates (cluster L).

The efficiency of the field method chosen by Cornwall is obvious. From 'an apparently inextricably tangled mass of human remains' as first described by him (Cornwall 1956a, 117), a superimposition of several coherent anatomical segments appears, when using the 'serial sections' filter. Cornwall's expertise does not end here; the quality of his methodical interpretation of what he saw, is even more remarkable.

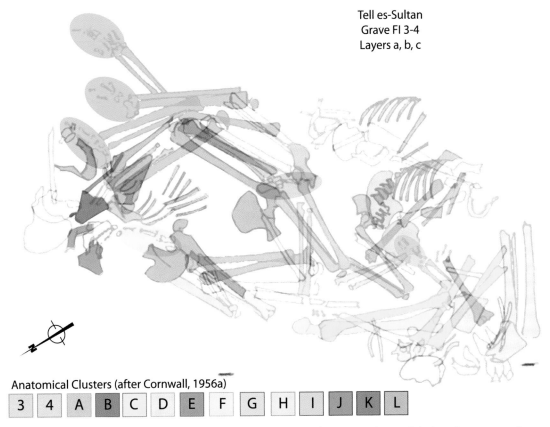

Tell es-Sultan
Grave FI 3-4
Layers a, b, c

Anatomical Clusters (after Cornwall, 1956a)

| 3 | 4 | A | B | C | D | E | F | G | H | I | J | K | L |

Figure 6.18: Anatomical clusters according to the description of Cornwall (1956a). The three layers of the burial are seen in the same re-fitted scheme. Each cluster has a different colour and a different label, see our text (drawing by F. Bocquentin).

Table 6.1: List of the anatomical clusters described by Cornwall and bones as identified in the drawings (cf. Figs 6.17 and 6.18).

CLUSTERS	BONES INVOLVED
N° 3	7, 8, 9, 10, 11, 12, 13, 14?
N° 4	1, 2, 3, 4, 5, 6
A	19, 20, 21, 22, 23, 24, 25?, 30?, 31?, 46, 47, 48, 49, 54
B	29, 55?, 56?, 58
C	37, 39, 40, 41, 68
D	59, 60, 63, 64, 65, 66, 67
E	80, 81, 82, 83, 84, 85, 86, 87
F	32, 50, 53?
G	52
H	70
I	71, 72
J	90, 91
K	92, 93
L	95, 96

Interpreting grave FI 3-4: decay processes and time span considerations

Commingled piles of bones are often interpreted in archaeology as secondary burials or ossuaries. Most of the time funerary acts – such as the wrapping of the body, the complex positioning of the corpse, or of perishable structures (wooden box, bed, etc.) – are not taken into consideration. These various elements can only be recognised and determined if the dig is performed by an anthropologist who is an expert in *archaeothanatology*.[4] But the knowledge derived from this specific taphonomic context due to corpse decay is currently still almost non-existent.

Nonetheless, Cornwall had a very pragmatic approach to interpreting the bone assemblage. Skeletons n° 3 and 4, articulated for a large part, gave him reasons to believe that they are the remains of previously disturbed primary burials. This explains why he was very careful and meticulous in looking for preserved anatomical segments while digging out the rest of the grave. Even though the two upper skeletons were relatively undisturbed, he concluded that, based on the anatomical clusters he identified, the disturbance concerned the whole assemblage and all three layers. Subsequently, Cornwall introduced a very important idea, namely that the deposit provided evidence for different events: 'It appears therefore, that the burial of these [n° 3 and 4], at least, must be subsequent to the major disturbances in the deeper layers. At the other end of the area there is nothing to show that the disturbance did not all take place on a single occasion, for all three layers are involved' (Cornwall 1956a, 119). This marks the introduction of a dynamic view of a funerary deposit. His description suggests at least four events: lower burials, disturbances, upper burials, disturbances. Nevertheless, the hypothesis of possible secondary deposits is not ignored but legitimately discredited: 'the fact that an originally orderly burial is discernible in many badly-disturbed cases suggests that the majority, at any rate, were not dismembered when first placed in the ground' (Cornwall 1956a, 120). Moreover, Cornwall noticed that limbs had been disturbed as units which kept a correct anatomical relation and that 'it scarcely seems likely…, that limb bones, or even two bones in the same segment of a limb, would remain articulated if decay of the body had proceeded so far as to permit separation of the parts of the pelvis or of mandibles from the skulls' (Cornwall 1956a, 120). Therefore, he had no doubt that the excavated pile of bones was not the initial organization of the deposit but was the result of later disturbances.

From the fact that crania were missing, even though nine isolated mandibles were unearthed, Cornwall presumed that the disturbances were caused by a deliberate re-opening of the grave in order to remove the skulls. Some explanations suggested for this practice include the idea that these skulls could have served as trophies or mementoes of the deceased (Kenyon 1954c, 108; idem 1971, 6; Cornwall 1956a, 119–20; idem 1981, 397–98) or the belief that, if the cranium was detached from the body, the ghost would not haunt its former body (Kenyon 1981, text, 78). These interpretations must be, of course, superseded by the very specific context of research. A year earlier, Kenyon had found at Tell es-Sultan the first

specimens of plastered skulls, re-modelled faces on human cranium, interpreted as the portrait-effigies of revered ancestors. Since then, other plastered skulls have been found in southern Levant PPN B sites (for a review: Bonogofsky 2006); their interpretation is still being debated (most recent articles: Stordeur and Khawam 2007; Testart 2008 and replies; Bocquentin 2013). However, the fact that some graves were re-opened in order to remove the skull at the end of the decay process is today recognised as a practice in this region during the Pre-pottery Neolithic and even earlier. Cornwall was the first to describe this process. It is worth noting that the time of removal was taken into consideration: 'that this grisly search took place not longer after the original burials than a few weeks at most is shown by the many parts displaced….,and yet still correctly articulated with their neares[t]…..Nevertheless decomposition of the bodies must have been fairly well advanced, otherwise how to account for separated innominate bones, femora and humeri separated from their respective distal fragments, reversed in relation to their fellows, and the numerous disarticulated mandibles?' (Cornwall 1956a, 119). Puzzled by the apparent contradiction of what he observed, he left the question unanswered. We can speculate about a possible explanation that the grave may have been re-opened several times, each corpse buried successively and each removal done one after the other, causing more and more disturbances over time on different types of articulation.

I. W. Cornwall: a vanguard field anthropologist or pioneer of archaeothanatology

Cornwall's approach to both the excavation and interpretation of human remains placed him at the forefront of funerary archaeology. Regrettably, as far as we know, his methodology remained practically unnoticed and the benefits of his work are only now being recognised. About ten years after Cornwall's innovative work at Tell es-Sultan, specific methodologies for handling archaeological graves began to develop (Leroi-Gourhan *et al.* 1962; Brothwell 1963). This field of funerary archaeology received a great deal of attention in France towards the end of the last century where systematic ways of study (field methods, vocabulary, population studies, and forensic considerations) were developed through workshops (Duday and Masset 1987; Duday *et al.* 1990; Castex *et al.* 1996), collective publications (e.g. Sellier and Masset 1990; Pereira 2013), field schools, and theoretical instruction. Today the field is well-established covering all chronological periods and known as 'field anthropology' ('anthropologie de terrain'), and was recently renamed as 'archaeothanatology' (Boulestin and Duday 2006; Duday 2009). This specific approach has, quite recently, been adopted more widely, also by the Anglo-Saxon research world (e.g. Roksandic 2002; Stutz 2003; Willis and Tayles 2009; Harris and Tayles 2012). For a better understanding of mortuary behaviour, human remains are the focal point of the study, as the corpse was for the burial ceremony. A great emphasis is laid on the spatial distribution of the bones and on their anatomical inter-relation. State of connection/dislocation forms one of the clues for interpretation. Taking into account the decay process of the corpse allows us to understand the evolution of the burial over time, and to re-construct the context of burial (initial position, possible envelope or ephemeral structures) and of later events (re-opening, removals, deliberate reorganisation or other kind of disturbances). The burial is not just studied for itself but also for reconstructing all the processes of handling the deceased from the moment of death to oblivion.

The manner in which Cornwall handled the graves at Tell es-Sultan clearly shows that his goals match modern objectives. The fact that he exposed the bones, layer by layer, identified them *in situ*, drew and numbered them (although it is unclear if he numbered them all *in situ* or at a later time, for the purpose of precise description) places him ahead of his time. The most remarkable aspect of his work is the way in which he referred to anatomical connections and disarticulations throughout the description of the grave. It led him to believe that the burials were all primary (i.e. corpses buried straight after death) but that major disturbances had occurred while the corpses were still in the process of decaying. In order to understand the original organisation of the grave he looked for preserved anatomical connections. It is worth noting that he also looked for coherent anatomical clusters, based on both spatial distribution of the remains and anthropological criteria (such as robustness and pairing of symmetrical bones). All

these aspects are still used today for interpreting plural burials. Cornwall also introduced the idea that different rates of decay of human articulations could be useful for assessing the time of the disturbances, particularly the time of removal of the skulls. The notion of enduring joints and labile joints is today the mainstay of archaeothanatology.

Cornwall has provided us with a very interesting description of the burial together with published data which is detailed enough to allow us to draw our own conclusions. We agree with his interpretation: grave FI 3-4 received primary burials, later disturbed for removal of the skulls. However, the removal of the skulls does not explain all the disturbances which he saw amongst the bones: a pair of long bones reversed, segments of skeleton pushed aside, disarticulation of most of the joints, etc. What we observe here is typical of collective burials where corpses are buried successively over a long period of time. During the use of the structure, skeletons were moved in order to free some space for the next ones. For Cornwall only the two upper skeletons were introduced at a later time in the grave. In fact, each burial may have been a different event, each time disturbing the previous deposits a bit more. Was a new death the occasion for removing the skull of the previous dead, or was the removal planned according to a funeral calendar? What is certain is that when the grave was opened the last time, it was done in order to take the skull of the (two) last skeleton(s).

The approach developed by Cornwall is not specific to burial FI 3-4. All graves dug at Tell es-Sultan in 1954 attest to his interest in burial practices and his goal to understand the evolution of the burial after deposits and observable disturbances have been made (Bocquentin 2013). Two years later, Cornwall published a book entitled *Bones for the archaeologist* (1956), which focused on comparative anatomy (human as well as animal) with a very interesting last chapter on 'study and interpretation'. It is a lesson of great value on the approach to field work. Some sentences in particular are noteworthy:

'apart from the information intrinsic to the collection as seen on the laboratory bench, there may be much to be gleaned from an examination of the material while it is still in position'...'photographs [must] be taken before anything is moved'...'there must be somebody present who knows enough about anatomy to notice anything out of the ordinary'...'each layer as it is exposed should be described verbally in the notebook'...'there is a chance that something, at first inexplicable, may lead to an eventual conclusion of importance, as to the state of the bodies when buried or disturbed, evidence of violent death, dislocations or other injuries or abnormalities. Once the bones have been lifted this evidence is lost if not noted and sufficiently recorded at the time'...'drawings on a sufficiently large scale are desirable'...'it is not enough to show that a particular bone is a femur. It should be clear that it is a right femur with its posterior aspect uppermost'...'there will often emerge results which constitute a contribution of real value to the excavation-report, and not merely a largely irrelevant Appendix'...'What is wanted is a more widespread interest among archaeologists in the bones material found on their excavations and closer liaison between excavators and osteologists, to their mutual benefit' (Cornwall 1956b, 238–39 and 245).

Therefore, Cornwall should be recognised as a fore-runner of modern funerary archaeology, a forgotten pioneer to whom we owe a debt of gratitude. Kenyon also deserves our appreciation as she gave Cornwall the opportunity to work in the field with a highly innovative approach which took an inordinate amount of valuable time.

Ackowledgemets

We are grateful to Imogen Gunn, Wendy Brown and Liz Haslemere of the Museum of Archaeology and Anthropology in Cambridge for their hospitality and help during our visits to the archives. We would also like to thank Rachael Sparks of the Institute of Archaeology Collections in London and Liora Kolska Horwitz of the Hebrew University in Jerusalem for providing records and information for this contribution.

Notes

1　In contrast with the assertion of Dorrell, Kenyon alleged that no trough querns were ever found in the PPN A phase in Tell es-Sultan (Kenyon 1993, 677).

2　Kenyon describes stage XVII as a bricky fill that was succeeded by new buildings in the whole area in the next stage. These skeleton remains were found in the mass of the fill (Kenyon 1981, Text, 77–78). The premise that the bones were not located at an occupation level seems to be confirmed by an observation from Cornwall. He noticed that 'the bodies were simply buried in the rubble and debris of their own houses, during a levelling of the site immediately following their deaths (Cornwall 1956a, 112; see also Kenyon 1954a, 48; idem 1956c, 186).

3　See Kurth 1981, 409 for complications from the hardening of human remains *in situ* during the campaigns 1955–1957 and 1957–1958.

4　Archaeothanatology is the reconstruction of decay process which altered the characteristics of the grave in order to determine the original burial context and infer acts linked to the management and treatment of the corpse and ultimately of the bone remains.

Bibliography of Tell es-Sultan (Jericho)

Bliss, F. J. 1894. "Notes on the Plain of Jericho." *Palestine Exploration Fund Quarterly. Quarterly Statements* 26:175–83.

Bliss, F. J. 1906. *The Development of Palestine Exploration.* London: Hodder and Stoughton.

Bocquentin, F. 2013. "Après la Mort, avant l'Oubli : le Statut des Crânes dans la Mémoire Collective au Néolithique Précéramique du Levant Sud." In *Une Archéologie des Temps Funéraires? Hommage à Jean Leclerc,* edited by G. Pereira. Special Issue of Les Nouvelles de l'Archéologie 132:54-59. Paris.

Bonogofsky, M. 2006. "Complexity in Context: Plain, Painted and Modeled Skulls from the Neolithic Middle East." In *Skull Collection, Modification, and Decoration,* edited by M. Bonogofsky, 15–28. Oxford: Archeopress.

Bouchain, J. 1999. *Endangered Cultural Heritage in the West Bank Governorates.* Ramallah: MOPIC.

Boulestin, B. and Duday, H. 2006. "Ethnology and Archaeology of Death: from the Illusion of References to the Use of a Terminology." *Archaeologia Polona* 44:149–69.

Brothwell, D. R. 1963. *Digging up Bones: the Excavation, Treatment and Study of Human Skeletal Remains.* London: British Museum.

Castex, D., Courtaud, P., Sellier, P., Duday, H. and Bruzek, J. (eds). 1996. *Les Ensembles Funéraires. Actes du Colloque "Méthodes d'Étude des Sépultures", Gujan-Mestras, Girond, 27-29 Septembre 1995.* Société d'Anthropologie de Paris, Bulletins et Mémoires de la Société d'Anthropologie de Paris, nouvelle série, tome 8, n° 3–4. Paris: Masson.

Conder, C. C. and Kitchener, H. H. 1881-1883. *The Survey of Western Palestine: Memoirs of the Topography, Orography, Hydrography, and Archaeology. Volume I-III.* London: Committee of the Palestine Exploration Fund.

Cornwall, I. W. 1956a. "The Pre-Pottery Neolithic Burials, Jericho." *Palestine Exploration Quarterly* 88:110–24.

Cornwall, I. W. 1956b. *Bones for the Archaeologist.* London: Phoenix House Ltd.

Cornwall, I. W. 1981. "The Pre-Pottery Neolithic Burials." In *Excavations at Jericho, Vol. III: The Architecture and Stratigraphy of the Tell. Text,* edited by K. M. Kenyon, 395–406. London: The British School of Archaeology in Jerusalem.

Dorrell, P. G. 1983. "Stone Vessels, Tools, and Objects." In *Excavations at Jericho, Vol. V: The Pottery Phases of the Tell and Others Finds,* edited by K. M. Kenyon and T. H. Holland, 487–575. London: British School of Archaeology in Jerusalem.

Dorrell, P. G. 1993. "The Spring of Jericho from early photographs." *Palestine Exploration Quarterly* 125:95–114.

Drinkard, J. F., Mattingly, G. L. and Maxwell Miller, J. (eds). 1988. *Benchmarks in Time and Culture. An Introduction to Palestinian Archaeology Dedicated to Joseph A. Callaway.* Atlanta: American Schools of Oriental Research.

Duday, H. 2009. *The Archaeology of the Dead.* Lectures in Archaeothanatology. Oxford: Oxbow Books.

Duday H. and Masset, C. (eds). 1987. *Anthropologie Physique et Archéologie. Méthodes d'Étude des Sépultures.* Paris: Éditions du CNRS.

Duday, H., Courtaud, P., Crubézy, E., Sellier, P. and Tillier, A-M. 1990. "L'Anthropologie de "Terrain": Reconnaissance et Interprétation des Gestes Funéraires." *Bulletins et Mémoires de la Société d'Anthropologie de Paris* 2:29–50.

Garstang, J. 1927. "The Date of the Destruction of Jericho." *Palestine Exploration Fund Quarterly Statement* 59:96–100.

Garstang, J. 1930. "Jericho, Sir. Charles Marston's Expedition of 1930." *Palestine Exploration Fund Quarterly Statement* 62:123–32.

Garstang, J. 1931. "The Walls of Jericho: the Marston-Melchett Expedition of 1931." *Palestine Exploration Fund Quarterly Statement* 63:186–96.

Garstang, J. 1932. "Jericho: City and Necropolis. 1. Late Stone Age. 2. Early Bronze Age. 3. Middle Bronze Age." *Liverpool Annals of Archaeology and Anthropology* 19:3–22, 35–54.

Garstang, J. 1933. "Jericho: City and Necropolis. 4. Tombs of MBAii. 5. Tombs of MBAii and LBAi. 6. The Palace Area." *Liverpool Annals of Archaeology and Anthropology* 20:3–42.

Garstang, J. 1934. "Jericho: City and Necropolis. 6. The Palace Area (cont.). Palace and Store Rooms, MBii Pottery and Houses LBi. Upper Stone Building, EBi." *Liverpool Annals of Archaeology and Anthropology* 21:99–136.

Garstang, J. 1935. "The Fall of Bronze Age Jericho." *Palestine Exploration Fund Quarterly Statement* 67:61–68.

Garstang, J. and Garstang, J. B. E. 1948. *The Story of Jericho.* London: Marshall, Morgan & Scott.

Garstang, J., Droop, J. P. and Crowfoot, J. 1935. "Jericho: City and Necropolis (Fifth Report)." *Liverpool Annals of Archaeology and Anthropology* 22:143–84.

Garstang, J., Ben-Dor, I. and Fitzgerald, G. M. 1936. "Jericho: City and Necropolis (Report for the Sixth and Concluding Season, 1936)." *Liverpool Annals of Archaeology and Anthropology* 23:67–100.

Greenberg, R. and Keinan, A. 2009. *Israeli Archaeological Activity in the West Bank 1967-2007. A Sourcebook.* Jerusalem: Rahas Press.

Harris, N. and Tayles, N. 2012. "Burial Containers – A Hidden Aspect of Mortuary Practices: Archaeothanatology at Ban Non Wat, Thailand." *Journal of Anthropological Archaeology* 31.2:227–39.

Hunt, E. D. (ed.). 1982. *Holy Land Pilgrimage in the Later Roman Empire, AD 312-460.* Oxford-New York: Oxford University Press.

Kenyon, K. M. 1953. "Excavation at Jericho, 1953." *Palestine Exploration Quarterly* 85:81–95.

Kenyon, K. M. 1954a. "Excavations at Jericho, 1954." *Palestine Exploration Quarterly* 86:45–63.

Kenyon, K. M. 1954b. "Ancient Jericho." *Scientific American* 190:76–82.

Kenyon, K. M. 1954c. "Excavations at Jericho." *The Journal of the Royal Anthropological Institute of Great Britain and Ireland* 84:103–10.

Kenyon, K. M. 1956a. "Excavation at Jericho, 1956." *Palestine Exploration Quarterly* 88:67–82.

Kenyon, K. M. 1956b. "Review of *Photography for Archaeologists* by M. B. Cookson." *Antiquaries Journal* 36:135–36.

Kenyon, K. M. 1956c. "Jericho and its Setting in Near Eastern History." *Antiquity. A Quarterly Review of Archaeology* 30:184–95.

Kenyon, K. M. 1957. *Digging Up Jericho*. London: Ernest Benn Limited.

Kenyon, K. M. 1960a. *Excavations at Jericho, Vol. I: The Tombs Excavated in 1952-1954*. London: The British School of Archaeology in Jerusalem.

Kenyon, K. M. 1960b. "Excavations at Jericho, 1957–58." *Palestine Exploration Quarterly* 92:88–108.

Kenyon, K. M. 1965. *Excavations at Jericho, Vol. II: The Tombs Excavated in 1955-1958*. London: The British School of Archaeology in Jerusalem.

Kenyon, K. M. 1971. "Burial Customs at Jericho." *Annual of the Department of the Antiquities of Jordan* 16:5–30.

Kenyon, K. M. 1981. *Excavations at Jericho, Vol. III: The Architecture and Stratigraphy of the Tell*. 1. Text, 2. Plates. London: The British School of Archaeology in Jerusalem.

Kenyon, K. M. 1993. "Tell es-Sultan." In *The New Encyclopedia of Archaeological Excavations in the Holy Land*, edited by Ephraim Stern, Ayelet Lewinson-Gilboa and Joseph Aviram, Vol. 2, 674–81. Jerusalem: The Israel Exploration Society and Carta.

Kenyon, K. M. and Holland, Th. A. 1982. *Excavations at Jericho, Vol. IV: The Pottery Type Series and Others Finds*. London: The British School of Archaeology in Jerusalem.

Kenyon, K. M. and Holland, Th. A. 1983. *Excavations at Jericho, Vol. V: The Pottery Phases of the Tell and Others Finds*. London: The British School of Archaeology in Jerusalem.

King, P. J. 1983. *American Archaeology in the Middle East. A History of the American Schools of Oriental Research*. Winona Lake, In.: Eisenbrauns.

Kurth, G. and Röhrer-Ertl, O. 1981. "On the Anthropology of the Mesolithic to Chalcolithic Human Remains from the Tell es-Sultan in Jericho, Jordan." In *Excavations at Jericho, Vol. III: The Architecture and Stratigraphy of the Tell*, Text, edited by K. M. Kenyon, 407–99. London: British School of Archaeology in Jerusalem.

Leroi-Gourhan, A., Bailloud, G. and Brézillon, M. 1962. "L'hypogée II des Mounouards (Mesnil-sur-Oger, Marne)." *Gallia Préhistoire* 5:23–133.

Marchetti, N. and Nigro, L. 1998. *Scavi a Gerico, 1997. Relazione preliminare sulla prima campagna di scavi e prospezioni archeologiche a Tell es-Sultan, Palestina (Quaderni di Gerico 1)*. Roma: Università degli Studi di Roma "La Sapienza".

Marchetti, N. and Nigro, L. 2000. *Excavations at Jericho, 1998. Preliminary Report on the Second Season of Excavations and Surveys at Tell es-Sultan, Palestina (Quaderni di Gerico 2)*. Rome: Università degli Studi di Roma "La Sapienza".

Moorey, P. R. S. 1991. *A Century of Biblical Archaeology*. Cambridge: Lutterworth.

Nigro, L. 2003. "Tell es-Sultan in the Early Bronze Age IV (2300–2000 BC). Settlement vs Necropolis – A Stratigraphic Periodization." *Contributi e Materiali di Archeologia Orientale* IX:121–58.

Nigro, L. 2004. "In the Shadow of the Bible. Archaeological Investigations by the Deutsches Palästina Vereins before

the First World War: Taannek, Megiddo, Jericho, Shechem." In *Archéologie dans l'Empire Ottoman Autour de 1900: Entre Politique, Économie et Science*, edited by V. Krings and I. Tassignon, 215–29. Bruxelles-Rome: Institut Historique Belge de Rome.

Nigro, L. 2009. "The Built Tombs on the Spring Hill and The Palace of the Lords of Jericho ('dmr Rha) in the Middle Bronze Age." In *Exploring the Longue Durée. Essays in Honor of Lawrence E. Stager*, edited by J. D. Schloen, 361–76. Winona Lake, In.: Eisenbrauns.

Nigro, L. and Taha, H. 2009. "Renewed Excavations and Restorations at Tell es-Sultan/Ancient Jericho. Fifth Season – March–April 2009." *Scienze dell'Antichità* 15:731–44.

Nigro, L., Sala, M., Taha, H. and Yassine, J. 2011. "The Early Bronze Age Palace and Fortifications at Tell es-Sultan/ Jericho. The 6th–7th seasons (2010–2011) by Rome "La Sapienza" University and the Palestinian MOTA-DACH." *Scienze dell'Antichità* 17:185–211.

Nigro, L. and Taha, H. (eds). 2006. *Tell es-Sultan/Jericho in the Context of the Jordan Valley: Site Management, Conservation and Sustainable Development. Proceedings of the International Workshop Held in Ariha 7th-11th February 2005 by the Palestinian Department of Antiquities and Cultural Heritage - Ministry of Tourism and Antiquities, UNESCO Office - Ramallah, Rome "La Sapienza" University*. Rome "La Sapienza" Studies on the Archaeology of Palestine & Transjordan, 2. Rome: "La Sapienza" Expedition to Palestine and Jordan.

Nigro, L., Sala, M. and Taha, H. (eds.). 2011. *Archaeological Heritage in the Jericho Oasis. A systematic catalogue of archaeological sites for the sake of their protection and cultural valorization*. Rome "La Sapienza" Studies on the Archaeology of Palestine & Transjordan, 7. Rome: "La Sapienza" Expedition to Palestine and Jordan.

Pereira, G. (eds). 2013. *Une Archéologie des Temps Funéraires? Hommage à Jean Leclerc*. Special Issue of Les Nouvelles de l'Archéologie 132. Paris.

Riklin, S. 1996. "Jericho 1992." *Excavations and Surveys in Israel* 5:68–70.

Robinson, E. 1841. *Biblical Researches in Palestine, Mount Sinai, and Arabia Petraea*. London: John Murray.

Robinson, E. and Smith, E. 1856. *Biblical Researches in Palestine, Mount Sinai, and Arabia Petraea*. London: John Murray.

Roksandic, M. 2002. "Position of Skeletal Remains as a Key to Understanding Mortuary Behaviour." In *Advances in Forensic Taphonomy: Method, Theory and Archaeological Perspectives*, edited by W. D. Haglund and M. Sorg, 99–117. Boca Raton: CRC Press.

Sellier, P. and Masset, C. 1990. "La Paléoanthropologie Funéraire." *Les nouvelles de l'Archéologie* 40:5-48.

Sellin, E. and Watzinger, C. 1913. *Jericho. Die Ergebnisse der Ausgrabungen*. Wissenschaftliche Veröffentlichung der Deutschen Orient-Gesellschaft 22. Leipzig: Hinrichs.

Sellin, E., Watzinger, C. and Langenegger, F. 1908. "Vorläufiger Nachrichten über die Ausgrabung in Jericho im Frühjahr 1908." *Mitteilungen des Deutschen Orient-Gesellschaft zu Berlin* 39:1–41.

Sellin, E., Watzinger, C. and Nöldecke, A. 1909. "Vorläufige Nachrichten über die Ausgrabung in Jericho im Frühjahr 1909." *Mitteilungen des Deutschen Orient-Gesellschaft zu Berlin* 41:1–36.

Stordeur, D. and Khawam, R. 2007. "Les Crânes Surmodelés de Tell Aswad (PPNB, Syrie). Premier Regard Sur l'Ensemble, Premières Réflexions." *Syria* 84:5–32.

Stutz, L. N. 2003. *Embodied Rituals and Ritualized Bodies. Tracing Ritual Practices in Late Mesolithic Burials.* Acta Archaeologica Lundensia Series altera: 46. Stockholm:Almqvist & Wiksell Intl.

Taha, H. 1999. "Le Département des Antiquités de Palestine." *Dossier d'Archéologie* 240:14–17.

Taha, H. 2010. "Tell es-Sultan (Jericho), the Oldest City in the World." *This Week in Palestine* 144:36–39.

Taha, H. and Qleibo, A. 2010. *Jericho, A Living History, Ten Thousand Years of Civilization.* Ramallah: The Palestinian Ministry of Tourism and Antiquities.

Testart, A. 2008. "Des Cranes et des Vautours ou la Guerre Oubliée." *Paléorient* 34.1:33–58.

Warren, C. 1869a. "Notes on the mounds of Jericho." *Palestine Exploration Fund Quarterly Statement* 2:209–10.

Warren, C. 1869b. *Notes on the Valley of the Jordan and Excavations at ʿAin es-Sultan.* London.

Watzinger, C. 1926. "Zur Chronologie der Schichten von Jericho." *Zeitschrift der Deutschen Morgenländischen Gesellschaft* 80:131–36.

Weippert, H. and Weippert, M. 1976. "Jericho in der Eisenzeit." *Zeitschrift des Deutschen Palästina-Vereins* 92:105–48.

Willis, A. and Tayles, N. 2009. "Field Anthropology: Application to Burial Context in Prehistoric Southeast Asia." *Journal of Archaeological Science* 36:547–54.

CHAPTER 7

KHIRBET QUMRAN

In 1947 the first cave containing manuscripts of the Dead Sea Scrolls was discovered by Bedouin shepherds, north of an ancient ruin known as Khirbet Qumran near the Dead Sea. The manuscripts and other artefacts from Qumran Cave 1 (1Q), originally known as the 'Ain Feshkha Cave', illuminated both the history of the biblical text and the variety of thought in early Judaism, and caused an international sensation. The nearby site of Khirbet Qumran itself was excavated over five seasons from 1951 onwards, under the directorship of Father Roland de Vaux, one of Leo Boer's lecturers at the *École Biblique et Archéologique Française de Jérusalem*. De Vaux concluded that this remote and unusual site was occupied by a little-known 'sect' of Judaism mentioned by Josephus, Philo, Pliny and Dio Chrysostom: the Essenes. It was suggested that they hid the Dead Sea Scrolls in nearby caves ahead of the Roman army's arrival in 68 CE, but continued for a time afterwards.

Unfortunately, De Vaux never published the final report of his findings and, in addition, there are many aspects of the site that remained unclear during the course of excavations, and there are even areas undocumented by photographs. This has led to many disputes among archaeologists, particularly in regard to the site's chronology, although it is clear that occupation started in the Iron Age, and that a new settlement was built there after a hiatus of some 500 years. The site was destroyed by the Romans in 68 BCE, but continued for a time afterwards.

Controversies also surround the identification of the site's occupants, and the function of the settlement. Most scholars adhere to the idea that the site was a settlement of the Essenes or another Jewish sect. Some scholars have suggested that Qumran was a commercial centre, located on a significant cross point of trade routes (to En Gedi and Jericho, as well as to Hyrcania and Jerusalem). Others argue that Qumran was a fortress, a villa or even a pottery manufacturing centre.

Given these controversies new data that shed light on the excavations are very welcome. Scientific technologies may be of help here, as will be demonstrated in this chapter.

The Archaeology of Khirbet Qumran

Joan E. Taylor

In 1954, as a 26-year-old student of the *École Biblique et Archéologique Française de Jérusalem*, Leo Boer took the opportunity to join the excavations at Qumran, the site associated with the Dead Sea Scrolls. He was there for the week of 20–27 March, during the third campaign of excavations (13 February–14 April 1954) directed by Father Roland de Vaux. His photographs record the huge energy of the operations, which, thanks to the large number of Bedouin workers, proceeded rapidly, and they also provide evidence of obscure areas of the site. These photographs have already been made available to the world via the website of the Palestine Exploration Fund, http://www.pef.org.uk/qumran, with captions illustrating their significance – and have been reproduced here. In addition, the editor of this volume and the present author have explored how the photographs can help solve archaeological problems in relation to the site (Wagemakers and Taylor 2011).

The scrolls cave

When Boer visited Qumran, it was already of great interest. Only two and a half years earlier in 1951, it had been identified as being linked to the Dead Sea Scrolls.

Seven years earlier, in 1947, the first of the scrolls had come to light in a cave one kilometre north of Qumran. Bedouin shepherds, Mohammed ed-Dhib and his associates, had found jars with ancient scrolls wrapped in linen. As the world learnt of this sensational find, local Bedouin continued to discover more manuscript fragments in the cave, releasing them lucratively into the antiquities market. In January 1949 the Arab legion, under Captain Akkash el Zebn, carried out a careful search and discovered the location of the cave, whereupon Gerald Lankester Harding, chief inspector of the Department of Antiquities of Jordan, invited Father Roland de Vaux of the École Biblique to excavate this important site with him.

In the sensational atmosphere surrounding the finding of the scrolls, Harding and de Vaux worked methodically, and found that the cave (later called Cave 1Q; see Fig. 7.1) had been very thoroughly gone over by Bedouin and others searching in and around it for anything of value. Broken pottery had been thrown outside. However, there was evidence that the cave had already been disturbed in antiquity, given the presence of over 40 smashed jars and lids, and a significant layer of fill (deposits of earth and animal droppings). They spent fifteen days excavating the cave meticulously and found 600 manuscript fragments in the half a metre of accumulated earth, later identified as coming from some 70 different Hebrew manuscripts,[1] along with a great deal of pottery. They also found many pieces of linen used to wrap up scrolls and seal the jars. They even found one decomposed scroll still inside its linen wrapper, stuck to the broken neck of a jar (see the photograph in Barthélemy and Milik 1955, pl. I: 8–10). They identified the pottery – jars and bowls – as coming from the end of the Hellenistic period, from the second century BCE to the beginning of the first century CE, although there were also potsherds apparently dating to the second and third centuries CE (see Harding 1949; de Vaux 1949a; idem 1949b; idem 1949c; Barthélemy and Milik 1955).

Boer visited this cave with his associates from the École Biblique, and we see two pictures of their arrival there (Figs 7.2 and 7.3). The small hole above the head of the man in the beret in Figure 7.2 was the original cave entrance. The lower entrance was first dug out by the Bedouin, and expanded by the archaeologists.

Boer would have been familiar with its history and also with de Vaux's analysis. De Vaux himself had suggested that it was most likely that this was a valuable library or archive, hidden away at a critical moment, probably when the Romans came to this area to quash the First Revolt in 68 CE (Josephus, *War* 4:437–39).

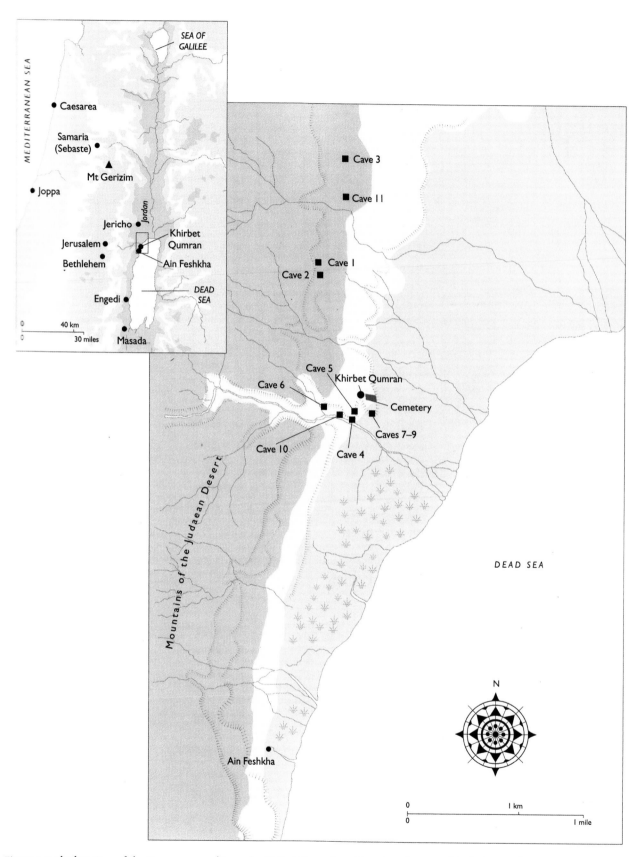

Figure 7.1: The locations of the Qumran caves (Drawn by Philip Winton from The Complete World of the Dead Sea Scrolls *by Philip R. Davies and George J. Brooke. Thames & Hudson Ltd., London).*

Figure 7.2: The man with the beret is standing outside the lower opening of cave 1Q. An additional entrance had been created below the small top opening.

Figure 7.3: Three persons – probably students of the École Biblique – posing around cave 1Q.

Dating issues were key, right from the start, given the fact that some scholars were suggesting that the scrolls from the cave were medieval. In 1951 the antiquity of the scrolls had been confirmed by one of the earliest successful radiocarbon dating experiments. Harding and de Vaux handed over four ounces of 'scrap linen' wrappers to Willard Libby, the father of radiocarbon dating. The resulting date was given as 1917 ± 200 Before Present, that is an uncalibrated age of 33 CE ± 200 (Libby 1951; Sellers 1951). The results roughly confirmed de Vaux's pottery dating in the cave and signalled from the start the important role of scientific analysis in understanding the site of Qumran. This result is now calibrated to be 200 BCE–350 CE (cf. Doudna 1998, 432).

The place was called the 'Ain Feshkha cave', since it was defined by the nearest well-known locality on the north-western shore of the Dead Sea: an oasis irrigated by natural freshwater springs, comprising large pools, a great variety of plants and trees, and a rich bird and fish life. The cave was not connected to the tumble of ruins at Khirbet Qumran, because up until that time the general view was that these ruins represented a Roman fort, dated to the third or fourth century CE. The spring and pool of Ain Feshkha seemed a more appropriate landmark. Christian travellers used to stop at Ain Feshkha en route between the Jordan River and Mar Saba monastery, further inland on the edge of the Kidron ravine. There was a large pool of drinkable water; such a resource was important to the Bedouin who lived in this territory. The ruins of Qumran themselves were called Khirbet ('ruin of') Feshkha by Bedouin (see Taylor 2002, 148, 156).

Khirbet Qumran

The site of Khirbet Qumran is situated on the western shore of the northern part of the Dead Sea. It lies on the edge of a marl platform with steep hills to the west, where a pass zig-zags up to the Buqeiʻa (Judaean wilderness). On the south side is the ravine of the Wadi Qumran, through which a torrent of water gushes once or twice every year when heavy rains fall in the distant Judaean hills. The edge of the plateau to the east is now about three kilometres from the western shores of the Dead Sea, although in the past,

when the sea level was higher, the water used to come close to base. Qumran is placed strategically, with a commanding view. There seemed no reason initially to connect ancient Hebrew and Aramaic texts with this Roman military outpost.

The first identification of Qumran ('Goumran') as a Roman defence post was made by Albert Augustus Isaacs, who visited the site on 23 December 1856, along with a party including the British consul James Finn and the photographer James Graham. Isaacs noted an aqueduct, tower and wall (Isaacs 1857, 66). The tower was built with 'roughly hewn stones' and '[t]he stones at the base are still cemented together, and it can hardly be doubted that this formed a tower or stronghold of some kind. The situation is commanding, and well adapted for defensive operations'. Isaacs also mentioned two small water reservoirs to the west of the tower which were in a very ruined condition, and another on the south-eastern side which was 'of considerable size, and very deep. The masonry of this was excellent, and, at a trifling cost, it could be made water-tight'. The wall was one which was 'regularly built of masonry, similar to that of which the tower is composed, and now between three and four feet in height' which ran 'from north to south, to the east of the reservoir.' Fortunately, Isaacs' team provided an etching – based on a photograph that no longer exists – showing the site as it was (Fig. 7.4), from the south-eastern corner of the pool, and showing the western wall of this locus and the tower beyond it. Isaacs noted the adjacent cemetery, but he believed the graves were Bedouin – a reasonable notion, given their similarity in form to Bedouin graves, and given the Bedouin practice of locating cemeteries in or close to ruins. Isaacs was the first to suggest that the remains were Roman defensive structure, and this was a view that continued to the time that the site was excavated by de Vaux. As C. W. M. Van der Velde stated in the same year as Isaacs' visit, following his information: 'The ruins called Ghomran are those of a small fortress which has been built to guard the pass above; and around it, on the E. and S., a few cottages have stood, which probably afforded shelter to the soldiers, the whole having been surrounded by a wall for defence' (Van der Velde 1856, 257). This identification was repeated by Gustaf Dalman in the chronicle of his travels (1914, 9–11), and also in Michael Avi-Yonah's 'Map of Roman Palestine' (1936, 164).[2]

REMAINS OF TOWER AND RESERVOIR AT GOUMRAN.

Figure 7.4: An etching made by Isaac's team shows Khirbet Qumran from the south-eastern corner of the pool L71.

Because of this old assumption that Qumran was a Roman fort, de Vaux and Harding initially rejected the site as relevant to the scrolls cave[3], although they did a surface inspection and dug up two tombs (de Vaux 1953a, 89; idem 1973, vii). In 1951 they went back to the site, digging from 24 November to 12 December with only fifteen workers, for three weeks. Before starting the digging, de Vaux made a careful record of what he could see at the site, confirming what Isaacs had recorded long ago (de Vaux 1953a, 89–90): the most apparent ruin was that of a rectangular building 30 by 37 metres, with secondary constructions on the north-west, west and south. Two small cisterns (later called L117, L118) could be seen in the west and a large, stepped cistern was plainly visible in the south (L71, shown in his pl. II b, and see Fig. 7.5). This was fed by an aqueduct leading up the Wadi Qumran, from which water was captured during the rainy season. He noted a long wall stretching north-south from the big pool and building, which isolated the ruin from the eastern area of the plateau, where there was a large cemetery. Photographs were taken (Humbert and Chambon 1994,

pls 3, 6) showing the mound of the so-called 'tower' visible in the north, and the side of a part of standing wall at the western side of L121, the corner of which has collapsed down the edge of the subsided hill; yet what is most obvious from the photographs is the huge amount of rubble all over the site. As with many sites, it is a large pile of fallen stones, with a few structures that can be distinguished only upon closer inspection. The top layer has tumbled down.

Harding and de Vaux excavated three rooms in the south-west corner of the building in which the tower was located (L1, L2, L4), two in the north-east corner (L5, L6), and one around the entrance (L7), concluding in the end that the construction of field stones and mud plaster was too rough for a Roman fort, and – importantly – there were a number of occupation levels prior to the final form of the structures. Most excitingly, they found embedded in the floor of L2 a cylindrical jar identical to the type of jar in which scrolls were said to have been found, and a coin dated to 10 CE. Pottery that came to light was of the same type as the pottery found in the cave (de Vaux 1953a).

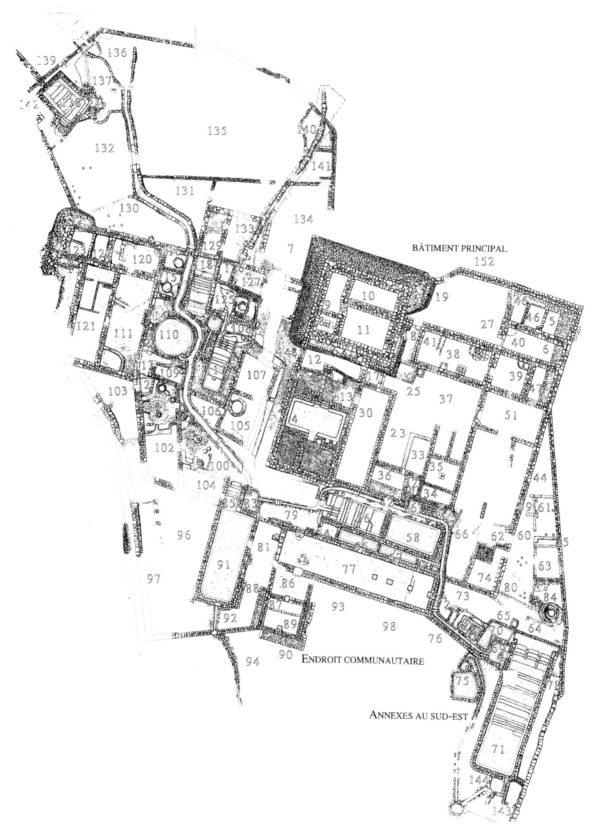

Figure 7.5: Qumran in Period II (Courtesy of Jean-Baptiste Humbert, EBAF, Jerusalem).

Excavations at Qumran began in earnest with the second season in 1953, which continued in 1954 with a third one, and with two more seasons in the subsequent years 1955 and 1956, jointly undertaken by the Palestine Archaeological Museum (the present Rockefeller Museum), the Department of Antiquities of Jordan, and the École Biblique, headed by Roland de Vaux. Preliminary reports were published (de Vaux 1953a; idem 1953b; idem 1954; idem 1956) along with two books (French and English) of de Vaux's Schweich Lectures at the British Academy – synthesising some of the material from the site (1961, 1973). De Vaux's excavations are currently being published in a series under the direction of Jean-Baptiste Humbert of the École Biblique: a series that will culminate in full final reports (Humbert and Chambon 1994; Humbert and Gunneweg 2003). Some important details are also found in the discussions by Laperrousaz (1966; 1976; 1980) and de Vaux's associate J. T. Milik (1959).[4] Since not all final reports have yet been published, Boer's photographs of Qumran are particularly interesting, and can be used to reflect on what de Vaux observed in

the field (Wagemakers and Taylor 2011). Furthermore, Boer has pictures of the charismatic de Vaux in action on the site (Figs 7.6, 7.7, and 7.8).

De Vaux soon observed that the earlier levels of Qumran were indeed associated with the scrolls cave, on the basis of pottery types, as he had decided after the initial excavation of 1951. He distinguished five periods of development, from the final form to the earliest:

Period III: 68–73 CE
Period II: *c.* 4 or *c.* 1 BCE to 68 CE
Abandonment phase following an earthquake and fire 31 BCE–*c.* 4 or 1 BCE
Period Ib: *c.* 100–31 BCE
Period Ia: *c.* 130–100 BCE
Iron Age (Israelite) – late eighth–sixth centuries BCE

When Boer visited the site this basic identification of phases was already in place, and de Vaux was refining his understanding as new parts of Qumran opened up. In addition, de Vaux noted that, underneath the Period III form of the settlement, the peculiarities of

Figure 7.6: Pay-day. De Vaux is sitting in front of a tent, paying a local worker. Presumably the recipient is signing for a receipt.

Figure 7.7: Tea break. Roland de Vaux (with beard) and Józef Tadeusz Milik are sitting on the right. The photograph shows Leo Boer himself at the far left.

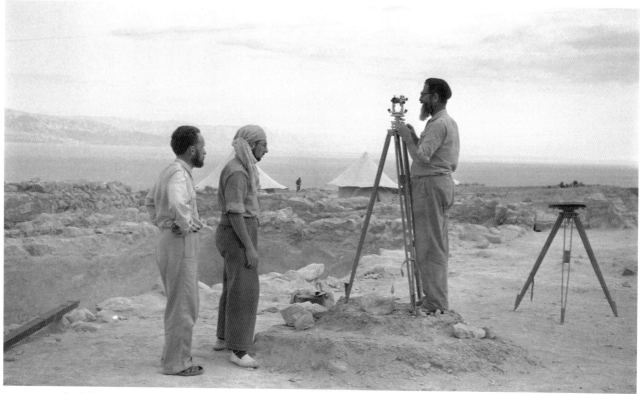

Figure 7.8: Roland de Vaux, accompanied by two students of the École Biblique, is surveying at L96. The men are standing next to the cistern (L91) that was being excavated that week.

the Period Ib and II structures – large rooms suitable for communal eating, sizeable pools that would fit the requirements of ritual purification baths, and so on – seemed to match an Essene identification (de Vaux 1973, 126–38). A cemetery with largely adult male skeletons was also suggestive of this identification. The Essenes were understood to be a 'sect' of Jews who lived an isolated yet communal life (see Philo of Alexandria, *Prob.* 72–91; *Hypoth.* 11:1–18; Josephus, *War* 2: 119–61; idem *Ant.* 18:22), particularly concerned with ritual purity and common meals, and were associated with this area of the Dead Sea coast on the basis of what was stated by the Roman writer Pliny (*Hist. Nat.* 5:15 [73], cf. Dio Chrysostom, in Synesius, *Dion* 3.2, cf. Solinus, *Collectanea* 35:1–12).[5]

The scrolls themselves had already been widely defined as Essene, especially given the contents of the so-called Community Rule, which spoke of some kind of 'union', *yahad*, and which provided regulations about a pure meal and community gatherings. Thus, in associating the site with the scrolls cave, Roland de Vaux naturally began to interpret Qumran in line with what was widely supposed about the ancient Essenes. Harding (1952, 105), following the initial excavations of 1951, had already expressed the view that Qumran represented a 'closed settlement'.

The number of workers de Vaux employed for the excavations from 1953 to 1956 – as indicated in Boer's pictures – shows how eager he and others were to define Qumran, and to make good progress to illuminate the context of the Dead Sea Scrolls. In the second season of excavations, de Vaux had discovered a large ancient rubbish dump north of the buildings, which he called 'Trench A'. This mainly contained older material, including Hasmonean coins from the second and early first centuries BCE. Referencing an earthquake in 31 BCE mentioned by Josephus (*War* 1:370; *Antiquities* 15:121), de Vaux suggested that the site had been damaged at this time, and needed to be cleared out and restored subsequently. An earthquake crack, revealed in the pool of L48-L49, seemed to confirm this (de Vaux 1954; idem 1973).

As work progressed through the 1954 season, in which Boer participated for a week, de Vaux discovered more evidence of this earthquake in L86, where a huge number of bowls were found under a fill, indicating that people dealt with the destruction by simply sealing off this area; de Vaux would call this higher level in the southern part of

the locus 'L89'. Boer was there just before the broken pottery was discovered, and took photographs of the area of L86-L87 after a separating wall had been removed, exposing a central pilaster (see Figure 7.5; Wagemakers and Taylor 2011). He saw fellow students excavating the continuous floor of the lower level on which the pottery was later found (Period Ib floor), and he also photographed the remains of a piece of fallen ceiling of palm rafters, and a central support column (Figs 7.9 and 7.10). Then he turned his camera to snap the contents of baskets in L87 (Fig. 7.11; the man with the wooden pole appears in the previous photo as well), before photographing what he saw above the wall of L89 to the west (Fig. 7.12). The baskets contain the broken storage jars and cooking pots referred to by de Vaux in his field notes for L87, but it seems he only recorded more complete objects, unless these could be fitted together (Humbert and Chambon 1994, 319).

It is clear that a great mass of rubble was cleared in the course of excavations, exposing both the interior and exterior of the buildings and cisterns to view, and we see in Boer's photographs this operation in progress, with a picture showing a worker tipping his basket of rubble over the ravine (Fig. 7.13). However, the topmost levels of crumbled remains relate to the final period of a site's existence, and because these periods are critical for understanding the stratigraphy, very special care should have been taken in removing this debris, so that no important material was lost. As far as can be determined, no sifting was done to look for small remains. There would have been a very natural tendency to press on and clear the surface as soon as possible so that excavation could progress, especially as the top layer was one that de Vaux considered peripheral to the scrolls. Boer's photographs can be illuminating for the rubble of Period III itself.

Cave 4Q and other scroll caves

Boer also shows us an image of a cave found at a stone's throw away from the buildings of Qumran, now known as Cave 4Qa. Boer's photograph (Fig. 7.14) shows a view out to the Dead Sea from the 'window' of this cave.

By 1954, the original 'Ain Feshkha' scroll cave had lost its status as unique, as new caves with

Figure 7.9: View from L86 to the north. Two students of the École Biblique are laying bare wooden remains in front of a block in L86-87, 89, known as the 'pantry'. The close-up recording of the block's condition before its restoration during the excavation campaign of 1954 is unique.

Figure 7.10: A Bedouin man is posing while he is exposing wooden remains which lie against the eastern wall of L86. At the same time, others next to him are uncovering wooden remains in front of a block (Fig. 7.9). In his field notes de Vaux wrote a day after Boer took this picture: 'Upon this floor in locus 86 were remnants of charred beams found'. The mass of wood in situ - carbonised palm logs - contains pieces of plaster.

Figure 7.11: Baskets filled with fragments of pottery found in L87 and referred to by de Vaux in his field notes for this locus.

Figure 7.12: This picture is taken from L89 (as in Period II, written on the wall) to the west. It looks over the top of a basin on the exterior western wall of this locus to where men are excavating pool L91 and walking in L96 to tip out their baskets into the ravine. This picture shows the very large number of workmen employed by de Vaux, enabling an extremely rapid excavation of areas of the site.

Figure 7.13: Throwing away debris coming from inter alia *L91 and 93 (see caption Fig. 7.12) down the ravine.*

manuscripts had been discovered, and so the first cave became known as Cave 1, or Cave 1Q ('Q' for 'Qumran' was a short way of indicating it had scrolls). After the initial excavation of 1Q Harding and de Vaux were well aware that the local Bedouin were searching for further manuscripts, and they mounted their own search. The survey successfully brought to light Cave 2Q (100 metres south of Cave 1Q, see Fig. 7.1) – where, along with manuscripts, there were fragments of over six scroll jars, a lid and three bowls – and 3Q, which had, along with the manuscripts, some fragments of hide and papyrus, a large quantity of pottery (over 30 broken scroll jars, over 20 lids, two jugs and a lamp), as well as the mysterious Copper Scroll.

However, the Bedouin managed to discover Caves 4Qa and b right beneath the plateau on which the ruins were located, cut into the marl of the Qumran plateau, just four months after the caves survey was completed. They are actually two separate caves. However, because the manuscripts, originally deriving from these and found by Bedouin, could not be assigned to one or the other, they were simply given the joint identification '4Q' and distinguished as 'a' and 'b'. De Vaux thought these artificial cavities were archaeologically barren

(de Vaux 1973, 52), and was therefore surprised to find they contained scrolls. In Cave 4Qa, there were also four almost complete jars, rims of a further four, three cooking pots, three lids, five bowls, three carinated bowls, three jugs and one lamp (de Vaux 1973, 52). He had not yet looked in other possible caves adjacent to 4Qa and b, even as he excavated at Qumran. De Vaux searched for collapsed caves only three years later, in 1955, after he found the remains of a rock-hewn staircase, leading from the plateau to the artificial caves to the south of the buildings; and thus caves 5Q–10Q came to light, while at the same time the Bedouin discovered Cave 6Q lying close to the Wadi Qumran itself, which contained manuscript fragments, a jar, and a bowl of the 'Qumran type'. In Cave 7Q there were manuscript fragments, as well as parts of two storage jars, a lid, a large bowl and a lamp, matching types in existence at Qumran from Period Ib to Period II. In Cave 8Q, which had two openings, fragments of manuscripts were found, phylactery texts, a prayer and mezuzah, with 100 leather strips used for scroll fastening, indicating the use of the caves for manuscript storage. There were also three storage jars, four lids, a handled jar and a lamp with a

Figure 7.14: This photograph was taken after Leo Boer entered cave 4Qa. This is the southern window of cave 4Qa, which looks out on a ledge. The western side of this ledge protrudes to the right. The view is to the south-east, and to the dirt road to Feshkha, where a building can be seen (compare with Humbert and Chambon 1994: fig. 427).

pared nozzle. In Cave 9Q, there was a small fragment of Hebrew or Aramaic writing (Baillet, Milik and de Vaux 1962, 163, pl. xxxv), dates and date-stones, three pieces of cord and sherds (Baillet, Milik and de Vaux 1962, 31). Date stones were also found in Cave 10, the remaining part of a cave on the west face of the spur in which Cave 4 was hollowed out (Baillet, Milik and de Vaux 1962, 164; de Vaux 1973, 53). Cave 10Q had a woven mat, a lamp with a pared nozzle, an ostracon with Hebrew letters (cf. Baillet, Milik and de Vaux 1962, 124) and sherds. In 1956 Cave 11Q was discovered by Bedouin, a cave containing the Temple scroll apparently within a scroll jar, among other important finds. This cylindrical jar, in which the Temple Scroll and other manuscripts were preserved, was associated with two jar covers, as well as linen scroll wrappers and other items (de Vaux 1956, 573–77; idem 1973, 51). Other items included a small mattock, a chisel or file, a knife, and some pottery including a small jug (contemporaneous to periods of Qumran

occupation, first century BCE to first century CE), bits of linen and basketry, pieces of rope, and a hardened and blackened scroll very tightly wound, now known to be of Ezekiel.

Boer visited Qumran not long after Cave 4Q was identified as a manuscript cave, but before the other marl caves close by were brought to light. At this point, in March 1954, only four manuscript caves were known.

Khirbet Qumran after Boer

Unfortunately, after the completion of his excavations and the publication of his preliminary reports, de Vaux did not make quick progress and died, unfortunately, in 1971, before he could publish his final report. His successor, Pierre Benoit, did not manage to move the publication forward. The responsibility for publishing this final report then fell to his successor, Jean-Baptiste Humbert, who first published de Vaux's field notes with the photographs taken at the excavation (Humbert and Chambon 1994), followed by a scientific volume (Humbert and Gunneweg 2003). One of the problems for Humbert, however, was that he realised that de Vaux's categorisation of phases was wrong in some fundamental way, and his full report would need to sort out some of the inherent problems (Humbert 1994; idem 2006). For example, de Vaux's assumption that the earthquake of 31 BCE was responsible for the fissure that split the pool L48–L49 is now considered to be incorrect (Humbert 2003, 437). The large earthquake crevice across the eastern part of the site, which cracked structures, most likely occurred after the site was abandoned or indeed led to the abandonment of the site, that is after Period III, since the same crevice in pool L48–L49 cracked the water channel leading to L71, still used in Period III. In addition, Humbert became convinced that the dating for the development of the site in the Hasmonean era was not as early as de Vaux assumed, and that de Vaux's chronology needed refinement.

Humbert instead defined a Hasmonean square enclosure through to an expanded form with complex water systems and industrial units. In this sequence (Humbert 2003), the building of the initial Hasmonean villa is dated to the time of Alexander Jannaeus (after 104 BCE; his Level 2, Phase A). Humbert determined that the major expansion of the site took place under the reign of Herod the Great (between 34 and 31 BCE): his Level 3, Phase A, punctuated by the earthquake that caused damage but not the great crevices, with subsequent rapid expansion in a phase he called Level 3, Phase B, from 31 BCE onwards.

In the absence of full reports of the site of Qumran, various investigations have continued at the site. In January 1992 a small team under the supervision of Robert Eisenman of the California State University Long Beach conducted a ground-penetrating radar survey to test the extent of earthquake damage, and located a fissure not recorded by de Vaux veering off to the east through L74 (Baigent and Eisenman 2000, 131–38).

From 1994 to 1996 Magen Broshi and Hanan Eshel considered the caves of the marl terrace, on which the ruins of Khirbet Qumran are located. Six collapsed caves were investigated north of the Qumran buildings (Eshel and Broshi 1997; idem 2004), with Caves C and F providing many fragments of jars, pots, bowls, and lamps dated to the first century CE, with the latest

coin dated to Year 2 of the First Revolt (67/68 CE). Along the pathways leading from the buildings to the caves they also found a large number of nails from sandals, pottery and coins, as well as an iron tent peg, all located with the help of a metal detector (Broshi and Eshel 1999a; idem 1999b). The artificial caves are very close to the structures of Qumran and would have been only a few minutes walk away, accessed by rock-cut stairways and ladders (Broshi and Eshel 1999b, 333, 335). Numerous other artificial caves have now disappeared: they noted how stairs from cave 10Q led to a further cave which is now eroded (Broshi and Eshel 1999b, 334). Their work has shown how the artificial marl caves are integrally related to the buildings of Qumran, and this ultimately also demonstrates how the manuscript fragments found in these caves (4Qa and b, 5Q, 7Q–10Q) are also connected to the buildings, being in the occupation area of the site. In the view of Eshel and Broshi, inhabitants of Qumran lived in these caves in the first century CE, as well as in tents.

Also in 1996, James F. Strange of the University of South Florida undertook a ground-penetrating survey of the Qumran plateau and excavated a small area just outside the eastern wall of the Qumran settlement, where he found an ostracon with a deed of gift, possibly referring to the 'yaḥad', though this reading has been disputed (Cross and Eshel 1997; idem 2000; Yardeni 1997; Callaway 1997; Strange 2006). This soil was compacted in this area following a trench dug by de Vaux, but it is possible this was in its original location. Strange also found some other interesting sherds, almost all from the Iron Age.

In 1993 and from 1996–1999, 2001 and through to 2004, Yizhak Magen, Military Staff Officer for Archaeology in Judaea and Samaria, and his assistant Yuval Peleg, excavated in a number of areas in and around Qumran (Magen and Peleg 2006; idem 2007). They brought to light a paved area beyond L77, and worked in various parts of the buildings. They excavated two further ancient refuse dumps missed by de Vaux, and re-excavated 'Trench A'. In the course of these investigations they brought to light more Iron Age remains, and found another earthquake fissure in the eastern refuse dump, which they say post-dated the abandonment of the site by perhaps centuries. They expanded the evidence of Qumran in the Iron Age (Phase A, late eighth to sixth centuries BCE), and re-dated the Qumran phases in a different system, in some ways similar to Humbert, although they were slightly dismissive of a phase corresponding to de Vaux's important Period III, most likely because most of this phase has been largely obliterated. Like Humbert, Magen and Peleg determined that the initial re-settlement phase as a military outpost took place at the time of Alexander Jannaeus, in the first part of the first century BCE (Phase B), followed by developments in the mid-first century BCE (Phase C), again from the time after the Roman conquest to the earthquake (63 to 31 BCE), from the earthquake of 31 BCE to 68 CE, when the site was destroyed by the Romans (Phase E); and that thereafter the damaged site was reoccupied by Jews prior to the Bar Kochba Revolt in 132–135 CE (Phase F). Magen and Peleg have rejected any association between Essenes and the site, or indeed the scrolls and the buildings, seeing the scrolls as entirely separate from the site. They believed that the military site became a pottery manufacturing centre in the Herodian period.

In addition, Randall Price and Oren Gutfeld have excavated on the Qumran plateau, and to the east of the wall, in a ten-year project from 2002 and 2012. They discovered deep pits with installations dating from the Iron Age to the first century CE (Price 2004; idem 2005). Observations and notes online indicate that the latest excavations located a floor beyond the north-south wall and worked around a number of graves located very close to this wall.

Such new excavations and also the publication of de Vaux's field notes with photographs, along with further revisions and analyses, have led to a great deal of debate about de Vaux's sequence of phases and the dates of these, as well as to alternative ideas of what the ruins of Qumran may represent.

Alan Crown and Lena Cansdale (1994) suggested that Qumran was a commercial *entrepôt* located on a significant trade route, with the settlement serving as a fort designed to guard an important pass or villa. However, my recent study with Shimon Gibson (Taylor and Gibson 2011) has indicated that the pathways are in fact a legacy of Iron Age settlements in the region and that these were maintained (but not developed) by the Hasmoneans and later occupants.

Norman Golb argued that Qumran was a secular fortress (1995), a view adopted by Magen and Peleg (2006; 2007) and Robert R. Cargill (2009a; 2009b) for the initial Hasmonean phase, although Cargill, like Humbert, sees this as changing to a Jewish communal settlement – associated with the scrolls – later on. Cargill, however, dates the initial Hasmonean phase to circa 140 BCE.

According to Yizhar Hirschfeld (1998; 2000; 2002; 2004; 2006), following the suggestions of Pauline Donceel-Voûte (1994; 1998), Qumran was in the Hasmonean and Herodian periods a fortified manor house, which functioned in connection with the lucrative opobalsam trade, being connected by roads to En Gedi and Jericho, as well as to Hyrcania and Jerusalem. Like Crown and Cansdale, Hirschfeld assumes that the paths were more sophisticated than they actually were, and various slightly 'luxurious' features of the site (often involving second-hand columns or paving, brought in from other sites) were over-emphasized in this reconstruction.

Both Jodi Magness (1996; 1998a; 1998b; 1998–9; 2000; 2002; 2004) and Hanan Eshel (2002; 2009; Broshi and Eshel 2004) have continued to defend many of de Vaux's most significant conclusions, and have stressed the key identification of the site as an Essene community centre, with Jodi Magness being the most outspoken defender of what is commonly known as the 'Qumran-Essene hypothesis' which links Qumran with both the scroll caves and the ancient Essenes. Most recently, I myself have broadly defended this hypothesis (Taylor 2012), with some modifications to de Vaux's chronology, after examining the historical and archaeological evidence for the Essenes, Qumran, the caves and the Dead Sea context. Overall, it is Humbert's chronology that seems most convincing, although with a slightly later date for the beginning of the Hasmonean phase in the reign of Alexander Jannaeus. In its Herodian phase, I have identified Qumran as being a place where scrolls were prepared for burial in the natural caves, though there were other industries too. I have also argued for the artificial integration of the caves with the site of Qumran (Taylor 2011), and have stressed the longer duration of Period III (Taylor 2006).

Khirbet Qumran, the scrolls and scientific study

With this great debate about Qumran continuing, about its use and its dating, and in the absence of the final full reports of de Vaux's excavations, scientific analyses have been very important. These have been publicised at a number of conferences as well as in collections of papers and individual articles. Many new, cutting-edge techniques have been used to identify the dating of the scrolls, the origin of the pottery clay, the glass material, bones from the cemetery, wood, ash, and so on (see Gunneweg in this chapter).

The refinements developed in radiocarbon dating have been of particular interest to me. When Libby first developed the technique, he used four ounces of linen to get an approximate probable date spanning 400 years. In 1990 a small amount of linen thread was all that was needed from the stitching on the Testament of Levi to obtain a result. This was dated at the Institute of Technology, Zurich, which produced a calibrated age range of 146–120 BCE (one standard deviation or 65% probability) (Bonani *et al.* 1992).

In 1994 a series of radiocarbon datings was carried out on Dead Sea Scrolls and other items at the University of Arizona in Tucson. A linen scroll wrapper attached to a leather thong, of the type used to wrap scrolls, was dated to 2069 ± 40 Before Present, which after calibration by today's standards means between 170 and 40 BCE at one standard deviation, or between 200 BCE and 20 CE at two standard deviations or 95% probability (Jull *et al.* 1995, 16).

I managed to find some of the linen from cave 1Q myself and had it radiocarbon dated. After the publication of the linen (Crowfoot 1951; idem 1955), much of it was donated by Harding to British academic institutions, one of which was the Palestine Exploration Fund, where it was labelled as coming from the 'Ain Feshkha Cave'. In 2001 I was able to identify this and send a sample for C14 testing to two laboratories (Risø National Laboratory, Copenhagen, and Centrum voor Isotopen Onderzoek, Groningen). This yielded a result with 95.4% confidence in the date range 50 BCE to 80 CE (Taylor *et al.* 2005). Prior to this, Jean-Baptiste Humbert had kindly allowed me to arrange radiocarbon dating for some bone from the Qumran cemetery (which is another subject, not discussed here). Also, the University of Waikato Radiocarbon Laboratory and

the National Museum of Denmark Carbon-Dating Unit collaborated on new tests on date stones found in the marl terrace caves, probably from cave 9Q (KhQ 519 and KhQ 2989). The Waikato University radiocarbon dating of half of one of the charred date stones indicates that the date (the fruit) was consumed and thrown into a fire sometime in the period 37 BCE–212 CE (95%) or 29–126 CE (68%). The Copenhagen/Groningen results on the other half and second date stone indicate dates of 40 BCE–125 CE (95% probability) and 5–85 CE (at 68% probability; Van der Plicht *et al.* 2003; Higham, Taylor, and Green 2003; Taylor and Doudna 2003).

This was followed by a large number of textiles, wood and linen being radiocarbon dated by the Risø National Laboratory and the Centrum voor Isotopen Onderzoek, Groningen. A new battery of radiocarbon dates of linen, wood, and parchment excavated at Khirbet Qumran and in the caves from de Vaux's excavations followed, which yielded interesting results, showing a variety of dates, often with a 68% probability (two sigma standard deviations) of a date between the first century BCE to early first century CE rather than a date overlapping with the destruction of the settlement by the Romans in 68 CE; sometimes there were later dates, which shows that the site was visited in the Byzantine and later periods.

Science-based approaches in general have been very much led pro-actively by Jan Gunneweg who hosts the website 'Qumran Science Center'[6] which publicises all the work on Qumran which focuses on nuclear, optical, chemical, biological, geological, computerised palaeographical and restorative techniques, and has a current list of 82 publications of the team associated with Gunneweg. In addition to numerous articles published in the journal *Archaeometry,* major collections of articles have appeared, with new techniques being used in various ways to extract the maximum amount of information from Qumran materials (see Gunneweg in this chapter).

In addition, digital models of Qumran have been created by both Robert Cargill in the UCLA's Qumran visualisation Project (Cargill 2009a);[7] and by Stephen Pfann (University of the Holy Land/the Orion Center), and the Katholische Universitat Eichstätt.[8] It is now possible to wander through the rooms of Qumran on your own computer.

The amount of energy expended on the Qumran site, both in the field and in numerous scholarly investigations, has been enormous, and quite beyond what is usually given to a small collection of rough buildings, pools and installations located far from a town. The association with the Dead Sea Scrolls makes Khirbet Qumran one of the most visited of all archaeological sites in Israel-Palestine, and one of the best known ancient places in the world. Boer came to this site long before it would develop into a tourist centre and attract a daily consort of roaring coaches. He arrived at a crucial moment, walking into the middle of an excavation that would be talked about ever since.

Notes

1   The scrolls include fragments of Genesis, Deuteronomy, Judges, Ezekiel, and Daniel. There were also fragments of the Book of Jubilees, the Testament of Levi and the book of Enoch as well as a fragment of the manuscript of Leviticus written in palaeo-Hebrew characters. Some documents were written on papyrus (as opposed to the usual parchment of the scrolls), some in Aramaic or Greek, and there were also unknown writings including *pesharim* (commentaries) on Micah, Zephaniah and the Psalms.

2   See also the review by Cargill 2011.

3   In 1949, de Vaux wrote of Qumran: 'il suffira de dire ici qu'aucun indice archéologique ne met cette installation humaine en relation avec la grotte où furent cachés les manuscrits', 'it suffices to say here that there is no archaeological indication to place this human settlement in relation with the cave where the manuscripts were hidden' (de Vaux, 1949c, 586, n. 2). It is interesting that de Vaux uses the verb 'cachés' here already, which shows how he had decided early on that the scrolls were purposely hidden away.

4   Some additional excavations and restorations were done in the 1960s by R. W. Dajjani for the Department of Antiquities of Jordan, with John M. Allegro and Solomon H. Steckoll, see Laperrousaz 1976, 14, 135.

5   For a detailed examination of the ancient sources on the Essenes, see Taylor 2012.

6   http://micro5.mscc.huji.ac.il/~msjan/qumransciencecenter.html

7   http://etc.ucla.edu/research/projects/qumran/

8   http://www1.ku-eichstaett.de/KTF/qumran/simu/sim_d.htm

Qumran Archaeology and Science: a Trans-Disciplinary Combination that Bore Fruit

Jan Gunneweg

On the very day of Christmas Eve 1973, the Archaeometry Unit was set up in the Institute of Archaeology at the Hebrew University of Jerusalem by the late Isadore Perlman, a leading member of the Manhattan Project.[1] The aim of the unit was to establish a 'handshake' between science and archaeology since scholars in these domains speak different languages, as Iz told me.

A 'handshake', however, is a *hapax* phenomenon that only takes place when people meet or leave or as a token of a gentlemen's agreement in such professions as the diamond industry, the cheese or animal market. Even the name 'Taskforce', which was adopted at a later stage, implies a group of people given the task to complete the scientific study of a single project until its bitter end, supported by advice from one or more archaeologists who have an interest in the project. However, these archaeologists do not on the whole promote real persistent collaboration.

A short history of archaeological development

Since the Crusader period and the following centuries, roaming armies, colonists or simply rich individuals have ransacked ancient sites, looted them, or later on in fact bought art objects in the countries they happened to be in and then brought the booty home. As soon as their mansions got overcrowded with, they would sell the stolen goods to museums who were only too happy to buy them. There, artefacts were exhibited, to be seen by many instead of a few privileged and were kept there for a century until scholars started to investigate the foreign artefacts by asking some questions, such as where they came from, who made them and how they were made.

The next step towards archaeology becoming functional for history was to verify whether the cultural heritage as described by the classical writers bore any

foundation on history, which is how archaeology became a study of digging the ground. For instance, Heinrich Schliemann took the writings of the Greek Pausanias as his travel guide and discovered the capital of Agamemnon's Mycene as well as Troy, following Homer's Iliad (Runnels 2002). Jean-François Champollion deciphered the Rosetta Stone (Rumford 2000) with twelve letters of the 26 Egyptian hieroglyphs (recognising the name *Kliopadra* as Cleopatra as well as Ramses and Thutmosis, respectively), without which the great Egyptian civilisation would have remained a *terra incognita*, since no one had been able to decipher its wall-writings.

In the nineteenth century archaeology developed even further as archaeologists started to systematically unearth tells (ruins). Flinders Petrie succeeded in distinguishing various civilisations in Tell el-Hesi (ancient Lachish in Israel) by adopting a technique called stratigraphy, based on the excavation of superimposed floors. The pottery found in these floors were then compared with Egyptian pottery which had been well-dated by cartouches of pharaohs in Egypt (Petrie 1891).

Once stratigraphy became known, architects and army officers started to dig for hidden cities, palaces and villas all over Europe and the Middle East, studying the interrelations between cities and peoples. Edward Robinson and Charles W. Wilson excavated in and around the Temple precinct at Jerusalem's Ophel and their names live on in Robinson's and Wilson's arch, which is located on both sides of the Wailing Wall in Jerusalem. Charles Warren even managed to excavate beneath the temple mount (Warren 1890).

Archaeological expeditions were sent from Sweden, Germany, and Great-Britain to such countries as Cyprus, Syria, Palestine, Egypt, Iran, and Iraq, the cradle of civilisation of the West. Charles Leonard Woolley even suggested he found the basis for the story of the Big Flood, as told in the Old Testament, at Ur (Woolley 1929). Biblical scholars tried to link the Ugaritic legends of Anat and Akhad (Patai 1990), the Gilgamesh epic (Kovacs 1989) and the Enumah Elish (Friedman 2003) account to comparable stories in the Hebrew Bible.

In the last quarter of the twentieth century, material scientists became interested in art and archaeology, as a spin-off from chemistry. In the mid-1950s, when trace elements could be measured by making matter radioactive, the discipline of physics was also added to the study of archaeological and art objects because scientists were now able to detect matter that cannot be seen with the naked eye or a microscope. The data were quantified by the invention of a pottery standard (Perlman and Asaro 1969).

Archaeology, science and Qumran

From 2001–2010, I represented Israel in two COST Actions[2] and became acquainted with 34 scholars, primarily of the natural sciences. On their request for a new project, I proposed the study of Qumran and the Dead Sea Scrolls from a scientific point of view. Today, 157 scholars from 45 institutions in 17 countries have collaborated on the project. Four books have been published, covering three Qumran workshop meetings

(Gunneweg and Greenblatt 2012; Gunneweg, Adriaens, and Dik 2010; Gunneweg, Greenblatt, and Adriaens 2006; Humbert and Gunneweg 2003). Why Qumran?

Qumran manuscripts represent the oldest complete backbone of monotheism for about four of the seven billion people on earth. Until 1947, Qumran had been just a ruin on the north-west shore of the Dead Sea (Fig. 7.15) where once a Jewish sect used to live, surrounded by cliffs containing eleven caves in which approximately 930 manuscripts were found in 1947 and the following years, dating from the third century BCE to the first century CE and written in ancient Phoenician-Hebrew script, '*Quadratschrift*'– Hebrew, Aramaic and Greek. These manuscripts contain the Jewish writings from the Hebrew Bible and Apocrypha as the books of Enoch and Jubilees, and a commentary on the book of Habakkuk, whereas a third of the texts refer to a Jewish sect, which are generally considered to be the Essenes referred to by the first century Jewish historian Josephus.

We wanted to obtain some hard evidence for or against certain archaeological hypotheses that had circulated since the late 1950s, when Qumran was excavated by Lancaster Harding and Roland de Vaux. Qumran has been classified as many things: a villa, farm, type of religious convent, site for producing

Figure 7.15: The ruins of Qumran with the Dead Sea and the mountains of Jordan in the background. Photograph by Leo Boer on 26 March 1954.

balsam, indigo or parchment, or a pottery production place (see Taylor in this chapter). From the moment that the COST Action project was approved, I changed the nomenclature of 'handshake' and 'taskforce' to the term 'trans-disciplinarity'. This term indicates a holistic approach on dealing with Qumran and its manuscripts by means of applying all relevant analytical techniques available in the various domains of natural sciences, as well as the disciplines in the humanities, such as history, exegesis, restoration, conservation, art and archaeology.

For this new approach I formulated four questions which cannot be solved solely in the domain of humanities, including archaeology:

1. Is there a connection between the settlement of Khirbet Qumran and the caves surrounding it?
2. In the light of the contents of some scrolls, can the inhabitants been classified as sectarians?
3. Who wrote the scrolls, where and when were they written?
4. How do we save the manuscripts for posterity?

A set of specific analytical techniques may be able to answer these questions: Ad 1. Connections between the settlement, the caves and other sites, are studied by analysing the provenience of the pottery found; Ad 2. Sectarian behaviour is not only established by written records, but also by biological and material cultural relics found *in situ*; Ad 3. Dating of the manuscripts is analysed by palaeography, but especially by radiocarbon (C14) dating, while the provenience of the scrolls is established by DNA, and by the analysis of the parchment and ink; Ad 4. The scrolls fragments are best preserved and conserved by cleaning and piecing them together, photographing them and looking at the in- and outside of the skin by Synchrotron Radiation (SR) and not just under a microscope.

The laboratory techniques used for solving pending archaeological questions are nuclear, optical, biological and chemical of character. These will be discussed one by one in the following sections.

Nuclear archaeology

In police archives all around the globe fingerprints of criminals and potential lawbreakers are stored to be recognised, judged, and sentenced to incarceration. A fingerprint is made up of many lines and it is the pattern of the lines that identifies a specific individual. The more lines of a fingerprint detected at a crime scene, the closer the criminal's identification. Such fingerprints are unique to an individual.

Likewise, when trying to obtain a chemical fingerprint of a ceramic pot (for instance Fig. 7.16), it is important to detect a pattern of many chemical elements in the clay which the potter used for making such a pot. The premise is that there are no two identical clay sources on earth and they can be differentiated by analysing them. As a consequence, pottery made of these clay sources can also be differentiated in the same way. The differences between the various clays (and thus between pots made of these clays) largely lie in the chemical elements found in them, such as Ca, Si, Al, Na, and Fe. However, for a site-specific fingerprint, we need to find trace elements which cannot be seen with the naked eye, yet can be calculated by means of radioactivity.

Trace elements constitute only 0.1% of clay and actually of anything that exists. They cannot be seen with a microscope. Here the nuclear reactor comes into the picture. When clay and pottery are irradiated by a flux of neutrons in a reactor, the majority of the elements in clay or ceramic become radioactive and can be measured due to the specific energy irradiated by each isotope. When these energies are compared to those from a known standard – irradiated simultaneously with the samples of unknown provenance – it is then possible to quantify the energies into numbers for each element, whether a major, minor or trace element, by comparing the two sets of spectra.

This analytical technique has been used successfully to identify ceramic, obsidian, amber and basalt, and has provided chemical fingerprints of such matter for the past 50 years. It is called 'instrumental neutron activation analysis' (INAA).

The second nuclear application much needed for the archaeology of Qumran is the dating of organic material; for example, the dating of bone and tooth (biological) specimens as well as textile and parchment (material of character) by 'radiocarbon mass spectrometry', better known as C14 dating.

A *case study*

According to the classical approach, pottery is studied by the ceramist who establishes visually that, for example, a certain pot, found in Israel, was an import

Figure 7.16: A photograph of a Bedouin man in Qumran uncovering a vessel, taken by Leo Boer on 21 March 1954.

from Cyprus, on the base of style, workmanship, finishing, and decoration as characteristic for Cypriote ware.

The breakthrough to achieve a more objective way of establishing the provenience of pottery came in the late 1960s, when archaeologists were given access, on the one hand, to a nuclear device, a nuclear reactor, and, on the other, a high-power light source, the so-called Synchrotron. Each of the two devices is of enormous importance for archaeology and geology because they provide cutting-edge information of almost everything on earth, and on a scale that usually cannot be observed with the naked eye. Both devices are able to trace the origin of biological and material matter.

Analysis of the connection site and cave by pottery provenience

In 1997, a pottery provenience study was started, headed by Marta Balla of the Nuclear Reactor at the University of Technology and Economics in Budapest and by the author of this article at the Hebrew University, in order to determine with whom the inhabitants of Qumran had been in contact.

Following the classical archaeological approach, Roland de Vaux concluded that the pottery found in the caves and at the Qumran settlement was identical and that they, therefore, belonged together (de Vaux 1973, 53–54). This suggested that the manuscripts could be used for interpretation of the settlement and, in turn, the archaeological relics could be used for interpretation of the manuscripts. This approach was satisfactory in the 1950s and 1960s, but presently it is considered insufficient to reconstruct the history of a site; facts are needed, not a dogmatic statement by a certain authority.

It was therefore important to corroborate or refute the existing theories. The task seemed enormous, because we would have to deal with the provenance of the finds, their dating, all sorts of statistics, and a survey of similar sites in the neighbourhood as well as further away. We decided to start with establishing the provenance of pottery found at Qumran, a procedure that has often provided information regarding the individual and group relations of people(s) during their lifetime.

First, water and mud from the Dead Sea, as well as marl, stucco, jar stoppers and the like, were sampled to find the type of clay of which local Qumran pottery was made. Two kiln wasters from the kiln waste garbage heap outside the walls provided the basis in order to establish what type of pottery was produced locally at Qumran (Fig. 7.17). The composition of the clay of this pottery turned out to be dissimilar to the marl/clay from Cisterns 58, 59, and 71, which was described as real clay from the rain flood deposits (Balla 2012; Gunneweg 2012a; Gunneweg and Balla 2003), and proved contrary to what was published by Magen and Peleg (2007). So this floot clay was not used for the locally made pottery.

Pottery provenience with the aid of INAA showed that most pottery from Qumran came from the vicinity of two cities, Jericho and Hebron, and some from the region of Edom. The remaining pottery has chemical fingerprints that differ widely from one another. It must be emphasised that there was no trace of a connection to the important sites of Jerusalem, Masada, or En Gedi, nor was there any similarity to the pottery found in the Cave of Letters, in which documents of the second Jewish rebellion (132–135 CE) were found, nor to the pottery from the 'Christmas Cave' near Qumran. We concluded that the inhabitants observed a self-inflicted isolation, only had a few trade relations with centres such as Jericho and Hebron, whereas the Jerusalem connection is entirely missing. These conclusions could never have been drawn by means of the traditional archaeological methods only.

Small jars

A series of small-sized jars, about fifteen centimetres smaller than the cylindrical jars usually considered as the real scroll jars, were determined as scroll jars by de Vaux, because they had a lid that could be fastened to the jar and they looked like the prototype of a scroll jar (Fig. 7.18). However, these small jars found at the Qumran site not only differ from one another – as far as their chemical composition is concerned – but also the only one jar found at En Gedi, and two others, one from the Martin Schøyen

Figure 7.17: Presumably the same vessel as in Figure 7.16, but now restored.

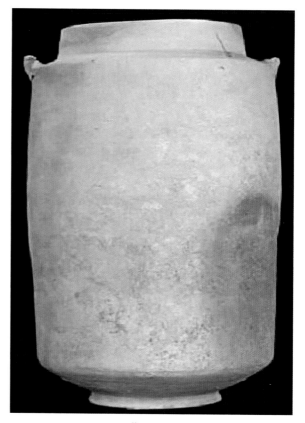

Figure 7.18: A small-sized jar found in Qumran.

collection and the other in the possession of Judy Brown at Manchester, analysed all differently from one another and from the real scroll jars. First, these jars found at Qumran are different in shape, size and are characterised by having either two-, three- or four-pierced knob handles. Only a single type of small Qumran jar was indeed made locally, the others failed to match anything from our data bases.

Optical archaeology

In order to get information on textile fragments, one must move from the nuclear to the optic domain. INAA would not be able to provide any information on the fiber of the yarn or the dyes used for tinting the fabric. A Synchrotron 'sees' the surface of artefacts as well as cross-sections of thin slivers of matter, about two-ten or more microns, by means of X-Ray fluorescence and diffraction on a nano-scale. Each material has its own specific pattern of reflection as well as diffraction. Let us explain what the Synchrotron technique is able to accomplish when applied to a fragment of textile.

For the identification of a fibre, one has access to a series of analytical techniques that either involve a microscope or one or more of the following options: a scanning electron microscope (SEM), a transmitting electron microscope (TEM), Fourrier-transmitted Infra-Red (FT-IR), Raman Spectroscopy and Synchrotron Radiation (hence SR). These all have in common that they analyse by X-Ray Fluorescence (XRF) and X-Ray Diffraction (XRD), in contrast to a microscope. The importance of the technique, its analysis-time involved in producing data, and the costs of equipment and skilled labour are linear, which means that the better the technique the more costly it will be. In the past, textiles from Qumran and the Cave of Letters were submitted to Synchrotron radiation at the ESRF (European Synchrotron Radiation Facility) in Grenoble, France.

A Synchrotron is basically an enormous strong light source with a concentrated light beam of a diameter of 50 down to two microns, making it possible to look at the molecular level of the material of which Qumran textile is made. A fibril, a tiny fraction of a single textile fibre, of five millimetres in length is spanned over a U-shaped – and inside open – sheet of hard kapton[3] and is bombarded with a SR-based XRF and XRD beam, which will scatter on a detector placed at an angle of 45 degrees from impact. The

latter then captures the secondary X-Rays, which, after having been processed, will provide a spectrum that is typical for linen, or wool, cotton, ramie, hemp and other fibres.

The reason for using the Synchrotron was that the textile samples, such as of wool and linen, could not be identified with certainty by means of a microscope or a SEM. For two of the samples in particular, as we shall see, the use of the Synchroton was crucial, as various textile experts disagreed about the identification of the samples, varying from linen to cotton.

If one is unsure about the age of a site, which is thought to belong to the first century CE, then the knowledge that there is cotton would be striking, because linen and wool have been around for millennia, yet cotton was only introduced into the Middle East in the seventh century CE. Therefore, cotton should not be present at the first-century site of Qumran.

The Synchrotron gave a definitive answer: the subjected textiles that were found in the caves at Qumran were made of linen and in the Christmas Cave of wool. However, two of the 24 samples from the Qumran caves that were analysed were made of cotton, even though the presence of cotton was not expected at Qumran. So, it opened an interesting discussion as to what cotton was doing at Qumran in the first century BCE and CE, while cotton was believed to have been introduced by the Arabs via Egypt into Israel as late as the seventh century CE. Could the experts have been wrong regarding the start of the presence of cotton in Israel?

Synchrotron radiation has also been of enormous help in comparing the strength of textile with the place where the textiles were found (Fig. 7.19). Those that were better protected from the Dead Sea environment were also better preserved. It also showed that artificial ageing of matter is undesirable since it is impossible to imitate what impact nature has on materials over centuries or millennia (Müller *et al.* 2007).

Dating and Qumran archaeology

Dating the settlement of Qumran was a long and arduous process; we were being hampered by the lack of dateable bone and teeth samples from the cemetery, because the soil, in which the bones had been buried for two millennia, was too dry, and the skeletons had also adsorbed a lot of calcium from

Figure 7.19: Martin Müller with the author (left) testing the strength of textiles at the ESRF in Grenoble in 2006.

the environment. We therefore put our hope on the dating of the textiles, which would, indeed, provide us with certain, but not easily obtainable, dates, as we shall see. There are two nuclear techniques that can provide dates for artefacts: radiocarbon dating, usually called C14 dating, and Thermoluminescence Dating, abbreviated to TL dating.

Radiocarbon dating

As we wanted a final answer to the question whether the identified cotton belongs to the Second Temple Period settlement, we submitted the entire batch of tested Qumran textiles to AMS Radio carbon dating, to the AMS Isotope Research lab at Groningen University, headed by Hans van der Plicht (Müller *et al.* 2006).

The dating of textiles and parchment was hampered by the fact that the scientists were unaware of what had happened to the parchment and the textiles in the early 1950s. When the newly obtained C14 date for all the Qumran textiles and date kernels arrived,

we noticed something alarming: the dates differed greatly from one another and after immediate consultation with Van der Plicht at Groningen and K. L. Rasmussen at Copenhagen, it was suggested that there could have been a contaminant that had interfered with the dating process. Rasmussen asked me whether I still had enough material left from the original batch of textiles to repeat the C14 analyses. Subsequently, I sent a second batch taken from the same textiles. After some historical detective work, it was discovered that in the 1950s the Rockefeller Museum had used either beeswax or paraffin or castor oil to consolidate not only the textile remains but also part of the Dead Sea Scrolls; concerning the latter it was done in order to facilitate the deciphering of the written text.

The standard way of removing the above-mentioned contaminants from the textiles proved insufficient and so the Risø laboratory in Copenhagen was asked to lend a hand. Helmut Egsgaard spent nine months painstakingly cleaning the textiles, using the Acid-

Alkaline-Acid cleaning process, supplemented by cleaning with ethanol and hexane, eight hours each respectively. After this, the batch of textiles was re-submitted for C14 to the AMS lab in Groningen. Soon after, I received a sheet with the new data on the dating of the textiles (Müller *et al.* 2007; Van der Plicht and Rasmussen 2010).

It was decided to publish the un-cleaned and the double cleaned textiles data sets side by side, thus showing what contamination can do to unclean organic matter. The data were published in the 2006 publication of the Qumran Proceedings of Jerusalem, and added credibility to C14 dating (Van der Plicht and Rasmussen 2010; Rasmussen *et al.* 2006, 142).

Among the dates were the two cotton samples which turned out to belong to the ninth and seventeenth century CE respectively. This indicates that, on two occasions at least, 'visitors' from later periods entered the very same caves where the manuscripts were found. This strengthened my opinion that the first visitors to the caves since antiquity were not the Ta'amireh Bedouins in 1947–1953, but others, much earlier, during the past two millennia.

A spin-off of this research is the uncertainty created surrounding earlier dating trials carried out at Oxford (UK), Zürich (CH) and Tucson (Arizona), whose scientists were unaware of the contamination by oil. A re-run of all these scroll fragments would be welcome. Hopefully, the Israel Antiquity Authority (IAA) still possesses the second half of these parchment/textile samples.

Thermoluminescence dating

However, for a site as Qumran, it is important to try to obtain corroboration of a C14 date by analysing a different material by means of a different technique; for example analysing pottery, in the context of which the textiles were found, by means of Thermoluminescence dating.

When clay is fired into a ceramic in a kiln, the elevated temperature of seven to nine hundred degrees Celsius wipes out all radioactive radiation accumulated in the clay. This indicates that the moment the pot leaves the kiln, its radiation is set to zero. During the lifespan of a ceramic vessel, it accumulates gamma radiation from the sun and when the vessel is abandoned and buried in the soil, it receives alpha and beta radiation. Part of this radioactive material is trapped in the ceramic.

Thermoluminescence's (TL) data acquisition is obtained by re-firing the pot(shard) in an electric kiln, starting at low temperatures, while simultaneously measuring how much radiation is lost with increased temperature. Gamma radiation derives from the element uranium (U) that is present in ceramic, whereas the alpha and beta radiation is due to the elements potash (K) and thorium (Th) that have been taken from the soil in which the pot was buried. These abundances are obtained by submitting the pot and its surrounding soil first to INAA. Since we know the half-lives of U, K and Th, we can calculate how old a pot is. At Qumran, we only have a few TL dates at present.

Restoration and conservation in archaeology

Excavating a site is necessary for gathering information about the settlement. Taking care subsequently of what has been found is another matter. In the end, we need to preserve what archaeology has brought to light. This includes the cleaning of human relics, keeping them in the best condition and preserving them for as long as possible so that curious people like you and me can see what our forefathers were able to accomplish.

In the past, artefacts were cleaned and then preserved in showcases, with a particular level of humidity and temperature. We now know that this is not satisfactory. The regulation of humidity and temperature levels alone cannot deal with the many deterioration processes that take place on the surface as well as deep into the core of matter, such as ceramics, glass, metals, parchment, papyrus, and ink, not to mention the destructive forces at work caused by bacteria and various fungi. Therefore, during the last two decades, conservation laboratories are being set up all over the world to deal with deterioration processes using new techniques.

Deterioration on the surface of an artefact can usually be observed with the naked eye or by the use of the bi- or con-focal microscope. The core of an object, however, is invisible and in order to discover the state of deterioration inside, cutting-edge analytical techniques are necessary, which will provide information on its lifespan. There must also be a continuous collaboration between the museum, the science department and the archaeologist who excavated the site. The European Synchrotron Radiation Facility (ESRF) in Grenoble used parchment and ink data to reveal deterioration of the scrolls on the inside of the parchment (Murphy *et al.* 2010).

Another interesting find at Qumran and in the Christmas Cave were wooden combs containing dandruff, soil, hair and lice. The hair would not have any DNA left, because of the heat and dryness of the desert as well as the long time that has expired, although in the case of the Christmas Cave some DNA could still be present. Lice, however, are bread and butter to a pathologist. A living louse, whether a body or head louse, has to eat every three hours, and its food is the blood of the person on which it lives. For analysis the lower part of the louse is required, the part that contains its guts. The guts still contain the last supper the louse had before dying. The blood can be extracted and may provide the DNA of the Qumranite who played host to the lice (Mumcuoglu and Gunneweg 2012).

Chlorine-bromine (Cl/Br) ratio as tracer for tracing the origin of a manuscript

The Berlin-based team of scientists used the chlorine/bromine (Cl/Br) ratio in the Dead Sea to trace where exactly the scrolls were written. Our team, however, did not consider this to be a constant ratio, making it difficult to trace the origin of the scrolls. We can only prove that the textile or parchment came from the Dead Sea area, which is superfluous information, since they were found there (Gunneweg 2012b).

Conclusions

When I was asked to write this paper, the editor asked me to show what science can add to archaeology. Well, I think that science has changed the way we look at Qumran. I also think that science can be invaluable for any excavation where enough material is found and preserved which can be analysed to provide scientific results.

In the twenty-first century there are many ways to find answers to old and new questions. However, first, one should ask the right questions. Second, one must have easy access to the artefacts that need to be analysed and to obtain the necessary permission to

start scientific research with minimally destructive intervention; yet it seems to me that an entirely non-destructive analysis of an object is a *contradictio in terminis*. Third, one should discuss the required analyses with a scientist who is an expert in her/his field and who will suggest the best analytical technique(s) likely to provide the greatest results. For example, if something can be solved by using a microscope, an expensive synchrotron analysis is unnecessary. Fourth, the budget at hand is a very important parameter. For example, if one intends to conduct a large research project to determine the provenance of pottery, it is wise to calculate the costs involved. It is possible to start with 200 samples, which will then first be submitted to a cheaper thin-section technique, called Petrography. With this technique 40-micron thick slides of ceramic may be studied under the microscope for their mineral distribution, and in doing so, one may discern roughly ten different pottery groups. Following that, one may apply neutron activation on a selection of the groups of pottery already established, in order to collect a quantitative abundance of the pottery's fingerprints, which can then be placed into a database to find a match with other profiles of this specific ceramic.

What the team of trans-disciplinary science collaborators working on Qumran material has accomplished so far is only of value if there will continue to be a collaboration within the team and if new and young collaborators will continue to be recruited to join the Qumran project.

I am grateful that it was Qumran that was chosen by the COST Actions for collaboration on a global scale because at Qumran there are all the possible samples in the domain of bio- and material cultures. Most of man-made artefacts as well as the pathogens (bacterial, viral or fungal) have been preserved, due to the climatic conditions that are characteristic of the Dead Sea area, and in this sense a gift of Mother Nature. The deterioration of parchment and papyrus is not a process that started in the 1950s, when the manuscripts were removed from their original cave habitat, as is believed by some. Deterioration started when the scrolls were used and subsequently hidden, two millennia ago. We first have to investigate the outdoor environmental conditions before we look at what the present museum conditions have attributed to stopping or slowing down deterioration. How much of it depends on what was the outdoor environment back in time (see the latest Qumran Proceedings, Gunneweg and Greenblatt 2012).

So far, DNA-extraction from human bones and teeth at Qumran has been unsuccessful, due to their extended burial in a calcium-bearing soil (marl) and due to the heat and dryness of the Dead Sea area. However, a good louse might provide the DNA of its host, and this might contain the alleged specific Y-chromosome that is said to be characteristic of the priestly clan (*cohanim*). This piece of information could then yield additional proof that Qumran was inhabited by a sectarian community.

Even if the link with the Essenes will never be established, one might be able to prove the sectarian character of the site, which is entirely different from that of En Gedi, Jericho, or Masada. In short, while plain archaeology had its merits at Qumran, trans-disciplinary Qumran archaeometry will prove indispensable for interpreting the possible or even probable provenance of the Judean Desert manuscripts when real and reliable tracers will be found that are site-specific. A single Cl/Br ratio is not enough for establishing the provenience of parchment or ink.

This paper has emphasised that the available analytical techniques should be understandable to and performed by skilled scientists, they should be relatively cheap and completed within a reasonable timeframe, leading to a prompt publication of the finds. The Qumran project has been and remains a valid example of scientific collaboration on a trans-disciplinary level. Its effects will only be really appreciated in the future when the scientific reports of Qumran have been engrained into archaeology, which for the time being remains a *desideratum*.

Notes

1 The Manhattan Project was the code name for a group of scientists in the USA, who, in the 1940s, went on to develop the atomic bomb which later was used on Hiroshima and Nagasaki in order to finish the war in Japan.

2 COST is an abbreviation for Cooperation in Science and Technology, an initiative that was started in the European Community to establish multi-disciplinary research in every possible domain, in our case Cultural Heritage.

3 Kapton is a polymer of imide monomers that does not interact with X-rays, which any other plastic would.

Bibliography of Khirbet Qumran

Avi-Yonah, M. 1936. "Map of Roman Palestine." *Quarterly of the Department of Antiquities in Palestine* 5:139–96.

Baigent, M. and Eisenman, R. 2000. "A Ground-Penetrating Radar Survey Testing the Claim for Earthquake Damage of the Second Temple Ruins at Khirbet Qumran." *The Qumran Chronicle* 9.2:131–38.

Baillet, M., Milik, J. T. and de Vaux, R. 1962. *Les "Petites Grottes" de Qumran.* Discoveries in the Judaean Desert 3. Oxford: Clarendon Press.

Balla, M. 2012. "First Neutron Activation Data on Christmas Cave Pottery Compared to Other Ceramics of the Dead Sea Region." In *Outdoor Qumran and the Dead Sea. Its impact on the Indoor Bio- and Material Cultures at Qumran and the Judean Desert manuscripts, Proceedings of the joint Hebrew University and COST Action D-42 Cultural Heritage Workshop held at the Hebrew University of Jerusalem in May 25–26, 2010,* edited by J. Gunneweg and Ch. Greenblatt. Jerusalem: Hebrew University. http://micro5.mscc.huji.ac.il/~msjan/qumranproceedings2010.html

Barthélemy, D. and Milik, J. T. 1955. *Qumran Cave 1.* Discoveries in the Judaean Desert 1. Oxford: Oxford University Press.

Bonani, G., Ivy, S., Woelfi, W., Broshi, M., Carmi, I. and Strugnell, J. 1992. "Radiocarbon Dating of Fourteen Dead Sea Scrolls." *Radiocarbon* 34:843–49.

Broshi, M. and Eshel, H. 1999a. "How and Where did the Qumranites Live." In *The Provo International Conference on the Dead Sea Scrolls: Technological Innovations, New Texts, and Reformulated Issues,* edited by D. W. Parry and E. Ulrich, 267–73. Leiden: Brill.

Broshi, M. and Eshel, H. 1999b. "Residential Caves at Qumran." *Dead Sea Discoveries* 6:328–48.

Broshi, M. and Eshel, H. 2004. "Qumran and the Dead Sea Scrolls: The Contention of Twelve Theories." In *Religion and Society in Roman Palestine: Old Questions, New Approaches,* edited by D. R. Edwards, 162–69. London/New York: Routledge.

Callaway, P. R. 1997. "A Second Look at Ostracon No. 1 from Khirbet Qumran." *Qumran Chronicle* 7:145–70.

Cargill, R. R. 2009a. *Qumran through (Real) Time: A Virtual Reconstruction of Qumran and the Dead Sea Scrolls.* Bible in Technology 1. Piscataway, NJ: Gorgias Press.

Cargill, R. R. 2009b. "The Qumran Digital Model: An Argument for Archaeological Reconstruction in Virtual Reality and Response to Jodi Magness." *Near Eastern Archaeology* 72:28–47.

Cargill, R.t R. 2011. "The State of the Archaeological Debate at Qumran." *Currents in Biblical Research* 10:101–18.

Cross, F. M. and Eshel, E. 1997. "Ostraca from Khirbet Qumran." *Israel Exploration Journal* 47:17–28.

Cross, F. M. and Eshel, E. 2000. "KhQOstracon." In *Qumran Cave 4 XXVI: Cryptic Texts and Miscellanea, Part 1,* edited by Philip S. Alexander *et al.*, 497–507. Discoveries in the Judaean Desert 36. Oxford: Clarendon Press.

Crowfoot, G. 1951. "Linen Textiles from the Cave of Ain Feshkha in the Jordan Valley." *Palestine Exploration Quarterly* 83:5–31.

Crowfoot, G. 1955. "The Linen Textiles." In *Qumrân Cave I,* edited by D. Barthémlemy and J. T. Milik, 18–38. Discoveries in the Judaean Desert 1. Oxford: Clarendon Press.

Crown, A. D. and Cansdale, L. 1994. "Qumran: Was it an Essene Settlement?" *Biblical Archaeology Review* 20:24–35, 73–74, 76–78.

Dalman, G. 1914. *Palästinajahrbuch des Deutschen evangelischen Instituts für Altertumswissenschaft des heiligen Landes zu Jerusalem.* Berlin: Ernst Siegfried Mittler.

Donceel-Voûte, P. 1994. "Les Ruines de Qumrân Réinterprétées." *Archéologia* 298:24–35.

Donceel-Voûte, P. 1998. "Traces of Fragrance Along the Dead Sea." *Res Orientales* 11:93–124.

Doudna, G. 1998. "Dating the Scrolls on the Basis of Radiocarbon Analysis." In *The Dead Sea Scrolls after Fifty Years. A Comprehensive Assessment* I, edited by P. W. Flint and J. C. VanderKam, 430–71. Leiden: Brill.

Eshel, H. 2002. "Qumran Studies in Light of Archaeological Excavations between 1967 and 1997." *Journal of Religious History* 26:179–88.

Eshel, H. 2009. *Qumran: Scrolls, Caves, History.* Jerusalem: Carta.

Eshel, H. and Broshi, M. 1997. "The Archaeological Remains on the Marl Terrace around Qumran." *Qadmoniot* 30:129–33 (Hebrew).

Eshel, H. and Broshi, M. 2004. "Three Seasons of Excavations at Qumran." *Journal of Roman Archaeology* 17:321–32.

Friedman, R. E. 2003. *The Bible with Sources Revealed. A New View into the Five Books of Moses.* San Francisco: Harper.

Galor, K, Humbert, J.-B. and Zangenberg, J. (eds). 2006. *Qumran, the Site of the Dead Sea Scrolls: Archaeological Interpretations and Debates. Proceedings of a Conference Held at Brown University, Nov. 17–19, 2002.* Leiden/Boston: Brill.

Golb, N. 1995. *Who Wrote the Dead Sea Scrolls? The Search for the Secret of Qumran.* New York: Scribner.

Gunneweg, J. 2012a. "Engedi-Qumran-Schøyen and Allegro Jars." In *Outdoor Qumran and the Dead Sea. Its impact on the Indoor Bio- and Material Cultures at Qumran and the Judean Desert Manuscripts, Proceedings of the joint Hebrew University and COST Action D-42 Cultural Heritage Workshop held at the Hebrew University of Jerusalem in May 25–26, 2010,* edited by J. Gunneweg and Ch. Greenblatt. Jerusalem: Hebrew University. http://micro5.mscc.huji.ac.il/~msjan/qumranproceedings2010.html

Gunneweg, J. 2012b. "Outdoor Versus Indoor Environment at Qumran and the Dead Sea. A Trans-disciplinary Approach." In *Outdoor Qumran and the Dead Sea. Its Impact on the Indoor Bio- and Material Cultures at Qumran and the Judean Desert Manuscripts, Proceedings of the Joint Hebrew University and COST Action D-42 Cultural Heritage Workshop Held at the Hebrew University of Jerusalem in May 25–26, 2010,* edited by J. Gunneweg and Ch. Greenblatt. Jerusalem: Hebrew University. http://micro5.mscc.huji.ac.il/~msjan/qumranproceedings2010.html

Gunneweg, J. and Balla, M. 2003. "Neutron Activation Analysis: Scroll Jars and Common Ware." In *Fouilles de Khirbet Qumrân et de 'Ain Feshkha II: Études d'Anthropologie, de Physique et de Chimie*. Novum Testamentum et Orbis Antiquus 3, edited by J.-B. Humbert and J. Gunneweg, 1–55. Fribourg: Academic Press Fribourg; Göttingen: Vandenhoeck and Ruprecht.

Gunneweg, J. and Balla, M. 2006. "Was the Qumran Settlement a Mere Pottery Production Center? What Instrumental Neutron Activation Revealed." In *"Holistic Qumran", Trans-Disciplinary Research of Qumran and the Dead Sea Scrolls, Proceedings of the NIAS-Lorentz Center Qumran Workshop, 21–25 April 2008*, edited by J. Gunneweg, A. Adriaens, and J. Dik, 39–62. Leiden: Brill.

Gunneweg, J., Greenblatt, Ch. and Adriaens, A. (eds). 2006. *The Bio- and Material Cultures at Qumran. Papers from a COST-Action G8 Working Group Meeting Held in Jerusalem Israel 22–23 May 2005*. Stuttgart: Fraunhofer Verlag.

Gunneweg, J., Adriaens, A. and Dik, J. (eds). 2010. *"Holistic Qumran", Trans-Disciplinary Research of Qumran and the Dead Sea Scrolls, Proceedings of the NIAS-Lorentz Center Qumran Workshop, 21–25 April 2008*. Leiden: Brill.

Gunneweg, J. and Greenblatt, Ch. (eds). 2012. *Outdoor Qumran and the Dead Sea. Its Impact on the Indoor Bio- and Material Cultures at Qumran and the Judean Desert Manuscripts, Proceedings of the Joint Hebrew University and COST Action D-42 Cultural Heritage Workshop Held at the Hebrew University of Jerusalem in May 25–26, 2010*. Jerusalem: Hebrew University. http://micro5.mscc.huji.ac.il/~msjan/qumranproceedings2010.html

Harding, G. L. 1949. "The Dead Sea Scrolls." *Palestine Exploration Quarterly* 81:112–16.

Harding, G. L. 1952. "Khirbet Qumran and Wady Muraba'at." *Palestine Exploration Quarterly* 84:104–09.

Higham, T., Taylor, J. E. and Green, D. 2003. "New Radiocarbon Determinations from Khirbet Qumran from the University of Waikato Laboratories." In *Khirbet Qumran and 'Ain Feshkha II: Études d'Anthropologie, de Physique et de Chimie*, edited by J.-B. Humbert and J. Gunneweg, 197–200. Gottingen: Vandenhoeck & Ruprecht; Fribourg: Editions universitaires.

Hirschfeld, Y. 1998. "Early Roman Manor Houses in Judea and the Site of Khirbet Qumran." *Journal of Near Eastern Studies* 57:161–89.

Hirschfeld, Y. 2000. "The Architectural Context of Qumran." In *The Dead Sea Scrolls: Fifty Years after Their Discovery. Proceedings of the Jerusalem Congress, July 20–25, 1997*, edited by L. H. Schiffman, E. Tov and J. C. VanderKam, 673–83. Jerusalem: Israel Exploration Society in cooperation with the Shrine of the Book, Israel Museum.

Hirschfeld, Y. 2002. "Qumran in the Second Temple Period. Reassessing the Archaeological Evidence." *Liber Annuus* 52:247–96.

Hirschfeld, Y. 2004. *Qumran in Context: Reassessing the Archaeological Evidence*. Peabody, Mass.: Hendrickson Publishers.

Hirschfeld, Y. 2006. "Qumran in the Second Temple Period: A Reassessment." In *Qumran, the Site of the Dead Sea Scrolls: Archaeological Interpretations and Debates. Proceedings of a Conference Held at Brown University, Nov. 17–19, 2002, edited by*

K. Galor, J.-B. Humbert and J. Zangenberg, 223–39. Leiden/Boston: Brill.

Humbert, J.-B. 1994. "L'espace Sacré à Qumrân: Propositions pour l'Archéologie." *Revue Biblique* 101:161–214.

Humbert, J.-B. 2003. "Reconsideration of the Archaeological Interpretation." and "Arguments en Faveur d'une Résidence Pré-Essénienne." In *Khirbet Qumran and 'Ain Feshkha II: Études d'Anthropologie, de Physique et de Chimie*, edited by J.-B. Humbert and J. Gunneweg, 419–44, 467–82. Gottingen: Vandenhoeck & Ruprecht; Fribourg: Editions universitaires.

Humbert, J.-B. 2006. "Some Remarks on the Archaeology of Qumran." In *Qumran, the Site of the Dead Sea Scrolls: Archaeological Interpretations and Debates. Proceedings of a Conference Held at Brown University, Nov. 17–19, 2002*, edited by K. Galor, J.-B. Humbert and J. Zangenberg, 19–39. Leiden/Boston: Brill.

Humbert, J.-B. and Chambon, A. 1994. *Fouilles de Khirbet Qumrân et de Ain Feshka I: Album de Photographies. Répertoire du Fonds Photographiques. Synthèse des Notes de Chantier du Père Roland de Vaux*. Novum Testamentum et Orbis Antiquus, Series Archaeologica 1. Fribourg: Editions Universitaires.

Humbert, J.-B. and Gunneweg, J. (eds). 2003. *Khirbet Qumran and 'Ain Feshkha II: Études d'Anthropologie, de Physique et de Chimie*. Gottingen: Vandenhoeck & Ruprecht; Fribourg: Editions universitaires.

Isaacs, A. A. 1857. *The Dead Sea: or, Notes and Observations Made During a Journey to Palestine in 1856-7*. London: Hatchard and Son.

Jull, A. J. T., Donahue, D. J., Broshi, M. and Tov, E. 1995. "Radiocarbon Dating of Scrolls and Linen Fragments from the Judean Desert." *Radiocarbon* 37:11–19.

Kovacs, M. G. 1989. *The Epic of Gilgamesh*. Stanford: Stanford University Press.

Laperrousaz, E.-M. 1966. "Brèves Remarques Archéologiques Concernant la Chronologie des Occupations Esséniennes de Qoumran." *Revue de Qumran* 12:199–212.

Laperrousaz, E.-M. 1976. *Qoumran, l'Etablissement Essénien des Bords de la Mer Morte, Histoire et Archéologie du Site*. Paris: Picard.

Laperrousaz, E.-M. 1980. "Problèmes d'Histoire et d'Archéologie Qoumraniennes: a Propos d'un Souhait de Précisions." *Revue de Qumran* 10:269–91.

Libby, W. F. 1951. "Radiocarbon Dates II." *Science* 114:291–96.

Magen, Y. and Peleg, Y. 2006. "Back to Qumran: Ten Years of Excavation and Research, 1993–2004." In *Qumran, the Site of the Dead Sea Scrolls: Archaeological Interpretations and Debates. Proceedings of a Conference Held at Brown University, Nov. 17–19, 2002*, edited by K. Galor, J.-B. Humbert and J. Zangenberg, 55–113. Leiden/Boston: Brill.

Magen, Y. and Peleg, Y. 2007. *The Qumran Excavations 1993-2004: Preliminary Report*. Judea and Samaria Publications 6. Jerusalem: Israel Antiquities Authority.

Magness, J. 1996. "What Was Qumran? Not a Country Villa." *Biblical Archaeology Review* 22:40–47, 72–73.

Magness, J. 1998a. "The Chronology of Qumran, Ein Feshkha, and Ein El-Ghuweir." In *Mogilany 1995: Papers on the Dead*

Sea Scrolls Offered in Memory of Aleksy Klawek, edited by Z. J. Kapera, 55–76. Kraków: Enigma Press.

Magness, J. 1998b. "Two Notes on the Archaeology of Qumran." *Bulletin of the American Schools of Oriental Research* 312:37–44.

Magness, J. 1998–9. "Qumran Archaeology: Past Perspectives and Future Prospects." In *The Dead Sea Scrolls after Fifty Years: A Comprehensive Assessment*, edited by P. W. Flint and J. C. VanderKam, Vol. 1, 47–77. Leiden: Brill.

Magness, J. 2000. "A Reassessment of the Excavations of Qumran." In *The Dead Sea Scrolls: Fifty Years after Their Discovery. Proceedings of the Jerusalem Congress, July 20–25, 1997*, edited by L. H. Schiffman, E. Tov and J. C. VanderKam, 708–19. Jerusalem: Israel Exploration Society in cooperation with the Shrine of the Book, Israel Museum.

Magness, J. 2002. *The Archaeology of Qumran and the Dead Sea Scrolls*. Grand Rapids, Mich.: Eerdmans.

Magness, J. 2004. *Debating Qumran: Collected Essays on its Archaeology*. Interdisciplinary Studies in Ancient Culture and Religion 4. Dudley, Mass.: Peeters.

Milik, J. T. 1959. *Ten Years of Discovery in the Wilderness of Judea*. Translation by J. Strugnell. Studies in Biblical Theology 26. London: SCM.

Müller, M., Murphy, B., Burghammer, M., Riekel, C., Gunneweg, J. and Pantos, E. 2006. "Structural and Elemental Analysis of Single Fibres from Qumran Using Modern Synchrotron Radiation X-ray Microdiffraction and Microfluorescence Techniques." In *Bio- and Material Cultures at Qumran*, edited by J. Gunneweg, Ch. Greenblatt, and A. Adriaens, 109–23. Stuttgart: Fraunhofer Verlag.

Müller, M., Murphy, B., Burghammer, M., Riekel, C., Pantos, E. and Gunneweg, J. 2007. "Ageing of Native Cellulose Fibres Under Archaeological Conditions: Textile From the Dead Sea Region Studied Using Synchrotron X-ray μ-Diffraction." *Applied Physics A, Materials Science and Processing* 89:877–81.

Mumcuoglu, K. and Gunneweg, J. 2012. "A Head Louse Egg, *Pediculus Humanus Capitis*, Found in a Comb in the Christmas Cave." In *Outdoor Qumran and the Dead Sea. Its Impact on the Indoor Bio- and Material Cultures at Qumran and the Judean Desert Manuscripts, Proceedings of the Joint Hebrew University and COST Action D-42 Cultural Heritage Workshop Held at the Hebrew University of Jerusalem in May 25–26, 2010*, edited by J. Gunneweg and Ch. Greenblatt. Jerusalem: Hebrew University. http://micro5.mscc.huji.ac.il/~msjan/qumranproceedings2010.html

Murphy, B., Cotte, M., Müller, M., Balla, M. and Gunneweg, J. 2010. "Degradation of Parchment and Ink of the Dead Sea Scrolls Investigated Using Synchrotron Based X-ray and Infrared Microscopy." In *"Holistic Qumran", Trans-Disciplinary Research of Qumran and the Dead Sea Scrolls, Proceedings of the NIAS-Lorentz Center Qumran Workshop, 21–25 April 2008*, edited by J. Gunneweg, A. Adriaens, and J. Dik, 77–98. Leiden: Brill.

Patai, R. 1990. *The Hebrew Goddess*. Third Enlarged Edition. Detroit: Wayne State University.

Perlman, I. and Asaro, F. 1969. "Pottery Analysis by Neutron Activation." *Archaeometry* 11:21–52.

Petrie, W. M. F. 1891. *Tell el Hesy (Lachish)*. London: Palestine Exploration Fund.

Price, R. 2004. "New Discoveries at Qumran." *World of the Bible News and Views* 6/3. http://www.worldofthebible.com/resources.htm#Bible studies

Price, R. 2005. "Qumran Plateau." *Hadashot Arkheologiyot: Excavations and Surveys in Israel* 117. http://www.hadashot-esi.org.il/report_detail_eng.asp?id=126&mag_id=110

Rasmussen, K. L., Gunneweg, J., Van der Plicht, J., Doudna, G., Taylor, J., Belis, M., Egsgaard, H. and Humbert, J.-B. 2006. "Cleaning and Radiocarbon Dating of Material from Khirbet Qumran." In *The Bio- and Material Cultures at Qumran. Papers from a COST-Action G8 Working Group Meeting Held in Jerusalem Israel 22–23 May 2005*, edited by J. Gunneweg, Ch. Greenblatt, and A. Adriaens, 139–64. Stuttgart: Fraunhofer Verlag.

Rumford, J. 2000. *Seeker of Knowledge. The Man Who Deciphered Egyptian Hieroglyphs*. Boston: Houghton Mifflin Harcourt.

Runnels, C. 2002. *The Archaeology of Heinrich Schliemann: An Annotated Bibliographic Handlist*. Boston: Archaeological Institute of America.

Sellers, O. R. 1951. "Date of Cloth from the 'Ayn Feshka Cave." *Biblical Archaeologist* 14:29.

Strange, J. 2006. "The 1996 Excavations at Quman and the Context of the New Hebrew Ostracon." In *Qumran, the Site of the Dead Sea Scrolls: Archaeological Interpretations and Debates. Proceedings of a Conference Held at Brown University, Nov. 17–19, 2002*, edited by K. Galor, J.-B. Humbert, and J. Zangenberg, 41–54. Leiden/Boston: Brill.

Taylor, J. E. 2002. "Nineteenth Century Visitors to Khirbet Qumran and the Name of the Site." *Palestine Exploration Quarterly* 134:144–64.

Taylor, J. E. 2006. "Kh. Qumran in Period III." In *Qumran, the Site of the Dead Sea Scrolls: Archaeological Interpretations and Debates. Proceedings of a Conference Held at Brown University, Nov. 17–19, 2002*, edited by K. Galor, J.-B. Humbert and J. Zangenberg, 133–46. Leiden/Boston: Brill.

Taylor, J. E. 2011. "Buried Manuscripts and Empty Tombs: The Genizah Hypothesis Reconsidered." In *'Go out and study the Land' (Judg 18:2): Archaeological, Historical and Textual Studies in Honor of Hanan Eshel*, edited by A. Maeir, J. Magness and L. Schiffman, 269–316. Supplements of the Journal for the Study of Judaism. Leiden: Brill.

Taylor, J. E. 2012. *The Essenes, the Scrolls and the Dead Sea*. Oxford: Oxford University Press.

Taylor, J. E. and Doudna, G. 2003. "Archaeological Synthesis of the New Radiocarbon Datings from Qumran." In *Khirbet Qumran and 'Ain Feshkha II: Études d'Anthropologie, de Physique et de Chimie*, edited by J.-B. Humbert and J. Gunneweg, 201–205. Gottingen: Vandenhoeck & Ruprecht; Fribourg: Editions universitaires.

Taylor, J., Rasmussen, K. L., Doudna, G., Van der Plicht, J. and Egsgaard, H. 2005. "Qumran Textiles in the Palestine Exploration Fund, London: Radiocarbon Dating Results." *Palestine Exploration Quarterly* 137:159–67.

Taylor, J. E. and Gibson, S. 2011. "Qumran Connected: The Paths and Passes of the North-Western Dead Sea." In *Qumran und*

Archäologie – wechselseitige Perspektiven, edited by J. Frey and C. Claussen, 1–51. Tübingen: Mohr Siebeck.

Van der Plicht, J., Rasmussen, K. L., Glastrup, J., Taylor, J. E. and Doudna, G. 2003. "Radiocarbon Datings of Material from the Qumran Excavation." In *Khirbet Qumran and 'Ain Feshkha II: Études d'Anthropologie, de Physique et de Chimie,* edited by J.-B. Humbert and J. Gunneweg, 193–96. Gottingen: Vandenhoeck & Ruprecht; Fribourg: Editions universitaires.

Van der Plicht, J., and Rasmussen, K. L. 2010. "Radiocarbon Dating and Qumran." In *"Holistic Qumran", Trans-disciplinary Research of Qumran and the Dead Sea Scrolls, Proceedings of the NIAS-Lorentz Center Qumran Workshop, 21-25 April 2008,* edited by J. Gunneweg, A. Adriaens, and J. Dik, 99–122. Leiden: Brill.

Van der Velde, C. W. M. 1856. *Memoir to Accompany the Map of the Holy Land.* Gotha: Justus Perthes.

de Vaux, R. 1949a. "Les Anciens Manuscrits Hébreux Récemment Découverts." *Revue Biblique* 56:204–33.

de Vaux, R. 1949b. "La Cachette des Manuscrits Hébreux." *Revue Biblique* 56:234–37.

de Vaux, R. 1949c. "La Grotte des Manuscrits Hébreux." *Revue Biblique* 56:586–609.

de Vaux, R. 1953a. "Fouille au Khirbet Qumran." *Revue Biblique* 60:83–106.

de Vaux, R. 1953b. "Exploration de la Région de Qumran." *Revue Biblique* 60:540–61.

de Vaux, R. 1954. "Fouilles au Khirbet Qumrân." *Revue Biblique* 61:206–36.

de Vaux, R. 1956. "Fouilles de Khirbet Qumrân." *Revue Biblique* 63:533–77.

de Vaux, R. 1959. "Fouilles de Feshkha." *Revue Biblique* 66:225–55.

de Vaux, R. 1961. *L'Archéologie et les Manuscrits de la Mer Morte.* London: Oxford University Press.

de Vaux, R. 1973. *Archaeology and the Dead Sea Scrolls.* Translation by D. Bourke. London: British Academy and Oxford: Oxford University Press.

Wagemakers, B. and Taylor, J. E. 2011. "New Photographs of the Qumran Excavations from 1954 and Interpretations of L.77 and L.86." *Palestine Exploration Quarterly* 143.2:134–56.

Warren, C. 1890. *Excavations in Jerusalem (1867-1870).* London: Palestine Exploration Fund.

Woolley, C. L. 1929. *Ur of the Chaldees: A Record of Seven Years of Excavation.* London: Benn.

Yardeni, A. 1997. "A Draft of a Deed on an Ostracon from Khirbet Qumran." *Israel Exploration Journal* 47:233–37.

CHAPTER 8

CAESAREA MARITIMA

In the year 22 BCE King Herod the Great began to build a new city on the coast, to which he gave the name Caesarea, in honour of his friend, the Roman emperor Caesar Augustus. Because of its setting next to the sea and to distinguish it from other places with the same name, the city was given the surname 'Maritima'.

The new city was located at Strato's Tower, a harbour town built by the king of the Phoenician town of Sidon, king Strato I. In late second century BCE this place came into the possession of the king of Dor and in 90 BCE it was taken over by the Hasmonaean king Alexander Jannaeus. After the invasion of this region by the Roman general Gnaeus Pompeius Magnus in 63 BCE, this town became part of the Roman province of Syria. The town was given to Cleopatra VII by Mark Antony, and, after the battle of Actium in 31 BCE, it was handed over to Herod by Augustus.

Caesarea Maritima was inaugurated in 10/9 BCE. The splendid city with its impressive port was lavishly decorated with temples, theatres and statues of gods and emperors. An inscription mentions governor Pontius Pilatus and the temple he built for Tiberius. After 6 CE it became the residence of the Roman procurators. It was the capital of the Province of Palaestina during the Byzantine period. After the Muslims conquered Caesarea in 639 in the name of Caliph Omar, they ruled the city for more than four and a half centuries. In 1101 the Crusader king Baldwin I captured and ransacked the place. In 1265 the Mamluk Sultan Beibars took Caesarea. The city was finally destroyed in 1291 by Sultan Mailik al-Ashraf.

Because of the presence of the imposing port, several of the archaeological teams working in Caesarea Maritima used underwater archaeology during their campaigns. An overview of their work will be given in this chapter.

The Archaeology of Caesarea Maritima

Kenneth G. Holum

For his visit to Caesarea on 2 May 1954 Leo Boer travelled by bus northward from Tel Aviv, past the small town of Hadera, inhabited mainly by German Jews, and past vast expanses of sand dunes, then turning off to the left onto a smaller road leading toward the sea four kilometres away. The passengers on the bus – teachers and students from the École Biblique – all noticed with delight clusters of yellow flowers half a metre high. These were beach evening primroses, still plentiful at Caesarea more than half a century later, lending a certain charm to the late spring landscape. But the young traveller would hardly have recognized the same route today, for a large development town, Or Akiva, has grown up on the road toward the coast, which now passes beneath a modern motorway before reaching the confines of the ancient site. From the spot where he and his companions had their lunch, 'in the shade of some trees' near the hippodrome, they had a clear view toward Kibbutz Sdot Yam on the shore to the south-west, and on the road straight ahead they could see the ruins of the Muslim village Qaysari, which has been abandoned since the early days of the 1948 war and is now known as the Old City (Fig. 8.6). If they glanced across open fields toward the north-east, they could see the site of the ancient aqueduct that once delivered water to Caesarea from the north, and which was at that time still concealed beneath the beach sand shimmering in the midday sun. Today, groves of tall trees, dense shrubbery, and banana plantations create an entirely different, strikingly verdant landscape.

A short history of Caesarea Maritima

Leo Boer arrived at Caesarea, armed with a detailed, literary knowledge of the city that lay beneath the sand.[1] He knew that King Herod, choosing the site of a derelict and older town, named Straton's Tower, had founded Caesarea between 22 and 10/9 BCE (Fig. 8.1). Writing in the next century, the historian Josephus relates (*Jewish War* 1.408–15, *Jewish Antiquities* 15.331–341) that the King ordered the new city's streets to be laid out 'at equal distances from one another' (i.e. on a grid plan), and that drainage channels should be installed beneath them, to be designed in such a way that they would be flushed out by the sea. New buildings included market places, a theatre, an amphitheatre, and other public buildings, as well as a royal palace, where Herod no doubt settled his court while he observed his architects and workmen setting about building a great city. Working outwards from the shore near the centre, the builders constructed the breakwaters for a man-made harbour, by lowering huge stones into the depths. They kept the harbour entrance on the north-west, Josephus tells us, protected from the prevailing west and south-west winds, and they added storehouses and towers on the broad upper surface of the breakwaters. On the adjacent shore, upon a 'kind of hill', Herod ordered the erection of a magnificent temple dedicated to the goddess Roma, personifying the might of Rome, and, as her temple-mate, to Emperor Caesar Augustus. In the emperor's honour Herod constructed the new city and named it Caesarea, and the harbour he called *Sebastos*, Greek for Augustus. Boer also knew of New Testament Caesarea, and that St. Peter had lodged there in the house of Cornelius the centurion, the first Gentile to be converted to Christianity (Acts 10), and he knew of the deacon Philip, who settled there and led Caesarea's earliest Christian community (Acts 8:4–20). It was also at Caesarea that the Roman governor Festus, after St. Paul had languished there for two years of house arrest, brought him to trial and, when he appealed, put him on a ship bound for Rome (Acts 21–25, cf. Krentz 1992).

Also familiar to Boer were a few details about Roman Caesarea, from 7 to 312 CE, where Vespasian was proclaimed emperor in 69 CE, where the provincial governors held their seat, and also, as the Christian community emerged, the metropolitan bishop of Palestine (Levine 1975). Most famous of these bishops was Eusebius of Caesarea, celebrated as

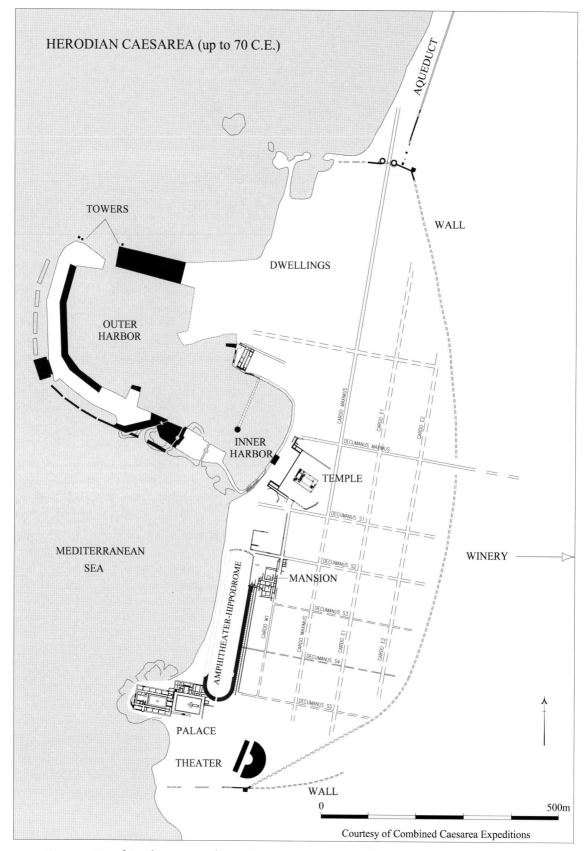

Figure 8.1: Map of Herodian Caesarea (drawn by Anna Iamim, courtesy of the Combined Caesarea Expeditions).

the first historian of the church, who in his *Martyrs of Palestine* described in gruesome detail the sufferings of Christians in Caesarea's amphitheatre during the Great Persecution of 304–311. In the written sources, the conversion of Constantine in 312 marked the onset of Caesarea's Byzantine period. During these centuries, from 312 to 640, the city hosted celebrated rabbis and accommodated the great library of Origen and Eusebius, renowned centre of biblical scholarship and the place where the ancient practice of reading texts from scrolls gave way, in the transmission of the Christian scripture, to the technology of the book (Grafton and Williams 2006; more generally Holum 2011a). Also attested in the written sources was the fall of Caesarea to the Arabs in 640, having held out longest among the ancient cities of Roman Palestine (Patrich 2011). Likewise documented, though not so richly, is Caesarea's subsequent Early Islamic period 640–1101 CE, when it survived as the smaller but still prosperous town of Qaysariyah (Hazard 1975, 79–80; Holum 2011b). Leo Boer saw nothing Early Islamic when he visited in 1954, but he did recognise ruins from the subsequent Crusader period 1101–1265, including vestiges of the town's fortifications (Figs 8.4 and 8.5); these were last strengthened in 1252 during the Sixth Crusade, when French King Louis IX carried some of the stones for the project on his own back (Hazard 1975).

The archaeology of Caesarea in the time of Leo Boer's visit

When Boer and his fellow-students arrived at Caesarea, archaeologists had only visited the site infrequently and possessed little knowledge of Caesarea's extent in the Roman and Byzantine periods or of the qualities of urban life there. Prior to 1948, the Muslims of the town Qaysari, originally refugees from Bosnia in Europe, had quarried the stones of the ancient city for their own houses, shops, a school, and a mosque. Occasionally an antiquities inspector of the British mandatory government or, after 1948, of the Israeli Department of Antiquities, would arrive to record the chance finding of a statue or of a Greek or Latin inscription (Vann 1992). The founding of Kibbutz Sdot Yam just to the south of Caesarea in 1940 brought to bear the enthusiasm and intelligence of Aaron Wegman, one of the original pioneers, who persuaded his colleagues to assemble chance finds from their

fields in a small museum. Boer enjoyed this collection very much, and it has now become one of the finest local museums in Israel.

Meanwhile, in 1930 the first reports appeared of an ancient synagogue, located on the coast just north of Muslim Qaysari (Fig. 8.2), but it was not explored systematically until Michael Avi-Yonah's excavations in 1956 and 1962. The poor remains did not receive definitive publication until half a century later (Govaars *et al.* 2008). In 1950 army trenching exposed an expanse of mosaic pavement displaying numerous species of bird and other animals. It was found in one of the suburbs outside the walls of the ancient settlement and which archaeologists more recently identified definitively as a suburban villa of the Byzantine period (Fig. 8.2). In its ruins they discovered remains of a dining table, decorated in gold glass, which served as a witness to the wealth of the city's elite on the eve of the Muslim conquest. It was reconstituted by expert restorers for museum display (Porath *et al.* 2005/2006).

Apparently unaware of the earlier discoveries, Boer and his companions visited the so-called 'Byzantine esplanade', just to the east of the Muslim village (Figs 8.2 and 8.3). In 1950 one of the kibbutz farmers had struck a massive statue here with his plough, and Shmuel Yeivin excavated the site on behalf of the Department of Antiquities, revealing in fact two Roman statues, which were reinstalled in the sixth century CE flanking the entrance to an apparent ancient shopping mall. When the group visited in 1954, the statue of Emperor Hadrian, executed in luxurious Egyptian porphyry, had been removed for display in a museum, but it has long since been put back in place. Leo Boer proposed identifying this ruin with the courtroom in which Festus had tried St. Paul, but unfortunately the date of the ruin was five centuries later (Holum 2008).

Systematic excavations in the 1960s

Through the 1950s, archaeological projects at Caesarea had been of the 'rescue' type, undertaken either to explore further and record chance discoveries, or to consolidate and preserve ancient ruins that threatened to succumb to natural or human destruction. In 1959–1964, for the first time, archaeologists from Israel and abroad managed to undertake systematic excavations on a much larger scale, which enabled

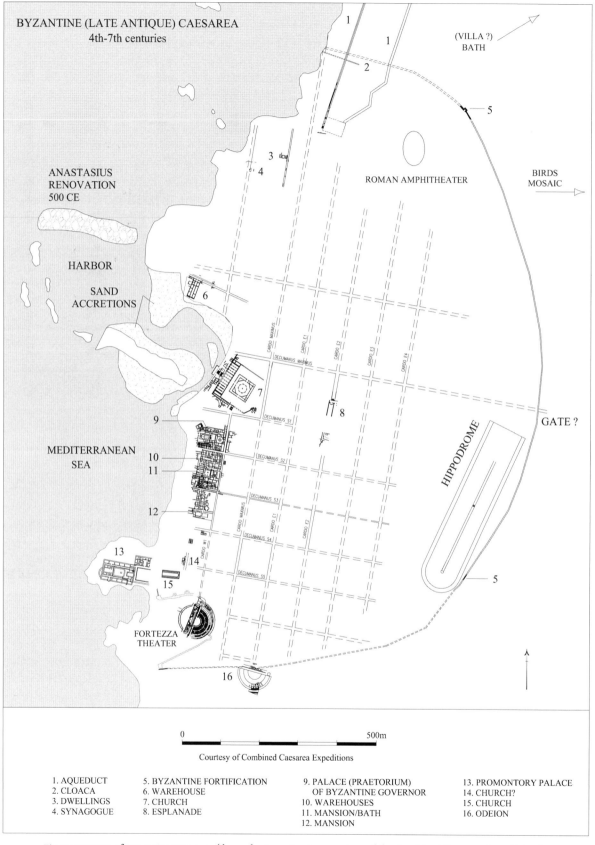

BYZANTINE (LATE ANTIQUE) CAESAREA
4th-7th centuries

ANASTASIUS
RENOVATION
500 CE

HARBOR

SAND
ACCRETIONS

MEDITERRANEAN
SEA

(VILLA ?)
BATH

ROMAN AMPHITHEATER

BIRDS
MOSAIC

GATE ?

HIPPODROME

FORTEZZA
THEATER

0   500m

Courtesy of Combined Caesarea Expeditions

1. AQUEDUCT	5. BYZANTINE FORTIFICATION	9. PALACE (PRAETORIUM)	13. PROMONTORY PALACE
2. CLOACA	6. WAREHOUSE	OF BYZANTINE GOVERNOR	14. CHURCH?
3. DWELLINGS	7. CHURCH	10. WAREHOUSES	15. CHURCH
4. SYNAGOGUE	8. ESPLANADE	11. MANSION/BATH	16. ODEION
		12. MANSION	

Figure 8.2: Map of Byzantine Caesarea (drawn by Anna Iamim, courtesy of the Combined Caesarea Expeditions).

Figure 8.3: The Byzantine Esplanade, looking north-west, excavated by S. Yeivin in 1950, photo by Leo Boer in 1954. Two colossal statues flanked the entrance to a building. The marble statue of a god is seated on the left, but the porphyry statue of Emperor Hadrian is missing, taken away for a museum exhibition. Note also the ubiquitous flowers, the beach evening primrose.

them to unlock the secrets of Caesarea as a site of ancient urbanism and, in particular, of Herod's remarkable harbour Sebastos, which Josephus had praised with such enthusiasm.[2]

Caesarea, of course, was a large urban site, extending over circa 95 hectares within the external (Byzantine-period) circuit of walls, which is why it was important to investigate extensive tracts in order to improve the understanding of the processes of urban development. Across the decades, as one project succeeded another, archaeological techniques gradually improved beyond the primitive methods employed in the 1960s and earlier. Teams adopted 'stratigraphic' archaeology, i.e. excavating by layers, and eventually the archaeologists learned how to record the layers more accurately, using laser surveying instruments. Gradually they began to employ ceramic chronologies with greater precision and to value every bit of material evidence that came out of the ground; not just pottery and coins, but glass, bone, and metal objects, and evidence for

human diet and the natural environment, such as animal and fish bones and the carbonized seeds of wild and domesticated plants.

The first impetus for large-scale projects came from abroad. In 1959 the Italian *Missione Archeologica Italiana*, directed by Antonio J. Frova of the University of Milan, undertook the first of five seasons of excavation, using a hired labour force and heavy-duty mechanical equipment. This project exposed completely the Roman-style theatre that Josephus had mentioned (Fig. 8.1), as well as a fortification, the so-called *fortezza*, which incorporated its ruins in the late sixth century after the theatre had fallen out of use (Fig. 8.2). The Italians also studied Caesarea's external circuit of fortification walls. By excavating a small segment, they demonstrated that the circuit, which, in 1954, was visible on the surface through much of its course, dated not to the Roman period but most probably to the fifth century CE. They also brought to light a length of city wall of a middle circuit north of the abandoned village Qaysari, now dubbed the Old

City, including a gateway flanked by two round towers and a polygonal tower further to the east (Fig. 8.1). The Italians proposed dating this circuit to the time of either Straton's Tower or King Herod.

In 1960, meanwhile, the American team of Edwin Link, using SCUBA gear ('self-contained underwater breathing apparatus') at Caesarea for the first time, proved that the ruins of Herod's harbour lay underwater just offshore from the centre of the Old City. Because of technical difficulties with the equipment and the crew, however, they accomplished little else.

Much more productive than Link's effort, and leaving a more profound imprint on the site's terrain, were the excavations conducted by Avraham Negev of the Hebrew University, Jerusalem between 1960 and 1964. Again, using hired labourers and mechanical equipment (bulldozers and large trucks), Negev cleared the moats, scarps, and counterscarps of the innermost fortification line, which dated to the Early Muslim period but was extensively rebuilt as late as 1252, the time of crusading King Louis IX (Figs 8.4 and 8.5). He also deployed his workmen inside the Old City to remove the fallen ruins of Bosnian houses on the high ground next to the three-apsed Crusader church, which Boer had seen, as well as the ruins on the slope to the west and along the east side of the lower ground. Earlier in the century this had been the *shuq* or market of Bosnian Qaysari (Fig. 8.6). Later, the archaeologists would discover that in antiquity this expanse of dry land had been the Inner Harbour (area I) of King Herod's Caesarea, and that, on the high ground near the Crusader church, later identified as the Temple Platform (area TP), had stood Herod's temple to Roma and Augustus, followed, four centuries later, by an octagonal Early Christian church. Negev did not know the location of these monumental buildings, but in removing the Bosnian ruins he exposed barrel-vaulted substructures, which, in the Byzantine period, formed the western façade of the Temple Platform and served later as the foundations of the Christian church.

While levelling a road along the south side of the Crusader moat, his workmen struck on ancient ruins, which Negev identified tentatively with the library of Origen and Eusebius. However, these ruins, including the mosaic pavements with Greek inscriptions, would turn out to be the governor's palace of Byzantine Caesarea. Negev often turned out to be wrong, but

Figure 8.4: Aerial view of Caesarea looking south-west, photographed by Aaron Levin in 1986. The Early Islamic/Crusader fortifications enclose the Old City. The site of the ancient harbour is visible on the upper right, the Negev excavation area on the upper left.

Figure 8.5: Eastern range of Early Islamic/Crusader fortifications looking north, photographed by Aaron Levin in 1986. Visible are the scarp, the moat, and the counterscarp, which date from the refortification under Louis IX of France in 1252.

Figure 8.6: Caesarea, looking west from Temple Platform (area TP), across the Inner Harbour (area I) to the Crusader jetty and Crusader citadel, photographed by Leo Boer in 1954. The deserted buildings that are visible date from the Bosnian Muslim occupation 1884-1948. The Bosnians reused the citadel as a police station.

he was a pioneer and had little to go on. To the north of the Old City, he excavated further trenches in the vicinity of the synagogue, but found little of significance. Finally, it was Negev who removed tons of sand from the double Roman aqueduct where it approached the city from the north, and which had eroded away from that point southward by the intruding waters of the North Bay.

A national park

In the meantime, even before Leo Boer paid his visit, the derelict and idyllic ancient site had been affected in new ways by the outside world: in 1952 Baron Edmund de Rothschild, whose grandfather had purchased great tracts of land in this part of Israel from the Turkish Sultan, deeded Caesarea and its surroundings, about 35,000 dunams, or 9000 hectares, to the State of Israel and formed a corporation, called the Baron Edmund Benjamin de Rothschild Caesarea Development Corporation to develop this land (CDC, visit www.caesarea.com).

The profits from this enterprise would go to benefit the State of Israel, especially to social, educational, and cultural programmes. Part of these programmes would include the development of the town of Or Akiva, the luxurious neighbourhoods of modern Caesarea to the east and northeast of the site, and a national park in the centre of the site, although much of the ancient urban space, outside the national park, is still farmed by the members of the Kibbutz Sdot Yam. The purpose of the national park, of course, was to attract tourists from all over the world to enjoy both the antiquities and the beaches that ancient Caesarea offered, and indeed it was the Department of Parks that had sponsored Negev's excavations.

Archaeology in the 1970s: the participation of volunteers and of the JCEM

Another positive development was the arrival of archaeological volunteers, first from North America and later from Israel itself and various countries in

Europe as well. Although the terms of participation varied, the motive for volunteer archaeology was to enable professional archaeologists and scholars to enlist archaeological enthusiasts, many but not all of them students, to sample the thrill of archaeology and its educational benefits under the guidance of professionals. Volunteer archaeologists worked without pay and in many cases actually paid themselves to get the chance to work long hours under the hot sun, at first several hundred dollars for three or four weeks, eventually several thousand.

The first group of volunteer archaeologists to arrive at Caesarea was the Joint Expedition to Caesarea Maritima (JECM) from North America, organised and directed by Robert J. Bull. This team arrived for the first time in the summer of 1972 and continued its work in alternate summers until 1985. Progress was slow, because the volunteers did not work with tractors, but with trowels, hoes, and buckets. Nevertheless, JECM turned a corner in the archaeology of Caesarea, as they for the first time comprehended the entire city in its plans. A major priority was to uncover the streets of the ancient city and its adjacent residential, commercial, and government buildings. The team excavated trenches to the north (field A) and south (field B) of the Byzantine esplanade that Boer had also seen. They discovered that this was indeed the line of one of the ancient paved streets, and brought to light (in area B) a colonnaded courtyard of the Byzantine period in which an important statue of the city goddess or Tyche had been displayed. This goddess, also known from coins, was from the Roman period and is now exhibited in the Caesarea Museum at Sdot Yam. To the north of the Old City, they continued the Avi-Yonah, Negev, and Italian excavations, exposing more of the fortification wall, which the Italians had discovered, dating it definitively to the time of King Herod (area G8). They also exposed the line of another street and adjacent domestic structures, in one of which they discovered a hoard of 99 gold coins, now displayed in the Israel Museum (Evans 2006).[3] To the south-east of the Old city, near the spot where Boer and his companions had had their lunch, the team conducted the first excavations of the ancient circus or hippodrome (field H), recovering significant elements in its design and showing that it had functioned from the second century CE to the sixth (Humphrey 1975).

Even more important were the JECM explorations south of the Old City. There the team expanded the Negev excavation, exposing important parts of a governmental complex, including the 'imperial revenue office' of Byzantine Palestine. Along the western slope above the shore, they discovered a complex of vaulted substructures, one of which had been in use as a *Mithraeum*, cult centre of the god Mithras, in the second and third centuries CE, and one of the first Mithraea known in the Middle East. In the productive season of 1979 (the first in which the author of this chapter participated), they discovered the network of city streets in what was to become known as Caesarea's South-west Zone (Figs 8.1 and 8.2). Indeed, JECM's main achievement was to recover, in isolated trenches across the site, fragments of the street plan, with the streets laid out 'at equal distances from one another', which permitted reconstruction of the urban plan of the ancient city.[4]

The campaigns of the Hebrew University and Haifa University

In the meantime, two Israeli projects also entered the lists of archaeological excavations at Caesarea, both of them employing volunteers. In 1975, 1976, and 1979, a team from the Hebrew University, Jerusalem, carried out excavations, directed by Lee I. Levine, a scholar of Jewish history and archaeology, who had written an important monograph on Caesarea (Levine 1975), and by Ehud Netzer, who was then in the process of becoming the leading authority on the architecture of Herod the Great (Levine and Netzer 1986).

Within the Old City, on the north side of its small, semi-protected harbour, Levine and Netzer excavated a large area employing careful stratigraphic techniques. A column inscribed with the single Hebrew word *shalom* had come to light here; it was suspected that this might be the location of the Jewish quarter of the ancient city. Instead, the excavators penetrated several layers of domestic architecture dated to the Early Muslim and Crusader periods, before exposing segments of still another street and, adjacent to it, a large public building of the Byzantine period, which they suspected to be a warehouse (*horreum*), a hypothesis that proved to be correct. To the south of the Old City, on a promontory jutting out into the sea adjacent to the Herodian-Roman theatre,

Levine and Netzer surveyed a mysterious pool cut into the rock, popularly known as 'Cleopatra's bath' (presumably because Mark Antony had presented this part of Judaea to his paramour), yet suspected by expert archaeologists to be a 'fishpond' (*piscina*). Against the consensus of earlier authorities, Ehud Netzer argued – and later, here too, he was proved right! – that this was the site, much damaged by the sea, of the spectacular maritime palace, mentioned by Josephus in his accounts of the founding of Caesarea, and from which the king observed the progress on construction of the harbour and the city to the north.

The idyllic surroundings of ancient Caesarea were affected yet again, in 1975, when the Israel Electric Company contracted scientists and scholars from Haifa University's Centre for Maritime Studies (CMS) to study the geomorphology of the sea floor along the coast at Caesarea. The initial plan was to construct a nuclear power plant west of Hadera and south of ancient Caesarea. Fortunately, the nuclear option was scrapped, and today the three lofty stacks of a conventional coal-fired plant dominate the skyline to the south (Fig. 8.7), and a jetty for unloading giant coal ships extends far into the sea – with so far unknown ultimate consequences for the beaches and coastline to the north.

In any case, the 1975 study was the first season of the long involvement of Avner Raban from Haifa University, first alongside his mentor and comrade Elisha Linder, with the archaeology of the harbour, which King Herod had built at Caesarea. By the time of his death in 2004, Raban had devoted nearly three decades of intensive research into Caesarea and the sea, and was in the process of writing up a final report.[5]

Underwater archaeology

At first, the CMS team limited its efforts to mapping and studying King Herod's breakwaters, but in 1979–1980 Raban collaborated with American underwater archaeologist Robert L. Hohlfelder, with whom he formed the Caesarea Ancient Harbour Excavation Project (CAHEP). This undertaking was later joined by R. Lindley Vann, also from America, John Oleson from Canada, and Israeli-American archaeologist Robert Stieglitz. In the summer seasons between 1980 and 1985, and in shorter fieldwork sessions until 1989, CAHEP explored shipwrecks and installations

underwater in the North Bay, the South Bay, and along the coast in between. Of most of the shipwrecks little survived apart from lead bottom sheathing, ballast stones, and concentrations of pottery. A better-preserved wreck of a merchant vessel in the North Bay was explored in detail by Michael Fitzgerald, a student at the Institute of Nautical Archaeology of Texas A. & M. University (Oleson *et al.* 2009, 163–223).

Nevertheless, CAHEP's directors had conceived their project not to study shipwrecks but as harbour archaeology, with its principal objective King Herod's harbour Sebastos, including its breakwaters, the outer and inner basins, and landward installations, which were components of the same harbour complex. In order to study Herod's project properly, the archaeologists developed new techniques, adapted from harbour archaeology at other sites. This included the use of air lifts and underwater dredges for excavation, and cylindrical steel caissons that were inserted into the sea floor as the divers worked through layers of deposition and enabled careful analysis of the stratification. Even more challenging were excavations in waterlogged contexts along the shoreline; here the archaeologists needed to build cofferdams and to apply constant pumping of water in order to dig stratigraphically. In this way they were able to recover ceramics and other finds and to record their progress in photographs and drawings. In these circumstances excavation was a costly process, made possible by generous subventions of the CDC and by the labour and monetary contributions ('dig fees') of hundreds of skilled SCUBA-certified divers who volunteered both their funds and their labour. During its main seasons, CAHEP completed mapping the great southern and northern breakwaters of Sebastos, the Inner Harbour (area I), and landward installations (Fig. 8.1) and began to explore the issue of the harbour's longevity and eventual demise (Raban 1989, 2009).

The Combined Caesarea Expeditions (CCE)

The excavations of JECM and CAHEP revealed much new data in the 1970s and 1980s, accomplishing great strides towards understanding King Herod's city and its later history, yet in archaeology as in other scholarly fields, continuing research always raises more questions than it can answer. In response

Figure 8.7: Caesarea, the South-west Zone, looking south, photographed by K. Holum in 2006. Visible on the left and in the foreground is one of at least four mansions of the Byzantine period. To the right and upper centre one can see the Herodian hippodrome or racing track, beyond it on the upper right the Promontory Palace, and in the upper left-hand corner the Byzantine fortezza, surrounding the reconstructed ruins of the theatre (not visible).

to newly-raised issues, the author of this chapter, historian and archaeologist at the University of Maryland in the United States, negotiated with Avner Raban of Haifa's CMS during the winter of 1989 in order to create a new project, the Combined Caesarea Expeditions (CCE). This project would continue the work of both CAHEP and JECM and would invite other projects to collaborate as equals in research on Caesarea antiquities. The negotiations were successful, and CCE began its work in 1989, continuing through a total of fifteen summer seasons until 2003.

The initial objectives were to renew the study of the main harbour breakwaters and basins, including the Inner Harbour (area I), and to return to the Negev excavations on the Temple Platform, which had left exposed a series of foundations that suggested an Early Christian church of octagonal plan. CCE also undertook to open an entire ancient city block to the

south of the Old City (area KK) in order to evaluate the evolution of urban settlement in a continuous tract through the entire occupation sequence.[6] In 1989 the excavators began work on the area KK at the top of one of the sand dunes lining the coast south of the Old City, which Boer visited in 1954 (Fig. 8.8), but we only found human burials dated to the Early Modern or Modern (Turkish) periods and probably representing a Bedouin population. After that we removed much of the dune, using mechanical equipment (a front loader and truck).

In subsequent seasons (1990–1992), at the level of ancient occupation, the first parts of an irrigation system became manifest, which was built shortly after the Muslim conquest of 640, when this tract of the ancient city was put to use for irrigated garden agriculture. In 1993 through to 1995, we also extended the KK excavation along the shore to the north (area CV) where a large building emerged which had one room showing a mosaic pavement, depicting animals, birds, and human figures, one of them a dancer (Lehmann 1999). We were surprised to find ancient buildings in such a good state of preservation beneath the dunes which Boer had photographed 40 years earlier (Fig. 8.8).

In the meantime, we had dated the foundations on the Temple Platform definitively to the Byzantine period (fifth to sixth century CE) and had identified them as a previously unknown Early Christian Church (Holum *et al.* 1992). In area I, the Inner Harbour, we began to explore buildings to the north and south of an ancient staircase, dated, like the church, to about 500 CE, while in the outer harbour basins divers directed their attention to the details of harbour construction, and to the slumping of the southern and western breakwater beneath the waves, which resulted in numerous ships that attempted to enter the harbour striking underwater ruins and sinking not far offshore.

The Caesarea Tourist Development Project

In 1992–1993 a new era began in the archaeology of Caesarea, and indeed of other major archaeological sites within Israel. This was the fourth influence from outside on what had been an isolated, idyllic archaeological site which Leo Boer visited, and it was equally welcome. Immigration from the former Soviet Union and from Ethiopia was bringing a large population of intelligent and industrious Jews into the Jewish state who needed to be employed. Under the leadership of General Amir Drori, director of the newly created Israel Antiquities Authority (IAA), the National Parks Authority, several government ministries, and local interests, including the CDC, were joined together to create the Caesarea Tourist Development Project (CTDP). The aim of this new Development Project was to create a more engaging archaeological park, while providing employment for the new immigrants. Starting late in 1992, the

Figure 8.8: Caesarea, view from the Crusader jetty towards the south-east, photographed by Leo Boer in 1954. The dunes along the shore conceal the surviving ruins in the South-west Zone, excavated in the 1990s.

funding sufficed to permit year-round excavations and to employ hired immigrant labourers, and the excavations continued on a large scale until 1998.

The Development Project engaged two archaeological teams to organise and direct the work. One was the IAA project, headed by Yosef Porath, and which received as its assignment parts of the western façade of the Temple Platform inside the Old City, and, in the South-west Zone to the south, the tract from area KK in the north to the theatre in the south, including part of Herod's Promontory Palace. The other team was sponsored by CMS at Haifa University, soon to be renamed the Recanati Institute for Maritime Archaeology (RIMS), and Avner Raban was appointed director, who invited Joseph Patrich, then working at Haifa's Department of Archaeology, to join him as co-director. Alongside the CTDP there were two teams of volunteer archaeologists, who received welcome logistic support from the CTDP. One was the University of Pennsylvania ('Penn') Project, headed by Kathryn Gleason and Barbara Burrell of the U.S., and the other was the continuation of Holum and Raban's CCE, now with the addition of Joseph Patrich as a third director. The volunteer teams, of course, excavated only during the summer seasons, but the dense array of archaeologists, engaged in research at Caesarea, actually worked well together, both in the summer and throughout the year.

It will be best to summarise the excavation results of the 1990s according to the excavation areas within the Old City and the harbour and in the South-west Zone (Figs 8.1 and 8.2). Continuing excavation on the Temple Platform (area TP) enabled CCE to announce in 1995 that it had discovered the foundations of King Herod's temple dedicated to Roma and Augustus. Studying the foundations and architectural fragments of the superstructure permitted project architect Anna Iamim to present a reasonable reconstruction of the temple in its architectural setting and indeed this had been one of the most imposing structures of its type in the Middle East, as Josephus indicated (Fig. 8.9). By the end of the 2000 season the architecture of the Early Christian church was also coming into focus, permitting likewise a reconstruction of the church and its setting above the Inner Harbour (Fig. 8.10). Like the temple this was a truly magnificent structure. Marble slabs clad its interior walls, which were also decorated with panels displaying vegetal motifs in multi-coloured stones, and beneath the

dome was a martyr shrine containing the bones of an unknown saint (Stabler *et al.* 2008).

In the meantime, the IAA project had excavated a Roman *nymphaeum* or fountain sanctuary on the northern extent of the Temple Platform façade, and had dated the construction of the vaulted substructures along the façade, discovered by Negev, to about 300 CE. In adjacent area I the CCE excavators had brought to light the foundations of an earlier staircase that linked the Inner Harbour with the Temple compound in a single architectural complex, also evident from the orientation of the temple and the harbour in the urban plan (Figs 8.1 and 8.9). Working throughout the year, the Haifa University team discovered the full length of the original Herodian quay on the east of the Inner Harbour, as well as flushing channels designed to prevent buildup of silt in the basins. And indeed they took on the huge project of excavating the Inner Harbour basin completely. It turned out that the basin had silted up at the beginning of the Early Islamic period and that an entire quarter of streets and dwellings had been built on the new dry land, and which were still occupied at the end of Crusader Caesarea (Arnon 2008). Eventually, this quarter fell to ruin and became the *shuq* of the ruined Bosnian town which Boer visited (Fig. 8.6). Today it is a pleasant lawn of Zoysia grass sloping downwards toward the inner quay of Herod's harbour and the façade of the Temple Platform.

Out at sea, beyond the beach, Avner Raban and his colleagues had already recovered the overall design of the original harbour, so the diving archaeologists turned in the 1990s to resolving other issues. On the one hand, they discovered that during the construction process Herod's builders had floated wooden caissons built on shore – the so-called 'single mission barges' – into position at the outboard ends and along the line of the breakwaters; had then filled these barges with concrete in a special mixture that would harden underwater, sinking them into position; and finally had built up the breakwater segments between these 'islands' out of large stones laid upon the sea floor. Some of these were presumably the huge stones on which Josephus reported in his descriptions of Herod's harbour project. In addition, the harbour archaeologists investigated the harbour's longevity, and discovered, for example, that a tsunami early in the second century CE had caused serious damage

Figure 8.9: Reconstruction of the Inner Harbour and the Temple Platform in the time of Herod the Great, drawn by Anna Iamim. The temple of Roma and Augustus stands in its courts. In front is the staircase connecting the temple esplanade with the Inner Harbour quay. On the quay in the centre, we position the altar of sacrifice.

Figure 8.10: Reconstruction of the octagonal martyr church on the Temple Platform built about 500. The Inner Harbour quay is still visible (cf. Fig. 8.9), as are a staircase leading upward to the church, and, next to the church, the shops of craftsmen and tradesmen, who sold goods and services to merchants and sailors in the harbour.

to the main breakwaters. As they focused more on geo-archaeological issues, the harbour archaeologists adopted the analysis of foraminifera (the exoskeletons of tiny marine organisms, as common as the grains of sand on a beach) and several other scientific techniques in order to improve accuracy in dating harbour sediments (Reinhardt and Raban 2008).

In 1996, when the international component of CCE had finished work in area CV to the south of the Old City, we undertook to expand the Levine and Netzer excavation of the quarter north of the Inner Harbour, which we designated area LL. Here we confirmed the existence of a large warehouse designed for storing grain and other commodities, dating to the time of King Herod, and no doubt associated with his new harbour. We also discovered that the original warehouse was reconstructed from its foundations at the beginning of the fourth century CE and remained in service to the end of antiquity. After that the entire area was given over to Muslim dwellings which were then occupied continuously during the Crusader period. Together with the results in area I, the LL excavation has vastly increased our knowledge of dwellings and commercial activities in Early Islamic Qaysariyah (Stabler *et al.* 2008).

Most impressive, however, of all the discoveries during the period of the Tourist Development Project in the 1990s, were the rich finds in the South-west Zone, between the fortifications of the Old City and the theatre. In the north of this zone, Joseph Patrich finished excavating the building complex which was uncovered by JECM in the 1970s and 1980s, proving beyond doubt that this had been the *praetorium* or palace of the provincial governor in the Byzantine period. It was organised around an elegant audience hall on the west which people approached from a north-south street through a monumental entrance via courtyards on two levels. Immediately south of this lay an entire *insula* or city block of warehouses (*horrea*), apparently six separate establishments, but, unlike the one in area LL, these were apparently privately owned. The discovery cast a flood of light on the economy of Byzantine Caesarea (Patrich 1999).

South of the warehouses were the excavations of Yosef Porath's IAA project. The next ancient building to be uncovered was a luxury structure of the Byzantine period containing many rooms decorated with marble floor slabs and multi-coloured stone wall coverings as well as a well-preserved Roman-style bath, featuring hot rooms and cold pools of the usual type. The IAA excavators thus identified the entire building as a *thermae*, a public bathhouse, and they still insist on this identification today. Other archaeologists, however, think that this structure was an elegant urban mansion, because it was likewise furnished with a grand internal court, lined with marble columns. Opening onto it were two of the normal apsidal dining rooms of mansions of the Byzantine period, designed to accommodate semi-circular dining couches (*stibadia*). Adjacent, on the south side, was another pair of warehouses, and to the south of them again a luxurious urban mansion, and perhaps still another, not well-preserved. On a ridge above the shore to the west, wafted by fresh sea breezes, the entire zone south of the governor's palace appears to have hosted an elegant quarter of mansions and (perhaps) of recreation facilities in the Byzantine period.[7]

Equally impressive was the adjacent complex that survived from Herod's original construction project at Caesarea (Gleason *et al.* 1998). During the 1990s Gleason and Burrell's team investigated the Promontory Palace which Ehud Netzer had first identified as Herod's residence at Caesarea. On a lower terrace jutting out into the sea, this palace had rooms for dining and accommodating guests and which surrounded a fresh-water pool. The upper terrace contained a courtyard flanked by marble columns, on the north side of which rose an audience hall where Herod himself held court. Since the first Roman governors inherited this palace from the Herods, this was most likely the very spot where St. Paul stood before Festus during his trial, which Leo Boer had proposed to have taken place in the Byzantine Esplanade. To the east of the palace's upper terrace, the IAA project excavated other facilities that had formed part of an expanding Roman government compound. Finally, on the other side of the palace wall, and at right angles to it, King Herod's racecourse extended northwards along the shore, which was also an IAA excavation. From its starting gates on the north end, horses bolted toward the turning post on the south in front of thousands of spectators who occupied seats on the east and around the south end, which were still in remarkably good condition (Fig. 8.8). In the second century, when the large eastern hippodrome was built, where Boer had his lunch, the smaller racecourse near the sea would undergo conversion for use as an amphitheatre for gladiators and animal fights.

The current archaeological state of affairs

The four archaeological projects accomplished much at Caesarea during the decade of the 1990s, the most productive period in its history of archaeological excavations. Since then, the various teams have been engaged in writing their final reports, and large-scale excavation has all but ceased. Dr. Peter Gendelman of the IAA, an alumnus of 1990s excavations, has undertaken several short-range rescue excavations, on occasions when agricultural operations or intrusive construction activity have exposed ancient ruins. In 2010 one of these rescue operations discovered that another amphitheatre, identified in early aerial photographs but since neglected, is actually well preserved and dates from the second century CE. It will require only a new team of archaeologists and large-scale financing in order to re-equip Caesarea with yet another major tourist attraction. This amphitheatre was likely to have been the location of Christian martyrdoms during the Great Persecution.

Over four seasons, starting in 2007, a team led by Nicolas Faucherre and Jean Mesqui of the Centre d'Études Supérieurs de Civilisations Médiévales of Poitiers, France, conducted a highly detailed survey of Crusader Caesarea. Meanwhile, geo-archaeologist Dr. Beverly Goodman, alumna of Avner Raban's harbour excavations, and her colleague Dr. Henrik Dey have pursued underwater research on the impact of natural processes along Caesarea's coast, especially on the destructive power of tsunamis (Goodman-Tchernov and Dey 2011). Hence a new generation of Caesarea archaeologists has emerged. Leading a new team of volunteers who are residents of the modern Caesarea villas, is Yosef Porath himself, veteran leader of Caesarea archaeologists, who continues to excavate from time to time inside the Old City. Therefore, the story of archaeology at Caesarea is far from over, and it will no doubt lead to even more exciting discoveries, which young Leo Boer could hardly have imagined, when he visited this idyllic place on a sunny day in May 1954.

Notes

1 For a general study of all periods see Holum *et al.* 1988, though recent archaeological research makes this work outdated. See the bibliography for a selection of the large literature that has appeared since the mid-1970s.

2 For the details of the projects between 1959 and 1995, with bibliography, see Raban and Holum 1996. This volume also contains a series of aerial photographs and site maps, as well as a map (Fig. 8.1) showing the locations of the various projects.

3 This discovery was made in 1993, when Joint Expedition archaeologists were continuing work in the framework of the CCE (below).

4 For a recent study of the urban plan of Caesarea and how it developed through the Roman and Byzantine periods, see Holum 2009.

5 Raban died in London whilst working on the final report, which was published posthumously by colleagues and students; see Raban 2009.

6 All the areas previously excavated and now studied by the CCE, were designated a new code, by simply doubling the letter. In this case, JECM's earlier field K now became KK.

7 For brief preliminary reports on the IAA excavations see Porath 1996, 2000.

Bibliography of Caesarea Maritima

Arnon, Y. 2008. *Caesarea Maritima in the Late Periods (700-1291 CE)*. British Archaeological Reports, International Series, no. 1771. Oxford: British Archaeological Reports.

Evans, J. DeRose. 2006. *The Coins and the Hellenistic, Roman and Byzantine Economy of Palestine*. Vol. 6 of *The Joint Expedition to Caesarea Maritima: Excavation Reports*, edited by R. J. Bull and O. J. Storvick. Boston: American Schools of Oriental Research.

Gleason, K., Burrell, B., Netzer, E., Taylor, L. and Williams, J. H. 1998. "The Promontory Palace at Caesarea Maritima: Preliminary Evidence for Herod's Praetorium." *Journal of Roman Archaeology* 11:22–52.

Goodman-Tchernov, B. and Dey, H. 2010. "Tsunamis and the Port of Caesarea Maritima over the *longue durée*: A Geoarchaeological Perspective." *Journal of Roman Archaeology* 23:265–84.

Govaars, M., Spiro, M. and White, L. M. 2008. *Field O: The "Synagogue" Site*. Vol. 9 of *The Joint Expedition to Caesarea Maritima: Excavation Reports*, edited by R. J. Bull and O. J. Storvick. Boston: American Schools of Oriental Research.

Grafton, A. and Williams, M. 2006. *Christianity and the Transformation of the Book: Origen, Eusebius, and the Library of Caesarea*. Cambridge (MA) and London: Harvard University Press.

Hazard, H. W. 1975. "Caesarea and the Crusades." In *Studies in the History of Caesarea Maritima*, edited by C. T. Fritsch, 79–114. American Schools of Oriental Research, Supplementary Studies, no. 19. Missoula (MT): Scholars Press.

Holum, K. G. 2008. "Caesarea's Fortune: Ancient Statuary and the Beholder in a Late Antique City." In *The Sculptural Environment of the Roman Near East: Reflections on Culture, Ideology, and Power*, edited by Y. Z. Eliav, E. A. Friedland, and S. Herbert, 535–54. Louvain: Peeters.

Holum, K. G. 2009. "*Et Dispositione Civitatis in Multa Eminens*: Comprehending the Urban Plan of Fourth-Century Caesarea." In *Man Near a Roman Arch: Studies Presented to Yoram Tsafrir*, edited by L. Di Segni, Y. Hirshfeld, J. Patrich and R. Talgam, 187–207. Jerusalem: The Israel Exploration Society.

Holum, K. G. 2011a. "Caesarea Palaestinae: A Paradigmatic Transition?" In *Shaping the Middle East: Jews, Christians, and Muslims in an Age of Transition 400-800 C.E.*, edited by K. G. Holum and H. Lapin, 11–31. Studies and Texts in Jewish History and Culture, no. 20. Bethesda (MD): University Press of Maryland.

Holum, K. G. 2011b. "Caesarea in Palestine: Shaping the Early Islamic Town." In *Le Proche-Orient de Justinien aux Abbasides: Peuplement et dynamiques spatiales*, edited by A. Borrut, M. Debié, A. Papaconstantinou, D. Pieri and J.-P. Sodini, 169–86. Bibliothèque de l'Antiquité tardive, no. 19. Turnhout: Brepols.

Holum, K. G., Hohlfelder, R. L., Bull, R. J. and Raban, A. 1988. *King Herod's Dream: Caesarea on the Sea*. New York and London: W. W. Norton & Co.

Holum, K. G., Raban, A., Lehmann, C. M., Berrurier, D. le, Ziek, R. and Sachs, S. F. 1992. "Preliminary Report on the 12889–1990 Seasons." In *Caesarea Papers: Straton's Tower, Herod's Harbour, and Roman and Byzantine Caesarea*, edited by R. L. Vann, 79–111. Journal of Roman Archaeology, Supplementary Series, no. 5. Ann Arbor (MI): Journal of Roman Archaeology.

Humphrey, J. H. 1975. "A Summary of the 1974 Excavations in the Caesarea Hippodrome." *Bulletin of the American Schools of Oriental Research* 218:1–24.

Krentz, E. 1992. "Caesarea and Early Christianity." In *Caesarea Papers: Straton's Tower, Herod's Harbour, and Roman and Byzantine Caesarea*, edited by R. L. Vann, 261–67. Journal of Roman Archaeology, Supplementary Series, no. 5. Ann Arbor (MI): Journal of Roman Archaeology.

Lehmann, C. M. 1999. "The Governor's Palace and Warehouses, West Flank (Areas KK7-9, CV, 1993-1995 Excavations." In *Caesarea Papers 2: Herod's Temple, the Provincial Governor's Praetorium and Granaries, The Later Harbor, A Coin Hoard, and Other Studies*, edited by K. G. Holum, A. Raban, and J. Patrich, 136–49. Journal of Roman Archaeology, Supplementary Series, no. 35. Portsmouth (RI): Journal of Roman Archaeology.

Levine, L. I. 1975. *Caesarea Under Roman Rule*. Studies in Judaism in Late Antiquity, no. 7. Leiden: Brill.

Levine, L. I. and Netzer, E. 1986. *Excavations at Caesarea Maritima 1975, 1976, 1979-Final Report*. Qedem: Monographs of the Institute of Archaeology, The Hebrew University of Jerusalem. Jerusalem: The Hebrew University.

Oleson, J. P., Fitzgerald, M. A., Sherwood, A. N. and Sidebotham, S. E. 1994. *The Finds and the Ship*. Vol. II of *The Harbours of Caesarea Maritima: Results of the Caesarea Ancient Harbour Excavation Project 1980-85*, edited by J. P. Oleson. British Archaeological Reports, International Series, no. 594. Oxford: British Archaeological Reports.

Patrich, J. 1999. "The Warehouse Complex and Governor's Palace (Areas KK, CC, and NN, May 1993–December 1995." In *Caesarea Papers 2: Herod's Temple, the Provincial Governor's Praetorium and Granaries, The Later Harbor, A Coin Hoard, and Other Studies*, edited by K. G. Holum, A. Raban, and J. Patrich, 70–107. Journal of Roman Archaeology, Supplementary Series, no. 35. Portsmouth (RI): Journal of Roman Archaeology.

Patrich, J. 2011. "Caesarea in Transition: The Archaeological Evidence from the Southwest Zone (Areas CC, KK, NN)." In *Shaping the Middle East: Jews, Christians, and Muslims in an Age of Transition 400-800 C.E.*, edited by K. G. Holum and H. Lapin, 33–64. Studies and Texts in Jewish History and Culture, no. 20. Bethesda (MD): University Press of Maryland.

Porath, Y. 1996. "Expedition of the Antiquities Authority." *Excavations and Surveys in Israel* 105:39–47.

Porath, Y. 2000. "Caesarea–1994–1999." *Excavations and Surveys in Israel* 112:34–40.

Porath, Y., Goren-Rosen, Y. and Neguer, J. 2005/2006. "'The Birds Mosaic Mansion' in the Suburbs of Caesarea Maritima, Israel." *Musiva et sectilia* 2/3:171–89.

Raban, A. 1989. *The Site and the Excavations.* Vol. I of *The Harbours of Caesarea Maritima: Results of the Caesarea Ancient Harbour Excavation Project 1980-85.* Edited by J. P. Oleson. 2 parts. British Archaeological Reports, International Series, no. 491. Oxford: British Archaeological Reports.

Raban, A. 2009. *The Harbour of Sebastos (Caesarea Maritima) in its Roman Mediterranean Context.* Edited by M. Artzy, B. Goodman and Z. Gal. British Archaeological Reports, International Series, no. 1930. Oxford: British Archaeological Reports.

Raban, A. and Holum, K. G. 1996. "Introduction." In *Caesarea Maritima: A Retrospective after Two Millenia,* edited by A. Raban and K. G. Holum, xvii–xliv. Leiden, New York, and Köln: Brill.

Reinhardt, E. G. and Raban, A. 2008. "Site Formation and Stratigraphic Development of Caesarea's Ancient Harbor." In *Caesarea Reports and Studies: Excavations 1995-2007 Within the Old City and the Ancient Harbor,* edited by K. G. Holum, J. A. Stabler and E. G. Reinhardt, 155–82. British Archaeological Reports, International Series, no. 1784. Oxford: British Archaeological Reports.

Stabler, J., Holum, K. G., Stanley, Jr., F. H., Risser, M. and Iamim, A. 2008. "The Warehouse Quarter (Area LL) and the Temple Platform (Area TP): 1996–2000 and 2002 Seasons." In *Caesarea Reports and Studies: Excavations 1995-2007 Within the Old City and the Ancient Harbor,* edited by K. G. Holum, J. A. Stabler and E. G. Reinhardt, 1–39. British Archaeological Reports, International Series, no. 1784. Oxford: British Archaeological Reports.

Vann, R. L. 1992. "Early Travelers and the First Archaeologists." In *Caesarea Papers: Straton's Tower, Herod's Harbour, and Roman and Byzantine Caesarea,* edited by R. L. Vann, 275–90. Journal of Roman Archaeology, Supplementary Series, no. 5. Ann Arbor (MI): Journal of Roman Archaeology.

CHAPTER 9

MEGIDDO

The imposing mound of Tel Megiddo (Tell el-Mutesellim), located in the Jezreel Valley, rises about 40 to 60 metres above the surrounding plane and covers an area of six hectares. Its strategic location at the place where the Iron Pass enters the Jezreel Valley gave the city control over the Via Maris, the international road that ran from Egypt via Gaza and traversed the land of Israel all the way to Damascus, and beyond, to Mesopotamia. Because of this strategic location, Megiddo would become an important city in the Bronze and Iron Ages up to the end of the Assyrian period.

The site is first mentioned in inscriptions of the Egyptian Pharaoh Thutmose III in the fifteenth century BCE. These texts describe the defeat of the king of Megiddo when a confederation of Canaanite city-states led by the kings of Kadesh and Megiddo revolted against Egyptian rule. The decisive battle was fought in the vicinity of Megiddo, after which Megiddo became an Egyptian stronghold in the Jezreel Valley.

According to the biblical accounts Megiddo remained the most important Canaanite city in the Valley in the time of the Judges. During the reign of King Solomon – traditionally dated to the tenth century BCE – the city was fortified, together with Hazor and Gezer (1 Kings 9:15).

In 733/732 BCE, the Assyrians invaded the northern part of Israel and made Megiddo the capital of the Assyrian province of Magiddu. After the battle of Josiah against pharaoh Necho in 609 BCE (2 Kings 23:29; 2 Chronicles 35:22), Megiddo is no longer mentioned in historical sources and after the Assyrian period the site ceased to have any importance. It is mentioned in the Book of Revelations 16:16 as Armageddon, the site of the final battle between the forces of good and evil (Ha Megiddon, 'the Mountain of Megiddo').

Several large archaeological expeditions have tackled the site and left their traces on the tell. In this chapter we will follow in the footsteps of Leo Boer when he visited the site of Tel Megiddo in the spring of 1954.

A Visit to Tel Megiddo in the Spring of 1954

Norma Franklin

Archaeological campaigns at Megiddo (1903–2012)

The first excavation of the site of Megiddo, then known as Tell el-Mutesellim, was conducted by Gottlieb Schumacher from 1903 to 1905 on behalf of the *Deutsche Orient-Gesellschaft*.[1] The second, much larger expedition was launched in 1925 by the prestigious Oriental Institute of the University of Chicago. The mound had been used by farmers from the neighbouring village of Lejun and the law demanded that excavation trenches must always be backfilled and the land returned to a usable condition. Fortunately, the Oriental Institute expedition was generously funded by John D. Rockefeller, Jr., which enabled them to purchase the entire mound in 1927 from the Agrabiah family of Umm el Faham in order to facilitate an extensive excavation programme concerning the whole mound. Later on their grandiose plans of peeling away strata after strata across the mound were shelved and excavation was concentrated on a number of key areas. The purchase of an archaeological mound was a unique event and this is the reason why Megiddo is the only site excavated during the British Mandate whereby the excavation trenches were not routinely backfilled. The Oriental Institute was also the first to build an administrative, residential, and laboratory building complex; located on the northern terrace of the mound.[2]

Unfortunately, in 1939 they were forced to abandon the site in a hurry due to the onset of the Second World War. The British Mandate Department of Antiquities, established in 1920, did not have the manpower to protect the site and it is debatable whether the site was even considered to be under their protection. The site lay dormant until 1948 when its strategic location provided the scene of a battle between the soldiers of the Arab Liberation Army and the fledgling Jewish state. Communication trenches were dug and on the southeast of the mound some of the exposed Stratum III buildings were adapted to serve as gun emplacements (Cline and Sutter 2011, 160–67). An area in the centre of the mound was turned into a field hospital and the administrative buildings were badly damaged, although this was caused mostly by post-war vandalism (Kletter 2008).

In 1949 an 'Antiquities Unit' was established by the newly founded State of Israel. This was initially part of the Public Works Department and later affiliated with the Ministry of Education.[3] The new unit started with a handful of workers, most of whom were former employees of the earlier British Mandatory Department of Antiquities, and their offices consisted of just a few rooms and a small reference library presided over by Dr. Shmuel Yeivin. In 1953, the government of the State of Israel, alerted to the fact that sites were in danger due to neglect and looting, established a nationwide contingent of guards. However, they were never more than twenty, and without any transport nor weapons, they had no real authority to protect large sites such as Megiddo (Kletter 2006, 117–32).

Consequently, at the time of Boer's visit in 1954, still no maintenance was conducted at Megiddo and no steps were taken to make the site accessible to visitors. In 1957, three years after Boer's visit, the Department of Antiquities, under the jurisdiction of the Israeli Ministry of Tourism, implemented a programme of site maintenance in preparation for the tenth anniversary of the State of Israel. In 1964 Pope Paul VI was welcomed at Megiddo[4] by Zalman Shazar, President of Israel and Levi Eshkol, Prime Minister of Israel. It was following this visit that most of Oriental Institute's administrative buildings were dismantled and the remaining buildings refurbished to serve as a visitors' centre.

In 1960 a small-scale archaeological investigation was resumed by Yigael Yadin on behalf of the Hebrew University of Jerusalem, and followed by further exploration in 1966, 1967, and 1971–1972 (see Yadin 1960; idem 1970; idem 1972). In 1992[5] a new large-scale expedition was launched by Tel Aviv University, directed by Israel Finkelstein, David Ussishkin and Baruch Halpern (Finkelstein, Ussishkin and Halpern 2000; idem 2006).[6]

Following in the footsteps of Leo Boer at Megiddo

When Boer arrived at Megiddo in the spring of 1954 he found the archaeological site neglected and overgrown with weeds. Approaching Megiddo from the north travelling on a quiet road, past Tel Yokneam, there would have been little traffic (Fig. 9.1). Today it is a busy highway (Route 66) yet the view across the valley to the east is still as beautiful.

Before tackling Megiddo, Boer and company wanted to have lunch and he records that they found a perfect spot shaded by a couple of large trees. In 1954 there were very few trees in the vicinity and none of them were very large. The one exception was a grove of eucalyptus trees, interspersed with smaller fig trees which flourished by the spring of Ain el Kubbi, located to the north-east of the mound on the opposite side of the road (Fig. 9.2, number 2). Boer would have already caught sight of Megiddo and before pulling over to the side of the road to his 'perfect place' for a picnic. Although Boer does not mention anything about water, this would have been the only shady place and a perfect choice.

Boer does not record how they gained entry to the site. A clue, however, is provided by his first comment which mentions the 'chambered gate'. This means that the group probably crossed the road from their picnic spot and walked up the path (situated opposite the spring) to the now deserted administration buildings of the Oriental Institute (Fig. 9.2, route I A). An 'Antiquities Unit' guard would have been stationed there, whose duties would also have included working as a guide for the occasional visitors. The fact that Boer does not mention a guide probably means that the guard was not on duty at the time and that the gate was locked; a circumstance which was not unusual! In that case, Boer and his party may have climbed up the gradual slope of the lower mound to the west of the buildings and arrived just below the 'chambered gate' (Fig. 9.2, route I B).[7]

It is interesting that he called the gate, the northern gate or the 'chambered gate' (Fig. 9.3). This is the gate named Iron Age II, Stratum IV, (2156). It was excavated by Robert S. Lamon in 1935–1936, when he served as temporary director[8] after the dismissal of the second director P. L. O. Guy[9] by the Oriental Institute. In the late 1920s P. L. O. Guy had excavated a city gate (500) in the same, low-lying area. It was a four-chambered gate and he immediately declared it to be evidence of the building work of Solomon as related in 1 Kings

Figure 9.1: Road 66. On the far left of the picture, the foothills of the Mount Carmel range and Yokneam. On the right the Jezreel plain.

Figure 9.2: Aerial view of Tel Megiddo with route and stops of Leo Boer added (Courtesy 'The Megiddo Expedition, Tel Aviv University'). 1. Route 66; 2. Spring, picnic area?; 3. Oriental Institute's buildings; 4. Gate 2156 (Figs 9.4 and 9.5); 5. Viewpoint (Figs 9.6 and 9.7); 6. Area of Late Bronze Age palace; 7. Spoil heap; 8. Water system crater (Fig. 9.9); 9. Southern stables (Fig. 9.10); 10. Cultic area (Fig. 9.11); 11. Deep section (Fig. 9.13).

Figure 9.3: Detail of the northern section of the tell (Courtesy 'The Megiddo Expedition, Tel Aviv University').

9:15 (Guy 1931, 24–27). When Lamon recommenced excavation in the same area he realised that the four-chambered gate must be attributed to Stratum III, the Assyrian City, and that a newly revealed six-chambered gate (2156) be attributed to Stratum IV (Loud 1948, 46–57). The six-chambered gate was the only major Stratum IV element exposed after the dismissal of Guy and stands in stark contrast to the rhetoric of *Megiddo I.* There is no mention in *Megiddo*

II of Stratum IV, nor of the six-chambered gate having been built by Solomon.

This explains why Boer – who was presumably familiar with the *Megiddo II* excavation report on the Stratum IV gate – does not mention anything about the six-chambered gate having a connection with Solomon and the biblical narrative. Instead, Boer observes that the gate resembles the (chronologically much earlier) Tell Balata gate (see Campbell in this volume). Boer's visit in 1954 serves to remind us that it was only after Yigael Yadin's excavations at Hazor and his discovery there of a six-chambered gate which he attributed to Solomon's building activities (Yadin 1960), that the controversial idea arose that the Megiddo six-chambered gate must also be Solomonic. Only the built-up foundations[10] of the gate were preserved and in Boer's photograph only the north end of the eastern half of the gate is visible (Fig. 9.4). The western half of the six-chambered gate was excavated away by the Oriental Institute.

It is interesting to compare Boer's photograph with the one taken by David Biven, (Fig. 9.5) who was a photographer excavating at Megiddo with Yigael Yadin in May 1967. The outer pier of the gate, leaning and with at least one ashlar missing, appears to have been reinforced in the interim, and extra stones have been added to the structure.

Boer and his group moved on and enjoyed the view from Megiddo over the Jezreel Valley (Fig. 9.3, 'Viewpoint photo'). In Boer's photograph (Fig. 9.6) Mount Tabor is easily recognisable on the horizon, and on the extreme right of the photograph is the Hill of the Teacher (Givat Hamoreh). His photograph can be compared with one taken by Biven in 1967, with a slightly wider-angle lens (Fig. 9.7). The girl is standing on a section of the city wall above the gate area and slightly further east than what can be seen in Boer's photograph. One may conclude that Boer probably took his picture from the Bronze Age buildings in Area DD (Loud 1948, 113–16). As this was one of the last areas to be excavated by the Oriental Institute, it would have been relatively easy to access.

There were no visitor's paths around the site, and the easiest way to negotiate the mound was to follow the 'beds' which had been prepared for the old railway tracks.[11] These railway tracks ran from the different excavation areas to the spoil heaps. The excavation debris from Area DD was taken via the gate area to the smaller and more recent spoil heap located on

Figure 9.4: The foundations of the eastern half of the Iron Age II six-chambered gate. Resting on the gate are the partial remains of the later Assyrian gate.

Figure 9.5: Yigael Yadin and students sitting by the 'Solomonic' gate in May 1967 (Courtesy David Bivin/LifeintheHolyLand.com).

Figure 9.6: A view from Area DD of the Jezreel Valley. Mount Tabor on the horizon.

Figure 9.7: A view of the Jezreel Valley and Mount Tabor taken in May 1967 to the east of the previous photo (Courtesy David Bivin/ LifeintheHolyLand.com).

the north-west edge of the Tel, adjacent to Area AA (see rail track in Fig. 9.3). It seems reasonable to assume that Boer and his party initially walked eastward after leaving the gate area following the track to Area DD and then, when the track stopped, retracing their steps back to the gate area (Fig. 9.2, route II). The track continued west along the edge of the mound and ran over the top of the Late Bronze Age gate (3178; Fig. 9.3, 'LB Gate') connecting Area DD to Area AA and the spoil heap (Loud 1948, 21, Fig. 43). The gate had been purposely blocked by the Oriental Institute in order to support the rail track to the spoil heap adjacent to Area AA.[12] Today the magnificent Late Bronze Age Stratum VIII gate (3178) serves as the tourist entrance to the upper city, yet when Boer visited it was still blocked.

The metal rails had been removed[13] some years prior to Boer's visit and the track itself now served as a convenient path, skirting the edge of the tell and leading to Area AA, the area of the partly excavated Late Bronze Age Palace with its ivory treasure (Fig. 9.3).[14] Boer's photograph (Fig. 9.8) shows the area of the palace and the treasury but he is strangely silent about it in his diary. It is possible that he was disappointed that the Oriental Institute had excavated down to the Middle Bronze Age levels. The huge section visible in Boer's photograph contains strata from the Assyrian period down to the Middle Bronze Age and apart from a few large ashlars in the section no sign of the famous palace remained. There are, in fact, two sections, the sunlit west-facing section and the shady north-facing section, separated by a deep north-south trench (Loud 1948, 6, Fig. 5).[15]

Boer and his group apparently continued to follow the rail track westward along the edge of the mound until it reached its final destination at the spoil heap (Fig. 9.2, route III).

Their next stop was the water system, called the 'sinnor' by Boer (Fig. 9.2, number 8). The distance from the spoil heap up to the water system entrance is not large. Boer complains that the water system is not easily accessible but it is not clear whether he is referring to their route from the spoil heap to the area of the excavation crater or to the treacherous path which they would have had to take if they had tried to descend to the actual water-shaft opening.

Figure 9.8: The location of the Late Bronze Age palace in Area AA. The giant sections dominate the scene.

Although Boer did not take a photograph of this, we know what the area looked like based on a photograph taken the previous year by Fritz Schlesinger on behalf of the Israel Government Press Office (Fig. 9.9).

The water system was excavated by Robert Lamon during the directorship of P. L. O. Guy. Lamon's excavation methods were severely criticised by the Oriental Institute, especially because of the creation of a massive excavation crater which, according to the Institute, destroyed any hope of reaching a comprehensive stratigraphic analysis of the area

(correspondence between the Oriental Institute and Guy: Oriental Institute archives, Chicago).[16]

Boer used the biblical term 'sinnor' for the water system which he would have known with regard to David's conquest of Jerusalem (2 Samuel 5:8). When Charles Warren, who was working on behalf of the Palestine Exploration Fund, discovered a karstic fissure leading up from the Gihon spring directly to a tunnel into the city of Jerusalem, he used the Hebrew word 'sinnor' (it is now known as 'Warren's shaft'). In this way the word 'sinnor' came to represent a water

Figure 9.9: The perilous descent to the water system in 1953. This is what Boer and party would have encountered (Courtesy Central Zionist Archives).

system dating from the tenth century BCE or even earlier. The Oriental Institute attributed the Megiddo water system to the Late Bronze Age and so Boer's use of the term 'sinnor' is in keeping with the knowledge at that time. Once again it was Yigael Yadin, who, in the aftermath of his excavation of the water system at Hazor, declared that all water systems must have originated in the ninth century BCE (Yadin 1972, 89–93). In this way the Megiddo water system was attributed summarily to the ninth-century building exploits of Ahab.[17]

Schlesinger's photograph of the water system crater is taken looking east, which is the direction Boer would have arrived from. In the distance a number of palm trees are visible; these mark the area of the 'stables' and are Boer's next stop (Fig. 9.2, number 9).

The set of 'stables' visited by Boer are known as the southern stables, and consist of five tripartite units (Fig. 9.10). This was the second stable complex excavated by the Oriental Institute. The first, the northern stables, were a set of twelve tripartite units, excavated early on under the direction of P. L. O. Guy. Guy was an equestrian himself and he immediately

recognised that these tripartite structures resembled modern horse stabling facilities. Therefore, despite the absence of any horse (or chariot) accoutrements, he declared them to be stables. Stratigraphically they were in the fourth layer down from the surface of the tell, today known as Stratum IVA.[18] Guy attributed the stables to the building exploits of King Solomon primarily on the basis of the biblical text in 1 Kings 9:19 (Guy 1931).[19]

The northern stables were partially excavated away by the Oriental Institute in order to reach the earlier levels, but the still-existent five most northerly set of tripartite units would have been better preserved than the southern stables at the time of Boer's visit. However, Boer does not seem to have visited those stables nor that part of the tell. Instead, the photograph shows the group clambering over the most westerly of the southern stable units.

The southern stables were attached to a large rectangular courtyard and the whole area, stables and courtyard, had been excavated down to the earlier Stratum V level, leaving the Stratum IV architecture, superstructure and foundations still *in situ* and exposed.[20] The Stratum IV architecture

Figure 9.10: The southern stables of Stratum IV; the area exposed down to Stratum V.

appears superimposed precariously over the Stratum V remains and this state of affairs would have seemed confusing to any visitor. The situation is best shown in an aerial photograph taken by Guy (Lamon and Shipton 1939, 155, fig. 123).[21]

In short, the walls seen in Boer's photograph are the foundation walls of the tripartite units. These walls once supported the stylobates, which, in turn, supported the pillars and feeding troughs of the stable. Today we know that the stables, together with the rest of Stratum IV, cannot be attributed to Solomon. In fact it was, once again, Yadin in the 1970s who first changed their attribution, from Solomon to Ahab, in other words, from the tenth century to the ninth century BCE. Then in the 1990s, following Israel Finkelstein's major revision of Iron Age chronology (Finkelstein 1996), and the excavation of the northern stables during the new excavations (Cline 2006; Cline and Cohen 2006), they were dated to the eighth century BCE. And today all the stables (and Stratum IVA) are attributed to the eighth century BCE and possibly represent the building exploits of Jeroboam II.

The function of the tripartite buildings as stables was challenged by some scholars, but the work of Deborah Cantrell has now firmly established them as stables; specifically stables for chariot horses which require stabling at close quarters as part of their training regime (Cantrell 2011, 87–113). In 2006, one of the tripartite stable units (1612) was reconstructed by the Israel National Parks Authority and because all the southern units had been excavated down to below-floor level, unit 1612, restored to its original height, now towers over the other stable units.

The next diary entry and photograph concern the cultic buildings in Area BB of the Oriental Institute (Fig. 9.2, number 10).[22] The cultic area was located in the far east of the tell and the walk from the southern stables to Area BB would not have been straightforward. The group probably left the area of the southern stables from the north-east corner of the stable's courtyard and followed the west-east rail bed track that led to the main spoil heap off the eastern edge of the tell (Fig. 9.2, route IV). Before reaching the spoil heap they would have had to turn north onto a north-south rail bed track which ran down the centre of the mound and led past the west end of Area BB. It would have been relatively easy to enter Area BB from the middle of the mound as there was little difference in elevation of the track in relation to Area BB according to the local topography of the Tel at the time.

The photograph (Fig. 9.11) shows the Early Bronze Age III Altar (4017) from Stratum XVII–XV (looking south-west), as excavated by Loud (see Loud 1939, 74, figs 164 and 165). Boer writes in his diary that they saw the remains of two religious buildings. However, he should have recognised more than two. If, as we must presume, the party entered the cultic area from the west, they would have passed the two 'megaron' temples (5289 and 5192), located west of the altar. They were possibly covered in weeds, but the third, better preserved, 'megaron' temple must have caught his eye: Temple 4040, located directly north of the altar (Fig. 9.12). The only other building clearly visible would have been the Early Bronze Age Ib long-room temple (4050), built parallel to the edge of the mound. Attributed to Stratum XIX, the long-room temple was located alongside the 'picture pavement': a paved area that led down from the tell to the valley below (Fig. 9.2, route V).[23]

Boer's group apparently followed the same route as the Early Bronze Age worshippers because his last photograph shows the group walking down the side of the mound and the great gaping section, which distinguishes Area BB, clearly visible behind them (Fig. 9.13).

The archaeology of Megiddo today

Although Megiddo had been extensively excavated prior to Boer's visit, the correct evaluation of the strata at Megiddo were severely hindered by the excavation techniques that were employed and by the pre-conceived conceptions of the early excavators. They were always eager to connect their finds to the biblical narrative, especially any biblical reference regarding the building activity of Solomon at Megiddo. Consequently, since the first excavation led by Gottlieb Schumacher at the dawn of the twentieth century until today, the dating of the Iron Age monuments has fluctuated between the tenth and eighth centuries BCE. In addition, in Boer's day, the Megiddo ceramic assemblages formed the cornerstone of pottery typology; yet the pottery typology established by the Oriental Institute was based on the stratigraphic location of the pottery vis-à-vis the architecture. This meant that, when the

Figure 9.11: The Early Bronze Age III altar in the cultic area, Area BB.

Stratum IVA stables were attributed to Solomon, the associated pottery was used to formulate the ceramic corpus for the tenth century, and so on. Needless to say things have moved on drastically since then.[24]

The cultic area exposed by Gordon Loud was and still remains unique. The great cut that defined Area BB, provided a wide exposure of an amazing area which had a continuous succession of temples from the Early Bronze Age to the end of the Late Bronze Age. The renewed excavations conducted by Tel Aviv University have revealed yet another, even earlier, Temple beneath the remains that Boer visited.[25]

Despite the continued excavation of Megiddo, the exposure of new architectural features and the continual re-evaluation of the stratigraphy and chronology of the site, Boer would certainly have recognised the Megiddo he visited that afternoon in the spring of 1954, and we, in turn, must acknowledge the valuable information contained in his unofficial and, until now, unpublished photographs of Megiddo.

Figure 9.12: Detail of the eastern section of the tell (Courtesy 'The Megiddo Expedition, Tel Aviv University').

Figure 9.13: The mound of Megiddo viewed from the east. The great cut down to bedrock in Area BB.

Notes

1 See Schumacher 1908 and Watzinger 1929.

2 See the Oriental Institutes Publications, available on-line. Fischer 1929; Guy 1931; Lamon and Shipton 1939; Loud 1948.

3 It was only in 1955, a year after Boer's journey through Israel, that the Israel Department of Antiquities and Museums (IDAM) was established.

4 The pope entered Israel at the, unofficial, border crossing north of Jenin (at the time part of Jordan, now part of the Palestinian Authority). Megiddo was chosen as the venue due to its strong connection with the Hebrew Bible and to the Christian Book of Revelations. While logistically it was en-route to Nazareth, which was the Pope's main objective.

5 At the time of writing, summer 2012, the Tel Aviv Megiddo Expedition has just completed its eleventh bi-annual excavation season.

6 David Ussishkin retired as director in 2012 and Eric Cline took his place as director.

7 The ancient entrance to a tell is always located at a point of easy access, and the Iron Age-'chambered gate', is no exception.

8 Robert Lamon was originally employed as a surveyor. Following P. L. O. Guy's dismissal, Lamon was only appointed temporarily until the new director, Gordon Loud, was free to take over. It was during this change-over period that Lamon excavated Gate 2156, before he too was dismissed.

9 For a comprehensive biography of Guy see Green 2009.

10 For an explanation of this term and its importance regarding the Megiddo gate see Ussishkin 1980.

11 The paths laid down by the Israel National Parks Authority (NPA) follow the old rail tracks, laid down by the Oriental Institute in order to facilitate the removal of the excavation debris to the spoil heaps.

12 In 1992 the NPA decided to remove the blockage and open the gate to the public. Excavation was carried out (Area G) by the Megiddo Expedition of Tel Aviv University, followed by restoration work (Finkelstein, Ussishkin and Halpern 2000, 104–17).

13 The metal tracks and wagons were sold to the Atlit company (verbal communication Daniel Abutaseira).

14 See Loud 1939.

15 The deep north-south trench was backfilled in 1998 (Finkelstein *et al.* 2000, 10).

16 See Lamon 1935, 13 fig. 9 and 37 fig. 29 for the situation before and after the excavation.

17 For a re-appraisal of the original excavation report, see Franklin 2000.

18 The Oriental Institute attribution was Stratum IV but Yadin renamed it Stratum IVA a decade after Albright (1943, 2–3, n.1) had amalgamated Stratum V with Stratum IVB.

19 The association of Stratum IV with Solomon was preserved throughout the publication volume 'Megiddo I', while in 'Megiddo II' (as mentioned previously) the only documented major Stratum IV monument was Gate 2156, and the name Solomon is never mentioned in the text.

20 The Stratum V architecture was never drawn up and no plan is available. This was partially rectified by Franklin (2006).

21 Guy was the pioneer of aerial photography, see Guy 1932.

22 Area J of the current Megiddo Expedition.

23 The Stratum XIX temple (4050) was dated to the Chalcolithic period by Loud but further investigation by the Megiddo Expedition in 1992–1996 revealed that the temple had two building phases which existed in the EB1b (Finkelstein and Ussishkin 2000, 25–74).

24 See Arie (2013a and 2013b), for an up-to-date analysis of the Megiddo pottery typology.

25 See Finkelstein, Ussishkin and Halpern 2000, 29–53; Adams 2013.

Bibliography of Megiddo

Adams, M. 2013. "Part III: The Main Sector of Area J." In *Megiddo V: The 2004-2008 Seasons*, edited by I. Finkelstein, D. Ussishkin, and E. H. Cline. Monograph Series of the Institute of Archaeology of Tel Aviv University 31. Tel Aviv: Emery and Claire Yass Publications in Archaeology.

Albright, W. F. 1943. *The Excavation of Tell Beit Mirsim, Vol. 3: The Iron Age.* Joint Expedition of the Pittsburg-Xenia Theological Seminary and the American School of Oriental Research in Jerusalem. Annual of the American Schools of Oriental Research 21–22: 2–3. New Haven: American Schools of Oriental Research.

Arie, E. 2013a. "The Late Bronze III and Iron I Pottery: Levels K-6, M-6, M-5, M-4 and H-9." In *Megiddo V: The 2004-2008 Seasons*, edited by I. Finkelstein, D. Ussishkin, and E. H. Cline. Monograph Series of the Institute of Archaeology of Tel Aviv University 31. Tel Aviv: Emery and Claire Yass Publications in Archaeology.

Arie, E. 2013b. "The Iron Age IIA Pottery." In *Megiddo V: The 2004-2008 Seasons*, edited by I. Finkelstein, D. Ussishkin, and E. H. Cline. Monograph Series of the Institute of Archaeology of Tel Aviv University 31. Tel Aviv: Emery and Claire Yass Publications in Archaeology.

Cantrell, D. O. 2011. *The Horsemen of Israel: Horses and Chariotry in Monarchic Israel (Ninth-Eighth Centuries BCE)*. Winona Lake, Indiana: Eisenbrauns.

Cline, E. H. 2006. "Area L: The 1998-2000 Seasons." In *Megiddo IV: The 1998-2002 Seasons*, edited by I. Finkelstein, D. Ussishkin and B. Halpern, 104–123. Monograph Series of the Institute of Archaeology of Tel Aviv University 24. Tel Aviv: Emery and Claire Yass Publications in Archaeology.

Cline, E. H. and Cohen, M. 2006. "Area L, Appendix: The 2004 Season." In *Megiddo IV: The 1998-2002 Seasons*, edited by I. Finkelstein, D. Ussishkin and B. Halpern, 124–129. Monograph Series of the Institute of Archaeology of Tel Aviv University 24. Tel Aviv: Emery and Claire Yass Publications in Archaeology.

Cline, E. H. and Sutter, A. 2011. "Battlefield Archaeology at Armageddon: Cartridge Cases and the 1948 Battle for Megiddo, Israel." *The Journal of Military History* 75.1:159–90.

Fisher, C. S. 1929. *The Excavation of Armageddon*. Oriental Institute Communications 4. Chicago: University of Chicago Press. (http://oi.uchicago.edu/research/pubs/catalog/oic/oic4.html).

Finkelstein, I. 1996. "The Archaeology of the United Monarchy: An Alternative View." *Levant* 28:177–87.

Finkelstein, I., Ussishkin, D. and Halpern, B. (eds). 2000. *Megiddo III: The 1992-1996 Seasons*. Monograph Series of the Institute of Archaeology of Tel Aviv University 18. Tel Aviv: Emery and Claire Yass Publications in Archaeology.

Finkelstein, I. and Ussishkin, D. 2000. "Area J." In *Megiddo III: The 1992-1996 Seasons*, edited by I. Finkelstein, D. Ussishkin and B. Halpern, 25–74. Monograph Series of the Institute of Archaeology of Tel Aviv University 18. Tel Aviv: Emery and Claire Yass Publications in Archaeology.

Finkelstein, I., Ussishkin, D. and Halpern, B. (eds) 2006. *Megiddo IV: The 1998-2002 Seasons*. Monograph Series of the Institute of Archaeology of Tel Aviv University 24. Tel Aviv: Emery and Claire Yass Publications in Archaeology.

Franklin, N. 2000. "Relative and Absolute Chronology of Gallery 629 and the Megiddo Water System: A Reassessment." In *Megiddo III: The 1992-1996 Seasons*, edited by I. Finkelstein, D. Ussishkin and B. Halpern, 515–23. Monograph Series of the Institute of Archaeology of Tel Aviv University 18. Tel Aviv: Emery and Claire Yass Publications in Archaeology.

Franklin, N. 2006. "Revealing Stratum V at Megiddo." *Bulletin of the American School of Oriental Research* 342:95–111.

Green, J. D. M. 2009. "Archaeology and Politics in the Holy Land: The Life and Career of P. L. O. Guy." *Palestine Exploration Quarterly* 141, 3:167–87.

Guy, P. L. O. 1931. *New Light from Armageddon: Second Provisional Report (1927-29) on the Excavations at Megiddo in Palestine*. Oriental Institute Communications 9 Chicago: University of Chicago Press. (http://oi.uchicago.edu/research/pubs/catalog/oic/oic9.html).

Guy, P. L. O. 1932. "Balloon Photography and Archaeological Excavation." *Antiquity* 6:148–55.

Kletter, R. 2008. "The Friends of Antiquities (in Heb. ידידי העתיקות): The Story of an Israeli Volunteer Group and Comparative Remarks." *The Journal of Hebrew Scriptures* Vol. 8, article 2. doi:10.5508/jhs2008.v8.a2

Kletter, R. 2006. *Just Past? The Making of Israeli Archaeology*. London: Equinox.

Lamon, R. S. 1935. *The Megiddo Water System*. Oriental Institute Publication 32. Chicago: The University of Chicago (http://oi.uchicago.edu/research/pubs/catalog/oip/oip32.html)

Lamon, R. S. and Shipton, G. M. 1939. *Megiddo I. The Seasons of 1925-34; Strata 1-V.* Chicago: University of Chicago Press. Oriental Institute Publication 42. Chicago: The University of Chicago (http://oi.uchicago.edu/research/pubs/catalog/oip/oip42.html).

Loud, G. 1939. *The Megiddo Ivories*. Oriental Institute Publication 52. Chicago: The University of Chicago (http://oi.uchicago.edu/research/pubs/catalog/oip/oip52.html).

Loud, G. 1948. *Megiddo II. Seasons of 1935-39*. Oriental Institute Publication 62. Chicago: The University of Chicago (http://oi.uchicago.edu/research/pubs/catalog/oip/oip62.html).

Schumacher, G. 1908. *Tell el-Mutesellim, Band I: Bericht über die 1903 bis 1905 mit Unterstützung Sr. Majestät des Deutschen Kaisers und der Deutschen Orient-Gesellschaft vom Deutschen Verein zur Erforschung Palästinas veranstalteten Ausgrabungen*. Leipzig: Rudolf Haupt.

Watzinger, C. 1929. *Tell el-Mutesellim, Band II: Bericht über die 1903 bis 1905 mit Unterstützung Sr. Majestät des Deutschen Kaisers und der Deutschen Orient-Gesellschaft vom Deutschen Verein zur Erforschung Palästinas veranstalteten Ausgrabungen*. Leipzig: Rudolf Haupt.

Ussishkin, D. 1980. "Was the Solomonic: City Gate at Megiddo Built By King Solomon?" *Bulletin of the American School of Oriental Research* 239:1–18.

Yadin, Y. 1960. "New Light on Solomon's Megiddo." *The Biblical Archaeologist* 23.2:62–8.

Yadin, Y. 1970. "Megiddo and the Kings of Israel." *The Biblical Archaeologist* 33:66–96.

Yadin, Y. 1972. *Hazor: The Head of All Those Kingdoms*. London: Oxford University Press for the British Academy.

CHAPTER 10

BET SHE'AN

The occupation of the mound of Bet She'an first began in the Pottery Neolithic period during the fifth millennium BCE, represented only by pits dug into the bedrock. Remains of the following Chalcolithic period (fourth millennium BCE) are represented by scanty architectural remains and sherds. The first substantial occupation of the site started in the Early Bronze Age I, during which domestic structures and streets, as well as an oval-shaped building of a public nature, were built, indicating a well-developed and sedentary village. This settlement, which had no fortifications and occupied most of the summit, was violently destroyed and then partially rebuilt, only to be abandoned, possibly for ecological or socio-economic reasons, at the end of the Early Bronze Age IB or at the beginning of the Early Bronze II, sometime around 3000 BCE.

Following a gap during the Early Bronze Age II, the settlement was renewed in the Early Bronze Age III. This occupation ended non-violently and was followed by a transient seasonal settlement, dating to the Intermediate Bronze Age at the end of the third millennium BCE. Apart from one tomb in the cemetery to the north of the tell, including remains from the Middle Bronze Age IIA, the mound was left abandoned for some 200 years, until new occupation in the Middle Bronze Age IIB, around 1800 BCE. The Middle Bronze Age IIB–C occupation was characterised by densely-built domestic structures and streets, as well as open areas that may have been of a cultic nature. Surprisingly, in contrast to the urban nature of other sites, Bet She'an remained unfortified during this period.

The Egyptian occupation of the site began with the Eighteenth Dynasty in the fifteenth century BCE and lasted without interruption until the end of the Twentieth Dynasty in the second half of the twelfth century BCE. Thus, most finds of the Late Bronze Age at the site were characterised by distinct traces of the presence of the Egyptian garrison, which was stationed at the site, including many inscriptions, monuments, small finds and architectural remains in Egyptian style, and a public building, which apparently served as the Egyptian governor's ceremonial palace. During this period, a series of super-imposed Canaanite temples were also built on the summit, indicating the co-existence of an Egyptian and Canaanite population during the Late Bronze Age. At no point in the early history of occupation was the mound fortified and during the second millennium BCE, the settlement shrank and occupied about merely half of the summit's area.

With the departure of the Egyptians, the town reverted to Canaanite, and subsequently, Israelite rule in the eleventh century. In Iron Age II, during the tenth-eighth centuries BCE, an administrative complex was built which included ashlar stone construction and possibly a gate leading into the complex. The town was destroyed by the Assyrians Tiglath-pileser III in the late eighth century BCE.

In the early Hellenistic period, the mound of Bet She'an itself was only a very small settlement. Around 260 BCE a new settlement was established by Ptolemy II, the king of Egypt. This new city was built on two mounds separated by the Harod Stream: Tel Izttaba in the north and Tel Bet She'an in the south. The new Greek name of the site was Scythopolis, 'the city of the Scythians'. Later on, during the Seleucid dynasty, it developed and probably then received its title of Polis. This city was besieged and destroyed by the Hasmonean kings around 108/7 BCE. It was rebuilt by Gabinius, the Roman proconsul of Syria (57–54 BCE), a few years after the Roman conquest of Syria and Judea by Gnaeus Pompeius Magnus.

In the early Roman period a new city was established at the foot of the tell with the acropolis fortified on the mound. At that time a monumental temple was built on the summit. Roman Scythopolis greatly expanded and became the most important city in northern Palestine. New colonnaded streets adorned the city, as well as squares, temples, a *nymphaeum*, decorative pools, bathhouses, a large and a small theatre, a hippodrome and other institutions typical of the Roman urban tradition.

Around the end of the fourth century CE, in the early Byzantine period, a new province by the name of Palaestina Secunda was founded with Scythopolis as its capital. At that time the city became Christian and its temples were abandoned and replaced by churches. In the early fifth century the city reached its peak in terms of size and population, becoming the third largest city in Palestine after Caesarea and Jerusalem. Its walls encircled an area of some 140 hectares and its population was estimated at some 30,000. A round church was built on the mound on the site of the erstwhile Roman temple.

A series of calamities, most importantly the devastating bubonic plague of 541/542 CE, marked a downturn in the history of the city. In 635 the city was conquered by the Muslim army. The excavations revealed no signs of destruction or violence, but the character of the town, however, changed. The Greek name Scythopolis was replaced by the old Semitic name Bet She'an, in its Arabic form, Baysan.

Around 659/660 CE the city was damaged by a major earthquake; the city lost much of its classical urban appearance and its skyline was dominated merely by the old Roman monuments, left derelict. On 18 January, 749 CE, an enormous earthquake this time devastated the town completely. The central valley, once the centre of Roman Scythopolis, was abandoned to a large extent. Most of the inhabitants moved to the southern plateau, where the modern town of Bet She'an is located today.

During the Crusader period the fortified manor house of Count Adam de Bethune, the Baron of Bet She'an, was built on top of the mound, which was ultimately destroyed by Saladin in 1183.

This chapter focuses on the visible changes resulting from almost 60 years of archaeological activities at Bet She'an. Special attention is paid to the excavation and restoration of the Roman theatre, which was still overgrown when Leo Boer visited the site in 1954. Apart from showing the archaeological progression at the site, this chapter also discusses the 'regional approach', which considers the broader regional picture and the interrelationships between sites of various sizes and types within the region.

A Note on Boer's Visit to the Roman City of Bet She'an

Yoram Tsafrir and Benjamin Arubas

When Leo Boer and the group of the École Biblique were heading for Tel Bet She'an on 5 May 1954, they passed the ruins of the Roman city of Bet She'an (Nysa-Scythopolis), although the remains were barely noticeable at that time (Fig. 10.1). According to Boer's account the group arrived at the modern city of Bet She'an about noon and after a vain attempt to visit the museum – closed for an unknown reason – they proceeded on foot into northern direction, to the tell (Fig. 10.2). On the way they stopped at the remains of the Roman theatre and Boer noticed that 'unfortunately, besides a few pretty passageways and some gates, there was not much left to see there.' After a short break, the group continued their walk to the mound which they then climbed. Although Boer found the results of the University Museum of the

University of Pennsylvania Expedition, carried out at the tell in the 1920s and early 1930s, disappointing, he did, fortunately, take a photograph from the top of the mound into southern direction (Fig. 10.3).

From Boer's account we can conclude that, after their visit of Tel Bet She'an, the group left the mound through the northern Byzantine [actually Medieval] gate from which a paved road led to the round church on the summit of the tell further along. They followed a part of this paved road, which is still seen today. After leaving the tell towards the north-west, about 500 metres beyond the mound, they passed a Byzantine building beneath which traces of the Chalcolithic era had been found but not seen today. Further on, they passed the late Roman street of Bet She'an and eventually reached the main road at the

Figure 10.1: The group of the École Biblique walking towards the valley of Nahal Amal and Tel Bet She'an.

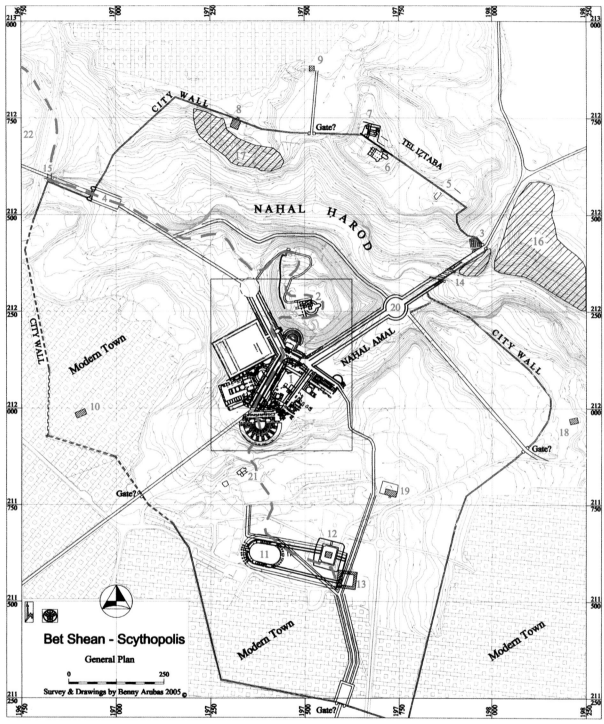

Figure 10.2: Site map of the Roman city of Bet She'an including the main features and the route taken by Leo Boer (Courtesy of Benny Arubas).

1. City center	8. Monastery of the Lady Mary	16. Eastern cemetery (Tel Hammam)
2. Tel Bet Shean: the acropolis	9. Samaritan synagogue	17. Northern cemetery
3. Northeast gate (Damascus Gate)	10. House of Kyrios Leontis	18. Monastery (?)
4. Northwest gate (Caesarea Gate) and	11. Amphitheater (previously hippodrome)	19. Great mosque (Jâmi'a al-Arba'in
marketplace	12. Crusader fortress	Ghǔzâwi)
5. Hellenistic city, residential quarter	13. Ottoman Serai	20. Circular plaza
6. Church of the Martyr	14. Northeast bridge (Jisr al-Maktu'a)	21. Southern bathhouse
7. Church of Andreas	15. Northwest bridge (Jisr al-Khan)	22. Extramural quarter (Tel Naharon)

Figure 10.3: The overgrown area of Bet She'an in the mid-1950s. In the centre the contours of the Roman theatre are visible.

place where it crossed the Wadi. Boer remarked that underneath the present-day bridge which they crossed to leave the area of Bet She'an, there was a Byzantine [actually Roman] one, made of the same stone as the old paved road mentioned above (Fig. 10.2).

Bet She'an in the 1950s

When Boer visited the site in 1954, Bet She'an was a small town, comprising of some old houses of the Late Ottoman and British Mandate periods and newly-built structures occupied by recent immigrants of Israel. The residential area extended over the southern plateau, above the central valley of Nahal Amal (Arabic: Wadi Asi), where the city centre of Roman Bet She'an was situated. As Boer's photographs show, the area was completely overgrown in the mid-1950s. In spite of this, there are two major elements clearly visible in the pictures. The first is Tel Bet She'an (Fig. 10.1), the ancient city, which had been excavated since 1922 (see Panitz-Cohen in this chapter). This high mound later became the acropolis of Roman-Byzantine Nysa-Scythopolis and Early Islamic Baysan.

This photograph shows the group of the École Biblique walking from the southern plateau in the northern direction of the central valley of Nahal Amal, towards the tell. The central valley is clearly visible but no monuments can be discerned, not even the theatre, which is located very close to the photographer.

This entire valley between the theatre and the tell used to be occupied by the city centre of Roman-Byzantine Nysa-Scythopolis and is now part of the large 'Bet She'an National Park'. The south-western part of this city centre has now been excavated by the Israel Antiquities Authority, headed by Dr. Gabriel Mazor and Rachel Bar-Nathan (Mazor and Najjar 2007; Mazor and Atrash forthcoming), while the other half has been excavated by a team from the Institute of Archaeology of the Hebrew University of Jerusalem, headed by Prof. Gideon Foerster and Prof. Yoram Tsafrir in the period 1986–2000 (Foerster and Tsafrir 1987-1988; idem 1988-1989; idem 1992). The excavation and extensive works of conservation and reconstruction together form the most extensive archaeological project carried out in Israel at the end of the twentieth century and was financed by public funds.

Comparing photographs

Figure 10.4, taken around the same time of the year in 2012 as Figure 10.1 in 1954, shows the same valley after excavation and with some restored buildings. The restored back wall of the theatre's stage is visible. In the centre we see the colonnaded Palladius Street (the street names were given by the excavators) connecting the main street junction near the tell with the amphitheatre. Palladius was the governor, under whose charge, probably in the early fifth century CE, a covered portico was built above the mosaic-paved sidewalk, as mentioned in an inscription; the street was originally constructed in the Roman period, but its renovation probably took place, as mentioned above, in the early fifth century, following the earthquake of the year 363 CE. On the left-hand side one can see the splendid semi-circular plaza, or 'sigma' according to its foundation inscription. It was built around 507 CE. On the right-hand side of the street one can see the flat area of the Byzantine agora and a line of shops along its north-western side.

The other monument, that can clearly be seen in Figure 10.3, is the Roman theatre. This photograph was taken from the lower slopes of the tell, looking south-west. In the centre we see the theatre before excavation. The semi-circular shape, typical of Roman theatres, can be detected clearly. Also visible are the vaulted passages (*vomitoria*) between the lower part and the upper part of the *cavea* (the stone benches for the spectators) and the line of the decorated backwall of the stage. Most interesting (and rather rarely seen in photographs of Bet She'an) are the poor stone buildings on the slopes of the southern plateau that were abandoned by the Palestinian residents in 1948, and some newly-built wooden shacks occupied by recent immigrants, who came mostly from eastern Europe and North Africa.

The theatre – built in the first century BCE and lavishly renovated at the end of the second century CE – was first excavated five years after Boer's visit, in the years 1960–1961, by S. Applebaum followed by A. Ovadiah and consequently by A. Negev. The excavations there were resumed in 1986 by an expedition on behalf of the Israel Antiquities Authority, headed by Dr. Gabriel Mazor and Rachel Bar-Nathan (see Mazor and Atrash in this chapter).

A recent photograph (Fig. 10.5) taken in 2009 from almost the same spot and into the same direction as Figure 10.3, clearly demonstrates the changes made by the excavations in the last 60 years. The Roman

Figure 10.4: Photograph taken from the same position as Figure 10.1, showing the theatre, the colonnaded Palladius Street, and the semi-circular plaza respectively (Photograph taken by Y. Tsafrir; spring 2012).

Figure 10.5: The Roman city of Bet She'an seen from Tel Bet She'an, almost 60 years after Leo Boer took Figure 10.3 from more or less the same spot (Photograph taken by B. Wagemakers; June 2009).

Figure 10.6: The semi-circular plaza, or 'sigma', Palladius Street, and Roman theatre (Photograph taken by Y. Tsafrir; spring 2012).

theatre is now clearly visible. The structure had a basalt core and the benches were made of limestone; only the benches of the lower part, buried under the surface, have survived. In the centre the line of Palladius Street can be seen, with columns restored on both sides. In the foreground of Figure 10.6 we see the semi-circular plaza of the 'sigma', covered with hard beaten earth, surrounded by the shops (those with a mosaic floor are protected by modern roofs). The buildings that are seen encroaching on the valley in the background of the old photograph were demolished when the area was declared a National Park.

The Roman Theatre at Nysa-Scythopolis (Bet She'an)

Gabriel Mazor and Walid Atrash

The civic centre of Nysa-Scythopolis of the Roman imperial period was located south of the mound and within the Amal Stream basin. It housed a forum in its centre surrounded by colonnaded streets and a theatre on its southern side (Fig. 10.7). The theatre was first surveyed, described and located with precision on the site map on April 1874 (Conder and Kitchener 1882, II, 106–7).[1] In his notes the British surveyor Claude R.

Conder states that the theatre is '... the best preserved specimen of Roman works in western Palestine'. A remarkable feature in the theatre auditorium (*cavea*;[2] see the theatre plan in Fig. 10.8 for architectural terms) were, according to Conder, 'the oval recesses half way up the cavea' and they were precisely drawn in the theatre plan by him. They were previously observed by C. L. Irby and J. Mangles, British navy officers,

Figure 10.7: Nysa-Scythopolis: aerial view of civic centre, looking north-east.

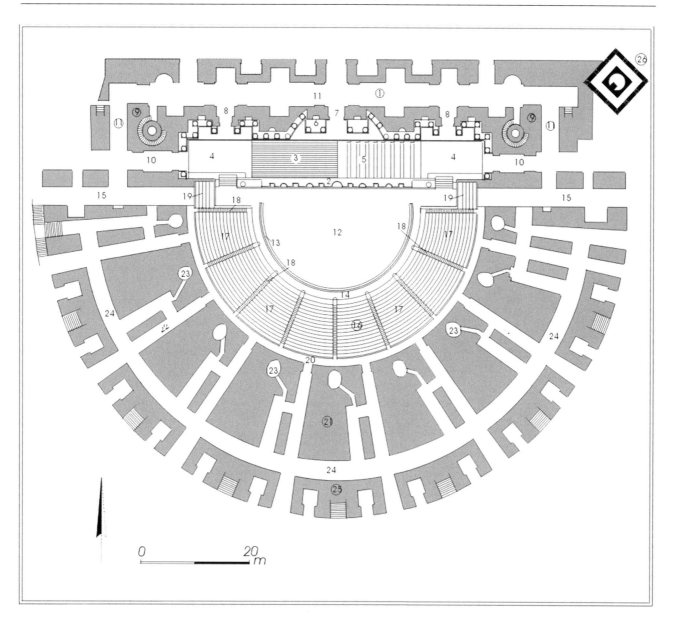

Figure 10.8: Plan of the Roman theatre in Bet She'an.

1. SCAENA	10. ITINERA VERSURARUM	19. TRIBUNALIA
2. PROSCAENIUM	11. CORRIDORS	20. PRAECINCTIO
3. PULPITUM	12. ORCHESTRA	21. MEDIA CAVEA
4. PULPITUM FLANKS	13. BISELLIA	22. VOMITORIA
5. HYPOSCAENIUM	14. BALTEUS	23. ACOUSTIC CELLS
6. SCAENAE FRONS	15. ADITUS MAXIMUS	24. AMBULACRUM
7. VALVAE REGIAE	16. IMA CAVEA	25. SUMMA CAVEA
8. HOSPITALIA	17. CUNEI	26. ROMAN TEMPLE
9. VERSURAE	18. SCALARIA	

E. Robinson, the pioneer of Biblical Geography and History, and V. Guérin, a French scholar, all of whom had already described the theatre in their earlier reports of the site (Irby and Mangles 1823, 301–3; Robinson 1856, 326–32; Guérin 1874, 284–98). The theatre was later photographed by the expedition of Penn University Museum in Philadelphia that conducted excavations on the mound during the years 1921–1933 (see Panitz-Cohen in this chapter).

The first excavations (1960–1962)

The theatre was first excavated by Simon Applebaum on behalf of the Israel Antiquities Department during the years 1960–1961 and by Abraham Negev in 1962 (Applebaum 1978, 77–97; Negev 1963, 585).[3] Applebaum's excavations revealed most of the theatre apart from its north-eastern entrance (*aditus maximus*[4]). The expedition work was conducted in a grid of squares of five by five metres, which first revealed the poor and derelict late Arabic houses that were built over the stage house and gradually exposed the lower earlier strata. The orchestra, surrounded by the semi-circle *cavea* which was partly exposed prior to the excavations, was first excavated at its upper layers by heavy equipment and, as the theatre remains became visible, the excavations were then continued by manual labour in a grid. Architectural members (columns and entablature) of the collapsed columnar façade (*scaenae frons*[5]) of the stage building, were removed from the theatre as the work progressed and the theatre underwent some minor restoration work.

A sporadic report from February 1954, found in the department archives, reports that Nehemia Tzori, an inspector of the Antiquities Department, conducted a trial trench along the theatre *cavea* but left no details, plan or photographs of his work. It is rather fortunate that the theatre photograph taken by Leo Boer several months later, on 5 May 1954, captured the trial trench in the western side of the *cavea* (see the white stripe along the auditorium in Fig. 10.3, in the contribution of Tsafrir and Arubas, which exposes the white limestone seats).

The Israel Antiquities Authority expedition (1986–2000)

Wide-scale excavations conducted in the city civic centre (1986–2000) by the IAA (Israel Antiquities Authority) expedition on behalf of the Bet She'an Archaeological Project, directed by Gabriel Mazor and Rachel Bar-Nathan, resumed the clearance of the theatre that was fully revealed and researched by Walid Atrash, the field supervisor. Recently the manuscript of the final report on the theatre was submitted for publication, including all the data regarding the earlier excavations and the architectural members of the *scaenae frons* columnar façade, as revealed by Applebaum (Mazor and Atrash forthcoming).

As the excavations were resumed, attention was focused first on the eastern *aditus maximus*, which was not previously excavated. This therefore presented an important trial excavation, in which Applebaum's stratigraphy and dating of the theatre's various strata were re-examined and challenged.

As the excavations proceeded, it became rather clear that both long and high walls of the eastern *aditus maximus,* including its covering vault sections, were leaning towards the north and in danger of collapse. In the restoration process both walls and vault sections were first recorded, their stone marked, and then dismantled, after which their foundations were reinforced. While exposing the foundations of the walls, the excavations revealed an unexpected surprise as the remains of an earlier theatre were unveiled underneath the current one. Further probes conducted in various other parts of the theatre confirmed the finds. The theatre that was first excavated by Applebaum and later by the IAA expedition and dated to the Severan period (late second to early third century CE; Fig. 10.9) was apparently built over, and entirely covered, an earlier theatre, in which two clear phases were observed.

The earlier theatre was first built during the reign of Tiberius (the early first century CE) and later enlarged during the Flavian period (third quarter of the first century CE). The widespread probes enabled its reconstruction and dating as they revealed some of its main foundations, walls

Figure 10.9: The Severan theatre: looking north-east.

and architectural members and thus furnished the required data for its comprehensive research. The early theatre constructed of basalt stone and soft limestone masonry was relatively small, its auditorium consisted of an *ima* and *media cavea*, and the décor of its *scaenae frons* columnar façade was rather simple. As was customary in the East, the theatre was built on a slope of a hill, facing north and was integrated into the first-century civic centre overlooking its forum.

Nysa-Scythopolis and the theatre

During the second century CE the civic centre of Nysa-Scythopolis was widely renovated and monumentalised. The city's main streets were rebuilt as colonnaded streets, furnished with *propylaea*[6], *nymphaea*[7] and *exedrae*[8], temples, *thermae*[9], and building complexes of the imperial cult were all erected in the new imperial architectural style, widely decorated in the elaborate Corinthian style and adorned by numerous marble statues (Fig. 10.10). New building materials were used: hard limestone of a superb quality, which was produced in the nearby Gilboa mountain quarries. At the end

of the century as the renovation of the civic centre reached its peak, the theatre, by then too small to accommodate the needs of a growing polis, was attended to and a new theatre was constructed on top of the earlier one.

The new theatre was a rather large one, its auditorium was divided into three horizontal sections (*ima*, *media* and *summa cavea*) crowned by a portico. The enlarged stage house was adorned by a three-storeys-high *scaenae frons*, the columnar façade of which was of the Corinthian order. Both this façade and its richly adorned entablature were entirely constructed out of imported marbles: light-grey marble from Proconnesos on the island of Marmara (Turkey), light-yellow marble from Aphrodisias (Turkey), green Cipollino from Carystos in Euboea (Greece), light-grey granite from the Troad (Turkey) and red granite from Syene (Egypt). The colourful columnar façade set against a background wall-plated with a colourful *opus sectile*[10] and statues in niches granted the baroque-styled *scaenae frons* a rich multi-coloured perspective scenic view, intensified by a strong light-and-shade effect (Fig. 10.11).

The auditorium was entered by a sophisticated system of six double and two triple passages (*vomitoria*[11]) set around the semi-circle peripheral

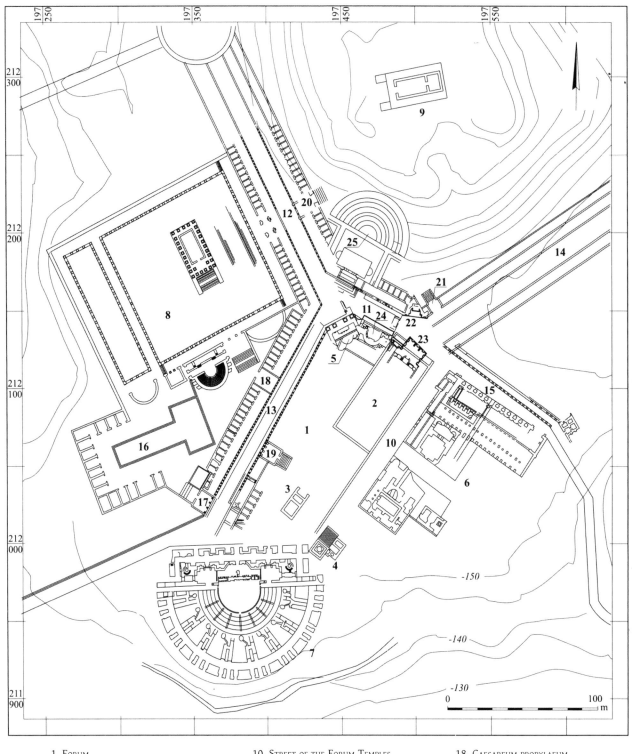

1. Forum
2. Basilica
3. Forum Temple I
4. Forum Temple II
5. Temple (?)
6. Eastern thermae
7. Southern theatre
8. Caesareum
9. Temple of Zeus Akraios

10. Street of the Forum Temples
11. Street of monuments
12. Northern Street
13. Palladius Street
14. Valley Street
15. Street of the Eastern Thermae
16. Western thermae
17. Thermae propylaeum

18. Caesareum propylaeum
19. Forum propylaeum
20. Temple of Zeus propylaeum
21. Valley Street propylaeum
22. Monument of Antonius
23. Altar
24. Nymphaeum
25. Northern theatre

Figure 10.10: Nysa-Scythopolis: civic centre, plan of the second century CE.

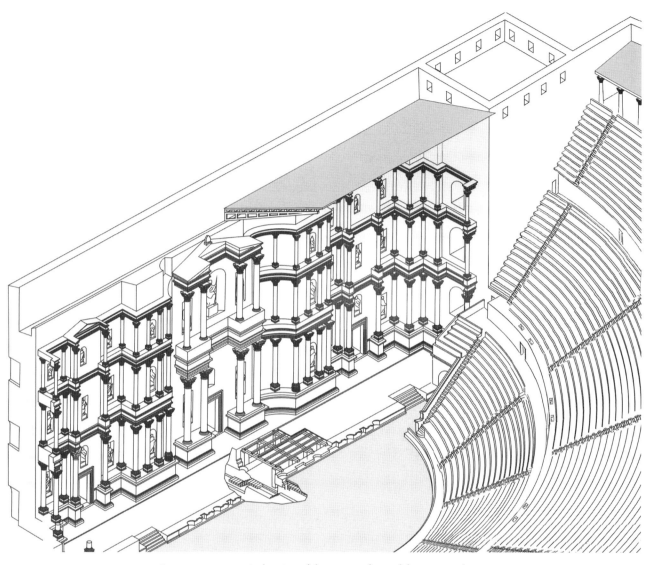

Figure 10.11: Isometric drawing of the scaenae frons of the Severan theatre.

wall of the theatre and under the *cavea* foundations. Half of the *vomitoria*, the right-side passages of each pair, entered the *cavea* via the circumference semi-circle passage (*ambulacrum*[12]) while the other passages entered nine oval-shaped acoustic cells that opened into the inner passage (*praecinctio*[13]) between the *ima* and *media cavea*. The cells constructed in line with the *cavea* staircases (*scalaria*[14]) served as amplifiers, which improved the theatre acoustics. References to this rather sophisticated system were found in Vitruvius, a first-century architect whose book on architecture included chapters relating to theatre construction and acoustics (Vitruvius *De Architectura* V 137–153).

Renovating and reconstructing the theatre

The theatre was renovated twice. On 17 May 363 CE an earthquake caused serious damage to the theatre resulting in the collapse of the *scaenae frons*, *summa cavea* and *portico*. In the following renovations, conducted in the early Byzantine period, the *summa cavea* and *portico* were not restored and the original capacity of the auditorium (10,000 spectators) was reduced by a third. The collapsed *scaenae frons* was rebuilt, albeit reduced to a two-storeys-high columnar façade. In the early sixth century CE the theatre was once again renovated with the *scaenae frons* reduced to a single-storey-high columnar façade. Along the northern outer façade wall a monumental portico was erected out of reused architectural members (spolia[15]) and in front of it a widespread paved square equipped with a *nymphaeum* was built next to the forum. In that setting, the theatre continued to serve the city as its main auditorium, presumably for secular and religious gatherings until the end of the Byzantine period. During the Umayyad period (661–750 CE), in which the city was renamed Beisan, a vast pottery workshop was built in the theatre's north-eastern premises. The theatre as well as the city were destroyed by an earthquake on 18 January 749 CE, an event that signified the end of Nysa-Scythopolis 994 year after its foundation as a Hellenistic polis.

Following the excavations of 1986–2000 wide-scale reconstructions were conducted in the theatre by a team from the IAA conservation department. The complex walls, foundations as well as superstructure were consolidated and sealed from future weather damage. The eastern *aditus maximus* walls and vaults were dismantled, their foundations stabilised and rebuilt. The entrance arch from the eastern *aditus maximus* leading to the orchestra, which was built of limestone masonry and voussoir, was reconstructed including its decorative profiles. The barrel vaults of all *vomitoria* were consolidated and reconstructed in various places. In the north-eastern side of the *cavea* a collapsed seats section (*cunei*), its accompanying staircase and tribune, were reconstructed mostly from the original elements – seats steps and banister elements with the addition of new limestone masonry and carved members. At the *media cavea* foundation, the north-eastern acoustic cell and its entering *vomitoria* were reconstructed. The *cavea* inner passage (*praecinctio*), the passage bordering podium and its inner staircases that mounted the *media cavea* and a section of its seats were reconstructed as well.

All the walls of the stage building were consolidated and the *versura*[16] towers that flanked the stage (*pulpitum*) were reconstructed. The round staircase, incorporated in the eastern *versura*, was partly reconstructed along with the *versura* second-storey room and its wide window that overlooked the stage. The stage low front wall (*proscaenium*[17]) composed of alternating semi-circle and rectangle niches was reconstructed and the stage was paved by a wooden floor. All three entrances into the stage (central – *valvae regiae* and both sides – *hospitalia*) were reconstructed along with the *scaenae frons* wall. Out

of the *scaenae frons* columnar façade two sections were reconstructed, erected over the renovated podium. Three red granite column shafts of the central composition façade were restored over newly-carved limestone bases. The north-eastern corner of the *scaenae frons* was fully reconstructed in its first-storey columnar façade. The columns of the Corinthian order were erected on top of decorated pedestals and crowned by magnificent marble capitals. Across the columns the richly-decorated marble architrave and friezes were reconstructed and on top of them the adorned cornices. The reconstructed section of the *scaenae frons* columnar façade, although small and partial, conveys the rich splendour of the *scaenae frons* façade, which a visitor can easily imagine, as it originally spread along the entire stage façade in three storeys to the height of over twenty metres (Fig. 10.11).

At the well-preserved *ima cavea*, the entire seats of which were preserved, only minor reconstructions were carried out of seats and steps, as the theatre was prepared for modern performances. Concerts of classical, opera and rock music have since taken place in the reused theatre in recent years, thus in part returning some of its ancient splendour to the magnificent complex. Hence during the 60 years since Leo Boer visited Nysa-Scythopolis as a former student of the *École Biblique et Archéologique Française de Jérusalem*, the magnificent Roman theatre was fully excavated and partly restored and today it is the best-preserved Roman theatre in Israel.

Notes

1   The survey was conducted in the framework of the SWP (Survey of Western Palestine) on behalf of the PEF (Palestine Exploration Fund).

2   The seating complex, generally divided into two or three horizontal sections: the lower section (*ima* cavea), the middle section (*media cavea*) and the upper section (*summa cavea*).

3   Apart from brief preliminary reports no final report regarding the work during 1960–1962 was ever published.

4   The *aditus maximi* (singular: *aditus maximus*) are the two barrel-vault-roofed entrances leading from outside the theatre (east and west) directly to the orchestra.

5   The wall of the stage building that closes off the stage and faces the *cavea*. It contained the three entrances

to the stage and its columnar façade rises to the height of two or three storeys and was outstanding in its rich architectural decoration.

6 Monumental entrance to a public building or staircase.

7 Water fountains, which were used to decorate colonnaded streets.

8 Semi-circular apse or rectangular niche.

9 Monumental imperial bath houses.

10 Marble plating of a wall.

11 A *Vomitorium* (plural *vomitoria*) is a radial passageway placed between two parallel walls that bear a continuous barrel vault. The *vomitoria* built under the *cavea* allowed easy entrance from outside the theatre.

12 A semi-circular corridor that runs between two concentric parallel walls roofed by a barrel vault. The ambulacrum supported an artificial slope on which the auditorium was built.

13 A semi-circular circumferential passageway that divided the seating complex (*cavea*) into horizontal sections.

14 Radial staircases that divided the *cavea* into wedge-like sections (*cunei*).

15 Architectural elements and masonry in secondary use.

16 The two tower-shaped wings of the stage building attached to its short sides thus closing the stage on both sides.

17 A low wall, usually decorated with alternating semi-circular and rectangular niches, that separates the stage from the orchestra.

The History of the Excavations at Tel Bet She'an and the Regional Surveys of the Bet She'an Valley

Nava Panitz-Cohen

When Leo Boer visited the site of Tel Bet She'an in 1954, it was an obvious place to stop during his tour of the country, as it lies at the junction of two much-travelled and important ancient (and modern) crossroads: the east-west route from the coast through the Jezreel and Harod (Wadi Jalud) Valleys leading eastward to Pella, and the north-south route running through the Jordan Valley. The same geographic location that helped to establish the importance of the site in antiquity prompted many modern scholars and travellers, among them Leo Boer, to visit the imposing tell that commands this strategic junction in the fertile Bet She'an Valley (Fig. 10.12).

Leo Boer's visit took place 21 years after the completion of the extensive excavations conducted at the site during 1921–1933 by the University Museum of the University of Pennsylvania (Fig. 10.13). Figure 10.1 in the contribution of Tsafrir and Arubas in this chapter, shows the group approaching Tel Bet She'an from the south. In his account of the visit, Boer relates:

'After a 25 minute drive we arrived in Bet She'an, a fairly unattractive modern town with remnants from the Crusader period. Its museum was closed for one or other reason so we left the town and proceeded on foot towards the Roman theatre, located north of the town and south of Tell Beisan. There was not much left to see

Figure 10.12: View of Tel Bet She'an from the north, looking south in 1921; the conical shape of the slopes is the result of the dump deposited by the University Museum Expedition. The trench dug by the UME is visible in the step delineating the summit (Courtesy of the Penn Museum, image 41647).

Figure 10.13: A member of the group of the École Biblique examining the remains of an ancient wall on the summit of the tell: apparently a Byzantine wall on the west side of the area, designated as Area R in the later Hebrew University excavations (photograph by Leo Boer).

there unfortunately, besides a few pretty passageways and some gates.

Behind the theatre lies Wadi Jalud and once we had crossed that, we found ourselves directly in front of the large mound of Tell Beisan, which still required a considerable climb in order to reach its top. Our visit to this place turned out rather disappointing for two reasons. The first one was that our tour guide clearly had neither enough time nor sufficient knowledge of the site to give us a systematic tour of it, and the second reason was that tall weeds covered the whole site – there just was not that much left to see. In addition to all that, the upper five strata had been removed completely! Except for a few remains of columns with capitals of Hellenistic sanctuaries, including one of Dionysus, and an altar in the ninth stratum, all the walls and other artefacts were made of clay.

The panoramic view from the top of the mound stretched from the Carmel on the one side to Ajlun in Transjordan on the other, and even the uplands around Pella were visible from here. Across the valley we could

see ruins of several ancient bridges. The recollection that five ancient trade routes used to come together here, made the significance of Tell Beisan's dominant position even clearer.

We left the mound through the northern Byzantine gate, from where a paved road used to lead to a church on a hill-top beyond. Part of this paved road still exists today, so we followed it more or less, and some 500 metres beyond the mound we passed a Byzantine structure beneath which traces belonging to the Chalcolithic era had been uncovered. Further on, we walked past the Cardo, the main street of Beisan, dating from the Late Roman period and eventually we reached the main road, at the point where it crosses the Wadi. Underneath the present-day bridge is a Byzantine one, made of the same stone as the old paved road mentioned above.'

In addition to this excerpt Boer notes that 'at the entrance of the museum of the knowledge of the plain of Esdrelon at a kibbutz in Tel Yosef, we encountered a stele of Ramesses II of which we were told that it was found at Bet She'an'. This is an interesting detail, since the *stele* is presently exhibited in the Rockefeller Museum in Jerusalem.

History of excavations

The University Museum, University of Pennsylvania Expedition

Between 1921 and 1933, the University Museum of the University of Pennsylvania conducted a pioneering wide-scale excavation on the mound of Bet She'an, called Tell el-Husn or 'the Mound of the Fortress' in Arabic. This endeavour stemmed from the desire of the University Museum to expand their archaeological work, which they had carried out in Egypt, to Palestine, and following a visit to the site in 1919 by George B. Gordon (Director of the Museum) and Clarence S. Fisher (Curator of the Egyptian section), it was chosen for excavation. The excavation permit was the sixth to be issued by the new British Mandatory Department of Antiquities and Bet She'an became the first American excavation in Palestine since the First World War (Mullins 2007, 23).

The excavations were directed consecutively by Clarence S. Fisher (1921–1923), Alan Rowe (1925–1928) and Gerald M. FitzGerald (1930–1933) (Fig. 10.14). During the first three seasons of excavations, most of the surface layers of the mound were removed, revealing the Early Islamic and Byzantine occupation levels. Among the important remains was a Byzantine dwelling quarter on the north-eastern side of the mound, and a circular Byzantine church as well as remains of a Roman temple on the summit. A medieval gate and fortification wall were also excavated in the north-western part of the summit.

After Fisher left Bet She'an to direct the University of Chicago's excavations at nearby Megiddo, Alan Rowe took over to and continued to excavate, but on a less-ambitious scale, limiting his work to the south-eastern part of the tell, exposing remains from Levels V (Iron Age II) to IX (Late Bronze IIA). The most important finds came from the Late Bronze Age and Iron Age I (fifteenth to twelfth centuries BCE), when Bet She'an served as a regional Egyptian administrative centre. The finds include three monumental basalt *stelae*

with inscriptions dating to the reign of Pharaoh Seti I and Pharaoh Ramses II, and a life-sized statue of Ramses III. Next to these, numerous other Egyptian monuments and objects were found that comprise the most significant of such assemblages ever found in Canaan. An imposing Egyptian 'Governor's Residency' (Building 1500) and quarters for the Egyptian garrison stationed at the town were revealed, as well as a series of four Canaanite temples attributed to Levels V, VI, VII/VIII and IX, which contained an invaluable group of cultic objects from these periods. Many tombs were excavated in the cemetery to the north of the mound, termed the 'Northern Cemetery', with rich finds including, *inter alia*, burials from the Intermediate Bronze Age and clay anthropoid coffins dating to the period of Egyptian control of the Nineteenth and Twentieth Dynasties, equivalent to Levels VIII–VI on the tell.

Following Rowe as dig director, Gerald FitzGerald limited the excavations to an even smaller area due to budget and time constraints. He concentrated on exposing Levels XVI to X (dating from the Early Bronze Age I to the Late Bronze Age I), ending the excavation in 1933 with a narrow trench excavated down to virgin soil and Late Neolithic pits dug into the bedrock. Bet She'an was the first excavation in Palestine to yield a continuous stratigraphic sequence from the Late Neolithic to the Medieval periods.

Some of the results of the University Museum Expedition were published relatively promptly in detailed, but not final, reports (FitzGerald 1930, 1931, 1932, 1934, 1935; Rowe 1928, 1930, 1940). The nature and quality of these reports were affected by the financial constraints of the Great Depression in the 1930s, as well as the outbreak of the Second World War. They reflect the state of the discipline of archaeology at that time: there were overly schematic plans (i.e. Fig. 10.15), numerous finds that could not be provenienced, loci numbers which were used during several strata (some of which were used more than once), lack of elevations, and objects that were discarded without proper documentation. Subsequently, comprehensive final reports were published on Levels VI to IV (James 1966), the Northern Cemetery (Oren 1973), Levels VIII to VII (James and McGovern 1993) and Strata XIX to XIII, the Chalcolithic and Early Bronze periods (Braun 2004).

Figure 10.14: University Museum expedition staff and others. From left: S. Yeivin, Mrs Rowe, Father L. H. Vincent, J. Teretieff, J. Garstang, C. Hiatt, A. Rowe, Mrs Garstang, G. FitzGerald; sitting: Rais Saleh and Abu el-Hassan (Courtesy of the Penn Museum, image 136435).

The Hebrew University excavations

The extensive excavations carried out at Bet She'an by the University Museum were one of the most significant archaeological projects ever to be conducted in the region between the two World Wars. However, in light of the fledgling state of the discipline, numerous problems relating to the interpretation of the results remained unsolved. The availability of new improved excavation methodology and research tools, prompted a new excavation, initiated by Yigael Yadin and Shulamit Geva of the Institute of Archaeology of the Hebrew University of Jerusalem in 1983. This brief season aimed to investigate the Iron Age I occupation levels, working on the eastern central part of the mound's summit, continuing to dig where the University Museum team had uncovered some of the most important Twentieth Dynasty Egyptian monuments. The untimely death

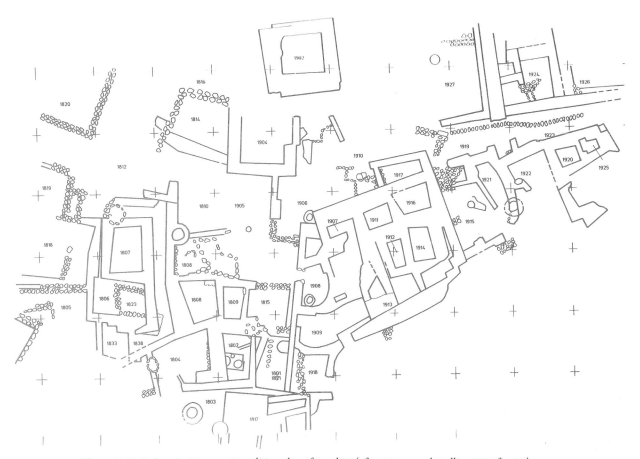

Figure 10.15: University Museum Expedition plan of Level XI (after Mazar and Mullins 2007, fig. 2.1).

of Yadin terminated this project, the results of which were published by Geva (Yadin and Geva 1986). Despite Yadin's expectations, no additional Egyptian monuments or inscriptions were found during this excavation. Most of the data recovered contributed to the definition of the Iron Age sequence, which was compared by Yadin and Geva to that of nearby Megiddo.

In 1984 a large-scale excavation was initiated by the Bet She'an Tourism Development Administration Authority, supported by the Israeli government, as a way to boost tourism and local employment. This excavation focused mainly on the areas to the west and south of the tell, between the tell and the extant Roman theatre. This excavation was divided into two expeditions: the Israel Antiquities Authority, under the direction of Gabriel Mazor and Rachel Bar-Nathan (for summaries and partial publication see Bar-Nathan and Mazor 1993; Mazor and Najjar 2007; Bar-Nathan and Atrash 2011) and the Institute of Archaeology of the Hebrew University in Jerusalem, under the direction of

Yoram Tsafrir and Gideon Foerster (for summaries see Foerster and Tsafrir 1987–1988; 1988–1989; 1992; Tsafrir and Foerster 1989–1990; 1997). They exposed important remains of the Hellenistic, Roman, Byzantine and Early Islamic periods in the lower city, and fully excavated the theatre (see also the preceding contributions in this chapter), the streets, bathhouses, monuments, a basilica, and more (Fig. 10.16). These excavations lasted from 1984 until 2000, with preservation and conservation work continuing until this day.

In the wake of these extensive long-term projects, it was only a matter of time before it was decided to excavate the tell of Bet She'an again, and in 1989 such a project was started under the direction of Amihai Mazar of the Institute of Archaeology of the Hebrew University of Jerusalem; nine excavation seasons were conducted until 1996.

The goals of the renewed excavation were manifold: to clarify the stratigraphic sequence related to the Bronze Age by re-examining the accessible University Museum records, to clarify the history and nature of

Figure 10.16: Tel Bet She'an viewed from the south, from the excavation of the city of the Roman-Byzantine-period (after Mazar and Mullins 2007, photo 1.1); compare this view to that in Figure 10.1, which Leo Boer saw in 1954, prior to the exposure of these remains.

the Egyptian administrative centre, to determine the Iron Age stratigraphic sequence, to investigate the post-Iron Age occupation levels, and to study the extent of settlement on the mound during the various periods of occupation. During the entire excavation, particular attention was paid to the conservation of the remains that were to become part of the archaeological park for tourists (Mazar 2006a, 10).

The results of these nine seasons of excavation were published in four comprehensive final reports (Mazar 2006b; Mazar and Mullins 2007; Panitz-Cohen and Mazar 2009; Mazar 2012).

Some of the important data collected showed that 1) there had been occupation gaps in the Early Bronze Age II and Middle Bronze Age IIA; 2) only the southern half of the mound had been occupied until the end of the Iron Age II when settlement expanded to the northern half; 3) the Egyptian presence began in the Eighteenth Dynasty (mid-fifteenth to fourteenth centuries BCE) and greatly expanded during the Nineteenth and Twentieth Dynasties (thirteenth to late twelfth centuries BCE), abruptly ending toward the end of the twelfth century BCE; 4) there was continuous occupation from the Persian to the Medieval periods; 5) the town on the mound had no fortifications prior to the Medieval period.

Employing the most up-to-date field excavation methods, the Hebrew University expedition focused on retrieval of most faunal and floral material, samples for C14 dating, which yielded important data concerning the Bronze and Iron Age chronological sequences, as well as local and regional patterns of trade and subsistence. Detailed studies of the finds yielded archeometallurgical analyses, pollen analyses, and petrographic and INAA proveniencing of pottery. Pottery studies included comprehensive, quantified typological registrations and distributional spatial analyses of completely excavated houses.

With the termination of the field excavation in 1996, Amihai Mazar began to direct the excavations at nearby Tel Rehov, the largest mound in the Bet She'an Valley, and the seat of a Canaanite city-state during the Late Bronze Age and Iron Age I, as well as an important administrative and economic centre in the Iron Age IIA. The choice to excavate Tel Rehov, about five kilometres south of Bet She'an, was part of a regional approach, providing a proper understanding of the site as it considers the broader regional picture and the relationships between sites of various sizes and types within the region. The excavations at Tel Rehov lasted from 1997 until 2012 and uncovered important remains dating from the Late Bronze Age until the Iron Age IIB, with the main finds coming from rich strata of the Iron Age IIA, tenth and ninth centuries BCE. Among the major discoveries was the establishment of the city during the Late Bronze Age, a virtually unique situation among the Canaanite cities,[1] and the presence of an industrial apiary (bee yard) dating to the late tenth century BCE, the only such establishment ever found in an archaeological excavation. The material culture of Tel Rehov was, on the one hand, entwined with that of contemporary Bet She'an, while on the other, various differences were found, in particular the virtual lack of Egyptian presence as opposed to its overwhelming intensity at Bet She'an.

Regional surveys

Extensive regional surveys of the Bet She'an Valley and its surrounding areas were conducted by Nehemiah Tsori in the 1940s and 1950s, identifying hundreds of sites dating to periods ranging from the Neolithic to the Medieval periods, including farms, villages, monuments, churches, synagogues, industrial installations and more (i.e. Tsori 1979). During the course of the Hebrew University excavations directed by Amihai Mazar at Tel Bet She'an, a comprehensive survey was conducted by Aren Maier as part of his doctoral research, including an in-depth spatial analysis of the valley with an emphasis on the second millennium BCE, particularly the Middle Bronze Age II. This study included environmental data and historical geographical observations, as well as a provenience study (INAA) of selected pottery and the compilation of detailed site distribution maps (Maier 1997; 2007; 2010). During the course of excavations at Tel Rehov, a survey was conducted around the site by Achia Cohen as part of his M.A. thesis.

Excavations at sites nearby Tel Bet She'an, such as Tel Amal (Edelstein and Feig 1993) and Tell el-Hammah (Cahill 2006), revealed material culture elements similar to those found at Bet She'an during the various periods of occupation, thus helping to define the Bet She'an valley as a cultural unit that developed trade and cultural relations in between the coast on the west-side and Transjordan on the east.

Currently, work is in progress on the publication of the results of the excavation at Tel Rehov by Amihai Mazar, emphasising the integrated nature of the sites in the valley over time.

The regional project

More or less from the beginning of modern archaeology, the concept of a survey has been part of the archaeological endeavour, alongside excavations. In fact, a survey is one of the main tools used to determine the location of ancient sites and to decide where to excavate, as well as establishing the chronological profiles and sizes of individual sites and regions. The main advantages of surveys are:

1) they can gather data more quickly and easily than by means of excavation, and to cover a much larger area than an excavation can;
2) they are more cost-effective, certainly in comparison with the much more expensive excavation;
3) they allow for future research, while excavations are in some ways destructive and do not leave archaeological evidence for future generations;
4) regional surveys can provide data taken from a broad geographic area and determine the chronological and regional profile of a region, as well as the type of site (city, farmhouse, cemetery, etc.).

The disadvantages of a survey are related to the rather large margin of error which is liable to occur. For example, if proper mapping tools are not used, the site may be marked incorrectly on the map. The reliability of the chronological profile depends on various factors that are difficult to control, such as the extent of familiarity with all the periods shown by the individual who interprets the collected pottery; in some cases, pottery dating to certain periods is easily identifiable, while other periods are not, which may result in an invalid representation of the chronology. Decorated pottery is more easily spotted than plain ware, and sherd size can be an issue as well. There is a tendency for the later periods to be better represented than the earlier ones. Often the season in which the survey is conducted affects the quality and quantity of the sherds collected, with high weeds in the summertime or thick mud in the winter often hindering progress (Uziel 2003, 14–18).

The survey of a specific region can be used to help define the material culture of the region during a given period, by analysing the artefacts gathered in a specific region and comparing them with sites or areas outside of that region (i.e. Wilkinson 2000; Cherry 2003; Given and Knapp 2003; Alcock and Cherry 2004; Liebner 2009; Maier 2010). Surveys conducted in the Bet She'an Valley, mentioned above, have established that the geographic borders of the valley, with the Gilboa mountains to the west, the Jordan River to the east, the hills of the lower Galilee to the north and the northern extreme of the Samaria Hills to the south, indeed represented a cultural unit during most of the Bronze and Iron Ages. The data collected from surveys, together with the rich finds from the excavation of various sites in the valley, have enabled a deeper and more informed understanding of the cultural and historical developments in the region.

An example of a study, carried out in the wake of data gathered from excavations and surveys, was conducted by A. Maier, focusing on the proveniencing of pottery gathered from various sites in the region, using the method of Instrumental Neutron Activation Analysis (INAA). The large sample of pottery from this period derived from a large number of sites in this well-defined region, providing a unique opportunity to study the subtle connections between the various sub-regions and sites, as well as to differentiate between fabrics found in this area and those from other areas (Maier 2007). The results showed that while in most of this region very similar clays were used to make the plain-ware vessels, there were micro-variations inferring the existence of localised pottery workshops. Another conclusion was that the potters in this region did not necessarily gather clay from their immediate vicinity, but rather selected their raw materials from particular locations within the region. Alternatively, the examined pottery may have been produced at a limited number of production sites in the region. A profile of fabric compositions was established according to periods, from the Intermediate Bronze Age until the Iron Age I, although most of the data came from the Middle Bronze Age II. A distinctive

pattern of pottery production was obtained for the region, showing a change in raw material in each period, with a relatively uniform clustering of fabrics within each period, confirming a high degree of unity within the region (Maier 2007, 561–62).

Another study conducted on data from excavations and regional surveys in the Bet She'an Valley pertains to the Iron Age II storage jar known as the 'Hippo' jar, named as such by the excavators of Megiddo because of the large size and tumid body of these jars (Alexandre 1995). These jars were very common at sites in the region, including Bet She'an, Tel Rehov, Tell el-Hammah and Tel Amal, as well as in the regional surveys. A comprehensive study conducted at the Institute of Archaeology of the Hebrew University by Ortal Haroch (as part of her M.A. thesis) has subjected some 150 of these jars to 3D scanning and analysis, enabling a precise comparison of the sizes and capacities of these jars. Together with petrographic provenience analysis, the scans have enabled the composition of micro-regional differences and similarities between these jars, identifying sites that were apparently supplied with jars from the same pottery workshop, as well as sites with their own types of 'Hippo' jars, suggesting separate production centres. These data allow us to relate excavated data to surveyed data, within the clear regional and chronological framework of the Bet She'an Valley. Similar jars were found outside the valley, for example at the site of Horbat Rosh Zayit near the Mediterranean coast. The size and shape, as well as the fabric, of these jars were identical to those of the jars in certain sites in the valley, indicating that they were sent to the coast from the same production centre that supplied the valley.

An additional regional aspect of the 'Hippo' jars is the appearance of the name 'Nimshi' inscribed on several jars of this type found at Tel Rehov and Tel Amal in the Bet She'an Valley and dating from the tenth and ninth centuries BCE. This name appears in the Bible, once as the father and once as the grandfather of Jehu, the usurper who ousted the Omride Dynasty from power in the Northern Kingdom of Israel. One of these inscriptions at Tel Rehov appears on a jar found in the industrial apiary uncovered at the same site and it was suggested that Nimshi was the name of a clan of landowners who lived in the valley and owned wide-scale industries, such as the apiary. This might have served as the power base for the coup staged by Jehu at nearby Samaria (Mazar and Panitz-Cohen 2007).

Yet another topic enriched by the regional perspective is the Egyptian occupation during the Eighteenth to Twentieth Dynasties in the Late Bronze Age. The excavation of Tel Bet She'an showed it to have been the seat of Egyptian rule, with an Egyptian garrison stationed there, particularly during the Nineteenth and Twentieth Dynasties (see references above). Excavations at sites near Bet She'an, such as Tel Rehov and Tel Amal, along with the regional surveys, have shown that the Egyptian presence was much less intense, or virtually non-existent, at many of these sites, reflecting much cultural differentiation: the material culture of the overlords did not appear to influence the surrounding population, who most likely paid their taxes and lived their lives as far away from the Egyptian culture as possible. Interestingly, somewhat further to the west, at the site of Megiddo in the Jezreel Valley, Egyptian presence at this time was relatively strong, reflecting the Egyptian interest in occupying strategic sites rather than disseminating its culture among the local population.

The example of the Bet She'an Valley regional project, initiated and directed by Amihai Mazar of the Hebrew University of Jerusalem in the wake of his excavations at Tel Bet She'an, shows the extreme value of such a regional approach.

Note

1   For the greater part, the Late Bronze cities in Canaan were smaller continuations of Middle Bronze cities and no new ones were established. One interpretation is that the Egyptians did not allow the establishment of new cities and also the construction of fortifications. Thus most of the Late Bronze cities were unfortified, or re-used earlier walls.

Bibliography of Bet She'an

Alcock, S. and Cherry, J. F. 2004. *Side-by-Side Survey: Comparative Regional Studies in the Mediterranean World*. Oxford: Oxbow Books.

Alexandre, Y. 1995. "The "Hippo" Jar and Other Storage Jars at Rosh Zayit." *Tel Aviv* 22:77–88.

Applebaum, S. 1978. "The Roman Theater of Scythopolis." *Scripta Classica Israelica* 4:77–103.

Arubas, B., Foerster, G. and Tsafrir, Y. 2008. "The Hellenistic to Early Islamic Periods at the Foot of the Mound." In *The New Encyclopedia of Archaeological Excavations in the Holy Land*, Vol. 5 (supplement), edited by E. Stern, A. Lewinson-Gilboa and J. Aviram, 1636–41. Jerusalem: The Israel Exploration Society & Carta.

Bar-Nathan, R. and Mazor, G. 1993. "The Bet She'an Excavation Project (1989-1991), City Center (South) and Tel Iztaba Area: Excavations of the Antiquities Authority Expedition." *Excavations and Surveys in Israel* 11:42–45.

Bar-Nathan, R. and Atrash, W. 2011. *Bet She'an II. Baysan. The Theater Pottery Workshop*. IAA Reports 48. Jerusalem: Israel Antiquities Authority.

Braun, E. 2004. *Early Beth Shan (Strata XIV–XIII): G. M. Fitzgerald's Deep Cut on the Tell*. Philadelphia: University of Pennsylvania Museum of Archaeology and Anthropology.

Cahill, J. 2006. "The Excavations at Tell el-Hammah: A Prelude to Amhihai Mazar's Beth-Shean Valley Regional Project." In *"I Will Speak the Riddle of Ancient Times". Archaeological and Historical Studies in Honor of Amihai Mazar on the Occasion of his Sixtieth Birthday*, edited by A. M. Maier and P. de Miroschedji, 429–60. Winona Lake, IN: Eisenbrauns.

Cherry, J. F. 2003. "Archaeology Beyond the Site: Regional Survey and its Future." In *Theory and Practice in Mediterranean Archaeology: Old and New World Perspectives*, edited by J. K. Papadopoulos and R. M. Leventhal, 137–59. Los Angeles: Cotsen Institute of Archaeology.

Conder, C. R. and Kitchener, H. H. 1882. *The Survey of Western Palestine* II. *Memoirs of the Topography, Orography, Hidrography and Archaeology*. London: Palestine Exploration Fund.

Edelstein, G. and Feig, N. 1993. "Tel Amal." In *The New Encyclopedia of Archaeological Excavations in the Holy Land*, Vol. 4, edited by E. Stern, A. Lewinson-Gilboa and J. Aviram, 1447–50. Jerusalem: The Israel Exploration Society & Carta.

FitzGerald, G. M. 1930. *The Four Canaanite Temples of Beth Shan. The Pottery (Beth Shan II/2)*. Philadelphia: University of Pennsylvania Press.

FitzGerald, G. M. 1931. *Beth-Shan Excavations: 1921-1923: The Arab and Byzantine Levels (Beth-Shan III)*. Philadelphia: University of Pennsylvania Press.

FitzGerald, G. M. 1932. "Excavations at Beth-Shan in 1931." *Palestine Exploration Fund. Quarterly Statement* (July):138–48.

FitzGerald, G. M. 1934. "Excavations at Beth-Shan in 1933." *Palestine Exploration Fund. Quarterly Statement* (January): 123–34.

FitzGerald, G. M. 1935. "The Earliest Pottery of Beth Shan." *Museum Journal* 24.22:5–22.

Foerster, G. 1993. "Beth-Shean at the Foot of the Mound." In *The New Encyclopedia of Archaeological Excavations in the Holy Land*, Vol. 1, edited by E. Stern, A. Lewinson-Gilboa and J. Aviram, 223–35. Jerusalem: The Israel Exploration Society & Carta.

Foerster, G. and Tsafrir, Y. 1987–1988. "The Bet Shean Project: B. Center of Ancient Bet Shean-North; C. The Ampitheater and Its Surroundings." *Excavations and Surveys in Israel* 6:25–43.

Foerster, G. and Tsafrir, Y. 1988–1989. "Bet Shean Project –1988: Hebrew University Expedition." *Excavations and Surveys in Israel* 7–8:15–22.

Foerster, G. and Tsafrir, Y. 1992. "The Bet Shean Excavation Project (1989–1991): City Center (North) Excavations of the Hebrew University Expedition." *Excavations and Surveys in Israel* 11:3–32.

Given, M. and Knapp, A. B. 2003. *The Sydney Cyprus Survey Project: Social Approaches to Regional Archaeological Survey.* Monumenta Archaeologica 21. Los Angeles: The Cotsen Institute of Archaeology.

Guérin, V. 1874. *Description Géographique, Historique et Archéologique de la Palestine* II. Paris: Impr. Impériale.

Irby, C. L. and Mangles, J. 1823. *Travels in Egypt and Nubia, Syria and Asia Minor During the Years 1817-1818.* London: John Murray.

James, F. W. 1966. *The Iron Age at Beth-Shan: A Study of Levels VI-IV.* Philadelphia: University Museum, University of Pennsylvania.

James, F. W. and McGovern, P. E. 1993. *The Late Bronze II Egyptian Garrison at Beth Shean: A Study of Levels VII and VIII.* Philadelphia: The University Museum, University of Pennsylvania.

Leibner, U. 2009. *Settlement and History in Hellenistic, Roman, and Byzantine Galilee: An Archaeological Survey of the Eastern Galilee.* Text and Studies in Ancient Judaism 127. Tübingen: Mohr Siebeck.

Maier, A. 1997. *The Material Culture of the Central Jordan Valley during the Middle Bronze II Period: Pottery and Settlement Patterns.* Ph.D. Dissertation. Jerusalem: Hebrew University of Jerusalem.

Maier, A. 2007. "Instrumental Neutron Activation Analysis of Selected Pottery from Beth-Shean and the Central Jordan Valley." In *Excavations at Tel Beth-Shean 1989-1996, Vol. II: The Middle and Late Bronze Age Strata in Area R*, edited by A. Mazar and R. A. Mullins, 554–71. Jerusalem: Israel Exploration Society and the Hebrew University of Jerusalem.

Maier, A. 2010. *"In the Midst of the Jordan": The Jordan Valley During the Middle Bronze Age (Ca. 2000-1500 BCE) - Archaeological and Historical Correlates.* Contributions to the Chronology of the Eastern Mediterranean, Vol. 26. Wien: Verlag der Österreichischen Akademie der Wissenschaften.

Mazar, A. 2006a. "Introduction." in *Excavations at Tel Beth-Shean 1989-1996, Vol. I: From the Late Bronze Age IIB to the Medieval Period*, edited by A. Mazar, 3–25. Jerusalem: The Israel Exploration Society.

Mazar, A. 2006b. *Excavations at Tel Beth-Shean 1989-1996, Vol. I: From the Late Bronze Age IIB to the Medieval Period.* Jerusalem: The Israel Exploration Society.

Mazar, A. 2012. *Excavations at Tel Beth-Shean 1989-1996. (Vol. IV): The Early Bronze and Intermediate Bronze Ages.* Jerusalem: The Israel Exploration Society.

Mazar, A. and Mullins, R. A. 2007. *Excavations at Tel Beth-Shean 1989-1996, Vol. II: The Middle and Late Bronze Age Strata in Area R.* Jerusalem: The Israel Exploration Society.

Mazar, A. and Panitz-Cohen, N. 2007. "It Is the Land of Honey: Beekeeping at Tel Rehov." *Near Eastern Archaeology* 70/4:202–19.

Mazar, G. 2008. "The Hellenistic to Early Islamic Periods: The Israel Antiquities Authority Excavations." In *The New Encyclopedia of Archaeological Excavations in the Holy Land*, Vol. 5 (supplement), edited by E. Stern, A. Lewinson-Gilboa and J. Aviram, 1623–36. Jerusalem: The Israel Exploration Society & Carta.

Mazor, G. and Najjar, A. 2007. *Bet She'an I. Nysa-Scythopolis. The Caesareum and the Odeum.* IAA Reports 33. Jerusalem: Israel Antiquities Authority.

Mazor, G. and Atrash, W. Forthcoming. *Nysa-Scythopolis: The Southern and Severan Theaters.* Bet She'an 3 IAA Reports. Jerusalem.

Mullins, R. A. 2007. "Reflections on Levels XI–IX of the University Museum Excavations." In *Excavations at Tel Beth-Shean 1989-1996, Vol. II: The Middle and Late Bronze Age Strata in Area R.*, edited by A. Mazar and R. A. Mullins, 23–38. Jerusalem: Israel Exploration Society and the Hebrew University of Jerusalem.

Negev, A. 1963. "Beth-Shean." *Revue Biblique* 70:585.

Oren, E. D. 1973. *The Northern Cemetery of Beth Shan.* Leiden: Brill.

Panitz-Cohen, N. and Mazar, A. 2009. *Excavations at Tel Beth-Shean 1989-1996, Vol. III: The 13th-11th BCE Strata in Areas N and S.* Jerusalem: The Israel Exploration Society.

Robinson, E. 1856. *Later Biblical Researches in Palestine and the Adjacent Regions: A Journal of Travels in the Year 1852.* London: John Murray.

Rowe, A. 1928. "The 1927 Expedition at Beisan. Final Report." *Museum Journal* 19:144–69.

Rowe, A. 1930. *The Topography and History of Beth-Shan (Beth-Shan I).* Philadelphia: The University Press for the University of Pennsylvania Museum.

Rowe, A. 1940. *The Four Canaanite Temples of Beth-Shan. The Temples and Cult Objects (Beth-Shan II/1).* Philadelphia: University of Pennsylvania Press.

Tsafrir, Y. and Foerster, G. 1989–1990. "Bet Shean Excavation Project – 1988/1989." *Excavations and Surveys in Israel* 9:120–28.

Tsafrir, Y. and Foerster, G. 1997. "Urbanism at Scythopolois-Bet Shean in the Fourth to Seventh Centuries." *Dumbarton Oaks Papers* 51:85–146.

Tsori, N. 1979. "Remains of Iron Age Sites in the Beth Shean and Jezreel Valleys, Mount Gilboa, Mount Tabor, Giv'at Hamore and the Plain of Issachar." *The Sixth Archaeological Conference in Israel (Tel Aviv, 14-15 March 1979).* Jerusalem: Israel Exploration Society (Hebrew).

Uziel, J. 2003. *The Tell es-Safi Archaeological Survey.* Unpublished M.A. Thesis. Bar Ilan University. Ramat Gan.

Vitruvius, *De Architectura* V 137–153, translated by M. H. Morgan. 1914. Cambridge: Harvard University Press.

Wilkinson, T. 2000. "Regional Approaches to Mesopotamian Archaeology: The Contribution of Archaeological Survey." *Journal of Archaeological Research* 8:219–67.

Yadin, Y. and Geva, S. 1986. *Investigations at Beth Shean: The Early Iron Age Strata.* Qedem 23. Jerusalem: Institute of Archaeology, The Hebrew University.

APPENDIX

List of Photographs from the Leo Boer Archive

Number	Caption	Date (dd-mm-yy)
2.1	Sicily seen from cruise ship Enotria	05-10-1953
2.2	The coast of Italy and Sicily	05-10-1953
2.3	Sunset over the Mediterranean Sea	05-10-1953
2.4	Port of Alexandria, Egypt	07-10-1953
2.5	Royal palace Alexandria	07-10-1953
2.6	Cruise ship Enotria in Alexandria	07-10-1953
2.7	Ras Beirut	08-10-1953
2.8	Port of Beirut	08-10-1953
2.9	Notre Dame du Liban at Jounieh	09-10-1953
2.10	Armenian patriarch and Mount Lebanon seen from Syrian seminary	09-10-1953
2.11	Syrian seminary nearby Jounieh	09-10-1953
2.12	Junior seminarists	09-10-1953
2.13	Senior seminarists	09-10-1953
2.14	View of Hammana and Falougha on the way to Baalbek	10-10-1953
2.15	Summit of Mount Lebanon	10-10-1953
2.16	Bekaa Valley and the road to Damascus	10-10-1953
2.17	Bedouins, Lebanon	10-10-1953
2.18	Rayak, Lebanon	10-10-1953
2.19	Islamic village, near Rayak, Lebanon	10-10-1953
2.20	Village of Ablah, church with the tomb of Noah, Lebanon	10-10-1953
2.21	Selling watermelons on the way to Baalbek	10-10-1953
2.22	Porters lodge, Baalbek	11-10-1953
2.23	Courtyard of Jupiter temple, Baalbek	11-10-1953
2.24	Capitals with 'eggs', symbols of life and regeneration, Baalbek	11-10-1953
2.25	Restored chapel Heliopolis, Baalbek	11-10-1953
2.26	Chapel vault, Baalbek	11-10-1953
2.27	View of Mount Lebanon, Baalbek	11-10-1953
2.28	Capital hewn from one piece, Baalbek	11-10-1953
2.29	Columns, Baalbek	11-10-1953
2.30	Entrance Bacchus temple, Baalbek	11-10-1953
2.31	Crusaders' crucifix in Bacchus temple, Baalbek	11-10-1953
2.32	Two types of columns, Baalbek	11-10-1953
2.33	Catholic quarter in Baalbek seen from the Bacchus temple	11-10-1953
2.34	Venus temple, Baalbek	11-10-1953
2.35	Panoramic view of Baalbek from the Anti-Lebanon	11-10-1953
3.1	Christian quarter, Damascus	12-10-1953
3.2	Christian quarter, Damascus	12-10-1953
3.3	Christian quarter, Damascus	12-10-1953
3.4	Courtyard, Great Mosque, Damascus	12-10-1953
3.5	Tower of the Last Judgment, Great Mosque, Damascus	12-10-1953
3.6	Via Recta, Damascus	13-10-1953
3.7	Bab Sharqi (Eastern Gate) seen from Via Recta, Damascus	13-10-1953
3.8	Bab Kisan; Kisan Gate through which Paul fled(?) Damascus	13-10-1953

Number	Caption	Date (dd-mm-yy)
3.9	Damascus seen from Salayeh	13-10-1953
3.10	Salayeh, Gebel Qasim, Armenian refugee camp	13-10-1953
3.11	Modern quarter Damascus; in the background refugee camp	13-10-1953
3.12	Inscription 'Iraq el-Emir	18-10-1953
13.3	Corridor in palace of 'Iraq el-Emir	18-10-1953
3.14	Vegetation of wadi in 'Iraq el-Emir	18-10-1953
3.15	Façade decoration of Qasr al-Mushatta palace	19-10-1953
3.16	Qasr al-Mushatta palace	19-10-1953
3.17	Group of École Biblique and the bus	19-10-1953
3.18	Desert at the height of Beer	19-10-1953
3.19	Picture of myself	19-10-1953
3.20	View of the Dead Sea from El-Kerak	20-10-1953
3.21	Crusaders chapel in fortress El-Kerak	20-10-1953
3.22	Part of castle seen from keep, fortress El-Kerak	20-10-1953
3.23	Crusaders' and Arabian features in foundation of fortress El-Kerak	20-10-1953
3.24	Nabataean temple seen from above, Dat Ras	20-10-1953
3.25	Group of École Biblique on top of Nabataean temple	20-10-1953
3.26	Wadi el-Hesa near El-'Ena (Aina)	20-10-1953
3.27	Vulcanic Gebel Eddakkar seen from Hirbet et-Tannur	20-10-1953
3.28	Cella of the sanctuary on Tannur	20-10-1953
3.29	Hirbet et-Tannur	20-10-1953
3.30	Et-Tafile and Dead Sea seen from a police station	21-10-1953
3.31	Guard at Et-Tafile	21-10-1953
3.32	Sela seen from El-Busera	21-10-1953
3.33	Araboth seen from El-Busera	21-10-1953
3.34	Group of Arabians in El-Busera	21-10-1953
3.35	Children of El-Busera	21-10-1953
3.36	Children of El-Busera	21-10-1953
4.1	Vulcanic mountain range at Wadi Dassa	21-10-1953
4.2	Shobak	21-10-1953
4.3	Shobak seen from about one kilometres	21-10-1953
4.4	Mountains near Petra. In background: Gebel Harun	21-10-1953
4.5	Setting up camp in Petra	22-10-1953
4.6	Roman legionair's tomb, Petra	22-10-1953
4.7	Garden tombs, Petra	22-10-1953
4.8	Altar high up, Petra	22-10-1953
4.9	Obelisk and Crusaders' ruins, Petra	22-10-1953
4.10	High place, Petra	22-10-1953
4.11	First city of Petra, Petra	22-10-1953
4.12	Wadi Musa, Petra	22-10-1953
4.13	Aqueduct, Petra	22-10-1953
4.14	Christian chapel with Nabataean façade, Petra	22-10-1953
4.15	Nabataean style, Petra	22-10-1953
4.16	Cult terrace, Petra	23-10-1953
4.17	Top of ed-Deir, Petra	23-10-1953
4.18	Ed-Deir, Petra	23-10-1953
4.19	Ed-Deir, Petra	23-10-1953
4.20	Tombs, seen from the Fort, Petra	23-10-1953
4.21	Main entrance Qasr al-Bint Fara'un, Petra	23-10-1953
4.22	High street, Petra	23-10-1953
4.23	Climbers at Umm el-Biyara	24-10-1953
4.24	Plain and mountains Er-Ram	25-10-1953
4.25	Wadi Er-Ram	26-10-1953
4.26	Block with Greek inscription in 'Aqaba	26-10-1953
4.27	View of Eilat	26-10-1953
4.28	View of 'Aqaba	26-10-1953
4.29	Camels near Isdruh	27-10-1953
4.30	Camels near Isdruh	27-10-1953
4.31	Rabbat-Moab	28-10-1953
4.32	Sel el-Mogib	28-10-1953
4.33	Two milestones in Sel el-Mogib on the side of Petra	28-10-1953
4.34	Dibon	28-10-1953
4.35	Basilica Nebo	29-10-1953

NUMBER	CAPTION	DATE (DD-MM-YY)
5.1	Forum at Amman	29-10-1953
5.2	Amman seen from Arabian Gate	29-10-1953
5.3	Arabian Gate, Amman	29-10-1953
5.4	Theatre of Amman seen from the Citadel	29-10-1953
5.5	Rock in temple of Zeus, Amman	29-10-1953
5.6	Jewish cemetery; valley of Jehosaphat; Gallicantu; Al Aksa mosque, Jerusalem	08-11-1953
5.7	Dome of the Rock, Jerusalem	08-11-1953
5.8	Gibea	12-11-1953
5.9	En-Nebi Samwil and Bet-Anot	12-11-1953
5.10	Route of Paul	12-11-1953
5.11	First and Second Walls, Ai	26-11-1953
5.12	Sally port, Ai	26-11-1953
5.13	Bethel seen from Burg Beitin	26-11-1953
5.14	Pool and wall, Bethel	26-11-1953
5.15	Et-Taiyibe; in background St George church	26-11-1953
5.16	Desert of Judah, seen from Rimmon	26-11-1953
5.17	Children in Rimmon	26-11-1953
5.18	Procession Delegato Apostolico	01-12-1953
5.19	Procession Delegato Apostolico	01-12-1953
5.20	Procession Delegato Apostolico	01-12-1953
5.21	Procession Delegato Apostolico	01-12-1953
5.22	Procession Delegato Apostolico	01-12-1953
5.23	Procession Delegato Apostolico	01-12-1953
5.24	Procession Delegato Apostolico	01-12-1953
5.25	Procession Delegato Apostolico	01-12-1953
5.26	Procession Delegato Apostolico	01-12-1953
5.27	The end of the Ophel valley and the Pool of Siloam	01-12-1953
5.28	Israeli tower (Salomon? Glacis of the Jebusites and wall of Nehemiah), City of David	01-12-1953
5.29	Two royal tombs, City of David	01-12-1953
5.30	École Biblique, Jerusalem	06-12-1953
5.31	Original depth of city moat, Jerusalem	06-12-1953
5.32	Rock on both sides of the street, Jerusalem	06-12-1953
5.33	Mount of Olives, Jerusalem	06-12-1953
5.34	Gethsemane and Russian church, Jerusalem	06-12-1953
5.35	Gethsemane and Russian church, Jerusalem	06-12-1953
5.36	Gate of Stephanus, Jerusalem	06-12-1953
6.1	Water supply system of Pilatus leading to Sur Bahir	09-12-1953
6.2	Solomon's Pools	09-12-1953
6.3	Solomon's Pools	09-12-1953
6.4	En 'Arrub	09-12-1953
6.5	En 'Arrub, refugee camp	09-12-1953
6.6	Mosque, Hebron	09-12-1953
6.7	Minaret of mosque, Hebron	09-12-1953
6.8	Mosque and Byzantine church, Hebron	09-12-1953
6.9	Old site of Hebron	09-12-1953
6.10	Abraham's castle, Hebron	09-12-1953
6.11	Pool, Hebron	09-12-1953
6.12	Wall of ancient Hebron	09-12-1953
6.13	View of Hebron seen from the ancient site	09-12-1953
6.14	View of the Eshkol and the Russian oak tree	09-12-1953
6.15	Deir el-Arbain	09-12-1953
6.16	Russian oak tree	09-12-1953
6.17	Russian oak tree	09-12-1953
6.18	Mambre	09-12-1953
6.19	Abraham's well	09-12-1953
6.20	En ed-Dirweh	09-12-1953
6.21	Beth-Sur	09-12-1953
6.22	Altar of the Birth, Bethlehem	13-12-1953
6.23	Altar of the Manger, Bethlehem	13-12-1953
6.24	Altar of the Birth, Bethlehem	13-12-1953
6.25	Altar of the Birth, Bethlehem	13-12-1953
6.26	Altar of the Birth, Bethlehem	13-12-1953

Number	Caption	Date (dd-mm-yy)
6.27	Basilica of Bethlehem	13-12-1953
6.28	View of Bethlehem	13-12-1953
6.29	View of Bethlehem	13-12-1953
6.30	Field of the Shepherds, Bethlehem	13-12-1953
6.31	École Biblique, Jerusalem	14-12-1953
6.32	École Biblique, Jerusalem	14-12-1953
6.33	Notre Dame de France, Jerusalem	14-12-1953
6.34	Tower of the Church of the Holy Sepulchre, Jerusalem	14-12-1953
6.35	Tower of the Church of the Holy Sepulchre, Jerusalem	14-12-1953
6.36	Tower of the Church of the Holy Sepulchre, Jerusalem	15-12-1953
7.1	Snow in Jerusalem	19-12-1953
7.2	Snow in Jerusalem	19-12-1953
7.3	Mandelbaum Gate	24-12-1953
7.4	Mandelbaum Gate	24-12-1953
7.5	Arrival Patriarch in Bethlehem	24-12-1953
7.6	Arrival Patriarch in Bethlehem	24-12-1953
7.7	Arrival Patriarch in Bethlehem	24-12-1953
7.8	Arrival Patriarch in Bethlehem	24-12-1953
7.9	Arrival Patriarch in Bethlehem	24-12-1953
7.10	Arrival Patriarch in Bethlehem	24-12-1953
7.11	Arrival Patriarch in Bethlehem	24-12-1953
7.12	Arrival Patriarch in Bethlehem	24-12-1953
7.13	W. Dussel	27-12-1953
7.14	W. Dussel	27-12-1953
7.15	Ploughing	29-12-1953
7.16	Street in El-Qubebe	29-12-1953
7.17	Roman road in El-Qubebe	29-12-1953
7.18	En-Nebi Samwil seen from El-Qubebe	29-12-1953
7.19	Ploughing	29-12-1953
7.20	Ploughing	29-12-1953
7.21	Palace wall, Ai	29-12-1953
7.22	Iron Age houses, Ai	29-12-1953
7.23	South corner and palace, Ai	29-12-1953
7.24	Third wall, Ai	29-12-1953
7.25	Church door, Et-Taiyibe	29-12-1953
7.26	Khan Hatrour	31-12-1953
7.27	Jerusalem and road to Jericho	31-12-1953
7.28	Qumran	31-12-1953
7.29	View from cave (4Qa) in Qumran	31-12-1953
7.30	Roof of the Souq, Jerusalem	02-01-1954
7.31	Dome of the Rock, Jerusalem	02-01-1954
7.32	Mount of Olives, Jerusalem	02-01-1954
7.33	Mount of Olives, Jerusalem	02-01-1954
7.34	Church of Holy Sepulchre, Jerusalem	02-01-1954
7.35	Damascus Gate, Jerusalem	02-01-1954
8.1	Mountains in front of Jericho	05-01-1954
8.2	Place of baptism upstream	05-01-1954
8.3	Place of baptism downstream	05-01-1954
8.4	Place of baptism downstream	05-01-1954
8.5	Jericho seen from Galgala	05-01-1954
8.6	Tell es-Sultan and Jericho seen from Qarantal	05-01-1954
8.7	Hillside Qarantal and Dead Sea	05-01-1954
8.8	Refugee camp seen from Tell es-Sultan	05-01-1954
8.9	Bedouin camp north of Jericho	05-01-1954
8.10	Setting up camp	05-01-1954
8.11	Sartabah and Jordan Valley	06-01-1954
8.12	Camping	06-01-1954
8.13	Tents Sartabah	06-01-1954
8.14	Shepherd	06-01-1954
8.15	Sheep in Jordan valley	06-01-1954
8.16	Jordan river downstream Tell ed-Damye	06-01-1954

NUMBER	CAPTION	DATE (DD-MM-YY)
8.17	Bridge Tell ed-Damye	06-01-1954
8.18	Jordan river upstream Tell ed-Damye	06-01-1954
8.19	Children in Jordan valley	06-01-1954
8.20	Road to Besan	06-01-1954
8.21	Women carrying branches on the way to Jerusalem	06-01-1954
8.22	Jerusalem seen from road to Bethlehem	06-01-1954
8.23	Mount of Olives seen from road to Bethlehem	06-01-1954
8.24	Silo	11-01-1954
8.25	Silo	11-01-1954
8.26	Silo	11-01-1954
8.27	Water bearers, Fara	11-01-1954
8.28	Fara	11-01-1954
8.29	Corn growing between stones, Fara	11-01-1954
8.30	Tell el-Far'a and Wadi	11-01-1954
8.31	View of Yasid and Siris	12-01-1954
8.32	Sichem	12-01-1954
8.33	Goats, Sichem	12-01-1954
8.34	Garizim	12-01-1954
8.35	Roman aqueduct between Nablus and Samaria	12-01-1954
8.36	Roman road between Nablus and Samaria	12-01-1954
9.1	Balata at foot of Garizim, seen from Ebal	13-01-1954
9.2	Well of Jacob and Wadi Far'a	13-01-1954
9.3	Well of Jacob and Sychar	13-01-1954
9.4	Wadi Far'a and location of Fara (police quarters)	13-01-1954
9.5	Woman and child	13-01-1954
9.6	Boy on donkey	13-01-1954
9.7	Landscape north of Tubas	14-01-1954
9.8	Hermon (just beyond Aqqabe)	14-01-1954
9.9	Plain, north of Zababida	14-01-1954
9.10	Mountainside vegetation Zababida	14-01-1954
9.11	Hermon seen from railtrack Afula	14-01-1954
9.12	Nazareth seen from railtrack Afula	14-01-1954
9.13	Esdrelom plain seen from railtrack Afula	14-01-1954
9.14	Genin	14-01-1954
9.15	Tell Dotan	14-01-1954
9.16	Tell Dotan and Hermon (and Tabor?)	14-01-1954
9.17	Silet ed-Dahr	14-01-1954
9.18	Scharon and Mediterranean Sea south of Silet ed-Dahr	14-01-1954
9.19	Scharon and Mediterranean Sea	14-01-1954
9.20	Scharon and Mediterranean Sea	14-01-1954
9.21	Samaria seen from the North	14-01-1954
9.22	Samaria seen from the South	14-01-1954
9.23	Balata seen from Gebel el Kebir	15-01-1954
9.24	Sheepdog seen from Gebel el Kebir	15-01-1954
9.25	Group seen from Gebel el Kebir	15-01-1954
9.26	Group seen from Gebel el Kebir	15-01-1954
9.27	Wadi Fara'a seen from Gebel el Kebir	15-01-1954
9.28	Ploughing seen from Gebel el Kebir	15-01-1954
9.29	Sheep seen from Gebel el Kebir	15-01-1954
9.30	Wadi Far'a seen from Gebel el Kebir	15-01-1954
9.31	Highlands of Transjordan seen from Tell el-Far'a	15-01-1954
9.32	Gebel el Kebir	15-01-1954
9.33	Yasuf	16-01-1954
9.34	Olive trees Samaria	16-01-1954
9.35	Bethoron Superior and coastal plain	16-01-1954
9.36	Looking down on Bethoron Inferior	16-01-1954
10.1	Wadi Selun and El-Lubban	03-02-1954
10.2	Road to Wadi Selun	03-02-1954
10.3	Wadi Bedan	03-02-1954
10.4	St. Mary's church on the Garizim	03-02-1954

Number	Caption	Date (dd-mm-yy)
10.5	Walled enclosure on the Garizim	03-02-1954
10.6	Apsis Basilica of Herod, Samaria	03-02-1954
10.7	Apsis Basilica of Herod, Samaria	03-02-1954
10.8	Forum, Samaria	03-02-1954
10.9	Wall of Ahab, Samaria	03-02-1954
10.10	Palace wall of Omri, Samaria	03-02-1954
10.11	Church of St John the Baptist, Samaria	03-02-1954
10.12	Colonnaded street, Samaria	03-02-1954
10.13	Muslims in prayer, Samaria	03-02-1954
10.14	Samaritan high priest with Codex	03-02-1954
10.15	Samaritan high priest with Codex	03-02-1954
10.16	Double wall, Sichem	03-02-1954
10.17	Carefully kept wall, Sichem	03-02-1954
10.18	Tomb of Joseph, Sichem	03-02-1954
10.19	Well of Jacob, Sichem	03-02-1954
10.20	Old road to Jericho	14-02-1954
10.21	Old road to Jericho	14-02-1954
10.22	Sheep on the road to Jericho	14-02-1954
10.23	Charub tree	17-02-1954
10.24	Almond blossom	17-02-1954
10.25	Almond tree	17-02-1954
10.26	East Jerusalem	21-02-1954
10.27	Dormition, Jerusalem	21-02-1954
10.28	South-East Jerusalem	21-02-1954
10.29	South-East Jerusalem	21-02-1954
10.30	North-East Jerusalem	21-02-1954
10.31	View from Calvary, Jerusalem	21-02-1954
10.32	Russian excavation site, Jerusalem	21-02-1954
10.33	Russian excavation site, Jerusalem	21-02-1954
10.34	Russian excavation site, Jerusalem	21-02-1954
10.35	Gate of Roman forum above Church of the Holy Sepulchre, Jerusalem	21-02-1954
10.36	Damascus Gate, Jerusalem	21-02-1954
11.1	Dominus Flevit: ancient Christian graves, Jerusalem	23-02-1954
11.2	Kedron Valley and temple, Jerusalem	08-03-1954
11.3	River-bed Kedron, Jerusalem	08-03-1954
11.4	Pool of Ezechias, Jerusalem	08-03-1954
11.5	Haceldama, Jerusalem	08-03-1954
11.6	Gehenna, Kedron, Tyropeon valleys, Jerusalem	08-03-1954
11.7	Wadi Kedron, Jerusalem	08-03-1954
11.8	Wailing Wall, Jerusalem	08-03-1954
11.9	Aqueduct on the old road to Jericho	10-03-1954
11.10	St George Monastery (Choziba)	10-03-1954
11.11	Wadi el-Qelt	10-03-1954
11.12	Herodian Jericho	10-03-1954
11.13	Skeleton in Tell es-Sultan	10-03-1954
11.14	Spring of Jericho (Elisha's Spring)	10-03-1954
11.15	Hirbet el-Mafgar	10-03-1954
11.16	Cisterns, Geba	14-03-1954
11.17	Michmas	14-03-1954
11.18	Wadi es-Suwenit: Bozez en Seneh	14-03-1954
11.19	Wadi es-Suwenit	14-03-1954
11.20	Wadi es-Suwenit	14-03-1954
12.0	Wadi es-Suwenit	14-03-1954
12.1	Farmland boundary	14-03-1954
12.2	Garden Tomb, Jerusalem	16-03-1954
12.3	St. Salvatore and Tyropeon, Jerusalem	18-03-1954
12.4	Via Dolorosa seen from the fifth Station, Jerusalem	18-03-1954
12.5	Modern Jericho	20-03-1954
12.6	Modern Jericho	20-03-1954
12.7	Excavations Qumran	21-03-1954
12.8	Excavations Qumran	21-03-1954

NUMBER	CAPTION	DATE (DD-MM-YY)
12.9	Excavations Qumran	21-03-1954
12.10	Excavations Qumran	21-03-1954
12.11	Excavations Qumran	21-03-1954
12.12	Excavations Qumran	21-03-1954
12.13	Excavations Qumran	21-03-1954
12.14	Excavations Qumran	21-03-1954
12.15	Excavations Qumran	21-03-1954
12.16	Excavations Qumran	21-03-1954
12.17	Excavations Qumran	21-03-1954
12.18	Excavations Qumran	21-03-1954
12.19	Dead Sea, direction of Jericho	22-03-1954
12.20	Dead Sea, direction of Transjordan	22-03-1954
12.21	Bedouin resting-place, Qumran	23-03-1954
12.22	Pay day Qumran	25-03-1954
12.23	Tea break Qumran	25-03-1954
12.24	Measurement of the site, Qumran	25-03-1954
12.25	Measurement of the site, Qumran	25-03-1954
12.26	Cave 1, Qumran	26-03-1954
12.27	Cave 2, Qumran	26-03-1954
12.28	Swimming in the Dead Sea, southern direction	26-03-1954
12.29	Swimming in the Dead Sea, southern direction	26-03-1954
12.30	Qumran and the Dead Sea	26-03-1954
12.31	Sea level, Dead Sea	01-04-1954
12.32	Caravan Jericho-Damye	01-04-1954
12.33	Storks, Fara	01-04-1954
12.34	Woman carrying branches, Fara	01-04-1954
12.35	Hellenistic Tower, Samaria	01-04-1954
12.36	Ivory house, Samaria	01-04-1954
12.37	Stairs of Temple of Augustus, Samaria	01-04-1954
13.0	Gifna	01-04-1954
13.1	Landscape Samaria, Gifna	01-04-1954
13.2	Shepherd near Qalandiyeh	01-04-1954
13.3	Dome of the Rock seen from the Church of the Flagellation, Jerusalem	06-04-1954
13.4	Mar Saba	08-04-1954
13.5	Wadi Kedron and Mar Saba	08-04-1954
13.6	Mar Saba and desert of Judah	08-04-1954
13.7	Wadi Kedron	08-04-1954
13.8	Palm Sunday procession, Jerusalem	11-04-1954
13.9	Palm Sunday procession, Jerusalem	11-04-1954
13.10	Palm Sunday procession, Jerusalem	11-04-1954
13.11	Palm Sunday procession, Jerusalem	11-04-1954
13.12	Palm Sunday procession, Jerusalem	11-04-1954
13.13	Palm Sunday procession, Jerusalem	11-04-1954
13.14	Palm Sunday procession, Jerusalem	11-04-1954
13.15	Arrival Greek Orthodox Patriarch, Jerusalem	17-04-1954
13.16	Arrival Greek Orthodox Patriarch, Jerusalem	17-04-1954
13.17	Arrival Latin Patriarch, Jerusalem	17-04-1954
13.18	Arrival Armenian Patriarch, Jerusalem	17-04-1954
13.19	Baptisterium Church of Holy Sepulchre, Jerusalem	20-04-1954
13.20	Calvary (twelfth Station), Jerusalem	22-04-1954
13.21	Rock of Calvary beneath the Mary altar, Jerusalem	22-04-1954
13.22	Altar of the Crucifixion (eleventh Station), Jerusalem	22-04-1954
13.23	Mary altar and Calvary (thirteenth Station), Jerusalem	22-04-1954
13.24	Stone of the Anointing, Jerusalem	22-04-1954
13.25	Dome of the Rock, Jerusalem	23-04-1954
13.26	Dome of the Rock, Jerusalem	23-04-1954
13.27	Dome of the Rock, Jerusalem	23-04-1954
13.28	First Station, Jerusalem	23-04-1954
13.29	First Station, Jerusalem	23-04-1954
13.30	Second Station, Jerusalem	23-04-1954
13.31	Third Station, Jerusalem	23-04-1954
13.32	Fourth Station, Jerusalem	23-04-1954

NUMBER	CAPTION	DATE (DD-MM-YY)
13.33	Fifth Station, Jerusalem	23-04-1954
13.34	Sixth Station, Jerusalem	23-04-1954
13.35	Seventh Station, Jerusalem	23-04-1954
13.36	Eighth Station, Jerusalem	23-04-1954
13.37	On the way to the 9th Station	23-04-1954
14.0	Synedrion, Jerusalem	26-04-1954
14.1	Dormition seen from Pontificio Instituto Biblico, Jerusalem	26-04-1954
14.2	South Jerusalem and King David Hotel, Jerusalem	26-04-1954
14.3	Modern Jerusalem	26-04-1954
14.4	Notre Dame de France and San Salvatore, Jerusalem	26-04-1954
14.5	High place (?), Hirbet Mazmil	26-04-1954
14.6	En Kerem	26-04-1954
14.7	Altar of the birth of John the Baptist, En Kerem	26-04-1954
14.8	Street in En Kerem	26-04-1954
14.9	En Kerem	26-04-1954
14.10	Church of the Birth of John the Baptist, En Kerem	26-04-1954
14.11	Mosaic, Church of the Visitation, En Kerem	26-04-1954
14.12	Monastery of the Holy Cross, Jerusalem	26-04-1954
14.13	Herodian family tomb, Jerusalem	26-04-1954
14.14	Land of Samson	27-04-1954
14.15	Mazor	27-04-1954
14.16	Antipatris	27-04-1954
14.17	Port Caesarea	27-04-1954
14.18	Port Caesarea	27-04-1954
14.19	Port Caesarea	27-04-1954
14.20	Caesarea	27-04-1954
14.21	Coast of Caesarea	27-04-1954
14.22	Court of Justice, Caesarea	27-04-1954
14.23	Wadi Mughara seen from third cave	27-04-1954
14.24	Mediterranean Sea seen from the Carmel	28-04-1954
14.25	View to the North East from the Carmel	28-04-1954
14.26	Mount Tabor seen from the Carmel	28-04-1954
14.27	Offer place of Elias	28-04-1954
14.28	Spot from where Elias saw a cloud	28-04-1954
14.29	Top of the Carmel	28-04-1954
14.30	Gate of Megiddo	28-04-1954
14.31	Mount Tabor seen from Megiddo	28-04-1954
14.32	Cross-cut in Megiddo	28-04-1954
14.33	Horse stables of Megiddo	28-04-1954
14.34	Altar of Megiddo	28-04-1954
14.35	Cross-cut in Megiddo	28-04-1954
14.36	Mountain pass between plain of Esdrelon and plain of Akko	28-04-1954
14.37	Akko seen from the plain	29-04-1954
15.0	Mosque Akko	29-04-1954
15.1	Minaret Akko	29-04-1954
15.2	Haifa from Akko	29-04-1954
15.3	Old port Akko	29-04-1954
15.4	Castle Montfort	29-04-1954
15.5	Mountain track in Galilee (environment Montfort)	29-04-1954
15.6	Hermon seen from highest point in Palestine	29-04-1954
15.7	Safed seen from Synagogue of Meron	30-04-1954
15.8	View from Dan	30-04-1954
15.9	Primary source of the river Jordan	30-04-1954
15.10	Primary source of the river Jordan	30-04-1954
15.11	Primary source of the river Jordan	30-04-1954
15.12	Primary source of the river Jordan	30-04-1954
15.13	Primary source of the river Jordan	30-04-1954
15.14	Border of Palestine	30-04-1954
15.15	Environment Dan	30-04-1954
15.16	Kibbuts Ai'Yelet Hashahar	30-04-1954
15.17	Hermon seen from the Qibbuts Ayyalet	30-04-1954

NUMBER	CAPTION	DATE (DD-MM-YY)
15.18	Sea level, Tiberias	30-04-1954
15.19	Port of Tiberias and Hermon	01-05-1954
15.20	Tiberias seen from the Lake	01-05-1954
15.21	Tiberias seen from the Lake	01-05-1954
15.22	Tiberias seen from the Lake	01-05-1954
15.23	Tiberias seen from the Lake	01-05-1954
15.24	Magdala seen from the Lake Tiberias	01-05-1954
15.25	Mount of Beatitudes from the Lake Tiberias	01-05-1954
15.26	Southern-most point of Lake Tiberias	01-05-1954
15.27	Mountains of Galilee from Lake Tiberias	01-05-1954
15.28	Capharnaum seen from Lake Tiberias	01-05-1954
15.29	Jordan estuary in Lake Tiberias	01-05-1954
15.30	Capharnaum seen from Lake Tiberias	01-05-1954
15.31	Mount of Beatitudes seen from Lake Tiberias	01-05-1954
15.32	Mount of Beatitudes seen from Lake Tiberias	01-05-1954
15.33	Mount of the Swines	01-05-1954
15.34	Synagogue at Capharnaum	01-05-1954
15.35	Synagogue at Capharnaum	01-05-1954
15.36	Synagogue at Capharnaum	01-05-1954
16.00	Synagogue at Capharnaum	01-05-1954
16.0	Road of Capharnaum to Heptapegon	01-05-1954
16.1	Catching fish, Lake Tiberias	01-05-1954
16.2	Catching fish, Lake Tiberias	01-05-1954
16.3	Lake Tiberias seen from Mount of Beatitudes	01-05-1954
16.4	Lake Tiberias from North-eastern shore	01-05-1954
16.5	Lake Tiberias from North-eastern shore	01-05-1954
16.6	Bet-Jerach	02-05-1954
16.7	Bet-Jerach	02-05-1954
16.8	Kibbutz Deganiya	02-05-1954
16.9	Church of Kana	02-05-1954
16.10	Church of Kana	02-05-1954
16.11	Street in Kana	02-05-1954
16.12	Street in Kana	02-05-1954
16.13	Street in Kana	02-05-1954
16.14	Spring of Kana	02-05-1954
16.15	Church of Joachim and Anna, Sepphoris	03-05-1954
16.16	View of modern Sepphoris and Carmel	03-05-1954
16.17	Landscape seen from Fort Sepphoris	03-05-1954
16.18	Landscape seen from Fort Sepphoris	03-05-1954
16.19	Nazareth seen from the road from Sepphoris	03-05-1954
16.20	Nazareth seen from the road from Sepphoris	03-05-1954
16.21	Nazareth seen from the road from Sepphoris	03-05-1954
16.22	Spring of Nazareth	03-05-1954
16.23	Apsis old Church of the Annunciation, Nazareth	03-05-1954
16.24	Apsis old Church of the Annunciation, Nazareth	03-05-1954
16.25	Cave of the Annunciation, Nazareth	03-05-1954
16.26	House in Nazareth	03-05-1954
16.27	Street in Nazareth	03-05-1954
16.28	Nazareth from the Church of Jesus the Adolescent	03-05-1954
16.29	Nazareth from the Church of Jesus the Adolescent	03-05-1954
16.30	Mount Tabor from the Church of Jesus the Adolescent	03-05-1954
16.31	Cave of the Annunciation, Nazareth	03-05-1954
16.32	Nazareth seen from the Notre Dame de l'Effroi	04-05-1954
16.33	Nazareth seen from the Notre Dame de l'Effroi	04-05-1954
16.34	Site of ancient Nazareth	04-05-1954
16.35	Mount Tabor, near Afulah	04-05-1954
16.36	Mount of Transfiguration	04-05-1954
16.37	Entrance gate of Mount Tabor	04-05-1954
17.0	Basilica on Mount Tabor	04-05-1954
17.1	Basilica on Mount Tabor	04-05-1954

NUMBER	CAPTION	DATE (DD-MM-YY)
17.2	Hermon and Naim seen from Mount Tabor	05-05-1954
17.3	Nazareth seen from Mount Tabor	05-05-1954
17.4	Nazareth and plain of Esdrelon	05-05-1954
17.5	Dabaritta and Gebel el-Qafze	05-05-1954
17.6	Way to travel (near Mount Tabor)	05-05-1954
17.7	Farming on the plain of Esdrelon	05-05-1954
17.8	Naim	05-05-1954
17.9	Jesreel	05-05-1954
17.10	Beisan	05-05-1954
17.11	Roman theatre and modern Beisan seen from the tell	05-05-1954
17.12	Various strata in Tell Beisan	05-05-1954
17.13	Spring of Gedeon	05-05-1954
17.14	Sidon, port of Dor	06-05-1954
17.15	Sidon, port of Dor	06-05-1954
17.16	Fort of Crusaders, Apollonia	06-05-1954
17.17	Israeli winepress Tell Qasile	06-05-1954
17.18	Israeli winepress Tell Qasile	06-05-1954
17.19	Old port, Yaffa	07-05-1954
17.20	Street in Lydda	08-05-1954
17.21	Strefelah seen from Tell Gezer	08-05-1954
17.22	El-Latrun seen from Tell Gezer	08-05-1954
17.23	Altar of Massoach	08-05-1954
17.24	Esthaol	08-05-1954
17.25	Yaffa-Tel Aviv	08-05-1954
17.26	Asdod	09-05-1954
17.27	Ascalon	09-05-1954
17.28	Coast of Ascalon	09-05-1954
17.29	Chalcolithic house in Bersabee	09-05-1954
17.30	Soubeita	10-05-1954
17.31	The Negev	10-05-1954
17.32	Arara	11-05-1954
17.33	Salt cave in Sodom	11-05-1954
17.34	El-Lisan seen from Sodom	11-05-1954
17.35	Gebel Usdum	11-05-1954
17.36	Near the Dead Sea	11-05-1954
18.0	Beersheba	12-05-1954
18.1	Beersheba	12-05-1954
18.2	Palace wall, Lachish	12-05-1954
18.3	Bet Guvrin	12-05-1954
18.4	Caves of Maresha	12-05-1954
18.5	Terebinthental Valley	12-05-1954
18.6	Sarea and Esthaol seen from Bet-Shemesh	12-05-1954
18.7	Qiryat-Y'arim	12-05-1954
18.8	Qiryat-Y'arim	12-05-1954
18.9	Jewish Jerusalem	13-05-1954
18.10	East Wall of Jerusalem	13-05-1954
18.11	Birket es-Sultan, Jerusalem	13-05-1954
18.12	Gehenna valley, Jerusalem	13-05-1954
18.13	Church of St. Peter in Gallicantu, Jerusalem	13-05-1954
18.14	Dormition, Jerusalem	13-05-1954
18.15	Double Gate seen from Akra, Jerusalem	18-05-1954
18.16	David's Gate (Zion Gate), Jerusalem	18-05-1954
18.17	Gallicantu, Jerusalem	18-05-1954
18.18	Haceldama, Jerusalem	18-05-1954
18.19	Royal gardens and En Rogel, Jerusalem	18-05-1954
18.20	North side Ophel, Jerusalem	18-05-1954
18.21	South side Ophel, Jerusalem	18-05-1954
18.22	Steps from Zion to house of Caiaphas, Jerusalem	18-05-1954
18.23	Triple Gate, Jerusalem	18-05-1954
18.24	Tombs in Kedron Valley, Jerusalem	18-05-1954
18.25	Gethsemane, Jerusalem	18-05-1954

NUMBER	CAPTION	DATE (DD-MM-YY)
18.26	Harvest in Bethlehem	20-05-1954
18.27	Bethlehem seen from the Field of Shepherds	20-05-1954
18.28	Entrance Church of Nativity, Bethlehem	20-05-1954
18.29	Street in Bethlehem	20-05-1954
18.30	Old Bethlehem and Bet Gala	20-05-1954
18.31	Sheep near Tekoa	23-05-1954
18.32	Bethlehem seen from Tekoa	23-05-1954
18.33	Threshing, near Tekoa	23-05-1954
18.34	Top of Herodion	23-05-1954
18.35	Herodion seen from Bethlehem	23-05-1954
18.36	Ascensio Domini (Chapel of the Ascension)	27-05-1954
18.37	Ascensio Domini (Chapel of the Ascension)	27-05-1954
19.0	Labourer in Jerusalem	28-05-1954
19.1	Street in Jerusalem	28-05-1954
19.2	Ninth Station, Jerusalem	28-05-1954
19.3	Street in Jerusalem	28-05-1954
19.4	Old entrance of the Church of the Holy Sepulchre, Jerusalem	28-05-1954
19.5	Street in Jerusalem	28-05-1954
19.6	'Pater Noster', Jerusalem	30-05-1954
19.7	Thorn bush at Pater Noster', Jerusalem	30-05-1954
19.8	Tomb of Lazarus, Bethany	30-05-1954
19.9	Bethany	30-05-1954
19.10	Robinson's Arch, Jerusalem	31-05-1954
19.11	Birket el-Hamra, Jerusalem	31-05-1954
19.12	Ein Rogel, Jerusalem	31-05-1954
19.13	Gihon Spring, Jerusalem	31-05-1954
19.14	Tomb of Mary, Jerusalem	31-05-1954
19.15	Church of the Holy Sepulchre, Jerusalem	01-06-1954
19.16	Citadel (Tower of David), Jerusalem	01-06-1954
19.17	Former site of the Hasmonean Palace, Jerusalem	01-06-1954
19.18	Former Jewish Quarter, Jerusalem	01-06-1954
19.19	St James Church, Jerusalem	01-06-1954
19.20	Armenian Quarter, Jerusalem	01-06-1954
19.21	Mograbi Gate (Dung Gate), Jerusalem	01-06-1954
19.22	North Jerusalem	01-06-1954
19.23	North Jerusalem	01-06-1954
19.24	'Ecce Homo' arch, Jerusalem	03-06-1954
19.25	Church of Saint Anne, Jerusalem	03-06-1954
19.26	Bethesda Pool, Jerusalem	03-06-1954
19.27	Bethesda Pool, Jerusalem	03-06-1954
19.28	Bethesda Pool and Church of Saint Anne, Jerusalem	03-06-1954
19.29	Church of the Holy Sepulchre, Jerusalem	04-06-1954
19.30	Church of the Holy Sepulchre, Jerusalem	04-06-1954
19.31	Church of the Holy Sepulchre, Jerusalem	04-06-1954
19.32	Church of the Holy Sepulchre, Jerusalem	04-06-1954
19.33	Church of the Holy Sepulchre, Jerusalem	04-06-1954
19.34	Dome of the Rock, Jerusalem	06-06-1954
19.35	East Jerusalem	08-06-1954
19.36	View from 'Amwas	10-06-1954
20.0	'Amwas	10-06-1954
20.1	'Amwas	10-06-1954
20.2	Lithostrotos, Jerusalem	12-06-1954
20.3	Lithostrotos, Jerusalem	12-06-1954
20.4	Dome of the Rock, Jerusalem	13-06-1954
20.5	Rachel's tomb	13-06-1954
20.6	Antilebanon (mountains) seen from Syria	16-06-1954
20.7	Homs	17-06-1954
20.8	Syrian village	17-06-1954
20.9	Citadel of Aleppo	17-06-1954
20.10	Citadel of Aleppo	17-06-1954

NUMBER	CAPTION	DATE (DD-MM-YY)
20.11	Aleppo seen from citadel	17-06-1954
20.12	Roman bridge over the Orontes River	19-06-1954
20.13	Orontes River	19-06-1954
20.14	On Mount Lebanon	19-06-1954
20.15	Old port of Lattaquia	19-06-1954
20.16	Old port of Lattaquia	19-06-1954
20.17	Rash Shamra	20-06-1954
20.18	Old port Rash Shamra	20-06-1954
20.19	Tripoli	21-06-1954
20.20	Tripoli seen from El Mina	21-06-1954
20.21	Old port Tripoli	21-06-1954
20.22	Church of the Franciscans, Tripoli	22-06-1954
20.23	Roman colonnade, Byblos	22-06-1954
20.24	Temples, Byblos	22-06-1954
20.25	Port of Byblos	22-06-1954
20.26	Masseboth, Byblos	22-06-1954
20.27	Adonis with Roman bridge	22-06-1954
20.28	Port Said	25-06-1954
20.29	Ferdinand de Lesseps	25-06-1954
20.30	Coptic museum, Cairo	28-06-1954
20.31	Old Cairo	28-06-1954
20.32	The Nile, Cairo	28-06-1954
20.33	Minaret, Cairo	29-06-1954
20.34	Mosque of Mohammed Ali Pasha, Cairo	29-06-1954
20.35	Minaret, Cairo	29-06-1954
20.36	Minaret, Cairo	29-06-1954
20.37	Minaret, Cairo	29-06-1954
21.1	Memphis	30-06-1954
21.2	Saqqara	30-06-1954
21.3	Saqqara	30-06-1954
21.4	Colonnade, Saqqara	30-06-1954
21.5	Tomb, Saqqara	30-06-1954
21.6	Entrance Pyramid of Unas	30-06-1954
21.7	Pyramid of Djoser	30-06-1954
21.8	Desert and Nile delta	30-06-1954
21.9	Site of the solar boat, Gizeh	01-07-1954
21.10	Sphinx	01-07-1954
21.11	Temple of the pyramid of Chephren	01-07-1954
21.12	Sphinx	01-07-1954
21.13	Strolling to the pyramid	01-07-1954
21.14	Pyramid of Cheops	01-07-1954
21.15	Syracuse	05-07-1954
21.16	Syracuse	05-07-1954
21.17	Madonna delle Lacrime, Syracuse	05-07-1954
21.18	Capri	06-07-1954
21.19	Naples	06-07-1954
21.20	St Peter's Basilica, Rome	08-07-1954
21.21	St Peter's Basilica, Rome	08-07-1954
21.22	Stazione Termini, Rome	08-07-1954
21.23	Station Valkenburg, Netherlands	12-07-1954
21.24	Map of north Israel	14-07-1954
21.25	Map of central Israel	14-07-1954
21.26	Map of south Israel	14-07-1954
21.27	Roadmap	14-07-1954
21.28	Map of the Old City of Jerusalem	14-07-1954
21.29	Map of Jerusalem	14-07-1954

INDEXES

INDEX OF ANCIENT SOURCES

Greek and Latin Authors

Josephus *Jewish Antiquities*

1.64–65	85
1.370	157
1.408–415	183
4.437–439	149

Josephus *Jewish War*

13.275–281	85
15.121	157
15.331–341	183

Philo *Quod Omnis Probus Liber Sit*

72–91	157

Philo *Hypothetica*

11.1–18	157

Pliny *Naturalis Historia*

5.15 [73]	157

Solinus *Collectanea Rerum Memorabilium*

35.1–12	157

Synesius *Dio, Sive De Suo Ipsius Instituto*

3.2	157

Vitruvius *De Architecture*

5.137–153	231

Old Testament/Hebrew Bible

Genesis

12:6–8	50, 90
13:3	50
33:18–20	90
34	90
37:14	90

Joshua

6	116
7:2	41, 50
7:3	51
7:5	51
8:9	41
8:11	51
8:25	51
8:28	40, 51, 90
12:9	41, 50
20	90
21	90
24:32	90, 96

Judges

9	90, 96, 104

1 Samuel

13:5	50

2 Samuel

4:12	11
5:8	209

1 Kings

9:15	202, 204–205
9:19	210
13:32	83
16	83
16:8–20	80
16:21–24	80
16:24	60, 77
16:25–33	76
16:28	63, 73
16:29–22:40	83
16:31	60, 80, 83
16:32–33	80
17–19	83
18	83
20	60, 80, 83
20:1–34	83
20:15	76
20:35–43	83
21	83
21:1	80
22	76, 80, 83
22:37	63, 73
22:39	60, 71 n. 4, 80

2 Kings

1	83
1:3	80
6	83
6:24–7:20	60
9	83
10	83
10:35	63, 73
13	83
13:9	63, 73
14:16	63, 73
14:29	63, 73
15	83
15:8–31	83
17	83
17:6	60
17:24–28	84
23:4	84
23:29	202
23:29–30	84

Isaiah

7	84

New Testament

General Index

Index of Modern Authors